Shame *in the* Therapy Hour

Shame *in the* Therapy Hour

Edited by
Ronda L. Dearing and
June Price Tangney

American Psychological Association • *Washington, DC*

2nd printing, December 2014

Published by
American Psychological Association
750 First Street, NE
Washington, DC 20002
www.apa.org

To order
APA Order Department
P.O. Box 92984
Washington, DC 20090-2984
Tel: (800) 374-2721; Direct: (202) 336-5510
Fax: (202) 336-5502; TDD/TTY: (202) 336-6123
Online: www.apa.org/pubs/books
E-mail: order@apa.org

In the U.K., Europe, Africa, and the Middle East, copies may be ordered from
American Psychological Association
3 Henrietta Street
Covent Garden, London
WC2E 8LU England

Typeset in Goudy by Circle Graphics, Inc., Columbia, MD

Printer: Maple-Vail Book Manufacturing Group, York, PA
Cover Designer: Naylor Design, Washington, DC

The opinions and statements published are the responsibility of the authors, and such opinions and statements do not necessarily represent the policies of the American Psychological Association.

Library of Congress Cataloging-in-Publication Data

Shame in the therapy hour/edited by Ronda L. Dearing and June Price Tangney. — 1st ed.
    p. ; cm.
  Includes bibliographical references and index.
  ISBN-13: 978-1-4338-0967-5
  ISBN-10: 1-4338-0967-2
  1. Psychotherapist and patient. 2. Shame. I. Dearing, Ronda L. II. Tangney, June Price. III. American Psychological Association.
  [DNLM: 1. Shame. 2. Psychotherapy—methods. BF 575.S45]

  RC480.8.S49 2011
  616.89'14—dc22

                              2011002248

British Library Cataloguing-in-Publication Data

A CIP record is available from the British Library.

Printed in the United States of America
First Edition

DOI: 10.1037/12326-000

Dedicated to the memory of Helen Block Lewis, whose innovative ideas on shame and guilt have provided guidance and inspiration.

CONTENTS

CONTRIBUTORS

Martin Bohus, MD, Department of Psychosomatic Medicine and Psychotherapy, University of Heidelberg; Psychosomatic Medicine and Psychotherapy Clinic, Central Institute of Mental Health, Mannheim, Germany

Brené Brown, PhD, LMSW, Graduate College of Social Work, University of Houston, Houston, TX

Milton Z. Brown, PhD, California School of Professional Psychology at Alliant International University, San Diego

Ronda L. Dearing, PhD, Research Institute on Addictions, University at Buffalo, The State University of New York, Buffalo

Norman B. Epstein, PhD, Couple and Family Therapy Program, Department of Family Science, School of Public Health, University of Maryland, College Park

Mariana K. Falconier, PhD, Marriage and Family Therapy Program, Department of Human Development, Northern Virginia Center, Virginia Technological Institute and State University, Falls Church

Emi Furukawa, PhD, Human Developmental Neurobiology Unit, Okinawa Institute of Science and Technology, Okinawa, Japan

Paul Gilbert, PhD, FBPsS, Mental Health Research Unit, Kingsway Hospital; Department of Clinical Psychology, University of Derby, Derby, England

Leslie S. Greenberg, PhD, Department of Psychology, York University, Toronto, ON, Canada

Judith Lewis Herman, MD, Department of Psychiatry, Harvard Medical School, Boston, MA

Virginia Rondero Hernandez, PhD, LCSW, ACSW, Department of Social Work Education, California State University, Fresno

Dennis J. Hunt, PhD, Clinical Psychologist and Consultant, Alexandria, VA

Shigeru Iwakabe, PhD, Graduate School of Humanities and Sciences, Ochanomizu University, Tokyo, Japan

Rebecca Klinger, MS, Counseling Psychology Program, College of Education, Lehigh University, Bethlehem, PA

Kelly Koerner, PhD, Evidence-Based Practice Institute; Private Practice, Seattle, WA

Lauren Kulp, BA, Counseling Psychology Program, College of Education, Lehigh University, Bethlehem, PA.

Nicholas Ladany, PhD, Department of Educational Support Services, Loyola Marymount University, Los Angeles, CA

Marsha M. Linehan, PhD, ABPP, Department of Psychology, University of Washington; Behavioral Research and Therapy Clinics, Seattle

Faith H. McClure, PhD, Psychology Department, California State University, San Bernardino

Andrew P. Morrison, MD, Department of Clinical Psychiatry, Harvard Medical School, Cambridge, MA; Boston Psychoanalytic Institute, Boston, MA; Massachusetts Institute for Psychoanalysis, Brookline

Ronald T. Potter-Efron, MSW, PhD, First Things First Counseling and Consulting, Eau Claire, WI

Theodore A. Powers, PhD, Department of Psychology, University of Massachusetts at Dartmouth, North Dartmouth

Shireen L. Rizvi, PhD, Graduate School of Applied and Professional Psychology, Rutgers University, Piscataway, NJ

Jennifer L. Sanftner, PhD, Department of Psychology, Slippery Rock University, Slippery Rock, PA

Elizabeth L. Shapiro, PhD, Department of Psychiatry, Harvard Medical School, Boston, MA

Elizabeth Simpson, MD, Massachusetts Mental Health Center, Jamaica Plain, MA; Harvard Medical School, Boston, MA

Michael Stadter, PhD, Private Practice, Bethesda, MD; Washington School of Psychiatry, Washington, DC; International Psychotherapy Institute, Chevy Chase, MD

June Price Tangney, PhD, Department of Psychology, George Mason University, Fairfax, VA

Mary Tantillo, PhD, PMHCNS-BC, FAED, Department of Clinical Nursing, University of Rochester School of Nursing, Rochester, NY

Edward Teyber, PhD, Psychology Department, California State University, San Bernardino

Mavis Tsai, PhD, Independent Practice; University of Washington, Seattle

Yolanda Villarreal, MSW, Graduate College of Social Work, University of Houston, Houston, TX

Robert Weathers, PhD, Psychology Department, California State University, San Bernardino

Shame *in the* Therapy Hour

INTRODUCTION: PUTTING SHAME IN CONTEXT

RONDA L. DEARING AND JUNE PRICE TANGNEY

Shame is a common emotion that contributes to many problems that bring clients into therapy, such as poor psychological adjustment, interpersonal difficulties, and overall poor life functioning (see Tangney & Dearing, 2002). Not only is shame a factor underlying many of the reasons that clients seek psychotherapeutic help, but clients may feel shame as a result of needing help with their emotional concerns. Once in therapy, clients may further experience shame while discussing intimate details about themselves. Shame is therefore likely to be elicited frequently in therapy, though signals of client shame may be subtle.

If a therapist fails to recognize client shame, the client's shame-related problems will likely continue. Furthermore, clients who experience unacknowledged shame in the context of therapy may feel misunderstood, resulting in an empathic failure on the part of the therapist. Such empathic failure may result in premature termination of therapy. Therefore, therapists must recognize, acknowledge, and address client experiences of shame—to both build a therapeutic alliance and resolve the shame.

The intent of this book is to provide clinicians with guidance for dealing with client shame. All aspects of shame are covered, including how shame develops, how it relates to psychological difficulties, how to recognize shame, and how to help clients resolve shame-related problems. The chapters bring together wisdom and insight gained from years of clinical experience, shared by master clinicians who have struggled to manage and positively transform shame in the therapy hour. In particular, the chapter authors provide specific strategies that they use to help their clients resolve shame-related issues, and they illustrate these techniques using detailed examples and clinical dialogue. We are delighted with the resulting volume of chapters by gifted authors who provide outstanding insights into the clinical presentation, management, and resolution of shame in the therapy hour.

The intended audience for this book includes clinical and counseling psychologists, psychiatrists, social workers, marital and family therapists, addictions counselors, and other mental health providers. The book should be of interest to clinicians in training as well as seasoned professionals, the majority of whom are unlikely to have had any specific training in shame-related issues but who almost certainly encounter clients' shame experiences on a daily basis. We expect that readers will benefit from the material on different levels; new therapists are most likely to benefit from the notion of being attuned to client shame as an important aspect of therapy, whereas experienced therapists are more likely to see the book as a much-needed set of tools for addressing the longstanding challenge of helping clients work through shame in a way that will prevent future negative consequences.

In the remainder of this introduction, we present a general overview of shame, including the many potential negative consequences associated with it. We begin by providing an empirically supported definition of shame and describing research evidence that demonstrates the relevance of shame to psychological symptoms and overall functioning. Next, we distinguish between shame and guilt, as originally conceptualized by H. B. Lewis (1971). Finally, we explain how the book is organized.

WHAT IS SHAME, AND WHY IS IT A PROBLEM?

Shame is a prevalent and painful emotion that arises frequently in everyday life and that can contribute to the psychological difficulties that cause people to seek treatment. Feelings of shame arise in situations in which an individual recognizes that he or she has committed an offense or violated a standard that is held to be important. Experiences of shame tend to be intense and overpowering because they evoke a sense of being bad, worthless, or contemptible. Shame is frequently associated with a sense of powerlessness, as well as sensations of shrinking, feeling small, being exposed, and wanting to disappear. People experiencing shame evaluate the eliciting mistake or transgression as being indicative of a self that is fundamentally flawed. For example, a client may feel shame after being rebuked by her boss, extrapolating that she is a terrible employee or even a failure at life.

Because shame tends to arise in conjunction with cognitive appraisals of the self, it falls into the category of self-conscious emotions (e.g., Fischer & Tangney, 1995; Tracy, Robins, & Tangney, 2007). This type of cognitive processing requires a certain level of developmental maturity, which explains why the propensity to experience shame is developed over time during early childhood rather than present from birth (M. Lewis, 1992). Although everyone experiences shame from time to time, some people have a greater tendency to experience shame than others. Thus, we distinguish between *in-the-moment* shame and *shame proneness,* with the latter being a dispositional tendency to experience shame across situations.

Feelings of shame in-the-moment are associated with a variety of characteristic behavioral indicators, such as having a slumped posture, lowering the head, covering the face, and blushing. It is believed that these outward expressions of shame are linked to a submissive stance that once served an evolutionary function to preserve basic safety and social standing (see Chapter 14, this volume; Gilbert & McGuire, 1998). As is seen throughout this book, therapists can benefit from becoming attuned to visible indicators of shame because these behaviors may serve as the only hint that a client is experiencing this painful yet clinically relevant emotion.

In addition to being a self-conscious emotion, shame is categorized as a moral emotion on the basis of the presumption that it limits or averts socially undesirable acts. However, although shame certainly influences one's actions, this influence may not always be in the direction of a higher level of moral behavior. The immediate action tendency when faced with shame is to hide or escape from the trigger that elicited the painful emotion. Subsequent action tendencies may include desperate attempts to eradicate the discomfort associated with shame by denying culpability, lashing out in anger, or blaming others. For example, a student feeling shame after failing an exam might think, "I've always hated this teacher—she's so unfair." Painful feelings of shame and the related action tendencies seem to result in a short circuit of the moral compass, which often causes things to go awry in the interpersonal realm.

Shame may interfere with establishing and maintaining healthy interpersonal relationships for a number of reasons. Among these are problems with empathy and anger. Empathy seems to be differentially related to both in-the-moment shame and dispositional shame proneness. Research consistently shows that the self-focus inherent in shame does not facilitate and may at times thwart a consideration for others who may have been wronged (for reviews, see Tangney & Dearing, 2002; Tangney, Stuewig, & Mashek, 2007a). Instead, when in the midst of a shame experience, the focus of cognitive and emotional energy is directed inward. At the dispositional level, being shame prone is negatively or negligibly related to perspective taking and empathic concern, both of which are essential to interpersonal connection. Moreover, when faced with the distress of another person, shame-prone individuals are likely to respond with self-focused personal distress, which tends to inhibit the ability to respond empathically to others.

Equally important, shame proneness is empirically linked to problems with hostility, anger, aggression, and a propensity to externalize blame (Ahmed & Braithwaite, 2004; Andrews, Brewin, Rose, & Kirk, 2000; Bennett, Sullivan, & Lewis, 2005; Harper & Arias, 2004; Harper, Austin, Cercone, & Arias, 2005; Paulhus, Robins, Trzesniewski, & Tracy, 2004; Tangney & Dearing, 2002). Specific types of negative anger management related to shame include direct physical aggression, verbal and symbolic aggression, displaced aggression, self-directed aggression, and ruminative unexpressed anger. Recent research has demonstrated that externalization of blame seems to mediate the relation of shame with verbal and physical aggression (Stuewig, Tangney, Heigel, Harty, & McCloskey, 2010). In other words, shame leads to blaming, which leads to aggressive behavior. This multitude of problems with anger can result in impaired social relationships with friends, coworkers, and loved ones.

Also of fundamental relevance to clients in therapy is the consistent association between a shame-prone dispositional tendency and psychological symptoms across diverse age groups and populations. Research findings using a variety of methods have shown a relationship between shame proneness and a multitude of symptoms ranging from low self-esteem (Yelsma, Brown, & Elison, 2002) to suicidal ideation (Hastings, Northman, & Tangney, 2000). These associations encompass the spectrum of symptoms commonly seen among clients in psychotherapy, such as depression, anxiety, eating disorder symptoms, posttraumatic stress disorder (PTSD), and substance abuse (Andrews et al., 2000; Ashby, Rice, & Martin, 2006; Crossley & Rockett, 2005; Dearing, Stuewig, & Tangney, 2005; Feiring & Taska, 2005; Ferguson, Stegge, Eyre, Vollmer, & Ashbaker, 2000; Harper & Arias, 2004; Leskela, Dieperink, & Thuras, 2002; Meehan et al., 1996; Murray, Waller, & Legg, 2000; Sanftner, Barlow, Marschall, & Tangney, 1995; Stuewig & McCloskey, 2005; for reviews, see Tangney & Dearing, 2002; and Tangney et al., 2007a). Thus, empirical findings confirm the long-standing clinical literature indicating that frequent experiences of shame contribute to individual vulnerability to psychological distress.

Although shame is associated with a host of potentially problematic action tendencies, interpersonal shortcomings, and psychosocial outcomes, it has seldom been the focus of attention in psychological interventions. We can only speculate as to why this is the case, but three reasons are likely to have contributed to this lack of consideration. First of all, the word *shame* is often avoided in everyday language. Second, shame is inherently linked to a desire to hide and conceal; thus, feelings of shame are frequently hidden and avoided, rather than brought up as the focus of attention during therapy. Third, as discussed throughout this book, it seems that therapists inadvertently avoid discussing shame-related issues with their clients. Therefore, despite its prevalence within the context of therapy, shame has rarely been a direct focus of intervention research or applied clinical writing.

Although shame can lead individuals into therapy, it is notoriously difficult to admit, discuss, and treat (H. B. Lewis, 1971; Lindsay-Hartz, 1984; Tangney & Dearing, 2002). The acute emotional pain associated with shame makes it likely that clients will avoid talking about shame-eliciting issues, yet shame experiences often have rich clinical relevance. Clinicians need to become adept at evaluating clients' tendencies toward shame and at recognizing subtle indicators of shame. Not only do clients seek therapy for shame-related issues, but the very process of entering and participating in therapy can be intensely shame inducing for the client. This is eloquently summarized by Greenberg and Iwakabe (Chapter 3, this volume) in the following statement: "The mere act of acknowledging that life is too difficult and the idea of laying bare one's deepest secrets to a relative stranger are fraught with shame."

Furthermore, shame isn't limited to clients—therapists experience shame, too. The notion of therapist shame runs throughout the book, with most of the authors acknowledging the ways in which therapist shame may influence the therapeutic encounter and providing insights into how best to manage and occasionally capitalize on therapist shame.

In summary, shame is a key factor that brings clients into therapy, can be elicited by the process of therapy, and can arise among therapists providing therapy. Thus, therapists need guidance to help them better understand shame and work with clients' and their own experiences of shame.

SHAME AND GUILT: WHAT IS THE DIFFERENCE?

In everyday parlance, the words *shame* and *guilt* are often used interchangeably (with *guilt* being used much more frequently). Clinicians, too, often use these terms interchangeably. However, shame and guilt differ in numerous ways. Therefore, we feel it is important to offer a specific, empirically based differentiation of the two. Helen Block Lewis (1971) proposed an elegant, yet subtle, distinction between shame and guilt that has withstood the test of time on the basis of evidence from abundant research using a variety of approaches (for reviews, see Tangney & Dearing, 2002; Tangney et al., 2007a). H. B. Lewis proposed that the key difference between shame and guilt hinges on whether the focus of attention is on the triggering behavior or attribute (guilt) or more generally on the self (shame). If, when faced with a misdeed or shortcoming, the focus of attention is on the event or behavior ("I *did* something bad"), guilt is the likely emotional outcome, whereas if the focus is on the self ("I *am* bad"), shame is the likely result.

Attribution theory supports this distinction and can provide for a more nuanced understanding of the differences between shame and guilt (e.g., Tangney, Wagner, & Gramzow, 1992; Tracy & Robins, 2006). Specifically, shame is the probable result when self-appraisals for negative events are attributed to internal, stable, uncontrollable, and global causes (e.g., "I am stupid"). Alternatively, guilt is to be expected when cognitive appraisals for negative events are attributed to internal, unstable, controllable, and specific causes ("I should have worked harder on that project").

Although H. B. Lewis's definition of shame (and its distinction from guilt) has been the conceptualization guiding our own work, we explicitly instructed chapter authors to feel free to use their own definitions of shame in addressing shame-related clinical issues. As it happens, most authors adopted the self versus behavior distinction that has been confirmed by much empirical research. But a number of authors expanded on this definition and further differentiated between different subtypes of shame, adding richness to clinical conceptualizations of this powerful and ubiquitous emotion. Where chapter authors opted to use slightly different or expanded definitions of shame, these differences are clarified within the applicable chapters.

Where Does Guilt Fit in?

Guilt tends to be less acutely painful than shame (because a specific behavior rather than the overall self is brought into question); nonetheless, guilt is associated with uncomfortable feelings of remorse and regret. As a result, the action tendencies associated with guilt typically involve wanting to make things better, for example, by apologizing, confessing, or making amends. This is in sharp contrast to the action tendencies associated with shame—to escape or to lash out. Thus, although shame and guilt are both linked to moral behavior, it seems that in the case of guilt, this connection is in a beneficial direction. In contrast to shame, guilt does not seem to be characterized by visible outward signs, but the action tendencies associated with guilt (e.g., confessions, apologies) make it more likely that guilt feelings will be brought up and discussed by clients within the context of therapy.

Research has shown that both the states of shame and guilt and the propensities toward shame proneness and guilt proneness differ greatly in terms of outcome. These differences occur in a variety of contexts, including psychological symptoms, interpersonal relations, and moral behavior. In most cases, the outcomes associated with guilt are more adaptive than those we have discussed as related to shame. For example, guilt, in contrast to shame, seems to be intricately and positively linked to empathic connection. People who are guilt prone are readily able to take the perspective of another person and to demonstrate other-oriented empathic concern in relation to others' feelings of distress (Joireman, 2004; Leith & Baumeister, 1998; Tangney, 1991; Tangney & Dearing, 2002). Furthermore, when feeling guilt about a specific behavior, the individual's focus of attention is often on the harm done (i.e., to another person) and on how to repair the situation. This urge to rectify matters leads to actions that facilitate strengthened interpersonal relationships.

People who are guilt prone are just as prone to experience anger as anyone else; however, when angered, guilt-prone individuals are less likely than their non–guilt-prone peers to engage in all types of aggression, and they are more likely to manage anger in constructive ways, such as nonhostile discussion and direct reparative actions (Ahmed & Braithwaite, 2004; Lutwak, Panish, Ferrari, & Razzino, 2001; Paulhus et al., 2004; Tangney, Wagner, Hill-Barlow, Marschall, & Gramzow, 1996). These healthier reactions to anger among guilt-prone persons seem to be attributable to the link between guilt and empathy (Stuewig, Tangney, Heigel, Harty, & McCloskey, 2010). Specifically, among guilt-prone individuals, anger seems to activate other-oriented empathy and a tendency to take responsibility, resulting in less aggressive behaviors. It seems that guilt-prone people manage anger by acknowledging and taking responsibility for their wrongdoings, resulting in healthier interpersonal outcomes.

Although the common clinical assumption is that guilt is a root cause of "neuroses" and other psychological problems, research has demonstrated that a predisposition to "shame-free" guilt is largely unrelated to psychological symptoms (for reviews, see Tangney & Dearing, 2002; Tangney et al., 2007a). Empirical studies that do suggest a link between guilt and psychological symptoms have typically failed to make H. B. Lewis's (1971) crucial self versus behavior distinction or have not used measurement instruments that differentiate shame from guilt. When using H. B. Lewis's operational definition, research findings have not shown a positive association between guilt proneness and psychological symptoms, including depression, anxiety, or symptoms of posttraumatic distress.

How Is the Shame–Guilt Distinction Relevant to Psychotherapy?

Clients and therapists alike are often unclear about the distinction between shame and guilt. Yet as the research evidence shows, shame brings with it vulnerability to a host of intrapersonal and interpersonal problems, whereas guilt appears to serve more adaptive functions. Thus, we believe therapists (and their clients) would benefit from recognizing the distinction between shame and guilt, rather than making the assumption that shame and guilt are both similarly problematic. Relative to guilt, shame (and especially dispositional shame proneness) is more likely to be detrimental to the therapeutic process, and it is also more likely to represent a significant part of the clinical picture presented by clients seeking help. By being aware of the risks and consequences associated with shame, as distinct from guilt, therapists can be better equipped to help their clients work through the difficult process of identifying, acknowledging, managing, and transforming problematic shame experiences.

We have found it useful to recognize shame and guilt at multiple levels (e.g., states, generalized dispositions, domain-specific propensities) occurring at different points vis-à-vis emotion-eliciting behavior (e.g., in anticipation or as a consequence of failures and transgressions). For example, like all emotions, shame and guilt can be conceptualized as states (i.e., feelings in the moment) and as affective traits (i.e., dispositional tendencies). Although everyone has the capacity to experience both shame and guilt (perhaps with the exception of the rare psychopath; see Tangney & Stuewig, 2004), people vary in their susceptibility to experience shame versus guilt in response to failure or wrongdoing. Some people are more likely to experience shame, others are more likely to experience guilt, and still others are inclined to experience a mix of the two—an experience we call *shame-fused guilt*. People aren't exclusively shame prone or guilt prone; rather, they fall somewhere on a continuum for each dimension, and these continua are moderately positively correlated. We refer to these dispositional tendencies as shame proneness and guilt proneness. These differing outcomes associated with shame- and guilt-prone dispositions make it particularly relevant for clinicians to evaluate clients' individual levels of shame proneness and guilt proneness (for reviews of different options for assessing shame- and guilt-prone dispositions, see Robins, Noftle, & Tracy, 2007; Tangney & Dearing, 2002).

Beyond generalized tendencies to experience shame and/or guilt across diverse situations, clinicians often find it useful to consider domain-specific sources of shame and guilt in their clients. Each client is apt to have unique areas of vulnerability—domains in which he or she is especially susceptible to feelings of shame, guilt, or both. For example, whether generally shame prone or not, a given client may be highly sensitive to body shame. Another client may be vulnerable to guilt vis-à-vis a demanding parent. Another may be susceptible to shame in connection with a psychological problem. In this volume, specific approaches for assessing clients' unique "shame triggers" are offered by Brown, Hernandez, and Villarreal (Chapter 15) and by Rizvi, Brown, Bohus, and Linehan (Chapter 10).

Not only do people have particular emotional reactions to specific events, they also can often imagine how they are likely to react to events that have not yet occurred. In this way, shame and guilt can exert their effects on behavior in anticipation of an event as well as following an event. Tangney, Stuewig, and Mashek (2007b) referred to these as *anticipatory* and *consequential* shame and/or guilt reactions, respectively. It seems probable that one reason clients are hesitant to bring up potentially shame-eliciting issues within therapy is the anticipated shame associated with discussing difficult shame-laden topics. This is apt to be most problematic for shame-prone clients because they are likely to anticipate that feelings of shame will arise across a variety of possible topics and thus are likely to avoid discussing issues that are potentially shaming. Providing a safe, caring therapy environment is essential for overcoming the obstacle of anticipatory shame among clients.

Shame-related concerns can be addressed within therapy both in-the-moment and at the dispositional level. For example, a client may be feeling shame about a recent incident of disciplining her child. Her cognitive interpretation may be, "I must be a horrible person to have yelled at my child." As a means of resolving this particular shame experience, the therapist can help the client shift her cognitive focus to specific eliciting events, associated behaviors, and ways of handling future events differently (e.g., "I had a stressful day at work. I was angry. I've never yelled at her before. Next time I should explain to her why I am upset using a calmer tone."). Similarly, at the dispositional level, therapists can teach their clients the vital difference in emotional outcome between evaluations of "I am bad" versus "I did a bad thing" so that clients can try to minimize their tendencies to think about negative events in terms of negative self-evaluation and instead evaluate the associated behaviors.

These are but a few examples of the approaches and techniques that clinicians have found useful when working with clients who are troubled by shame. The chapters in this book provide clinicians with several approaches, drawing on the wisdom and experience of a remarkable set of master clinicians working from diverse theoretical perspectives. By addressing shame in the context of psychotherapy, the therapist can help clients with the immediate symptoms that led them into therapy and also help clients develop the resources to prevent such problems from developing in the future.

ORGANIZATION AND OVERVIEW OF THIS BOOK

This book is divided into five sections, as follows.

Part I: Shame From Multiple Therapeutic Perspectives

The chapters in Part I illustrate how shame is managed from a variety of clinical orientations and within specific types of therapy. It would have been impossible to include all possible schools of psychotherapeutic thought, but we believe that these chapters offer ideas, suggestions, and specific techniques that will be helpful to therapists from a variety of backgrounds. Although common themes emerge throughout the book (e.g., empathy, therapist authenticity, recognition of shame), each chapter in this section provides a unique perspective on approaches for navigating shame within the therapy hour. Shame has long been recognized in the analytic and dynamic literature (e.g., H. B. Lewis, 1971; Morrison, 1989; Piers & Singer, 1953); careful readers may notice that several of the chapters have a psychodynamic underpinning (e.g., Chapter 1, by Morrison; Chapter 2, by Stadter; Chapter 7, by Epstein & Falconier; Chapter 11, by Herman). Nonetheless, chapter authors come from a variety of disciplines. Each was willing to take the risk of writing about shame, much as therapists must be willing to deal with their own shame before they are able to help their clients heal shame-related wounds. Indeed, the compilation of chapters clearly demonstrates that clients' (and therapists') experiences of shame during therapy are frequent and cut across therapeutic approaches.

Chapter 1 sets the stage by describing the psychodynamics of shame. In this chapter, Morrison, who has written extensively about shame, identifies the developmental processes and intrapersonal underpinnings of shame from a psychodynamic perspective. In addition, he discusses the many (often elaborate) defenses that people use to avoid painful feelings of shame. Morrison provides readers with strategies for looking beyond clients' defenses to help them overcome problematic shame.

In Chapter 2, Stadter contextualizes shame through an object relations lens. Namely, he describes how one's inner world centers on internalized self–other interactions, including interactions that result in shame. Furthermore, Stadter characterizes ways in which relations with others can be experienced as shaming (e.g., directly, indirectly, by neglect or abuse), and he describes the types of reactions that can result when shame is experienced (e.g., hyperarousal, dissociation, contempt). Stadter explains how internalized self–other patterns play out in the therapeutic interactions between client and therapist. He then demonstrates how the therapist can use these interactions to help the client change repetitive, maladaptive interaction patterns.

Greenberg and Iwakabe, in Chapter 3, place shame in the greater framework of emotion-focused therapy. The authors demonstrate ways that the therapeutic relationship can be used to help the client derive useful meaning from shameful experiences. They stress the necessity of a safe, trusting interpersonal context for healing shame within therapy.

Shifting to a different school of psychotherapeutic thought, in Chapter 4, Koerner, Tsai, and Simpson discuss shame from a functional analytic framework (which emerged from the radical behaviorism tradition). In this chapter, one sees the importance of meticulous assessment for understanding how the contributing factors to shame are unique for each individual client. Furthermore, Koerner and colleagues explain that it is insufficient to explain one behavior or emotion as resulting from another (e.g., "she felt shame because she felt worthless"); instead, the authors emphasize the importance of the confluence of specific antecedents that lead to a particular result. In other words, it is imperative to understand multiple relevant factors that contribute to the client feeling shame in one specific instance but not in another seemingly similar set of circumstances.

The next three chapters examine interpersonal dynamics in group, family, and couples therapy contexts. In Chapter 5, Shapiro and Powers demonstrate the unique power of group therapy both for eliciting shame and for healing it. As explained by the authors, dealing with shame in group therapy is, indeed, a paradox. Most clients are rendered virtually paralyzed by the notion of sharing their darkest secrets among a room full of relative strangers; yet, as the authors demonstrate, this very act of sharing shameful experiences, and feeling accepted by others, is critical to the process of recovering from the painful feelings of shame.

In Chapter 6, Teyber, McClure, and Weathers focus on family therapy. The authors illustrate how parents' shame can unintentionally result in profound shame in their children. By providing a safe environment for recognizing these patterns, family therapists can help heal and transform shaming family dynamics. Teyber and coauthors elegantly demonstrate this process using a case example that flows throughout the chapter.

In Chapter 7, Epstein and Falconier demonstrate how romantic partners are in a unique position to activate one another's shame triggers, whether by accident or by intention. Because of the intimacy inherent in couple relationships and the interpersonal nature of shame, shame dynamics are bound to occur within couples. The authors provide a detailed framework for assessing each individual's proneness to shame as well as the couple's communication patterns that may result from or elicit shame. The authors then discuss specific cognitive–behavioral techniques that can be used in couples therapy to replace maladaptive shame-based or shaming communication patterns with more constructive interactions.

In Chapter 8, the final chapter of this section, Furukawa and Hunt provide a unique perspective on working with shame among immigrant and refugee clients. Such clients often come from different cultural or ethnic backgrounds than their therapists; because cultural norms are often relevant to the emergence of shame experiences, cultural misunderstandings have enormous potential to result in client shame. Furthermore, the very idea of entering therapy may be profoundly stigmatizing for some cultural groups. Therapists must be uniquely attuned to the nuances of shame in clients from different cultures. Furukawa and Hunt's chapter offers a glimpse into challenging multicultural dynamics as well as useful suggestions for working with these clients in an informed, sensitive manner.

Part II: Challenging Problems in Therapy: Shame-Based Clinical Disorders

Part II provides an overview of disorders in which shame may cause specific challenges for the therapist. Shame is pervasive; therefore, the range of psychological issues and disorders in which it comes into play is vast. Part II shows how shame contributes to the development of certain disorders while the presence of the disorder fuels additional shame.

Few disorders are more stigmatizing than the addictive disorders. As discussed in Chapter 9, by Potter-Efron, the presence of an addiction is often intentionally hidden not only by the person with the disorder but all too often by his or her loved ones as well. It is no coincidence that avoidance and a desire to hide are hallmark action tendencies associated with shame. These attempts to conceal the underlying problem result in perpetuation of the cycle of shame. This *shame–addiction spiral* must be addressed in order to effectively treat addictions.

In Chapter 10, Rizvi, Brown, Bohus, and Linehan address one of the most inherently difficult presenting problems that therapists face: borderline personality disorder. In addition to discussing the manifold shame-related problems facing these clients, the authors introduce the therapeutic technique of *opposite action* as applied to shame (Rizvi & Linehan, 2005), which represents one of the few methods that have been empirically demonstrated to be effective at reducing shame.

Herman's chapter on PTSD—Chapter 11—highlights the developmental processes and relational disruptions that can lead to shame and severe psychological symptoms. In particular, Herman explains how certain violations (e.g., childhood abuse, violent crime) can result in profound shame, which, when unresolved, results in the symptoms of PTSD. Herman describes a series of steps for helping clients recover from these extreme relationship violations, including normalizing feelings of shame, exploring shame experiences, establishing a safe therapeutic environment, and learning to discuss shameful events.

Similarly, in Chapter 12, Sanftner and Tantillo conceptualize eating disorders as arising from chronic relationship disruptions. Consistent with many of the chapters in this book, the authors propose that healing from unremitting shame is contingent upon feeling understood and worthy of affection. Sanftner and Tantillo describe the importance of forming a healthy, validating relationship with the therapist in which the client can explore the shame-related triggers that lead to eating-disordered behavior. Furthermore, successfully establishing a safe relationship with the therapist can empower the client to begin to form additional meaningful connections with others.

Part III: Shame in the Other Chair

In Part III, consisting of Chapter 13, Ladany, Klinger, and Kulp present a promising model of supervision as one means of providing psychotherapy training in a nonshaming manner. As previously noted, many authors mention therapist shame (or their own shame) when working with clients. This discussion reflects the difficulty of immersing oneself in the shame experience, whether it involves writing a chapter, working with a client, or dealing with one's own experiences of shame. We believe therapists in training should be provided with instruction about how therapist and client shame can influence the therapeutic endeavor. Ladany and colleagues' chapter provides an initial foray into this largely unexplored and sensitive topic.

Part IV: Shame-Focused Strategies

The two chapters of Part IV focus on newly developed treatments explicitly designed to address and heal shame. In Chapter 14, Gilbert describes his work on compassion focused therapy (CFT). Gilbert proposes that individuals who are self-critical and shame prone have seldom experienced compassion from others and lack the necessary skills to practice self-compassion. CFT teaches clients shame reduction skills that include practicing mindfulness, developing self-soothing strategies, tolerating positive and negative emotion, and learning to be self-compassionate. CFT exercises use a combination of strategies, including psychoeducation, imagery, normalizing, and compassionate validation by the therapist.

In Chapter 15, Brown, Hernandez, and Villareal introduce the idea of *shame resilience*—namely, the ability to recognize shame experiences and endure them constructively. The authors posit that establishing connections with others and being empathically understood are essential to developing shame resilience. Forming these interpersonal connections hinges upon learning to be vulnerable and becoming comfortable sharing shame experiences with others. The *Connections* curriculum, based on shame resilience theory (Brown, 2005), allows clients to develop and practice these skills. (As previously mentioned, Chapter 10, on borderline personality disorder, also discusses a pilot-tested shame-specific treatment, opposite action.)

Part V: Shame: Future Directions

In the final chapter, Tangney and Dearing attempt to synthesize the common themes emerging from across chapters and summarize our thoughts on future directions for research and treatment. Because both of us have delved deeply into the research related to shame (e.g., Tangney & Dearing,

2002) and have done clinical work, we thought at the outset of this project that we had a reasonable understanding of how shame factors in with treatment. Certainly, we knew that it plays an important role in the therapeutic process; otherwise, we wouldn't have felt compelled to organize this book. However, over the course of reading and editing the chapters, we came to realize that the master clinicians who wrote these chapters have a deeper and richer understanding of shame than that which can be gained from reading the existing research literature alone. This is not to say that we discount the idea of empirically supported treatment; on the contrary, we are strong proponents of treatment that is supported by research data. Yet efforts to develop empirically supported treatment approaches focusing on shame are still in their early stages, with only three empirically based treatments described to date.

Although many therapeutic approaches offer specific techniques for dealing with shame (as is demonstrated throughout this book), there is much more work to be done in terms of developing new interventions and clarifying what works. We hope that the wisdom and insights of the entire set of chapters, taken together, will provide a firm basis for additional treatment development and evaluation efforts. We strongly subscribe to the notion that the best treatment and the best research evolve from the interplay inherent in the clinical science model. Researchers formulate their ideas based on observations of the real world; treatment research is no different.

REFERENCES

Ahmed, E., & Braithwaite, V. (2004). "What, me ashamed?": Shame management and school bullying. *Journal of Research in Crime and Delinquency, 41*, 269–294. doi:10.1177/0022427804266547

Andrews, B., Brewin, C. R., Rose, S., & Kirk, M. (2000). Predicting PTSD symptoms in victims of violent crime: The role of shame, anger, and childhood abuse. *Journal of Abnormal Psychology, 109*, 69–73. doi:10.1037/0021-843X.109.1.69

Ashby, J. S., Rice, K. G., & Martin, J. L. (2006). Perfectionism, shame, and depressive symptoms. *Journal of Counseling and Development, 84*, 148–156.

Bennett, D. S., Sullivan, M. W., & Lewis, M. (2005). Young children's adjustment as a function of maltreatment, shame, and anger. *Child Maltreatment: Journal of the American Professional Society on the Abuse of Children, 10*, 311–323.

Brown, B. (2005). Shame resilience theory: A grounded theory study on women and shame. *Families in Society: The Journal of Contemporary Social Services, 87*, 43–52.

Crossley, D., & Rockett, K. (2005). The experience of shame in older psychiatric patients: A preliminary enquiry. *Aging & Mental Health, 9*, 368–373. doi:10.1080/13607860500131252

Dearing, R. L., Stuewig, J., & Tangney, J. P. (2005). On the importance of distinguishing shame from guilt: Relations to problematic alcohol and drug use. *Addictive Behaviors, 30,* 1392–1404. doi:10.1016/j.addbeh.2005.02.002

Feiring, C., & Taska, L. (2005). The persistence of shame following sexual abuse: A longitudinal look at risk and recovery. *Child Maltreatment, 10,* 337–349. doi:10.1177/1077559505276686

Ferguson, T. J., Stegge, H., Eyre, H. L., Vollmer, R., & Ashbaker, M. (2000). Context effects and the (mal)adaptive nature of guilt and shame in children. *Genetic, Social, and General Psychology Monographs, 126,* 319–345.

Fischer, K. W., & Tangney, J. P. (1995). Self-conscious emotions and the affect revolution: Framework and introduction. In J. P. Tangney & K. W. Fischer (Eds.), *Self-conscious emotions: Shame, guilt, embarrassment, and pride* (pp. 3–22). New York, NY: Guilford Press.

Gilbert, P., & McGuire, M. T. (1998). Shame, status, and social roles: Psychobiology and evolution. In P. Gilbert & B. Andrews (Eds.), *Shame: Interpersonal behavior, psychopathology, and culture. Series in affective science* (pp. 99–125). New York, NY: Oxford University Press.

Harper, F. W. K., & Arias, I. (2004). The role of shame in predicting adult anger and depressive symptoms among victims of child psychological maltreatment. *Journal of Family Violence, 19,* 367—375. doi:10.1007/s10896-004-0681-x

Harper, F. W. K., Austin, A. G., Cercone, J. J., & Arias, I. (2005). The role of shame, anger, and affect regulation in men's perpetration of psychological abuse in dating relationships. *Journal of Interpersonal Violence, 20,* 1648–1662. doi:10.1177/0886260505278717

Hastings, M. E., Northman, L. M., & Tangney, J. P. (2000). Shame, guilt, and suicide. In T. Joiner & M. D. Rudd (Eds.), *Suicide science: Expanding boundaries* (pp. 67–79). Boston, MA: Kluwer Academic.

Joireman, J. (2004). Empathy and the self-absorption paradox II: Self-rumination and self-reflection as mediators between shame, guilt, and empathy. *Self and Identity, 3,* 225–238. doi:10.1080/13576500444000038

Leith, K. P., & Baumeister, R. F. (1998). Empathy, shame, guilt, and narratives of interpersonal conflicts: Guilt-prone people are better at perspective taking. *Journal of Personality, 66,* 1–37. doi:10.1111/1467-6494.00001

Leskela, J., Dieperink, M., & Thuras, P. (2002). Shame and posttraumatic stress disorder. *Journal of Traumatic Stress, 15,* 223–226. doi:10.1023/A:1015255311837

Lewis, H. B. (1971). *Shame and guilt in neurosis.* New York, NY: International Universities Press.

Lewis, M. (1992). *Shame: The exposed self.* New York, NY: Free Press.

Lindsay-Hartz, J. (1984). Contrasting experiences of shame and guilt. *American Behavioral Scientist, 27,* 689–704. doi:10.1177/000276484027006003

Lutwak, N., Panish, J. B., Ferrari, J. R., & Razzino, B. E. (2001). Shame and guilt and their relationship to positive expectations and anger expressiveness. *Adolescence, 36,* 641–653.

Meehan, W., O'Connor, L. E., Berry, J. W., Weiss, J., Morrison, A., & Acampora, A. (1996). Guilt, shame, and depression in clients in recovery from addiction. *Journal of Psychoactive Drugs, 28,* 125–134.

Morrison, A. (1989). *Shame: The underside of narcissism.* Hillsdale, NJ: Analytic Press.

Murray, C., Waller, G., & Legg, C. (2000). Family dysfunction and bulimia psychopathology: The mediating role of shame. *International Journal of Eating Disorders, 28,* 84–89. doi:10.1002/(SICI)1098-108X(200007)28:1<84::AID-EAT 10>3.0.CO;2-R

Paulhus, D. L., Robins, R. W., Trzesniewski, K. H., & Tracy, J. L. (2004). Two replicable suppressor situations in personality research. *Multivariate Behavioral Research, 39,* 303–328. doi:10.1207/s15327906mbr3902_7

Piers, G., & Singer, M. (1953). *Shame and guilt.* Springfield, IL: Thomas.

Rizvi, S. L., & Linehan, M. M. (2005). The treatment of maladaptive shame in borderline personality disorder: A pilot study of "opposite action." *Cognitive and Behavioral Practice, 12,* 437–447. doi:10.1016/S1077-7229(05)80071-9

Robins, R. W., Noftle, E. E., & Tracy, J. L. (2007). Assessing self-conscious emotions: A review of self-report and nonverbal measures. In J. L. Tracy, R. W. Robins, & J. P. Tangney (Eds.), *The self-conscious emotions: Theory and research* (pp. 443–467). New York, NY: Guilford Press.

Sanftner, J. L., Barlow, D. H., Marschall, D. M., & Tangney, J. P. (1995). The relation of shame and guilt to eating disorder symptomatology. *Journal of Social and Clinical Psychology, 14,* 315–324.

Stuewig, J., & McCloskey, L. A. (2005). The relation of child maltreatment to shame and guilt among adolescents: Psychological routes to depression and delinquency. *Child Maltreatment, 10,* 324–336. doi:10.1177/1077559505279308

Stuewig, J., Tangney, J. P., Heigel, C., Harty, L., & McCloskey, L. (2010). Shaming, blaming, and maiming: Functional links among the moral emotions, externalization of blame, and aggression. *Journal of Research in Personality, 44,* 91–102. doi:10.1016/j.jrp.2009.12.005

Tangney, J. P. (1991). Moral affect: The good, the bad, and the ugly. *Journal of Personality and Social Psychology, 61,* 598–607. doi:10.1037/0022-3514.61.4.598

Tangney, J. P., & Dearing, R. (2002). *Shame and guilt.* New York, NY: Guilford Press.

Tangney, J. P., & Stuewig, J. (2004). A moral emotional perspective on evil persons and evil deeds. In A. Miller (Ed.), *The social psychology of good and evil: Understanding our capacity for kindness and cruelty* (pp. 327–355). New York, NY: Guilford Press.

Tangney, J. P., Stuewig, J., & Mashek, D. J. (2007a). Moral emotions and moral behavior. *Annual Review of Psychology, 58,* 345–372. doi:10.1146/annurev. psych.56.091103.070145

Tangney, J. P., Stuewig, J., & Mashek, D. J. (2007b). What's moral about the self-conscious emotions? In J. L. Tracy, R. W. Robins, & J. P. Tangney (Eds.), *The self-conscious emotions: Theory and research* (pp. 21–37). New York, NY: Guilford Press.

Tangney, J. P., Wagner, P. E., & Gramzow, R. (1992). Proneness to shame, proneness to guilt, and psychopathology. *Journal of Abnormal Psychology, 101*, 469–478. doi:10.1037/0021-843X.101.3.469

Tangney, J. P., Wagner, P. E., Hill-Barlow, D., Marschall, D. E., & Gramzow, R. (1996). Relation of shame and guilt to constructive versus destructive responses to anger across the lifespan. *Journal of Personality and Social Psychology, 70*, 797–809. doi:10.1037/0022-3514.70.4.797

Tracy, J. L., & Robins, R. W. (2006). Appraisal antecedents of shame and guilt: Support for a theoretical model. *Personality and Social Psychology Bulletin, 32*, 1339–1351. doi:10.1177/0146167206290212

Tracy, J. L., Robins, R. W., & Tangney, J. P. (Eds.). (2007). *The self-conscious emotions: Theory and research*. New York, NY: Guilford Press.

Yelsma, P., Brown, N. M., & Elison, J. (2002). Shame-focused coping styles and their associations with self-esteem. *Psychological Reports, 90*, 1179–1189.

I

SHAME FROM
MULTIPLE THERAPEUTIC
PERSPECTIVES

1

THE PSYCHODYNAMICS OF SHAME

ANDREW P. MORRISON

Shame is a painful burden that permeates the whole body and envelops one's complete sense of self. It is, perhaps, the most agonizing of human emotions in that it reduces us each in stature, size, and self-esteem, such that we wish to disappear, to sink into the ground. "Shame settles in like a dense fog, obscuring everything else, imposing only its own shapeless, substanceless impressions" (Morrison, 1994, p. 19). We go to great extremes to overcome those shortcomings that lead to shame. If we can't hide, we attempt to change the very attributes that have caused this distress. Characteristically, these efforts fail, and we are left to suffer with our shame. Since we can never successfully hide ourselves from the world of observers, we employ defenses that aim at hiding our shame experience or those personal attributes that stimulate it. We get angry, contemptuous, or envious of the other; depressed; or, alternatively, grandiose. These defenses against shame are explored later, but suffice it to say that our personal efforts are aimed at minimizing the distress presented by shame.

What leads to shame? It is crucial to note that shame is about the self, the *whole* self (Lewis, 1971). Shame and self-experience reflect the subjective sense of defect, failure, flaw, weakness, dirtiness, insignificance, and many related qualities of imperfection. Among these other qualities, one in particular stands out: a sense of passivity and the many qualities that accompany it. Passivity often complements feelings of dependency, of need (for support, supplies, love)—feelings that one believes shouldn't be present. Gender becomes relevant here because, in American culture, it is particularly true that men believe they mustn't be dependent or needy, whereas women tend to be more tolerant of these yearnings.

For each of these noxious qualities of self-experience, one shared factor generates the sense of shame: the occurrence of falling short of one's aspirations or expectations for perfection and achievement. To put this more symbolically, shame reflects the degree to which we fall short of attaining our ideals. Sandler, Holder, and Meers (1963) wrote of an *ideal self*—the state of self reaching its ideal—contrasted with the *actual self*—the sense of self as we actually are. The distance or gap between the ideal and actual selves determines the presence and intensity of shame at any given time. The ideal may reflect a physical skill, a moral quality, or an intellectual achievement, but whatever its essence, it stands for some essential attribute of self. Without attaining the ideal, we are left feeling incomplete, inferior, or a failure—these experiences are the heart of shame.

In this chapter, I use a psychodynamic conceptualization of shame to demonstrate the interplay of shame with narcissism, the distinction between shame and guilt, the development of shame in a self-object context, and the role of ego and superego in the development of shame. I illustrate how patient shame is often disguised under a variety of defense mechanisms, such as contempt, envy, or grandiosity. Furthermore, I attempt to elucidate these concepts using representative clinical examples as a means of demonstrating how therapists can use acceptance and gentle interpretation to help their clients gain control over the painful grip of shame. Finally, I address the therapist's experience of shame.

THE ROLE OF NARCISSISM IN SHAME

Because shame is about self-experience, we inevitably encounter the psychodynamic phenomenon of narcissism—a complex but crucial construct that invites inquiry far beyond the reach of this chapter. This psychodynamic concept of narcissism is not to be confused with the narrower, and more pathological, personality disorder described in the *Diagnostic and Statistical Manual of Mental Disorders* (American Psychiatric Association, 1994). The essence of narcissism, I suggest, is a yearning to be unique—special to a significant other. When this yearning is fundamentally gratified in childhood, we grow up feeling satisfied, nurtured, and whole. It is the response of the caretaker that Kohut (1977) called "the gleam in the mother's eye" (p. 116).

Such a response from the mothering figure—called by Kohut the *mirroring self-object*—yields a sense of self that is coherent, stable, and well esteemed. Alternatively, in its absence, the self is felt to be chaotic or disrupted, with an overwhelming sense of deficit or fragmentation. It is this latter sense about oneself that leaves one sensitive to narcissistic vulnerability and to shame. In this way, shame is the negative feeling of narcissism, much as anxiety and guilt were seen in traditional psychoanalysis as the hallmarks of neurotic conflict.

Very broadly, I conceive of narcissism as reflecting all aspects of self-experience, including the two extremes of desire for perfection, grandiosity, and absolute lovability—the *expansive pole* of self—and feelings of inferiority, smallness, and insignificance—the *contracted pole* of self. These poles generate a dialectical tension between each other, a tension that I have called the *dialectic of narcissism* (Morrison, 1989). I suggest that the expansive and contracted poles of self-experience are both present for us all, with one being dominant (*foreground*) and the other more recessive (*background*) at any given time or for a particular individual. Experiences at either pole have the potential to result in feelings of shame.

SHAME VERSUS GUILT

Having introduced guilt into our discussion of shame, it is relevant now to consider the differences between shame and guilt. I have defined *shame* as a negative feeling about the state of the whole self, a noxious conviction that the self is bad, defective, a failure. *Guilt*, on the other hand, refers to a deed committed or omitted against someone else—an action that hurts or maims the other (Piers & Singer, 1953). Shame generally results in passivity or inaction; guilt often stimulates activity. Guilt usually invokes confession to remedy the feeling, whereas shame characteristically leads to hiding and concealment or withdrawal. The ultimate goal in healing guilt is forgiveness, whereas shame seeks acceptance. Frequently, the two feelings are simultaneously present, interacting with and eliciting the other in what Lewis (1971) called the *guilt–shame cycle*. For example, John (pseudonyms are used throughout) does something that harms his brother, for which he feels guilt. Simultaneous feelings of shame cause him to pull back and withdraw. In response to the shame, he gets angry and lashes out, feeling guilty once more. This is a fairly typical sequence involving guilt and shame in which the two coexist and interact.

Jackson was a recently graduated lawyer who was working long hours at a large firm. He was toiling over a defense document for one of the firm's clients, and he made one major error in judgment for which he was severely criticized by the senior partner in charge of the case. Jackson felt guilty for the excessive trouble he had caused the firm and, potentially, the client. At the

same time, he felt ashamed of himself for being so incompetent and ineffi-
cient in his work as an attorney. That night he went home feeling his ineptitude, and when his dog wouldn't stop barking in excitement, Jackson lashed
out and smacked the dog on the rump. Abruptly his mood had changed from
sheepish passivity to anger and aggression, after which he felt, again, the
familiar guilt.

HOW SHAME DEVELOPS

Having looked at the relationship between shame and guilt, it becomes
relevant to consider the developmental pathway of shame. Shame is generally considered the earlier to develop of the two affects, reflecting a sense of
ineffectiveness in gaining the love or attention of the early caregiver (usually
the mother). Thus, if the infant seeks a particular response from the mother—
a response that he or she might have reason to expect—and the mother fails
to react accordingly, the infant is likely to feel bad or unworthy. Repeated
rebuffs of this nature tend to generate an insecure, noncohesive sense of self
that readily becomes sensitive to and experiences shame. This development
is what Kohut (1971) referred to as *failure of the mirroring self-object*.

Later in development—from 12 to 18 months—the toddler begins to
differentiate himself or herself from the maternal environment. At this stage,
he or she experiences early individuality accompanied by some feelings of
autonomy and independence but also by feelings of separateness and isolation.
Broucek (1982, 1991) referred to this as the period of *objective self-awareness*, in
which the child first stands alone and becomes aware of comparison and competition with others. This period can represent a firming of sensitivity to shame,
especially if self-awareness is tarnished by negative experiences of competition
and comparison with playmates or siblings. At this point the toddler may yearn
for support, strength, or power from a caretaker (often the father), a function
that Kohut (1977) attributed to what he called the *idealized self-object*.

Finally, shame becomes internalized as one's gaze is turned inward. At
about 4 or 5 years of age, the child articulates particular ideals for himself or
herself, and thus shame becomes understood in relation to whether or not he
or she "lives up to" cherished ideals. These may have to do with being "good,"
"strong," "popular," or "smart"—whatever it is toward which the child aspires.
The point is that the child seeks to attain a chosen ideal and develops the
capacity to determine whether that aspiration has been reached. As we have
seen, this is the state described by Sandler et al. (1963) in which the ideal self
is compared with the actual self, sometimes leading to the shame of failure,
incapacity, or unworthiness as a result of failing to reach a given ideal. The
process leading to shame has been internalized with the judgment made of

whether or not the self has lived up to his or her own specific ideal. Certainly, it is true that we form our own ideals from attributes internalized from the expectations of caregivers and the broader culture—from the clatter of objects already residing within. Nonetheless, the shape of these ideals is created individually by, and for, each of us. From this point on, shame is formed by our own expectations of ourselves as well as those of our social and cultural surround and is a manifestation of our imagination, our fantasies, and our creativity.

I have been describing, then, a developmental sequence of shame previously spoken of as a developmental line, except for the fact that this sequence is hardly "linear." Although these stages always overlap, the sequence of shame is from infantile failure in merging or mirroring from the maternal caregiver; to independence and objective self-awareness, with potential inferiority that seeks support from an idealized, omnipotent parent/father; to the ideal self, in which we ourselves become the source of judgment about attaining our ideals. Certainly other affects and attributes besides shame develop in relation to these phases, but for the purposes of our discussion I have found this sequence to be useful in understanding the developmental evolution of shame. It also represents a fine-tuning of the shame experience, from a vague sense of inefficacy for getting a soothing response, to a more particular sense of self separate from the delineated world of others, to, finally, a more specific feeling of failure regarding particular ideals that we have shaped for ourselves.

THE ROLE OF EGO AND SUPEREGO IN SHAME

The developmental sequence also introduces the more traditional psychoanalytic model in its approach to shame—that is, the matter of superego and ego ideal as psychic structures that relate to the shame experience. Piers and Singer (1953) wrote about guilt and shame from a classical perspective, with guilt representing a transgression of the superego and shame reflecting a tension between the ego and the ego ideal. The danger from guilt is punishment and castration, whereas the danger from shame is abandonment and rejection. In this important article, Piers and Singer spoke both of the guilt–shame cycle emphasized by Lewis (1991) and also of ego failure with regard to the ego ideal.

Freud introduced the concept of the ego ideal in his monumental *On Narcissism* (1914/1957), at that point written as an effort to answer challenges to libido theory from Jung and Adler. The ego ideal is the structure against which the ego measures itself, and in falling short of attaining its ideal, the ego experiences failure and a drop in self-esteem. Much more is elaborated by Freud in this essay, but nowhere in his thoughts about narcissism does he explicitly point to shame. However, *On Narcissism* presents many ingredients for a potential examination of shame, including the ideal (as expounded in the ego ideal), self-esteem, and narcissism itself (which, as noted earlier, is the bedrock psychodynamic concept from which the shame experience evolves). It took future disciples of Freud to discover and describe the centrality of shame in clinical work (see Morrison, 1989).

IDENTIFYING SHAME WHEN PATIENTS PRESENT IN THERAPY WITH DEFENSE MECHANISMS

Much of the earlier discussion in this chapter of the psychoanalytic theory of shame only implied its essential role in psychotherapy. In this section, I examine the explicit manifestations of shame in psychodynamic treatment and suggest approaches to therapeutic intervention.

Patients may present for treatment with anger, despair, or self-loathing, feelings that frequently conceal underlying experiences of shame. Because shame is often experienced as the most potent and painful of human impressions, it often generates efforts intended to camouflage or disguise (Morrison, 1989). Because of its noxious and agonizing qualities, shame frequently stays hidden or unspoken in a patient's lexicon, just as for many years it remained unrecognized or minimized within psychoanalytic theory. So too does the pain of shame threaten us as therapists, often reminding us of faults or weaknesses that we have experienced at various points in our lives. This shared pain regarding shame can often lead to a collusion between therapist and patient to avoid acknowledging or identifying shame.

A first task in treatment, then, is often to recognize and name shame, which may necessitate overcoming our own hesitation or embarrassment to speak of it. When I have introduced the notion of shame, I often get a response from patients of surprise, followed by an excited exclamation of discovery—the "aha!" experience when shame is first identified. For example, when I first met with Carol, a rail-thin anorectic young woman who came for treatment of depression and of an eating disorder, she despaired of ever understanding and changing her problem with eating. She readily acknowledged how angry she was at her father, stating that she never felt she could live up to his expectations of her. As we talked about her sense of ineffectiveness in pleasing him, I wondered whether she might be feeling ashamed for not being able to do as well as she expected of herself or to achieve scholastically the grades that her father demanded. She became more energized as she felt recognized for these feelings of shame and then moved on to talking about her body and her need to be in perfect shape. "So if there's any extra skin or fat, you feel mortified and humiliated," I suggested. At this, she lit up and replied that she had never thought of it that way before, but she guessed that it was so. Much of her subsequent treatment focused on her tendency to experience shame, its roots in her relationship to her parents and to her "beautiful" sister, and ways that she might come to think differently about herself.

Of course, it is one thing to identify shame and another to treat and ease it in psychotherapy. Carol's course was difficult and challenging; I will continue to examine some of the problems in the long-term alleviation of shame. It is noteworthy, however, that one of Carol's initial symptoms was anger, particularly toward her father because of her perception that he expected so much of her. Shame is frequently disguised behind certain characteristic defenses, among the most prominent of which are anger and rage. The relationship of shame to anger and rage brings us back to the significant connection between shame and narcissism in that one major source of anger is an assault on or injury to the self. Kohut (1972) referred to this as *narcissistic rage*, pointing to anger as a response to narcissistic injury and wounding. However, I believe that Kohut omitted one important ingredient in his position on rage and narcissism— namely, the significant role that shame plays in eliciting rage and anger.

Narcissistic injury reflects a blow to the self and to self-esteem, leading first to a searing experience of shame, which then generates the rage in the rage–shame cycle of Piers and Singer (1953) and Lewis (1971). For example, in Carol's relationship to her father, we can imagine his upbraiding her for receiving a C in a history course. Her first reaction would likely have been searing shame for having let her father and herself down in her studies, but then this painful blow to her pride would have led to a lashing out, an explosion toward him along the line of "Damn it, Dad, leave me alone. Stop criticizing me!" In this, as in many similar instances, an assault on the self causes shame, which triggers a reaction of anger. Because anger is the more visible of the emotions, and because it is meant to conceal shame in the first place by turning passive into active, it is often the anger that gets noted and treated while the underlying shame is overlooked. In short, anger can stand as a principal defense against unrecognized shame (Morrison, 1989).

Another common clinical defense against shame is contempt. Not infrequently, patients conceal their own shame by projecting it onto the other, who becomes diminished and ridiculed. Thus, through projective identification one relieves oneself of the burden of shame by attributing it to the failures of another ("It's not me who's defective, but you, you poor slob"). The focus is shifted from one's own incompetence to that of the poor bystander. As in any use of projective identification, the recipient may bear some resemblance to those qualities of self (see Sands, 1997), but its purpose in contempt is essentially to rid the self of shame by attributing personal superiority in comparison with the other.

For example, Donald was a self-doubting, insecure young man who felt shy and uncertain in social situations. He felt particularly uncomfortable with his sense of passivity with regard to his boss. He found it difficult to think about these feelings, however, and often assumed a posture of superiority and grandeur in the presence of others. This was expressed in the transference when Donald suggested that his therapist must be uncertain and unsure of himself relative to his analytic peers. Although there were certain stylistic similarities between his therapist and himself, it became quite apparent that Donald was transferring his own feelings of insecurity onto his therapist. At one point his therapist wondered aloud whether Donald might sometimes feel insecure. Donald thought carefully about this question and eventually agreed that this might be the case. In this way Donald's shame sensitivity was brought into the treatment, and its various manifestations could be examined and worked on.

Similar to contempt in its function of concealing shame is envy. From a Kleinian perspective, envy is considered a fundamental expression of hostility and aggression with the goal of destroying the envied, coveted object. Although hostile attacks may play a part in envy, envy frequently represents a veiled expression of shame, by which the self is experienced as inferior to the other. Shame usually lies "upstream" from envy, shifting attention from the shamed self to the esteemed other (Lansky, 1997). For instance, early in his treatment, Dr. B, a psychologist, expressed great envy and anger at me for being a psychiatrist: "You lord that MD over everyone you contact," he proclaimed. In his treatment he expressed a longing to have become a physician, and it was readily evident that he felt shame that he had become "only" a psychologist. His envy became a handy way for us to explore his shame about the extent of his professional achievements and ultimately about many other of his personal attributes.

Another manifestation of problematic, unresolved shame is depression, which may itself be difficult to distinguish from shame. Bibring (1953) described depression in terms of "helplessness" in living up to "narcissistic aspirations," leading to feelings of failure, weakness, and inferiority. These qualities reflect equally shame and humiliation as well as depression, making it difficult to differentiate one from the other. Similarly, Kohut (1977) spoke of "guiltless depression" over failure to achieve ambitions and ideals, thus sounding a note about depression that reverberates with our understanding of shame.

This relationship between shame and depression is clinically important in that treatment implications and emphases differ considerably from those depressions that reflect loss and/or internally directed aggression and guilt. It behooves us to explore the differences between guilt and shame depressions and, in their extreme, shame suicides. As described by Bibring (1953), depressions initiated by shame reflect despairing convictions about the state of the self, about failure to live up to aspirations and cherished ideals, about a sense of self-defect. Therapy in these depressions focuses on feelings about the self, identifying the various ways that the patient feels he or she has "fallen short" and the sources of his or her loss of self-esteem. Often it is helpful to identify and explore the patient's shame over these identified shortcomings. Shame emanates from the threat of rejection and abandonment. Frequently the patient suffering from a shame-based depression feels isolated and alone, and this loneliness and sense of being rebuffed provide a handle to get at his or her conviction of worthlessness.

A major danger from shame depressions is the threat of suicide. The relationship of shame to suicide has been grossly underestimated in the psychodynamic assessment of suicidal potential. It is particularly prominent for those who feel exposed to public observation and condemnation, such as a government official about to be exposed for a scandal or an Asian American man who kills himself and his family over his loss of job and income. Suicide in Japan achieves a ritualistic significance in some cases toward the end of a productive life with the waning of personal powers. A prime example of this is the public self-immolation of the writer Yukio Mishima, for whom suicide seemed a means of redeeming and atoning for his shame.

Analogously, suicide can be a last resort for those who feel despairing over their failure to live up to their life aspirations and goals (e.g., Kohut, 1977). I am reminded of the suicide of Mr. G, a former patient of mine. Mr. G was a divorced man in his late 60s who had left treatment feeling much less depressed and despairing, with the hope of resuscitating his business and pursuing a new lady friend. Several years later, he was found dead of an overdose, alone in his office. I was informed by Mr. G's daughter that his business had failed, his girlfriend had left him, and he felt that he had nothing left. His suicide note spoke of his realization that he had been a failure in all of his dealings, that nothing had turned out the way he had expected for himself, and that it wasn't worth going on. His circumstances and his narcissistic vulnerability pointed clearly to his profound shame and humiliation.

Another defensive means of hiding shame is through grandiosity and a sense of unique specialness. We might say that a patient's grandiosity is frequently a manifestation of reaction formation (i.e., the tendency to act in a manner opposite to the feared emotion) as a defense: "I'm not a failure; I'm really something pretty outstanding." Stolorow (e.g., Morrison & Stolorow, 1997) spoke of *defensive grandiosity* in describing the noisy, haughty superiority of those who conceal shame and a sense of inferiority behind a shield of arrogant grandeur. In treating bellicosely grandiose patients, it is important, first of all, not to take at face value their self-aggrandizement or to be excessively affronted by their raucousness. When working with the perfectly coiffed narcissist of a traditional stripe, it is most useful to look for openings, cracks, in his or her defensive assuredness before attempting to gain entry into realms of self-doubt—for example, "I noticed a moment of hesitation there when you spoke of being the best salesman in the company. I wonder whether you were feeling some doubt about that. What do you think?" or "Did that turning away when you spoke of how beautiful you look in that new dress mean anything?" In this manner it may be possible to get under the patient's veneer of superiority and bring attention to self-doubt and concerns, initiated by the patient himself or herself, about inferiority and failure. Once these negative feelings become acknowledged and acceptable, they can be explored in subsequent treatment, and hidden shame becomes available for therapeutic examination.

A final effort aimed at controlling and concealing shame is the act of withdrawal, an attempt to hide experienced shame and the personal deficits that have generated it. The familiar comment "I could have sunk into the ground; I just wanted to disappear!" expresses this phenomenon succinctly. In this context, the social characteristic of shame is accentuated and with it the role of the observer, the audience, in generating shame. This public instigation of shame constitutes the specific attribute of humiliation. It is out of humiliation that we wish to sink into the ground, to disappear before the eyes of the other. This fantasy differs from the shame we feel before our own eyes as we fail to attain our own ideals, yielding to the defensive hiding of denial, disavowal, or dissociation.

Related to these defenses against shame we encounter a phenomenon by which shame is covered by a "sleight of hand"—that is, by the words that people use to describe their own ill feelings toward themselves. I have called this phenomenon the *language of shame* (Morrison, 1996). A broad shield of words that depict one aspect or another of shame is frequently used, but it behooves therapists to sensitize themselves to the possible presence of shame lurking behind the offerings of such descriptors as "I'm pathetic"; "I feel ridiculous"; "I am a loser, different, insignificant"; "I'm a failure, broken, worthless, defective, a reject." The reader can add his or her own favorites to this list of shame equivalents, but it is important to recognize the presence of shame that lies behind these self-negating epithets that patients frequently hurl at themselves. Once recognized by the therapist, it becomes beneficial to identify the shame experience that the patient is trying to express. Once named or equated with the noun or adjective that the patient has selected to describe himself or herself, the patient's shame becomes a palpable entity that can be explored, examined, and ultimately modified. As mentioned earlier, the identification of shame can itself lead to the "aha!" experience of recognition and relief that these long-held self-loathing feelings are, perhaps, tolerable and acceptable.

Another way of thinking about shame clinically is whether it is bearable or unbearable to the patient (Lansky, 1997, 2007). Unbearable shame is the shame I have been speaking about, the shame that demands concealment, causing hiding, fear of rejection, or abandonment. Unbearable shame may be concealed, as well, from the self as from the observing other through the defenses of disavowal, rage, contempt, envy, and grandiosity. Treatment consists of exploring the expressed, conscious feelings; looking for openings to the underlying experiences of shame; and gently pursuing these experiences in a way that conveys interest and acceptance on the part of the therapist. As the patient gradually recognizes that the therapist finds the patient's shame relevant, interesting, and tolerable, he or she can begin to identify with the therapist's acceptance of his or her shame and of the aspects of self that generate it. Through this measured process of exploration and acceptance, the patient can begin to tolerate shame, and it gradually becomes bearable. Shame then moves from unconscious to conscious and becomes a psychological problem that can be explored and discussed. Conscious shame may readily be accompanied by, or merge with, depression, and thus both feelings should be considered in the course of treatment.

There are certain familiar situational or emotional problems that frequently induce shame, and it becomes imperative to inquire about shame as we work with these conditions of our patients. Shame may reflect the societal or cultural disapproval with which such problems are viewed, or it may in fact play a part in generating the given emotional dilemma. Thus, shame can serve as instigator of the given difficulty or as a response to the problem itself. Often it functions both as instigator and response. For example, in alcoholism or drug abuse, shame and low self-esteem often play a large part in leading to the dependency or addiction as a means of diluting the painful feeling. However, once addicted, drug or alcohol abusers often feel steeped in shame over their role in society, in the family, or both. A person with anorexia may develop an eating disorder as a means of coping with a deep sense of personal or body shame but then may feel shameful over the designation as being sick or, alternatively, over interruptions in eating regimens.

Other examples of the role of shame in familiar symptoms or character syndromes include posttraumatic stress disorders, in which the victim may consider himself or herself responsible for physical or sexual abuse; racial or cultural stereotyping, in which the recipient may feel inferior or flawed; homosexuality, when individual preferences may have been associated with strangeness or difference; obesity in a social context that values slimness; or poor athletic performance when physical prowess had been encouraged. Such universal conditions as aging and illness also leave the individual in unfamiliar and undesirable states, thus instigating shame and humiliation. Many other conditions might be cited that underscore some deviation from an ideal or from the norm in which shame over such deviation is central to an individual sense of distress.

CLINICAL EXAMPLES

Here I present an hour with Carter, who left treatment some years ago when he moved to another city. The specific details of this session are somewhat blurred by time and memory, but the gist of the material accurately reflects issues as they evolved between us. I use this vignette as a means of drawing attention to the close association between shame and narcissism, as well as to the difficulties presented in the treatment and modification of shame. This snapshot will indicate, I hope, some of the therapeutic challenges that shame presents to those who seek to alter its devastating personal effects. Carter's profound narcissistic vulnerability, coupled with searing shame that penetrated his very being but was covered by defensive distractions, represents *primary shame* (Levin, 1967; Morrison, 1994). Primary shame is characterized by an enduring belief that the self is fundamentally and irreparably flawed (Levin, 1967; Morrison, 1994). This is in contrast to *secondary shame*, which everyone experiences from time to time and which often reflects a response to a specific flaw or failure or a temporary defensive reaction of passivity in response to a more assertive or aggressive act or inclination on the part of another.

Carter, a meaty man who always came to sessions dressed immaculately in a suit, white shirt, and tie, was standing in front of my office door, scowling as he tapped visibly on his watch. "I thought we had an 11:00 appointment," he said sharply. "We do," I replied as I opened the door and gestured him in; I realized that I was approximately 2 minutes late. Carter's eyes glared with hatred as he said, "Oh, it doesn't really matter if you're late. Nothing important; I think I'll leave now." He turned abruptly, snatched up his briefcase, and bolted down the hall and out of the building. I was startled, but without explicit thought about his vulnerability, resultant shame, and feelings of isolation, I ran out after him and caught up. "Carter, I'm sorry to have been away from the office when you arrived, but please come back so we can talk about it." We had recently been discussing his self-loathing, concerns about worthlessness, and humiliation at being ignored. He shrugged and, dejectedly, joined me in walking back to the office.

Once seated, Carter glared icily at me for several minutes and then looked down, his body arched forward, his voice trembling. "No one seems to think I'm important any more. My secretary called in sick today. I had needed her to process some important papers. I had a lot on my mind, but then you didn't seem to think it was worth being there on time for me." Internally I was thinking, "For God's sake; it was only a couple of minutes," but I nodded in understanding. "I can see that it was disappointing." "Disappointing? That's the least of it. I guess being there with me just didn't count for you." I apologized again and mentioned to him that we had recently been talking about how he felt small, insignificant. This incident seemed to confirm those feelings.

"I called the 'big man' again; you know, Boralski [an important client]. And again he hasn't answered me. God, 2 years ago I sold him a million worth of insurance; he took me out to dinner after we closed the deal. This time, he doesn't even respond to my call." I asked how it made him feel. "Shitty. I used to really have access to him. I don't know what's wrong, what's happened to me. I used to have plenty of money, friends. Now I can't seem to get any business going. Three or four years ago I was making more than $300,000. I don't have money now to get furniture for my apartment or even to keep up with my payments to you. I call some of my old business contacts to see if they need more insurance for their workforce, and if they return my call at all, they say they don't want any. One guy who I bailed out of a tough situation—got him insurance despite his having had a heart attack—he said that he had taken care of his needs elsewhere. Elsewhere? Ungrateful bastard—he must have gone to someone else. And Dianna's gone—took her things out of my closet when I was driving around, just trying to get away, to think. Boralski—I used to be able to just knock and walk into his office." His mortified despair saturated the room.

"You know, Carter, I understand that things just aren't the way they were supposed to be, the way they once were. You're used to respect from people, for friends to call, ask you out. Something's happened now—no calls, no sales, not much money. It feels pretty terrible and confusing." I was imagining downtrodden Willy Loman in Arthur Miller's *Death of a Salesman*.

"Yeah. I just feel like a grain of sand on the beach of humanity. Only a speck of dust."

"That can be brushed away," I opined. "So it must have felt like you were pretty insignificant to me, that I didn't think much about you when I came in late, after you had come to the door. Couldn't just walk into my office, like you used to be able to do with Boralski."

"Right. You didn't give a shit; you had better things to do with your time."

Then, with a flash, "What difference does any of this make? You're too busy to pay attention to me. And if you did, what could you do anyway? What good does it do to talk, to gripe about the way things are? You can't change things; you're not here to be my friend. Why don't you call Boralski—remind him that we used to take beers together before he became too big, too important, to spend time with me—that a couple of years ago, I was big enough for him to bother with. Oh, but this is crap. How is this supposed to help? So, I remember that I graduated from the University of California at Los Angeles business school, that I used to be on the board of directors there. Screw them. Screw you, Doc. You can't do anything to help, or you're not doing anything."

"It's like I don't do anything that makes you feel strong again, makes you feel like you matter," I concurred. "I don't take away your sense of insignificance, your feeling of humiliation."

And so the session continued, grinding slowly, painfully, to an end. I listened to Carter's tirade, absorbed his anger and despair, and did not attempt to contradict or confront or interpret. I tried essentially to empathically take in and to understand. When the meeting ended, I said to him that I was glad he had agreed to return to the office. "Yeah; a lot of good it did." But then, in a softer voice, as he walked through the door, he murmured, "I'm glad I did, too." "See you next week." "Yeah, OK."

This vignette of Carter offers a glimpse into treatment with a man of extensive narcissistic vulnerability and fragility and its expression through deep, despairing humiliation and shame. His self-conscious preoccupation was paramount, with personal lack of attention feeling overwhelmingly devastating—for example, "I just feel like a grain of sand on the beach of humanity." This judgment about himself was made not with existential acceptance but with suicidal despair. His self ideal was rigidly constructed in the most grandiose and perfectionistic manner. When in his life he came close to realizing his ideal and goal, he was ecstatic and exhilarated. When, like Icarus, he flew too high and inevitably fell, he became suicidally depressed and despairing. Carter's depression was that generated by failure and shame, instigating further paralysis and inability to work effectively.

A word about Carter's background and development: He described his mother as being aloof and critical, his father as punitive and demanding. There was no warmth or tenderness in his memories of his family, except by his mother toward his younger sister. He felt betrayed and bested by his sister in gaining attention from their parents. He described his high school years as having been reasonably happy; he had friends, was successful athletically and academically, and then went on to a good college. He worked hard at studies and set a goal for himself of financial success, planning to exceed his father in wealth. The one thing he shared with his father was a love of sailing, and after business school and beginning his own insurance business, he bought a sailboat that exceeded any boat that his father had ever sailed.

Carter's childless marriage lasted only several years, ending in an acrimonious divorce. He spoke of his ex-wife with the same excoriating hatred with which he described his mother. Women served him only as "trophies," whose beauty or sexiness he wore as a badge of his own worth. Friends were described in terms of their significance and importance, their capacity to enhance his own prominence. In recent years his business had receded, like a tide ebbing, leaving a dry bed of sand—the beach whose image Carter had used to describe his sense of insignificance. This diminished and shame-drenched sense of himself had intensified his depression, which itself impeded his own capacity to do business. His financial security receded, and ultimately he was forced to sell his sailboat to pay his bills. This loss, as well as the loss of stature that had accompanied his position at a local yacht club, intensified his humiliated depression and brought him into psychotherapy. He had selected me because he had heard of my affiliation with Harvard, so I "must be good."

If one takes Carter's tales of childhood and his parents seriously, one can well imagine that his efforts as an infant to gain their attention and response were rebuffed or ignored, that his affective expressions of anger or distress were criticized or punished, and that later his experiences in competition and comparison with peers (and his sister) were painfully degrading. Carter's sense of self, so dependent on feedback from his environment (congruent with Lewis's, 1971, construct of field dependency) was weak and fragile, requiring mirroring from and idealization of the supportive other (recall Kohut's, 1977, self-object responsiveness). His ego ideal was rigid and excessive, demanding perfectionistic achievement in order for him to feel at ease with himself. Wide swings between grandiose superiority and constricting insignificance dominated his self-experience, illustrative of the "dialectic of narcissism" (Morrison, 1989).

Carter also illustrated the association between narcissism and shame, particularly indicating the powerful defenses against shame such as grandiosity and dissociation. Any suggestion of weakness or failure (i.e., narcissistic injuries) and the accompanying shame became intolerable to him as he tried to reestablish connection with his esteemed associates or lashed out in rage (as he did at me when he felt ignored by my lateness). Shame and its instigators were unbearable for Carter to contemplate, but they generated his deep despair and depression. His despondency and despair reflect what I noted earlier in this chapter as shame depression, which is often the most lethal of depressions, not infrequently leading to suicide (Hastings, Northman, & Tangney, 2000). Writing of depression and "guiltless despair" in those who feel that they cannot atone for their lifelong failures, Kohut (1977) stated,

> The suicides of this period are not the expression of a punitive superego, but a remedial act—the wish to wipe out the unbearable sense of mortification and nameless shame imposed by the ultimate recognition of a failure of all-encompassing magnitude (p. 241).

With Carter, at the depth of his despair, I had to be watchful for indicators of possible suicide.

Carter represents those patients for whom shame is hidden and concealed; feelings of shame must be inferred from the language and defenses they use to protect against its unbearable essence. In this instance he did acknowledge feeling "humiliated," which presumably was more palatable because it could be attributed to the scornful other. His defenses against shame included rage, as turned against me for my presumed lateness and disrespect for his need. A sense of unjustifiable need is one major source of shame, particularly for the narcissistically grandiose individual like Carter, whose character is built upon not needing anyone or anything. The rage that Carter demonstrated—toward his therapist, the "big man," his ex-girlfriend—was his means of disavowing his shame by blaming the other and hence turning the shame-ridden passive into active.

Another defense that Carter used to hide shame was that of withdrawal, as when he fled from me down the hallway. By withdrawing from others, he could hide from his shame and interpersonally generated humiliation and also protect the other from his shame-produced rage and destructiveness. Carter expressed contempt through his attack on his therapist for not caring about him and not even coming on time for Carter's appointment. This contempt represents a projection onto the therapist of Carter's own sense of insignificance and shame in an effort to rid himself of that shame, turning the other into the defective one. Finally, one sees the crumbling of Carter's grandiosity as reality intrudes on his defensive maneuvers. The process of fragmentation of his self structure provides the therapist with openings to identify and work with Carter's deep sense of shame and low self-esteem, thus helping him in his attempt to work his way out of his false self (Winnicott, 1965).

Treatment of narcissistic vulnerability and shame is among the most difficult of challenges to psychotherapy. Antidepressant medication is, of course, one arm in treatment of this condition. Carter responded moderately to hefty doses of selective serotonin reuptake inhibitors, often requiring a merry-go-round of drugs until one would help, at least for a while. I tried to understand and accept the depths of his disappointments and despair, offering a companion to his isolation, his sense of insignificance, and his efforts at modifying and softening his rigid ideals. If together we could help Carter to become more flexible in what he demanded of himself, both through acceptance of his difficulties and clarification of their origins, perhaps he might ease his shame-infused burdens and self-criticisms. Might there be other, more genuine ways that he could approach closeness with friends or accomplishments in his work? We struggled with the loftiness of his expectations of worthiness in his companions, both within and outside of the transference. I remained sensitive to his experiences of my empathic failures (as in my "tardiness"), trying always to identify and resolve them as barriers causing disruptions in our relationship.

Carter was a tough nut to crack, representative of the obstacles that patients with severe narcissistic vulnerability and shame present to therapists. Nevertheless, these are the patients who frequently appear in our practices, and a careful understanding of their difficulties, along with a willingness to grapple with the problems that we each face in their treatment, behooves and ultimately benefits us. He left, with modest gratitude, to take a job in an office some distance away. I have not heard from him since his leaving some years ago, and I cannot be confident that our work together was of lasting benefit to him. I do know, however, that he remains vividly in my memory and also that much of what I learned about shame and narcissism was solidified through my relationship with Carter.

Not all instances of shame in our patients are as difficult to treat or alter as was the case with Carter. For example, Ashley was a bright, spunky young woman who was successfully teaching in an academic department. One day, she arrived late for a therapy appointment, cursing loudly at a truck driver who had cut her off and then laughed derisively at her as she had swerved to avoid hitting the truck. "He was just a big lug," she complained, adding that he had been such an "asshole" for thinking he could go wherever he wanted, pushing little folk out of his way. "Little folk?" I questioned. From this we got into how frightened Ashley had felt in the presence of this big man with his big, dangerous truck. The phallic implications of her concerns were apparent, and we made adequate note of these. But what seemed to connect most use-fully for Ashley were her particular associations to "little."

She was tiny in build, and she had always felt small and puny in comparison with her contemporaries (see Kilborne, 2002, for a discussion of size and shame). She had felt frightened and humiliated by her encounter with the truck and its driver, reminding her of her conviction that she was tiny and insignificant. "He didn't even bother to notice me, and then he mocked me when I was scared and angry." She went on to complain that she had felt humiliated by him and then pathetic and ashamed that this incident could cause her such discomfort. Her feelings regarding the encounter with the truck driver allowed us to consider her sense of smallness and insignificance, which were at the heart of experiences of shame that occasionally troubled her. We worked on this shame, which usually was connected with some trou-bling event in her outside life, and ultimately attained some understanding and relief of her feelings of trivialness and insignificance.

Ashley's shame was not the deeply ingrained despair represented by Carter's primary shame, bound up as his was in narcissistic vulnerability. Hers was less pervasive or destructive and represents reactive or secondary shame in response to a specific flaw or failure, as in feeling overwhelmed by the burly truck driver's aggressive act.

SHAME IN THE THERAPIST

Shame is a most contagious emotion, and it often emerges that the patient's shame reverberates with shameful experiences or feelings in the therapist (Morrison, 2008). The pain that is often generated within the therapist when confronting the patient's feelings of shame may lead to the therapist evading work on this emotion or circumventing consideration of the convictions that the patient holds about himself or herself that elicit the shame. In fact, much of the concealment of, and lack of attention to, the role of shame in psychoanalytic theory until the work of Lewis and Kohut can be attributed to an evasion of the pain it generates within patient and therapist alike. Thus, there tends to be a collusion between patient and therapist to avoid attention to shame, as there had been in the early history of psychoanalytic theorizing.

Shame can be instigated within the therapist through identification with the patient. Shameful feelings of failure or ineptitude can occur when treating difficult patients, including in response to unsuccessful efforts at modification of patients' shame. Shame can also result from comparing oneself with colleagues or when competing with colleagues (or, especially, with fellow trainees) for referrals, stature in the institutional hierarchy, and recognition of clinical excellence. Particularly in the world of psychoanalytic institutes, the role of training or supervising analyst has been regarded as the pinnacle of achievement, but what of the analyst who applies for, but does not attain, this exalted status? Similarly, how does the committed therapist respond when a patient to whom he or she has devoted much intense effort decides to quit or to seek treatment from someone else? What of the psychotherapist who is mocked by medically oriented colleagues for not simply dispensing drugs as the answer to patient problems? These are all among the issues that inevitably come up in the course of a psychotherapist's professional career, frequently causing shame.

These instances tend to elicit shame in the therapist by reflecting the discrepancy between the ideal self—in terms of professional efficacy—and the actual self—the therapist's self-perception as falling short of his or her professional aspirations. In this instance, one can identify parallels between the instigation of shame in therapist and in patient. Depending on the nature and intensity of the shame experience for each, this affect may remain covered and avoided, representing at times a mutual collusion to evade attention to it. In fact, there are instances in which a patient's willingness to confront shame may serve as a model to help the therapist face and work through elements of his or her own shame experiences and, in particular, to work through this collusion together with the patient.

I have considered instances of shame in the therapist generated within the therapeutic dyad itself and others that reflect the place of the therapist in relation to his or her professional community. There are other instances of shame in the therapist reflecting feelings about himself or herself alone. These tend to be universal limitations of life that we each face as we progress in our course. Here I think of two phenomena that we each face but that have special significance to us as therapists: aging and declining health. As psychologists age in our life and in our profession, we move from the stature of being esteemed expert to becoming weary, having less vigor, and being seen sometimes as "over the hill." Not infrequently, this process is coupled with illness of one sort or another, intensifying the sense of professional fading. Clinical referrals may recede, requests for teaching may decline, and more frequent inquiries come forth about whether one is still working or has retired. These factors confront each of us with receding prowess and realistic limitations, all potential sources of personal shame. How the therapist deals with these feelings may provide an ultimate challenge to his or her capacity to face inevitable limitations, testing the one benefit of aging—the development of wisdom and perspective.

CONCLUSION

Shame is one of the most excruciating of human emotions, and yet for many years it was ignored by psychoanalytic practitioners and theoreticians. The intense pain of shame may cause one to conceal, ignore, and hide from its sharp probing. Yet ultimately there seems to be no avoiding shame's searchlight, which inevitably catches us in its high beam like a deer paralyzed by the blaze of an oncoming car. We use many attempts—usually other feelings—to hide shame or the defective self elements that perpetrate it. We disguise it behind a multitude of substitutes and analogies, but these disguises fail to prevent it from exercising its doleful impact. Shame may seep to our very core, in the case of unbearable, primary shame, or cause only temporary torment in response to a particular insult, in the case of reactive, secondary shame.

The relationship of shame to narcissism and narcissistic phenomena is central to the psychodynamic perspective, and I have emphasized shame's embeddedness in feelings about the self as a whole. Narcissism reflects any and all referents to the self, whether in grandiose, bellicose superiority or in contracted, withdrawn smallness and insignificance. The tension between these two dimensions constitutes a dialectic of narcissism, with shame a potential reaction to either pole. We generate for ourselves an ideal self. The distance we measure between it and our sense of an actual self determines the degree of shame that we endure. Narcissistic injury (i.e., a threat to one's sense of self-worth) itself most frequently generates shame and rage, a lashing out to retaliate or destroy the offending other. Frequently the role of shame is overlooked as a trigger to rage and vengeance over a narcissistic insult.

These elements in the dynamic understanding of shame dictate the therapeutic approach to its attenuation. First of all, it behooves the therapist to recognize and identify shame, thus bringing it out of hiding and concealment.

Articulation of shame is frequently a startling and exciting revelation to the patient so accustomed to cringing concealment of this emotion. Then the gradual chipping away at the convictions of fault or failure to offer other ways of considering the state of the self or the dynamic sources of such noxious convictions takes place over the protracted period of time required to move shame from unbearable to bearable, from unacceptable to acceptable. The therapist must convey his or her own acceptance of the patient's shame or defects, sometimes even by sharing insights about the therapist's own shame. Interpretations may also focus on defensive structures that interfere with the patient recognizing personal achievements and on what the patient might do to alter the sense of incompetence or inefficacy that led to shame. Ultimately, shame never totally disappears from our repertoire of painful feelings, but its searing incisions can be dulled and eased through understanding and through attaining greater flexibility of ideals and aspirations. This process of easing of self-demands continues through the evolving stages of one's life.

Is shame always noxious, or can it at times be a useful stimulus to healthy growth? Kilborne (2002) differentiated between humanizing and toxic shame, attributing only to the latter those noxious elements that I have been discussing. I find it difficult to find any redeeming qualities in shame per se, in contrast with the clear benefits of self-awareness. Rather, I believe that what can be useful about shame lies only in its resolution. Through accepting and probing treatment, the toxicity of shame can be reduced, and its overwhelming blight can be minimized. Thus, it is the mastery of shame that can be palliative and humanizing. This should become the goal in the psychotherapy of shame, as I hope has been suggested throughout this chapter.

REFERENCES

American Psychiatric Association. (1994). *Diagnostic and statistical manual of mental disorders* (4th ed.). Washington, DC: Author.

Bibring, E. (1953). The mechanism of depression. In P. Greenacre (Ed.), *Affective disorders* (pp. 13–48). New York, NY: International Universities Press.

Broucek, F. (1982). Shame and its relationship to early narcissistic developments. *The International Journal of Psycho-Analysis, 63*, 369–378.

Broucek, F. J. (1991). *Shame and the self.* New York, NY: Guilford Press.

Freud, S. (1957). On narcissism: An introduction. In J. Strachey (Ed.), *The standard edition of the complete psychological works of Sigmund Freud* (Vol. 14, pp. 67–102). London, England: Hogarth Press. (Original work published 1914)

Hastings, M. E., Northman, L. M., & Tangney, J. P. (2000). Shame, guilt, and suicide. In T. Joiner & M. D. Rudd (Eds.), *Suicide science: Expanding boundaries* (pp. 67–79). Boston, MA: Kluwer Academic.

Kilborne, B. (2002). *Disappearing persons: Shame and appearance*. Albany, NY: State University of New York Press.

Kohut, H. (1971). *The analysis of the self*. New York, NY: International Universities Press.

Kohut, H. (1972). Thoughts on narcissism and narcissistic rage. *The Psychoanalytic Study of the Child, 27*, 360–400.

Kohut, H. (1977). *The restoration of the self*. New York, NY: International Universities Press.

Lansky, M. R. (1997). Envy as process. In M. R. Lansky & A. P. Morrison (Eds.), *The widening scope of shame* (pp. 327–338). Hillsdale, NJ: Analytic Press.

Lansky, M. R. (2007). Unbearable shame, splitting, and forgiveness in the resolution of vengefulness. *Journal of the American Psychoanalytic Association, 55*, 571–593.

Levin, S. (1967). Some metapsychological considerations on the differentiation between shame and guilt. *International Journal of Pyschoanalysis, 48*, 267–276.

Lewis, H. B. (1971). *Shame and guilt in neurosis*. New York, NY: International Universities Press.

Morrison, A. (1989). *Shame: The underside of narcissism*. Hillsdale, NJ: Analytic Press.

Morrison, A. P. (1994). The breadth and boundaries of a self-psychological immersion in shame: A one-and-a-half-person perspective. *Psychoanalytic Dialogues: The International Journal of Relational Perspectives, 4*, 19–35. doi:10.1080/10481889409539003

Morrison, A. P. (1996). *The culture of shame*. New York, NY: Ballantine Books.

Morrison, A. P. (2008). The analyst's shame. *Contemporary Psychoanalysis, 44*(1), 65–82.

Morrison, A. P., & Stolorow, R. D. (1997). Shame, narcissism, and intersubjectivity. In M. R. Lansky & A. P. Morrison (Eds.), *The widening scope of shame* (pp. 63–87). Hillsdale, NJ: Analytic Press.

Piers, G., & Singer, M. (1953). *Shame and guilt*. Springfield, IL: Thomas.

Sandler, J., Holder, A., & Meers, D. (1963). The ego ideal and the ideal self. *The Psychoanalytic Study of the Child, 18*, 139–158.

Sands, S. H. (1997). Self psychology and projective identification—whither shall they meet? A reply to the editors (1995). *Psychoanalytic Dialogues, 7*, 651–668. doi:10.1080/10481889709539210

Winnicott, D. W. (1965). *The maturational process and the facilitating environment*. New York, NY: International Universities Press.

2

THE INNER WORLD OF SHAMING AND ASHAMED: AN OBJECT RELATIONS PERSPECTIVE AND THERAPEUTIC APPROACH

MICHAEL STADTER

Writing is a relational activity, and it includes two relationships: one between writer and reader and the other between writer and self. The process for me is always a journey through the domains of exhibitionism and shame. I want my work to be seen and for me to be seen as worthwhile (or, if my narcissism is very active, to be seen as inspired and inspiring). But I also fear that I'll be viewed as not having anything to offer or, in a narcissistic mood, as being basically inadequate, defective, and unworthy. Writing an entire chapter on this primitive emotion concentrates those reactions for me and evokes many images of ashamed and shaming patients and of ashamed and shaming therapists, myself included. A frequent semihumorous comment from colleagues, when told about this chapter, is that they could help because they know so much about it—personally.

In this chapter, I describe how object relations theory and technique can inform psychotherapy with patients who struggle with high levels of shame. Too often, writing on shame has centered on a particular theoretical,

I acknowledge the valuable help I received on this chapter from Jane Prelinger, Steven Schulman, Ronald Vande Loo, David Scharff, and the members of my Thursday and Friday supervision groups.

45

research, or clinical approach, ignoring or devaluing other perspectives. Although object relations therapy has much to offer, so do other points of view, and I believe the object relations approach can augment and be integrated into other perspectives.

NOTES ON THE CONCEPT OF SHAME AND PSYCHOANALYTIC THEORY

In this chapter, I broadly follow the conceptualization of shame as developed by Lewis (1971) and Tangney and Dearing (2002). I concentrate on patients who have pathologically intense levels of shame rather than on patients with little or no shame (e.g., antisocial, psychopathic, some narcissistic personalities). I focus on the fragmenting, dysfunctional impact of shame but acknowledge that it can have significant benefits as well: hiding of the self when weakened or injured, modesty, social sensitivity, and conformity with social norms (Pines, 1987; Trumbull, 2003). Last, I am impressed, as are many clinicians, with the profoundly physiological aspects of shame in addition to the psychological (e.g., Ashbach, 2003; Beer, 2007; Schore, 1994). It is this physical power that often accounts for the depth of psychological disruption and fragmentation.

Trumbull (2003) characterized shame as interpersonal traumatization and noted that the physical and psychological symptoms of ashamed individuals are very similar to the clinical picture of acute stress disorder. Furthermore, she believed that repeated and prolonged patterns of interpersonal traumatization are a major etiological factor in the formation of pathological shame—shame that is overwhelming, fragmenting, and seriously damaging to self-esteem and interpersonal functioning. Freud did make a distinction between shame (social anxiety) and guilt (moral anxiety; Spero, 1984), but for much of the history of psychoanalytic theory, guilt was studied extensively while shame received little attention. That changed in the 1970s, especially with the influence of self psychology and its emphasis on narcissism. Although there are significant variations in psychoanalytic views of shame, there are some general points. Shame comes not from the superego but from the ego ideal (Ashbach, 2003) or the ideal self (Morrison, 1983; Chapter 1, this volume). In summarizing the differences between the ego ideal and the ideal self, Pines (1987) stated,

> The ego-ideal represents the classification of goals, ideals and valued-object representations which we internalize as a check-list against which to compare ourselves. The ideal-self is the more subjective, less specific and cognitive, sense of self to which we aspire with regard to ideals and standards (pp. 25–26).

Shame targets the whole person, whereas guilt is directed toward a transgression or doing something wrong. Vision seems prominent, literally and symbolically, in the experience of shame (Lewis, 1971; Pines, 1987; Spero, 1984): the shaming eyes, the way others see the self, the way the person views self, and so forth. The developmental importance of the infant and toddler reading the mother's gaze and facial expressions may account for this importance of sight in the shame experience (Schore, 1994). Note throughout this chapter how frequently I reference *seeing* and *being seen*.

Schore (1994, 2003) advanced a research-based neuropsychoanalytic theory on the genesis of pathological shame states and the mechanisms of psychotherapeutic change. Strong shame states in childhood cause serious, primitive problems in development if the caregiver can't or doesn't adequately promote the development of the child's adaptive affective regulation capacities. The psychotherapy of such individuals, according to Schore (2003), involves attention to dysregulated primitive affects such as shame; close attunement at the nonverbal, emotional level (right-brain functioning); appreciation of the centrality of therapeutic interactive repair; and an emphasis on process, among other factors.

OBJECT RELATIONS OVERVIEW

Object relations theory has much in common with other psychoanalytic theories, especially relational structural theories such as self psychology, but no other perspective puts as much emphasis on the human need to depend upon and relate to others. There are various object relations theories, but the one that I use in this chapter is based on the contributions of the British Middle School (Balint, 1968; Fairbairn, 1952, 1958; Guntrip, 1961, 1969; Winnicott, 1958, 1965), contemporary American writers (Bollas, 1987; Ogden, 1989, 1994; Scharff & Scharff, 1998), and my own previous work (Stadter, 1996; Stadter & Scharff, 2000).

The foundational premise of object relations theory is that we are social animals who need to depend upon and relate to other humans (Greenberg & Mitchell, 1983; Stadter & Scharff, 2000). Starting at least as early as birth, relating to others generates an unconscious process of cognitive–affective internalization in which multiple representations of self and other come to form the inner world. (Note that object relations theory has tended to use the terms *ego* and *object* rather than *self* and *other*. Although the two sets of terms are not totally identical, they are roughly equivalent, and I generally use the more modern terms of *self* and *other*. It is important to note that the terms *object* or *other* can refer to relationships in the external world or in the internal world.)

Therefore, the inner world of each of us is made up of numerous internalized pairings of self and other connected by feelings and thoughts. On the one hand, a child's repeated experience of being afraid and then being comforted by a mother causes the internalization of a containing, soothing other in relationship with a contained, safe self. On the other hand, a child's repeated experience of making a mistake and the parent then reacting angrily generates an internalization of an angry, perhaps shaming, other in relationship with an uncontained, inept, perhaps ashamed self. These various pairings in the inner world affect present functioning in three ways: through unconscious projection of the inner world onto external reality, through unconscious choice of other relationships that repeat the inner dramas, and through projective identification. The latter is an unconscious, subtle, nonverbal process of interpersonal cueing whereby one person influences another person to unconsciously play a role in a drama from their inner world. It has some similarities to the concept of self-fulfilling prophecy. For more on projective identification, see Stadter (1996) and Scharff (1992).

From these very simple building blocks, quite complex and textured patterns of relating to self and others emerge. Object relations therapy emphasizes the following (Stadter & Scharff, 2000):

- Each patient is unique, as is the distinctive relationship that develops with a specific therapist at a particular point in time. This emphasis on the uniqueness of the patient is crucial because many shame-ridden patients have found that their individuality and differences were either neglected or even specifically targeted for attack. Examples include a musically interested boy who is shamed by his family for not being a "real male" or an emotionally expressive girl in a family where there is a stoic prohibition on affective expression. In this sense, psychotherapy with shame-prone individuals is directed toward the whole self.
- The unconscious repetition of past patterns of relating is a focal point of exploration. For many patients, their inner worlds are closed systems, and interactions with self and others follow automatic, unconscious patterns. As I discuss below, this occurs as a defensive retreat from a too-threatening or neglectful outer world. Object relations therapy aims at freeing patients to have a present and a future that are different from an endlessly repeated past.
- The therapist studies both transferences and countertransferences to understand the patient and to promote change. In a sense, understanding relating is the way of relating in object relations therapy. The therapist works to be aware of the unconscious forces and patterns driving the patient's relationship with

the therapist (transference) and to be aware of the therapist's own feelings and modes of relating in response to the patient (countertransference). This approach holds that the therapist's countertransference is frequently a key in understanding patients because it can give the therapist an experiential sample of the patient's inner world as well as insight into how the patient affects others outside of the therapy. The therapeutic relationship is fundamental to the healing power of therapy. It is so fundamental that the effectiveness of any technical intervention depends upon the nature and depth of the therapeutic relationship and is secondary to it (Guntrip, 1969).

SHAME AND THE INNER WORLD

I next describe some of the more frequent varieties of shaming internal others and shamed selves. It is not exhaustive, and specific self-representations can pair with different, specific object representations. There are many possible combinations. These internalizations can come about at any stage in life but tend to be powerful in childhood development, and many of the examples originated during those years. I use examples of language to illustrate the types, but shaming–shamed interactions and representations largely involve tone, body posture, facial expression, eye contact, and other nonlanguage elements.

The Shaming Internal Others

Direct Shaming Other

The direct shaming other is the most obvious, classic shaming other. The other shows displeasure or even disgust ("How could you be so thoughtless?" "You make me sick." "What an idiot."). This can, of course, be very painful, but the interaction is at least clear and direct. Exploration of the internalization of this other can be relatively straightforward, with the patient intellectually agreeing that this wasn't a good way to be parented and it's not a good way to treat oneself. However, modifying it and letting it go can be very difficult.

Indirect Shaming Other

Interaction with the indirect shaming other may seem, on the surface, not consciously intended to shame but still does. The other may react with disappointment or sadness. An 18-year-old high school senior opens an envelope and finds that she was rejected by the Ivy League college of her choice.

She looks at her father, who breaks off eye contact, looks down, sighs, and says, "That's OK [pause] . . . I know you'll get into a good school." This is a more complicated internalization because the self is shamed but the other is seen as not shaming and even as being compassionate. The interaction may not even register consciously as noteworthy. I've frequently seen this in the backgrounds of patients who idealize their parents but have an eerie sense that they themselves are bad and they can't put it into words. The shaming is conveyed more in the unconscious atmosphere of the relationship than in specific interactions.

Karen (1992) noted that parents who are insecure about themselves and their roles as limit setters may shame their children through these unconscious, unspoken interactions. The parents' ambivalence and discomfort about being firm or their fear that the child won't like them gets communicated indirectly as an unnamed, unconsciously experienced, uneasy interaction that leaves the child having the previously noted eerie sense that something is not OK—"Maybe *I'm* not OK."

Another way that a child can feel indirect shaming is when a parent is very accomplished (e.g., successful, beautiful, wealthy) and the child feels the unspoken expectation to be as successful as the parent. As one of my patients said, both seriously and humorously, "I feel so much better since I've accepted that I'm downwardly mobile."

Neglectful Shaming Other

The two previous types of shaming others involve a negative response by the other. But a nonresponse can also be intensely shaming. When my patient Cynthia was 17, she came to her father in her prom dress and said excitedly, "What do you think, Daddy?" He looked up from his computer and said, distractedly, "You look fine," and then immediately returned to his e-mails. Children desire to be seen as worthwhile or special or simply to be noticed. If they get no response or a very weak one, these interactions can be internalized as a shamed self in response to being invisible to the other. Also, the simple desire to be acknowledged and affirmed can feel shameful, for being too needy. This type of interaction, even more than indirect shaming, may be difficult for the patient to process because it's not a presence of something that was shaming; rather, it's the felt absence of something desired that was shaming. In Cynthia's case, we were able to work with it only after it came up in the transference when she felt that I wasn't responding enough to her and that I didn't really see her for who she was. I invited exploration of this by saying, "You've noted that you think I'm helpful to you, but I get the impression that you also feel something's missing."

Grandiose Shaming Other

In their conscious desire to promote positive self-esteem in their children, many parents praise them in an unrealistic, effusive manner and resist giving negative feedback on their problem behavior. At an unconscious narcissistic level, the parents see the child as an extension of themselves, and the child has to be seen as "extraordinary" or "the best" for the parents' own self-esteem regulation. This can lead the child to feel that simply being ordinary is shameful, and the child is left unprepared for reality. As Karen (1992) stated,

> They [the parents] may neglect to teach him good manners, may give him the impression that certain of his obnoxious traits are cute, or may generally assure him that he is the most fantastic child who ever lived. They are unwittingly setting him up for shame. (p. 43)

Another frequent impact of the grandiose shaming other can occur when the person sees the self realistically, as not the brightest, handsomest, or most successful. If the other holds on to the grandiose view, the person feels ignored and not really known. The self is then interacting with a grandiose shaming other who is also a neglectful shamer.

Abusive Shaming Other

When a child is physically or sexually abused, there are many types of psychological damage (Perry, Pollard, Blakley, Baker, & Vigilante, 1995). Intense shame is frequently one of the injuries. In the case of physical abuse, the abuser is violent, punishing, and physically invasive. It conveys a sense of "You're so bad, you deserve this extreme treatment." In the case of sexual abuse, what is internalized is usually more complex and confusing. The sexual abuser may also be violent, punishing, and physically invasive but also can communicate that the child is special and chosen for the sexual abuse. If the child also feels sexual stimulation, the internalization is even more bewildering.

Why should physical and sexual abuse cause shame in the victim? There are a number of reasons. First, the child may have the unconscious question, "Why would this person act so outrageously toward me? It must be because I'm so bad." This question can be even more complex if the abuser is a parent: "Why would my mother, who loves me, be driven to beat me? It must be because I'm so terribly bad." The abuser may directly say such things. Second, the abuse may evoke feelings that are shameful. Sexual stimulation and/or some pleasure in being special can feel shameful. Alternatively, the child may hate the abuser and feel ashamed of that. Also, remember that shame is a primitive emotion, and the child likely may not be able to think about it at all but may feel a vague sense of badness or defectiveness. Third, many abusers do not feel conscious shame and may therefore act shameless. Through the process of projective identification, the shame reaction of the victim can be intensified as any unconscious shame of the abuser is disavowed and projected into the victim.

Self-Shaming Other

Children learn how they should relate to themselves not only by the way the parents treat them by also by how the parents treat themselves. In the previous types, children internalize how the other interacts with them. In this type, children take in how parents treat themselves, even if it is very different from the way the parent treats the child. So a father could convey to a son not to push himself too hard in school and to look for a career that makes him happy regardless of the status of the occupation. Yet the son could feel driven to excel if the father was rarely satisfied with his own successes and frequently expressed his own low self-esteem.

The Shamed Selves

In this section, I discuss six types of states. Three describe the content of shame (i.e., what the person is ashamed of), and three describe the subjectivity of shame (i.e., what shame feels like).

Content of Shame

What are people ashamed of? Karen (1992) stated that Silvan Tompkins, an early researcher on shame, believed that anything and everything about a person can be the source of shame—the good and the bad, the extraordinary and the ordinary. Therapy work is directed in part at trying to understand and helping to metabolize (process) what is shameful for this unique individual. Three self-states describe the content of shame: the bad shamed self, the defective shamed self, and the successful shamed self.

Bad Shamed Self. The bad shamed self is perhaps the self-experience that is most described in the shame literature (e.g., Ashbach, 2003; Morrison, 1989; Tangney & Dearing, 2002). In the classic distinction between shame and guilt, it is the shameful self-experience of "I *am* bad" rather than the guilt experience of "I *did* something bad." The badness may be a moral sense of unworthiness, existential badness, a disgust with self, or a nonverbal, vague sense of unworthiness.

Leonard, a 30-year-old devout Christian, consulted with me because of a debilitating major depressive episode. He had had a lifelong belief in his fundamental badness that intensified with his depression. He wanted to work alone and avoid contact with others, as he imagined them seeing him as unworthy. He cognitively knew that he was no worse than the average person and that his faith told him he would be saved. Yet he felt that he was worse than anyone else in the world and that not even Jesus could save him. Interestingly, despite his strong religious beliefs, his shame was not moral but rather existential. He didn't feel bad as a Christian; he felt bad as a person. Much of his shamed self came from his beloved, idealized, but directly shaming father and his neglectful shaming mother.

Defective Shamed Self. With the defective shamed self, the content of the shame centers on something lacking in the person. The person feels "not enough" in the arenas of attractiveness, intelligence, sensitivity, strength, success, maleness, femaleness, and so forth. The list is truly endless as the observed self painfully looks at the ego ideal and feels pathetic and shamefully lacking. Such defect shame is at times evoked by apparently small setbacks, but it also can be the result of a major crisis, such as a divorce or job loss; a traumatic loss of bodily integrity, such as debilitating illness or traumatic injury (e.g., amputation from combat injuries); or the aging process.

Successful Shamed Self. It can seem paradoxical, but the experience of being successful, accomplished, and honored can feel shameful. Eva, a 34-year-old administrative director of a humanitarian nonprofit group, was widely regarded in her organization as being indispensable by her colleagues. In therapy, she talked about desperately wanting to avoid a luncheon thanking her for her contributions. She went, was given a generous gift certificate, and was applauded by the group. She described sweating, blushing, not being able to look at them, and hurrying out of the room as soon as she could. We learned in her therapy that these situations evoked great difficulty in self-regulation. In her personal history, she experienced much parental grandiose shaming, and she felt that her successes, although substantial, didn't merit the lavish praise accorded her ("I'm not *that* good!"). At the other end of the self-regulation continuum, success and affirmation overstimulated her, and she felt flooded with pride and fantasies of extraordinary success. She became ashamed of her own grandiosity and feared it getting out of control—an unconscious identification with her grandiose parents.

Another variation on a self state of success shame is the shame of being the most successful member of a family. From a traditional analytic standpoint, this type of shame has often been described as oedipal guilt. Kevin, at 50, was the most successful member of his family. Independently wealthy through his own efforts, he was healthy and had a good, stable marriage. By contrast, his siblings and parents were more troubled in the arenas of health, wealth, and relationships. He was dreading the family Thanksgiving dinner. Kevin described his feelings as survivor guilt, but more accurately, he was success shamed. The distinction is as follows: The survivor guilt state of mind is,

"I feel guilty because I survived while others I care about didn't make it. I *did* something bad." The success shamed state of mind for Kevin was, "I am ashamed about *who I am* in relation to the others I care about." I think an important clinical consideration here is that these situations are frequently seen as simply guilt inducing, but they often also involve the more fundamental self-attack of shame. An additionally painful aspect of this for Kevin was that as he looked into the eyes of his less fortunate family members, he saw them feeling ashamed in comparison with him. For a man who himself has been so sensitive to shame, it is painful to see them viewing him as a shaming other (indirectly shaming).

When a person is in a success-shamed state of mind, there are many variations of shame and guilt beyond what was illustrated by Kevin's case. For instance, when working with other success-shamed patients, I have often seen them express shame and guilt for not having provided more to help the others who were not doing as well.

Subjectivity of Shame

What does shame feel like? Described next are three experiences of self: the hyperaroused shamed self, the dissociated shamed self, and the contemptuous shamed self.

Hyperaroused Shamed Self. The hyperaroused shamed self feels flooded with overwhelming physical and affective activation. Eva's success shame illustrates this state, which includes blushing, hunching the shoulders, shrinking the body, hiding the eyes, covering the face, and avoiding others' gaze (Ashbach, 2003). Of course, the hyperaroused state can be extraordinarily painful and even intolerable.

Dissociated Shamed Self. Another reaction to intolerable shame is at the other end of the continuum of arousal: dissociation. Indeed, one of the evolutionary benefits (and liabilities) of shame is that the person is impelled to hide (Trumbull, 2003). The dissociated shamed self goes into hiding not only from the outside world, but also from the inner world (see Guntrip's [1961, 1969] regressed libidinal ego, discussed later in this chapter). This shamed self shuts down, doesn't feel much, and, depending on the intensity of the dissociative state, experiences a strange calm, numbness, hazy thinking, decreased vitality, and depersonalization. An important aspect of this for psychotherapy is that the patient may not look ashamed, may seem especially relaxed, and may not be conscious of shame. This is an example of the fragmenting effects of shame as the patient splits off the intolerable experience and has difficulty integrating affect, memory, identity, and consciousness. The shame itself has gone into hiding from both the therapist and the patient.

Leslie, 49, a victim of childhood sexual abuse, was describing the events of the week in her session when a sudden shift occurred. I noticed it rather vaguely and sensed something was different. I asked her, and she said, "I just lost you; I'm floating and talking to you from the end of a tunnel." It had taken us considerable time to notice these shifts and to be able to think about them together. As we studied what happened in the session, she reported that the change commenced when she remembered an intensely shameful sexual encounter during an affair. As we talked, she shifted to the hyperaroused shamed self. One of the key sequences in the psychotherapy of shame then occurred: She reexperienced and processed the shameful experience, but at a more tolerable intensity and in the presence of a containing, supporting other—her therapist. Repeating this process with her many times over a period of years helped her to become more integrated and to have fewer states of dissociation.

Contemptuous Shamed Self. The frequent connection between shame and aggression has been well documented (Reed, 2001; Tangney & Dearing, 2002). The causal connection goes in both directions: People are sometimes overcome with shame over their hostility and aggression, and sometimes aggression is a reaction to feeling shamed. The contemptuous *shamed* self is a *shaming* self that has been evoked by an internal shaming other. This self is an example of identification with the aggressor. In other words, the contemptuous shamed self unconsciously identifies with the shaming other (identification with the aggressor) and acts contemptuous and shaming. The person's own shame is projected onto the target of the disdain, an external other who is seen as reprehensible and distasteful—a person worthy of being shamed. The person may not even be aware of shame because the aggressive response has become so automatic and immediate that the shame doesn't register in explicit memory. In the shaming–ashamed drama, the contemptuous shamed self takes the role of the shamer.

Nathan, 32, and I had been meeting for several months in therapy, three times per week. He announced that he was talking with a friend who was in analysis, and they both believed that he should come four times a week. My initial, unspoken, thought was that this might not be a good idea. Nathan had had great difficulty with boundaries and limits, and I had concerns that increased frequency might be overstimulating and destabilizing. In any event, I thought we should reflect on it. I said to him that maybe this would be useful, but that we should think about it together before we decided. He immediately got angry and said he couldn't understand why I wouldn't say yes right away. He felt consciously angry and contemptuous but unconsciously shamed and rejected. I said that more frequent sessions don't always mean better therapy and that our approach together was to reflect on issues before we act. I also acknowledged that my answers had been upsetting to him, and I wanted to understand that better. Nathan replied that it was obvious why he was angry; he derisively said that I was an incompetent, uptight therapist who didn't care about him. He threatened to quit and see another therapist who would jump at the opportunity to work with him. Nathan unconsciously felt shamed and repeated the shaming interaction by contemptuously shaming me. It took us an extended period to work this through.

GUNTRIP'S REGRESSED LIBIDINAL EGO: WITHDRAWAL FROM SELF

Two early theorists of the British Middle School, Fairbairn (1952, 1958) and Guntrip (1961, 1969), emphasized the key role of schizoid phenomena, and their work has much to offer in considering the inner world of the shamed individual. As I noted earlier, shame rarely found its way into psychoanalytic writing in the 1950s and 1960s, and shame did not specifically appear in the writing of these two theorists. However, in their case descriptions, they were often referring to shame when using the terms *fear, anxiety, threat, attack,* and *guilt*. Fairbairn (1952) developed a comprehensive object relations theory of personality derived in large measure from the study of the opposite of relationship seeking: schizoid phenomena, or the internal forces that impel the person to withdraw from relationships. Fairbairn and Guntrip used the term *schizoid* much more broadly than the diagnostic category of schizoid personality disorder in the following ways. First, we all have schizoid tendencies, but in some individuals, these tendencies have become particularly intense and dysfunctional. Second, Fairbairn and Guntrip believed that, actually, schizoid individuals frequently had quite strong dependency needs for others. In such instances, the schizoid style is a defense against how strong such needs are. Third, the withdrawal from the outer world into the inner world may be hidden and not overt. The person may appear interpersonally connected but, actually, is not. Narcissistic personalities, for instance, can seem very connected to others, but internally they feel isolated and empty. Finally, schizoid withdrawal is not viewed as a simple passive withdrawal but instead involves parts of the personality actively attacking (shaming) the self for attempting to relate to others ("How could I be so stupid to think that we could have been friends? I'm an idiot.").

I believe that individuals frequently develop strong schizoid strategies to manage shame. Guntrip (1969) detailed nine schizoid characteristics, and seven are prominent in many shame reactions: introversion, withdrawnness, loss of affect, disturbance in narcissism, loneliness, depersonalization, and regression. The other two, sense of superiority and retreat to self-sufficiency, also appear in contemptuous shamed selves.

From his work on the primary need to be in relationship and on the opposing schizoid forces of retreat from relationships, Fairbairn (1952) elaborated a theory of the internal world that was fully relational and made up of three self–other paradigmatic pairings in contrast to Freud's id–ego–superego (see also Scharff & Scharff, 1998; and Stadter, 1996):

1. *The central ego with the ideal object:* an internal object relationship between a self that calmly seeks and is satisfied by a good, responsive other. This part of the personality is the internalization of positive experiences of others in which needs are appropriately met. Dominant affects associated with these interactions include comfort, security, satisfaction, and positive relatedness.

2. *The antilibidinal ego with the rejecting object:* an internal relationship between an other that is frustrating and rejecting and a self that is attacking of the desire and need for others. This part of the personality develops from negative experiences in which needs are not met in relationships and in which affects of anger, abandonment, and frustration are prominent. Fairbairn's first term for the antilibidinal ego was the *internal saboteur,* which captures the aspect of a part of the self that attacks and sabotages relationship.

3. *The libidinal ego with the exciting object:* the self that wants and longs for a close relationship but is unfulfilled because it is relating to a desired, tantalizing internal other that stimulates need but ultimately frustrates it. This is that part of the personality that has internalized experiences in which hopes and desires have been stimulated but have been, in the end, frustrated. When there are many and/or intense experiences of this type, the subjective states of yearning, disappointment, and unfulfilled need are very strong. The actual need for others is then often felt to be shameful.

Consider this view of the inner world from two perspectives. First, this view describes internal, largely unconscious intrapsychic relationships between parts of self and internal others. Second, it describes types of interpersonal relationship patterns that may be reenacted and unconsciously chosen again and again. So it refers both to the intrapsychic and to the relational.

Schizoid individuals, in Fairbairn's view, withdraw into this inner world in response to a too-threatening external world, and we certainly see this clinically. Guntrip (1961, 1969), though, believed that the theory didn't adequately explain the schizoid problem. He noted that once the person withdrew into the inner world, there often was still no safety. There was an active attack from parts of the personality (the antilibidinal ego and the rejecting object) on a part of the self (the libidinal ego) that longed for relationships. The inner world itself became too threatening, and he described a further split in the personality with a part of self that retreats from the rest of the inner world.

He saw this inner retreat as a part of all of us but as especially strong in some individuals. This was his concept of the regressed libidinal ego, a part of the libidinal ego that self-protectively withdraws from even internal self–other relationships. In other words, there are two withdrawals. First, there is the generally observable schizoid withdrawal from the external world of relationships because it is too unsafe. The person then becomes preoccupied with the inner world behaviorally, cognitively, and affectively. The second withdrawal is from the inner world of object relations because it, too, is unsafe, frightening, and, at times, shaming. An individual can escape from the shaming eyes of other people when alone but still feel intense shame from the "eyes" of his or her own inner world. Escape from that shame requires a second withdrawal. The concept of the regressed ego depicts the predicament of the shamed individual—both the outer world and the inner world are threatening, unsafe, and shaming.

The withdrawal to the regressed libidinal ego state can function paradoxically both to promote and to impair the health of the individual. Think of it this way: The retreat of the shamed person into the regressed ego state can be a womb, or it can be a tomb. As a womb, it can be a state of isolation and safety. The person can escape from the pain and disorganization of shame and can stabilize and regulate affect and self-esteem. In positive development, the individual recovers and finds enough equilibrium to leave the regressed ego state. The person no longer needs this second withdrawal, can tolerate integration, and can manage the attacks from the various parts of the inner world.

But the regressed libidinal ego state can also be a tomb, in that such a profound internal retreat leaves this part of the self inaccessible to the rest of the personality. Also, the person may fear leaving this safe place and may stay concealed from the remainder of the personality and from the external world of relationships. The clinician may see this in patients with very diminished vitality, strong conscious fantasies of withdrawal, unconscious fantasies of return to the womb, dissociation, and depersonalization. What I described earlier as the dissociated shamed self is very similar to Guntrip's concept of the regressed libidinal ego.

Guntrip's (1969) view of psychotherapy was that the regressed libidinal ego needed to be addressed if "radical" change—personality change—could occur. He listed three elements of the therapist's work:

1. Support the patient's ego functioning of everyday life while the deeper issues are being dealt with. This aspect of therapy is supportive psychotherapy.
2. Analyze the internal world of bad object relations and uncover the regressed ego. This includes transference analysis.
3. Provide a "safe symbolic womb" in the therapy for the regressed libidinal ego as the patient struggles toward growth, vitality, and integration in the personality.

CLINICAL ILLUSTRATION: DONALD

The case summary of Donald illustrates the regressed libidinal ego, shame, and work with both in psychotherapy. In the first session, Donald averted his eyes, blushed, and in a nervous voice said he was feeling hopelessly inadequate with women. Over time, this narcissistic, shame-prone lawyer of 27 revealed two patterns of failure with women. He often would choose unattainable women and then feel rejected by them. His self states were a defective shamed self and, sometimes, an existentially bad shamed self. In a less frequent pattern, he would find a woman who wanted the relationship to continue. However, soon after Donald felt secure with her, he would begin to feel that she wasn't good enough for him, and he would end the relationship. His subsequent self states were a contemptuous self that was hostile toward the woman and eventually a defective self that judged that he had been stupid to waste his time on such an "obviously pitiful" relationship. Following both types of endings, he would retreat from women, not dating for several months. During these times he would also have brief periods of depersonalization and panic attacks.

His history revealed a number of interpersonal traumatizations (Trumbull, 2003), especially from his father. Donald described his father as a highly respected lawyer, a proud man who ruled the family and set exceptionally high standards. Their Jewish heritage and religion were central in the family life, and Donald was pleased to be a part of such a special family. However, he recounted many instances of his father directly shaming him and how he managed it.

For example, when Donald was 10, he had a play date at his house with some non-Jewish friends. His father overheard him using a Hebrew phrase with the friends and said, derisively, in front of the friends, "Donald's acting like a big man. He thinks he's the Rabbi." Donald felt overwhelming shame, left his friends for an indeterminate period of time, and literally retreated into a closet in the house. He burrowed into the warm soft clothing and felt safe in the darkness. He focused on his bodily sensations, trying not to think very much. He shifted from a hyperaroused self to a dissociated self. Eventually, his shame diminished, and he felt that he could rejoin his friends. He made up an excuse for his absence and resumed his play. This was a frequent way that he managed his ashamed self. In the family, Donald reported, they were so accustomed to him frequently retreating for a time that when he returned from the closet nothing was mentioned. It was partly helpful that they didn't further shame him on his return, but they also made no effort to provide interpersonal support in handling his shame (neglectful shaming others). The hiding in the closet was an external equivalent of his regressed libidinal ego. We also saw evidence of it in his need for a few months' break from dating following a breakup until he could adequately self-regulate. During those months, his vitality was low, and he frequently commented that he felt detached (a dissociated shamed self). He was out of contact not only with women but also with a part of himself.

His 3-year, twice-weekly therapy involved several repetitions of a four-stage cycle. Donald would first idealize me, feel very close to me, and see us both as special individuals. This would give way to the next phase in which he still idealized me, but now the high regard he had for me caused him to feel inadequate by comparison (indirect shaming other/defective shamed self). He also had felt inadequate by comparing himself with his father (indirect shaming other/defective shamed self) in addition to the direct shaming he suffered at his father's hands. Third, as yet another romantic relationship failed, he came to see me as an inadequate therapist, complained that I couldn't help him, and stated that coming to therapy reminded him that he was hopelessly flawed in relationships. He painfully felt a hyperaroused, defective self. During this phase, his distress was intensified because he felt ashamed of having to be in therapy, of disappointing me, and of failing at even a therapy relationship. In other words, he experienced therapy and me as indirectly shaming him. It is noteworthy that Donald did not stop therapy in this phase of the cycle. However, in the fourth phase, he did distance himself from me, women, and himself with a retreat into his regressed libidinal ego state. The therapy seemed to me to be rather superficial during this fourth phase in the cycle, and I wondered whether we were actually doing any work. It was significant, though, that he did continue the sessions and maintain contact with me while in the dissociated shamed state. Still, much of Donald was not available to me or the therapeutic process. He had retreated into the regressed libidinal ego state.

We went through several repetitions of this cycle, and, of course, the therapy was more messy than this simple outline would suggest. For his part, Donald maintained consistent attendance even when he felt ashamed of coming to therapy (hyperaroused defective shamed self) and even when he was not emotionally available, having retreated into his regressed libidinal ego (dissociated shamed self). I worked to be patient during the withdrawn periods and to not push him too hard. I had to manage my countertransference states of feeling ashamed of being an inadequate therapist (my defective shamed self). When possible, we worked together on putting into words the cycle between us and the patterns with romantic relationships. Another key aspect of the therapy was that he gradually came to see that I could be with him in a way that helped to regulate his shame. Unlike his family, Donald came to rely on me to interpersonally help him with the interpersonal traumatization of shame. The dream presented below facilitated that process.

I now return to Donald's boyhood retreat into a closet. As noted, this was the external equivalent of his internal retreat into his regressed libidinal ego state. Throughout the therapy, he had many dreams about hiding in closets. He usually felt safe in the closet and was always alone—until the following dream, which he reported about 2 years into the therapy:

> I'm in the closet again, but it's different than it's ever been before. Susan's in it, too! The closet's not peaceful this time. Somebody's coming to attack us. I don't know who. We're trying to clear off shelves—there are shelves in the closet—so we can move. You know, so we can maneuver when they attack us. But she's getting in the way! She's not helping at all, and I'm thinking, oh God! We're going to die! All because of her! I'm furious at her, and I'm scared shitless. It wakes me up.

At the time Donald had this dream, he had been dating Susan for 4 months. He was feeling secure and accepted by her and was at his characteristic point of thinking that his girlfriend wasn't good enough for him. However, through the therapy, he had been resisting the urge to break up and was trying to reflect on what he was feeling. His dream represented him beginning to let his regressed ego reconnect with others (internal and external). However, he was terrified about this intrusion into his "womb" and feared that his most private self might not survive. We came to understand that the attackers were internal others who would shame him for depending on and being emotionally intimate with Susan. He did persist in the relationship with Susan and was able to be more connected with parts of himself and with other people as well. Donald and Susan eventually married.

The dream also represented his struggle around intimacy with me. The "Susan" in the dream also symbolized me and his fear that some parts of himself would shame him for relying on and being vulnerable with me. The four-stage cycle in the therapy described above was partly about his idealization and subsequent disappointment and partly about expecting that I would shame him as his father, women, and Donald himself had done. In the therapy he had gradually come to realize that I was good enough to continue with and that he was safe enough to bring in deeper, more private material.

IMPLICATIONS FOR PSYCHOTHERAPY

The Basic Setting

There has been widespread acknowledgment that seeking therapy and continuing in it frequently induce shame (Karen, 1992; Lewis, 1971; Tangney & Dearing, 2002). However, clinicians often underestimate the potential for shaming–shamed experience in the therapy setting.

The shame of being in therapy may be hidden for various reasons, including being ashamed of feeling shame. Therapists should try to inquire sensitively about it so clients can put into words and thus have the opportunity to regulate the distress together with the therapist (see discussion of Schore, 1994, 2003, below). Attuned therapists try not to aggravate shame but accept that it will emerge and attempt to discuss it when tolerable. To this end, a therapist might observe, "Coming to talk to a psychologist for the first time can be difficult for many people. How was it for you?" "How has today's session felt to you?" "You've told me that you don't like to be the center of attention. What's it been like for us to focus so much on you each week?"

The very act of interpretation can be shaming (Spero, 1984). Patients may experience the interpretation process as either direct or indirect shaming. As Spero (1984) noted, "The shame personality, however, has too often experienced during early development intrusive shaming objects who, with 'insights' expressed during shaming tirades, appear inescapably omniscient and uncovering, second-guessing the self at every turn and destroying inner privacy" (pp. 275–276). The uncovering process of interpretative work can, therefore, feel like an intrusive shaming reenactment, implying inadequacy and lack of awareness or intelligence. Interpretations presented in a style conveying lack of certainty but also an invitation to explore can reduce this (e.g., "I'm not sure of this, but I had a sense that your daughter's comment hurt you more than you might have thought. Is there anything to that impression of mine?").

Also, therapists can be experienced as neglectful shamers when interpretations are off the mark and the patient feels not really seen. Therapists can be perceived as shamers through other interventions as well. Examples include when the patient is feeling like a diagnostic category, like the target of a "cookbook" approach, or as merely the therapist's 3 p.m. Monday appointment. This is not to say that such reactions are avoidable, and, indeed, they can be a key part of transference analysis. It does suggest that interpretation, diagnosis, and other interventions should be done in a manner that promotes collaboration rather than situations in which the expert therapist holds forth and is in total control.

Small, unconscious elements of the therapist's style can be needlessly shaming and may require self-examination by therapists and/or discussion with patients. For instance, a patient told me that she felt compassionately understood in the sessions. However, she felt insignificant and ignored when she would ask to reschedule an appointment and I would leave a message about a possible time in a "hurried, impatient, administrative tone." Although her response was multidetermined and had many transferential elements, I do think that my calls to her and other patients often had that tone. I have tried since then to be more aware and focused when making such calls.

Countertransference

Throughout this chapter, I have sought to emphasize the importance of the therapist's internal responses. As noted earlier, awareness and use of countertransference are key elements of the object relations approach described here (Scharff & Scharff, 1998; Stadter, 1996), and I view them as essential in managing the therapist's affective states, in directing interventions, and in deeply understanding the patient, cognitively and affectively.

Sometimes the therapist's internal responses are the only way for the therapist to sense split off parts of the patient's inner world (Bollas, 1987). In this way, the therapist can tune in to the deeply unconscious, nonverbal, implicit aspects of a patient even though he or she may not know what to make of these responses for an extended period of time. These countertransference responses may be the first impressions gleaned of the patient's regressed libidinal ego.

In relating intimately with a shame-prone person, therapists will be vulnerable to powerful states of being ashamed, of shaming, and of feeling contemptuous themselves. Thus, they are vulnerable to countertransference enactments, unconsciously playing a role in the patient's inner drama (e.g., the therapist unconsciously acting like the patient's indirectly shaming mother). In a sense, then, shame can be contagious and can distort therapists' self-concept and equilibrium. Therapists working intimately with shame-prone patients must understand, bear with, and make constructive use of these states.

Patients with strong shame issues may powerfully shame their therapists. Ashbach (2003) stated that "the experience of working with a shame-based individual frequently involves surviving the patient's attempts to shame the therapist into submission, or in more extreme cases, shame the therapist out of existence" (p. 84). Therapists can be attacked for not understanding, for not being competent, for not being well trained, for not helping enough, for not being experienced, for being too experienced, for the way they dress, for their office decor, for being too smart, for not being smart enough, for not being like a previous therapist—the list is endless. The ability of therapists to contain and tolerate these disturbing states of mind without retaliation or retreat creates an environment of safety and invites patients to face and explore their own ashamed and/or contemptuous selves. This permits regressed libidinal ego aspects of the patient's self to emerge. To do this effectively, it requires therapists to come to terms with, and develop awareness of, their own ashamed and shaming inner world.

Related to the previous point, therapists may be disappointed in the outcome of therapy and with patients' limited ability or desire to change. This disappointment could be especially likely when therapist and patient goals differ. The disappointment can be conveyed subtly and not so subtly, and the disappointed therapist–disappointing patient dynamic can be an indirect shaming other–defective shamed self pairing or a self-shaming other–defective shamed self pairing. Patients, then, depending on their own dynamics, may feel they have let their therapist down. Therapists need to take care that their own narcissistic needs for accomplishment and nurturance don't unconsciously create a shaming dynamic.

Other Implications

Finally, I emphasize a few additional aspects of the object relations therapy of shame. I am not claiming that these are unique to this approach; there is much in common with other psychodynamically informed therapies.

Therapists may be insightful about the various conflicts, deficits, and repetitive patterns of their patients. However, these issues frequently cannot be explored productively until shame material has been dealt with first. The concerns may have to do with shame in the therapy process itself or shame outside of the therapy room.

A reason why shame may need to be addressed before other issues can be explored is that avoidance of shame can consciously or unconsciously keep topics outside of the therapy process. Sensitive inquiry into what hasn't been discussed or fantasies of what can't be brought into the therapy can open up the therapy space ("I've been reflecting on the very significant topics we've been discussing this past month, and I was wondering if any areas come to mind that we haven't talked about." "You've really been pushing yourself to explore topics that are intensely painful. Can you imagine anything that you wouldn't feel you can bring in here?"). Such material is often shame laden and in the domain of regressed libidinal ego phenomena.

When patients are in a shame-based state, they may be too disrupted to be able to process it. As Zaslav (1998) noted, "Thus, it is useful to get into the habit with such patients of carefully reviewing previous sessions for shamed reactions, and to try to accomplish these reviews when the patient appears controlled and emotionally shored up" (p. 163). In other words, "strike while the iron is cold." For example, "Two weeks ago, you were so upset. You hated that you got drunk again and lied about it to your AA group. Maybe we could explore that a bit more today?"

I previously described connections between shame and contempt. Shame is linked to other states as well, and I would suggest that therapists especially consider possible shame connections with anger, social anxiety, envy, diminished empathy for others, and violence.

Shame may be involved when a patient is considering premature termination of therapy. Patients may consciously wish to stop treatment because shame has been stimulated and the patient wants to escape from it by ending therapy. Or the patient may have an unconscious sense of something shameful about to be touched and wishes to avoid it. I had seen Luis, 52, for about 6 months of weekly therapy concerning a family crisis. Although the crisis had been largely resolved, I was still surprised when he abruptly said he wanted to stop therapy. I acknowledged that the crisis and he were in a good spot but encouraged him to continue for a bit longer and see where we went. In the very next session, he brought up a shameful topic he had never mentioned before, a vague sense that he had been a very bad father (defective shamed self) to his now-grown children. We continued our work.

In patients' development of more awareness of self-in-relationship, it is often important for them to see that they sometimes unconsciously shame others the way they were shamed. This can be a much more painful realization than the awareness of their own shamed selves but can be explored empathically (e.g., "I can appreciate how deeply upset you were with your wife and with her rage at you. Any idea how she may have felt when you called her an 'awful mother'?").

A central point of this chapter has been for therapists to be sensitive to patients' shame and to not aggravate it. However, therapists should also not automatically avoid it and neglect facing crucial therapy issues. In fact, at times a shaming experience in therapy can be a major catalyst for change. I am not advocating intentionally shaming the patient as a confrontational technique but rather considering that if the patient does feel shamed by the therapist, it can have some positive effects. Earlier in the chapter, I presented Leonard, the 30-year-old devout Christian, as an example of a bad shamed self. Eight months into the twice-weekly therapy, we were looking at his lifelong belief in his fundamental badness, which had intensified with his serious depression. His usual openness with me was absent as he talked about various aspects of himself that were "good" but was steadfast in being convinced of his badness nonetheless. He felt to me like a rebellious teenager asserting himself through negation. I said to him, "My, you *are* stubborn on this!" He looked away and blushed but quickly recovered and continued talking. It was clear that I had shamed him. I suggested that a change had occurred between us, but he denied it and the session ended. I had unconsciously reenacted his experiences with his directly shaming father. He returned for his next session 2 days later and said he had almost not come and had seriously considered terminating. "Why should I come here? I can get treated this way by my father back home!" he said. Leonard was still upset with me but less so than he was in the previous session. As we processed it, he said that he had realized that there was a difference between his father and me: that I would at least listen to him, whereas his father wouldn't. So he thought he'd give me another chance. I said, "I'm glad you're giving me another chance. Can we look together at what this stirred up and what you felt about me?" This proved to be a turning point to some degree in our exploration of his bad shamed self, with him being more open to the possibility that he wasn't intrinsically bad.

The example of Leonard also illustrates a major way that psychotherapy can heal shame-prone patients. When an ashamed–shaming dynamic occurs between a patient and a therapist (and with others), the therapist works to help repair the damage by being able to regulate it together with the patient rather than the patient having to deal with it alone. This is consistent with Schore's (1994, 2003) neuropsychoanalytic theory concerning the mechanisms of psychotherapeutic change for such patients. As noted earlier, the psychotherapy of such individuals, according to Schore (2003), involves attention to dysregulated primitive affects such as shame; close attunement at the nonverbal, emotional level; appreciation of the centrality of therapeutic interactive repair; and an emphasis on process.

CONCLUSION

Because shame assaults the whole person, psychotherapy will either fail or be quite limited if the patient has not felt seen and valued as a unique person. Therapists must relate to the patient's idiom, the unique set of potentials of each particular person. In this sense, the psychotherapy of shame involves the psychotherapy of the whole person. Although I would argue that this is true of all depth psychotherapy, I think it is especially relevant in the treatment of shame. Guntrip (1969) captured the spirit of this object relations approach in the following quote: "Only when the therapist finds the person behind the patient's defences, and perhaps the patient finds the person behind the therapist's defences, does true psychotherapy happen" (p. 352).

REFERENCES

Ashbach, C. (2003). Persecutory objects, guilt, and shame. In J. S. Scharff & S. A. Tsigounis (Eds.), *Self-hatred in psychoanalysis* (pp. 69–87). New York, NY: Brunner-Routledge.

Balint, M. (1968). *The basic fault*. London, England: Tavistock.

Beer, J. S. (2007). Neural systems for self-conscious emotions and their underlying appraisals. In J. L. Tracy, R. W. Robins, & J. P. Tangney (Eds.), *The self-conscious emotions: Theory and research* (pp. 5–67). New York, NY: Guilford Press.

Bollas, C. (1987). *The shadow of the object*. New York, NY: Columbia University Press.

Fairbairn, W. R. D. (1952). *An object relations theory of the personality*. New York, NY: Basic Books.

Fairbairn, W. R. D. (1958). On the nature and aims of psycho-analytic treatment. *The International Journal of Psycho-Analysis, 39*, 374–385.

Greenberg, J. R., & Mitchell, S. A. (1983). *Object relations in psychoanalytic theory*. Cambridge, MA: Harvard University Press.

Guntrip, H. (1961). *Personality structure and human interaction: The developing synthesis of psychodynamic theory*. New York, NY: International Universities Press.

Guntrip, H. (1969). *Schizoid phenomena, object relations and the self*. New York, NY: International Universities Press.

Karen, R. (1992). Shame. *Atlantic, 269*(2), 40–70.

Lewis, H. B. (1971). *Shame and guilt in neurosis*. New York, NY: International Universities Press.

Morrison, A. P. (1983). Shame, the ideal self, and narcissism. *Contemporary Psychoanalysis, 19*, 295–318.

Morrison, A. P. (1989). *Shame: The underside of narcissism*. Hillsdale, NJ: Analytic Press.

Ogden, T. H. (1989). *The primitive edge of experience*. Northvale, NJ: Jason Aronson.

Ogden, T. H. (1994). *Subjects of analysis*. Northvale, NJ: Jason Aronson.

Perry, B. D., Pollard, R. A., Blakley, T. L., Baker, W. L., & Vigilante, D. (1995). Childhood trauma, the neurobiology of adaptation, and the "use-dependent" development of the brain: How "states" become "traits." *Infant Mental Health Journal, 16*, 271–291. doi:10.1002/10º7-0355(199524)16:4<271::AID-IMHJ2280160404>3.0.CO;2-B

Pines, M. (1987). Shame—what psychoanalysis does and does not say. *Group Analysis, 20*, 16–31. doi:10.1177/0533316487201004

Reed, G. S. (2001). Shame/contempt interchanges: A frequent component of the analyst–patient interaction. *Journal of the American Psychoanalytic Association, 49*, 269–275. doi:10.1177/00030651010490011801

Scharff, J. S. (1992). *Projective and introjective identification and the use of the therapist's self*. Northvale, NJ: Jason Aronson.

Scharff, J. S., & Scharff, D. E. (1998). *Object relations individual therapy*. Northvale, NJ: Jason Aronson.

Schore, A. N. (1994). *Affect regulation and the origin of the self: The neurobiology of emotional development*. New York, NY: Erlbaum.

Schore, A. N. (2003). *Affect regulation and the repair of the self*. New York, NY: Norton.

Spero, M. H. (1984). Shame—an object-relational formulation. *The Psychoanalytic Study of the Child, 39*, 259–282.

Stadter, M. (1996). *Object relations brief therapy: The therapeutic relationship in short-term work*. Northvale, NJ: Jason Aronson.

Stadter, M., & Scharff, D. E. (2000). *Object relations brief therapy*. In J. Carlson & L. Sperry (Eds.), *Brief therapy with couples and individuals* (pp. 191–219). Phoenix, AZ: Zeig, Tucker & Theisen.

Tangney, J. P., & Dearing, R. L. (2002). *Shame and guilt*. New York, NY: Guilford Press.

Trumbull, D. (2003). Shame: An acute stress response to interpersonal traumatization. *Psychiatry*, 66(1), 53–64.

Winnicott, D. W. (1958). *Through paediatrics to psycho-analysis*. New York, NY: Basic Books.

Winnicott, D. W. (1965). *The maturational processes and the facilitating environment*. New York, NY: International Universities Press.

Zaslav, M. R. (1998). Shame-related states of mind in psychotherapy. *Journal of Psychotherapy Practice and Research*, 7, 154–166.

3

EMOTION-FOCUSED THERAPY AND SHAME

LESLIE S. GREENBERG AND SHIGERU IWAKABE

Emotion-focused therapy (EFT) is an integrative approach to psycho-therapy designed to foster clients' emotional processing skills and emotional literacy. This helps people better use and regulate their affect and thereby enhance their well-being (Greenberg, 2002; Greenberg & Paivio, 1997; Greenberg, Rice, & Elliott, 1993; Greenberg & Watson, 2006). EFT has been shown to be effective in the treatment of depression (Goldman, Greenberg, & Angus, 2006; Greenberg & Watson, 1998; Watson, Gordon, Stermac, Kalogerakos, & Steckley, 2003), trauma, interpersonal injuries (Paivio, 2001), and couples distress (Greenberg & Goldman, 2008; Johnson, Hunsley, Greenberg, & Schindler, 1999). What is notable about the empirical basis of EFT is that not only has its efficacy been established, but also each step of the successful client change process has been supported through a series of task analytic studies (Greenberg, 2007). Originally, six major change tasks were identified in individual therapy (Greenberg et al., 1993), each dealing with a specific affective–cognitive problem, such as self-criticisms, self-interruption of emotional experience, and unfinished business. Shame was found to be a central ingredient in many of these problems. Recently Greenberg and Goldman (2008) also described the role of shame both in maintaining negative interactions in couples and in resolving emotional injuries.

69

In this chapter, we look at the role of shame in psychotherapeutic change. We begin by reviewing the theory of EFT and of shame. We then summarize EFT principles for working with shame, discussing relational validation, accessing and acknowledging shame, shame regulation, and the transformation of shame. We then look at differential intervention for different shame processes and for varieties of shame experience and discuss cultural issues in working with shame in EFT. We conclude with a case illustration.

EMOTION THEORY IN EMOTION-FOCUSED THERAPY

EFT emphasizes the central role of emotions in both adaptive and maladaptive psychological functioning. At the most basic level, emotions are seen as an adaptive form of information processing that orients people to their environment and provides action readiness. In EFT, the lives of human beings are viewed as profoundly shaped and organized by emotional experiences. When, for example, shame is activated, we feel our mind going blank and feel paralyzed on the spot, wishing that we could sink into the ground and disappear. We not only are acutely aware of others' gaze, but we also become intensely and rapidly aroused. Immediate physiological changes occur: Blood rushes to the head, and the face blushes. Shame causes the self to curl up and retreat into itself.

Central to EFT theory is the organizing function of emotion schemes. The term *emotion schemes* refers to cue-activated response-producing internal organizations that synthesize a variety of levels and types of information from sensorimotor stimuli, emotion memory, and conceptual-level information (Greenberg, 2002). In contrast to a cognitive schema that produces representations in language, the emotion scheme is an internal organization that is not mediated by thought and that produces nonverbal action tendencies and affective experience. For example, shame schemes, when activated, lead to feeling inferior or worthless, and this involves a tendency to bow one's head and shrink in an effort to sink into the ground and disappear so as to not be seen. At the same time, one becomes acutely and painfully conscious of oneself as gazed on and evaluated by others. Rather than simply believing that one is worthless or thinking that one is inferior, there is the sense of social disdain (real or imagined).

In EFT, affect regulation is seen as a core human motive. People seek to have the affects they want and to not have the affects they don't want because the emotions we seek and avoid promote survival and adaptation. Much human action and interaction, then, is seen as being driven by felt satisfaction—by the felt excitement and suspense of connection and striving and by the boredom, anxiety, and loneliness when these are absent. Emotion that results from appraisals of situations in relation to our well-being (Frijda, 1986, 2007; Greenberg et al., 1993) guides us as to what is good and bad for us, and we attach, act to maintain our identities, and pursue competence because of how these actions makes us feel.

In addition to being motivated to regulate affect, people also are seen as motivated to seek meaning (Greenberg & Goldman, 2008). People's goals therefore consist of more than simply "feeling good." Thus, at times, under certain circumstances people will seek "negative" emotions, tolerate pain, or sacrifice themselves in the service of higher-order feelings of virtue or love. EFT therefore does not propose a simple hedonistic theory of motivation (i.e., the seeking of pleasure and the avoidance of pain). Although people primarily do seek to feel positive emotions, "negative" emotions, such as sadness and anger, also are highly functional, and people self-regulate the emotions with the aim of achieving goals, not of simply seeking pleasure.

Finally, EFT takes a dialectical–constructivist view of human functioning and proposes that people are in a constant process of making sense of the emotional experiences that arise from scheme activation (Greenberg & Pascual-Leone, 2001; Greenberg et al., 1993). People thus seek to understand the meanings of their experience and actions and to create meaning out of these. Personal meaning, in this view, emerges by the self-organization and explication of one's own emotional experience. An ongoing circular process of making sense of experience—symbolizing bodily felt sensations in awareness and articulating them in language—leads to construction of new experience. Optimal adaptation thus ultimately involves an integration of head and heart, reason and emotion.

TYPES OF SHAME

Shame essentially relates to a person's sense of worth; it makes people want to hide, as opposed to guilt, which prompts apology or the making of amends (Lewis, 1971; Tangney & Dearing, 2002). Shame is connected to the evolutionary mechanisms that link to status and social rank, whereas guilt links to the evolutionary mechanisms that underpin caring behavior (Gilbert & McGuire, 1998). Shame makes us close down and avoid thinking too much about events because it makes us feel bad about ourselves. Guilt propels us to repair.

People feel shame when they feel small or diminished in the eyes of the other. People also feel shame when they feel overexposed, as if appearing naked in public or having lost control of themselves; they feel that other people see them as worthless or undignified. Shame can also arise when people reveal their emotions to another person or show their excitement and these expressions are not seen or responded to. Children feel shame when no one pays attention to their emotional excitement or their efforts at exhibiting their prowess (Kohut, 1977). When they excitedly yell "Mommy! Daddy! Look at me!" as they stand ready to jump from a diving board into a swimming pool and their parents ignore them, they might shrink away in shame.

In EFT, different classes of emotion, such as primary and secondary and adaptive and maladaptive emotions, are distinguished from one another to guide differential intervention. *Primary emotion* is the first response a person has to a stimulus; *secondary emotions* are those emotions that are reactions to more primary emotion, such as feeling secondary anger in response to feeling hurt or secondary rage in response to primary shame. Secondary feelings also are feelings about feelings, such as feeling ashamed of one's fear. Primary emotion, in addition, can be seen either as providing adaptive information and action tendencies, such as sadness in response to loss or anger at violation, or as being maladaptive. *Maladaptive* emotions are those that no longer enhance survival or are no longer functional, such as fear of loud noises based on combat posttraumatic stress disorder or fear of closeness based on prior childhood abuse that has left one unable to trust.

Thus, *primary adaptive shame* is seen as a person's most fundamental, direct, initial, rapid reaction to a situation of diminishment and in therapy is accessed for its adaptive information and capacity to organize adaptive action. Adaptive shame informs people that they are too exposed and that other people will not support their actions or that they have violated important standards or values. The display of shame also has the function of reducing others' aggression and increasing the likelihood of social reconciliation by evoking affiliative responses, sympathy, and forgiveness from others (Keltner & Harker, 1998).

Primary maladaptive shame, however, which often results from past trauma or a poor attachment history, leads to withdrawal and avoidance and results in treating the self and others badly. Almost all of us have some minitraumatic experiences from childhood, such as being the last player to be selected for a team. Such experiences can result in the internalization of the experience of being shunned. Maladaptive shame resulting from such experiences can be activated in adulthood. What once were adaptive emotional responses, developed as a survival strategy in reaction to abuse, humiliation, or rejection, are internalized and become maladaptive. This type of internalized core shame is one of the more frequently occurring primary maladaptive emotions in therapy, and it must be accessed in order to transform it. In therapy, it is also important to distinguish between external shame (generated by perceptions of how others view us) in reaction to events and internalized shame (generated by internalized judgments, criticism, and contempt; Gilbert, 1997). In EFT, primary maladaptive shame is one of the key negative emotions to be accessed and transformed. These shame responses are not mediated by thought or self-judgment. Emotion schematic memories, rather, are evoked when a set of cues match the scheme releasers independent of any judgment or automatic thoughts in language. Thus, the face of contempt of the other evokes an emotion scheme of shame, and the person has a sinking feeling in the stomach and begins to feel like hiding.

Secondary shame is an emotional reaction to a primary emotion, such as feeling ashamed of one's sadness or anger. Secondary shame needs to be explored to discover its root cause. Finally, *instrumental shame* is an emotional behavior pattern that the person has learned to use to achieve an interpersonal aim, such as feigning embarrassment in order to appear appropriate. Expressing shame to convey submission is often a cultural form of greeting. Instrumental shame, however, can be dysfunctional when it is used rigidly and repeatedly to satisfy unmet needs. In therapy, clients often need help to become aware of the goal of shame expressed in this manner.

In EFT, working with shame primarily is concerned with exploring and transforming internalized maladaptive primary shame that is part of a core sense of self as worthless, inferior, weak, vulnerable, and/or unlovable. In addition, secondary shame, which is generated by self-critical cognition, contempt, and disgust directed at the self, is also an important focus of therapeutic work. These two forms of shame often are related, and they form a spectrum of a shame-based syndrome, which generates a chronic sense of worthlessness and inferiority as well as a rigid shame-related cognitive-affective processing style.

EMOTION-FOCUSED THERAPY PRINCIPLES
FOR WORKING WITH SHAME

Overcoming shame leads to a strengthening of the self, including increased confidence and self-esteem. In addition, once people are deshamed, they are more open to change in different domains of their psychological functioning. Work with shame is thus crucial for many problems that people bring to therapy. Next, we discuss four major EFT principles for working with shame: relational validation, accessing and acknowledging shame, regulating shame, and finally transforming shame.

The first principle of EFT, designed to counteract shame, is the development of a supportive, validating, empathic, and affectively attuned relationship. When relational safety is established, the focus shifts to accessing shame, overcoming the avoidance of shame, symbolizing it, and allowing the painful feelings of shame to be experienced. Interventions then focus on helping clients stay in touch with their experiences of unresolved shame and humiliation and to symbolize these feelings in the immediacy of the session or to regulate the shame if it is too overwhelming. This then allows for the transformation of shame by exposing the activated maladaptive shame to new emotional experiences generated in the therapy. Mobilization of strengths and internal resources, such as self-compassion, self-empathy, self-respect, empowering anger, and pride, helps undo damaging shame experiences and helps the person construct new meaning from the shameful experiences. Treatment of shame thus aims at accessing the maladaptive shame schematic memories, transforming them by accessing strengths and emotional resources in the personality, and creating new meaning (Greenberg, 2002; Greenberg & Paivio, 1997; Greenberg & Watson, 2006).

Relational Validation

Shame operates everywhere in therapy because clients are constantly concerned about what part of their inner experience can be revealed safely and what part must be kept hidden. Clients' struggles with shame may start even before the therapy begins. The mere act of acknowledging that life is too difficult and the idea of laying bare one's deepest secrets to a relative stranger are fraught with shame. Seeking help from professionals about personal matters thus can evoke a sense of humiliation. It requires considerable trust for clients to reveal to the therapist what they consider to be their deepest flaws and those parts of self of which they are most ashamed. The first goal in counteracting shame therefore is to develop a supportive, validating, empathic, and affectively attuned relationship.

Shame is created within interpersonal relationships; therefore, it needs an interpersonal relationship to heal and transform it. To overcome the shame that interferes with self-acceptance, people have to come out of hiding and undo their tendency to bypass and avoid the experience of shame (Nathanson, 1992). An empathic validating relationship helps clients acknowledge and fully experience shame, humiliation, and embarrassment in the session so that these feelings can be exposed to disconfirming experiences with the therapist who is affirmative and compassionate. Clients learn that if they reveal their flaws and shortcomings, they will not be rejected or judged as worthless or defective.

Therapists need to be attuned and responsive to nonverbal as well as verbal indicators of shame-related experience in the session. Nonverbal indictors include downcast eyes, squirming or writhing in the seat, and laughter or shrugging off that covers embarrassment. Clients may joke about "hating" being there, or feel "reduced to paying for help," or give indications that it is somehow degrading to be in therapy. Immediacy in attending to these markers of reluctance is essential to establishing the therapeutic bond. Interventions such as "It's embarrassing to talk about such private things, but it's important" or "It's hard to ask for help; it makes you feel a bit like a child, but we all need help at times" validate the client's internal struggle and provide support.

Feeling shamed in therapy is highly dependent on the quality of the therapeutic relationship. It is important for therapists to be alert to whether they have unwittingly shamed the client by not being attuned to the client's feelings or by misunderstanding or missing something important. Shaming clients causes ruptures in the working alliance, which is so important to therapy outcome (Horvath & Bedi, 2005). Healing these types of ruptures in the relationship and correcting current misunderstandings can be highly therapeutic (Rhodes, Hill, Thompson, & Elliott, 1994; Watson & Greenberg, 1995). In these instances, an understanding, supportive relationship is not just a precondition to further work with shame but is the essence of the treatment itself, enabling a corrective interpersonal emotional experience.

Accessing and Acknowledging Shame

The second goal of EFT intervention is to help clients recognize and overcome avoidance and acknowledge painful feelings of shame. Clients automatically avoid and deflect from the experience of shame because shame is so painful (Nathanson, 1992). Shame avoidance interferes with people's ability to attend to their internal experience. People may talk about embarrassing or humiliating experiences but avoid the intense discomfort of the immediate experience. Drawing attention to the shameful experience often only intensifies the impulse to retreat and close down emotionally. The therapist thus needs to guide clients to attend to and acknowledge their shame. Responses such as "As you were talking about that, I was aware of how degrading that must have felt" refocus clients' attention on their own internal experience. Therapists also can reflect the discomfort of feeling small, worthless, and humiliated in the presence of another and normalize clients' desire to protect their dignity and the tendency to look away from their therapists while they speak. Clients who express anger that covers shame can be encouraged to express their reactive anger at being humiliated, but interventions should acknowledge their anger as a secondary reaction and a face-saving coping response and should highlight the underlying core experience of shame. An example of such a refocusing intervention would be as follows: "Yes, so angry at him for using you. That's a reaction to that awful feeling of being used like that. That's the most damaging part. I know it's hard, it hurts, it's degrading to feel . . . what . . . unvalued . . . unimportant, belittled?"

Drawing attention to and focusing attention on shame, however, can threaten a person whose self-esteem is fragile. It is therefore important to assess client ego strength; to be unintrusive, delicate, and sensitive to client fragility; and to be respectful of the client's inclination to withdraw in shame.

With many clients it may be necessary first to strengthen their self-esteem before they can tolerate exposing or acknowledging their experience of shame. It is sometimes necessary to provide a rationale for experiencing and disclosing shame because it feels like such a self-damaging emotional state and the client may perceive the therapist as coercive and punitive. For example, when clients express reluctance to talk about embarrassing or shameful material, therapists can encourage them with responses such as, "I know it's hard, but it's so important to say; otherwise, it eats away at you" or "keeps you so isolated."

Helping clients acknowledge shame that is on the periphery of their awareness requires particular sensitivity on the part of the therapist. Intervention involves, first, recognition of surface reactions that cover shame, such as cockiness, bravado at bad feelings, narcissistic anger, perfectionism, or other types of obsessiveness and then empathic conjecture about the underlying experience. A response to bravado about rejection might be "I hear the determination in your voice, like there's this part of you that puts on a brave front to protect against this other part that feels kind of insignificant." An empathic response to the shame underlying a client's social anxiety, for example, might be "It's almost like, if they saw you for who you really are, they'd reject you."

The therapist often can help the client access core shame by empathically highlighting the underlying pain of wounds to self-esteem and the pain of not belonging. Responses that validate how shaming things were and how the unmet longing to belong left one feeling so worthless, while also affirming the adaptiveness of this need, are very therapeutic. Responses that help evoke the shame a client feels include "Yes, as kids we all need so desperately to be accepted, to belong" or "How humiliating to be exposed like that, caught on the toilet, with them laughing at and pointing fingers at you." Clients then might disclose how abandoned and alone they felt as a child, wishing more than anything that they were liked or loved in spite of their deficits. Putting shame into words with a trusted other enables the client to step outside the emotional experience so that the shame no longer seems to permeate his or her entire being; this also helps self-compassion emerge.

Once avoidance and interruption of shame are overcome, interventions such as evocative imagery or psychodramatic enactments (Greenberg et al., 1993; Elliott, Watson, Goldman, & Greenberg, 2004) are needed to help clients bring the shame alive in the immediacy of the session and stay in touch with their particular experiences of shame long enough to symbolize these feelings in awareness. Activation of the shame makes it amenable to the input of new experience, and it is this new experience that can transform the maladaptive emotion schemes that produce shame. A powerful intervention for evoking shame consists of a two-chair dialogue in which the client enacts the harshly negative, contemptuous, self-evaluative processes that produce shame (Greenberg et al., 1993). In this intervention, therapists ask clients to enact the two parts of themselves—the critic or judge who directs contemptuous statements and the part of themselves that is the recipient of the contempt and disgust. This process heightens awareness of the specific internalized messages, the expressive quality, and the experiential impact of the internalized contempt and disgust—the shame and pain of such self-denigration and the damage to clients' self-esteem.

Regulating Shame

There are both implicit (right hemispheric) and explicit (left hemispheric) forms of affect regulation (Schore, 2003). In people who are more shame prone, the problem often is a deficit in implicit, automatic forms of shame regulation that modulate affect, nonverbal communication, and unconscious process. Although the primary therapeutic goal in EFT for shame-prone people is for them to learn to automatically regulate the intensity of their affective arousal so that shame does not become overwhelming, initially deliberate behavioral and cognitive forms of regulation—a more left hemispheric process—are useful especially for those who feel out of control. *Explicit shame regulation* refers to the processes by which people attempt to voluntarily control when, and how intensely, they experience shame. Helping clients to find ways consciously or purposively to cope with their shame often is a first therapeutic step, especially for people who are highly distressed. Thus, taking a warm bath to calm down (sensory regulation), learning to distract when feeling shame (cognitive regulation), or consciously reconstructing the situation can improve coping to limit distress to a more manageable level.

Over time, however, it is the building of *implicit* or *automatic emotion regulation* capacities that is important for shame-prone clients. Directly experiencing aroused shame being soothed by relational or nonverbal means—a more right hemispheric process (Schore, 2003)—is one of the best ways to build the internal capacity for implicit self-soothing. Soothing most centrally comes interpersonally in the form of empathic attunement and responsiveness to affect and through acceptance and validation by another person. Clients with underregulated affect have been shown to benefit both from validation and the learning of emotion regulation and distress tolerance skills (Linehan et al., 2002).

Forms of meditative practice and self-acceptance often are helpful in achieving a working distance from the overwhelming core maladaptive emotion of shame. The ability to regulate breathing and the ability to observe emotions and let them come and go are important processes to help regulate many types of emotional distress. As well as being mindful of internal experience, it is helpful to guide dysregulated clients to be mindful of what is going on outside of their immediate internal emotional experience by redirecting their attention to the external environment.

Shame thus can be regulated by developing tolerance for negative affect and by soothing at a variety of different levels of processing. Physiological soothing involves activation of the parasympathetic nervous system to regulate heart rate, breathing, and other sympathetic functions that speed up under stress. At more deliberate levels, promoting clients' abilities to allow and be compassionate to their emerging painful emotional experience is the first step toward tolerating shame and developing the capacity to self-soothe (Gilbert, 1997; Gilbert & Procter, 2006; see also Chapter 14, this volume). It often is the relationship with an attuned other that is essential in developing shame regulation, but as we have seen, self-soothing involves many components, including diaphragmatic breathing, relaxation, development of self-empathy and compassion, and positive self-talk (Greenberg & Watson, 2006).

Transforming Shame

The transformation of shame involves both generating new, more resilient emotional responses and validating the new feelings and the emerging more confident self-organization (Greenberg, 2002; Greenberg & Watson, 2006). One of the best ways of changing emotion is with another opposing emotion that acts to undo the first emotion (Greenberg, 2002). Once clients have accessed core dysfunctional emotion schemes that involve maladaptive shame, the scene is set for transforming the maladaptive state by mobilizing alternative emotional responses based on adaptive needs and goals to expand clients' emotional response repertoire. For example, withdrawal and avoidance responses of a defeated and demoralized self that come from core shame are paired with new approach responses associated with empowered anger, comfort-seeking sadness, or expansive pride and other positive emotions that undo the effects of paralyzing shame.

In promoting access to new emotions, therapists need to validate the spontaneous emergence of more adaptive emotion (Greenberg, 2002). Therapists need to shift clients' focus of attention to help them pay attention to background or subdominant more adaptive feelings. Accessing needs and goals is another key method to help undo shame. Therapists can ask clients what they need when they are in painful shame. Raising a need or a goal to a conscious self-organizing system evokes and heightens a sense of agency. If a client, in a state of shame, experiences a need for validation, an anger-based sense of pride often emerges at not having the need met. Expressive exercises such as positive imagery, expressive enactment of the emotion, and remembering another emotion can also help clients experience another more adaptive emotion in the present. Often the adaptive emotions that help transform shame are empowered anger and the sadness of loss that supports comfort seeking. Therapists also can suggest that a client focus on something in a different way; for example, the therapist may ask clients to focus on what they didn't like about their abusive parents instead of focusing on their own negative self-appraisals. Changing how one views a situation or talking about the meaning of an emotional experience often helps clients experience new feelings (Gross, 2002). Therapists might express on behalf of the client the outrage, pain, or sadness that the shamed client is unable to express. A new emotion can also be evoked in response to new interactions with the therapist. The therapist might, for example, self-disclose to create a sense of closeness or commonality to communicate acceptance and to evoke a feeling of calmness.

Shame also interrupts positive emotions such as joy, pride, and interest (Nathanson, 1992; Tomkins, 1987). Many clients who have a strong sense of shame tend to hide their strengths and joys. Therefore, it is helpful to have them own their strengths and enjoy them. The therapist's focus on a positive feeling will have an effect on the client and will deepen the positive feeling or evoke other feelings attached to it. Attempting at appropriate times to evoke and amplify positive emotions by asking clients to repeat certain self-affirming and self-expressive statements and to elaborate what they imply helps them overcome embarrassment at and constriction of the expression of these feelings. Encouraging clients to boast about their achievements, for example, helps them express pride and gives them permission to feel it. It is helpful to ask clients first to allow the positive feeling to flow in their bodies, to feel the excitement and let it build, and then to show it on their face and in their voice and express it in their bodies (Greenberg & Watson, 2006).

Therapists also need to be attuned to spontaneously emerging challenges to shame, such as a client's adaptive resources or positive emotional responses—for example, humor and pride—that can counteract shame. There often is a part of the self that doesn't quite believe the self-criticism. For example, a client who was berating herself for "chickening out" of a direct confrontation with her parents suddenly switched to "Oh, well, at least I sent the letter." The therapist could have focused on her self-criticism. Instead, the therapist chose to support the emergence of client strength by responding, "Yes, that seems like a real accomplishment. How did it feel to put all those things on paper?" The following week, the client brought in a copy of the letter, and this was used as an opportunity to explore her capabilities that had been often overlooked and devalued and to strengthen her self-respect.

The final aspect of therapeutic work transforming shame with EFT is the consolidation of new meaning and the reconstruction of narratives that confirm or change clients' identities and the views they have of their experiences. When clients who have experienced core maladaptive feelings of primary shame and worthlessness are able to symbolize these feelings in awareness and acknowledge that this is what they feel at their core, they begin to gain some reflective mastery over their experience. With the symbolization of their core feeling, they create a separation from it. The feeling now is not simply an overwhelming experience of "I *am* worthless," but rather an experience of "I *feel* worthless," which is a feeling I have, rather than who I am. The feeling becomes an object or product of the self, one that produces distress, rather than being the self, and thus can be regulated more easily. This symbolization creates an inner space for clients to reflect on themselves apart from the shame experience and to get to the core resilient self that wishes to survive and thrive.

When clients are able to reflect on their shame experiences, with the help of the therapist they make connections between different elements of their lives, begin to posit alternative explanations for their experiences, revise their views of themselves or their history, and develop new narratives (Greenberg & Angus, 2004). This process is often accompanied by a sense of greater connectedness and mastery in their lives. With clients troubled with varieties of shame-related problems, one important therapeutic goal is to help them develop a new set of lenses through which to view themselves, the past, and the future. Clients can develop narratives that emphasize their resiliency and newly acquired sense of agency, thus reconstructing their views of themselves. When this occurs, the self is no longer judged as a failure but rather as capable of success in the face of obstacles and able to thrive even when confronted with experiences that previously might have been perceived as threatening to survival. Thus, clients' views of the self, the world, and their experience are revised and reconstructed as these views become illuminated and reflected on in therapy.

DIFFERENTIAL INTERVENTION FOR VARIETIES OF SHAME EXPERIENCE

A number of different goals of shame work EFT have been distinguished, each requiring different sets of in-session interventions to facilitate change (Greenberg, 2002; Greenberg & Paivio, 1997). The major goals of shame work identified are (a) being informed by primary adaptive shame; (b) transforming primary maladaptive core shame and strengthening the self to overcome societal shame; and (c) overcoming secondary shame generated by self-critical cognitions.

Being Informed by Primary Adaptive Shame

Shame felt in response to violations of implicit or explicit personal standards and values, such as shame at engaging in deviant behavior, shame at a public loss of control, or shame at being a neglectful or abusive parent, is adaptive shame. It helps people not alienate themselves from their group and maintain a sense of connection and belonging while also protecting their privacy. It does this by preventing people from erring too much in public or breaking the rules that form the social fabric.

In therapy, feelings of adaptive shame need to be acknowledged because they provide valuable information about socially acceptable behavior and action tendencies that can be used to guide conduct. Recently we found that in couples suffering from emotional injury in which one partner felt betrayed or invalidated, the expression of shame by the injurer as part of the apology appeared to be a key ingredient to rebuilding trust and promoting forgiveness (Greenberg, Warwar, & Malcolm, 2010).

Transforming Primary Maladaptive Core Shame

Shame in therapy usually presents in its maladaptive form. Internalized maladaptive shame involves a pervasive sense of oneself as defective, worthless, or unacceptably flawed. This form of shame often is at the center of self-critical depression (Greenberg & Watson, 2006). Shame also is important in chronically shy clients; most people experience some shame, but a very high percentage of clients with social anxiety disorder suffer from excessive shame. If anxious and depressed clients are not helped to reduce their core shame, relapse often occurs very quickly. Core shame is a more enduring part of the person's self-experience that influences his or her personality. It forms the undercurrent of experience without emerging into awareness. An early learning history of rejection, ridicule, and criticism as well as abuse and neglect generally leads to the development of a core sense of self as flawed, worthless, unlovable, or bad. Repeated experiences of core shame lead to an overall sense of low self-esteem.

Maladaptive core shame also arises from child-rearing practices that teach children that their feelings, desires, or behaviors are unacceptable. Shaming is a common child-rearing practice, and to a certain degree we all are damaged by it. More intense core shame occurs as a result of abuse, neglect, and other forms of childhood maltreatment. People who were emotionally, physically, or sexually abused as children have internalized a sense of themselves as "spoiled goods" and feel defective, unlovable, and/or worthless (see Chapter 11, this volume). People who were harshly punished often feel debilitating shame for having transgressed moral standards, whereas others who were invalidated fear being the object of social denigration or stigma. People who were treated with contempt learn to treat themselves the way they were treated by significant others—that is, with self-contempt-and they often experience total humiliation for being who they are. The problem for many abused clients is the sense that somehow they were responsible for a shameful act over which they had no control, that they deserved the abuse and brought it on themselves. Pathogenic beliefs about the self as defective or spoiled were poignantly illustrated by one client who, speaking about having been sexually molested as a girl, cried, "Who would want me now?"

Sometimes core shame develops from experiences of rejection due to class, race, gender, or sexual orientation or being somehow "different" and judged inferior. One client, for example, felt deep shame about her infertility. Primary maladaptive shame from this type of social comparison or rejection is not essentially different from the internalized shame arising from childhood maltreatment except that the shame is not imposed by a primary caregiver. Nevertheless, the person has internalized a core sense of himself or herself as inferior, unacceptable, deviant, or somehow deeply flawed.

Intervention with shame-prone survivors of maltreatment and abuse, who often feel responsible for the abuse, involves appropriately externalizing the blame, or "putting the blame where it belongs." In addition, among people who have been abused, the abuse is often a closely guarded secret, yielding pervasive shame anxiety (anticipatory anxiety about feeling shame) and fear of intimacy. In psychotherapy, therapist empathic affirmation of vulnerability (Greenberg et al., 1993) is the initial therapeutic strategy of choice when the therapist notes indicators of maladaptive shame during therapy sessions. In such instances, the therapist helps clients stay with their shame so as to experience the acceptance of the therapist and find their own resiliency, for example, by allowing themselves to experience other adaptive emotions. Sadness or anger can be fundamentally growth producing in that they point to adaptive actions appropriate to the situation. For example, sadness can lead to reaching out to connect to others, or anger can lead to asserting one's right to live one's own life without shame (Greenberg, 2002; Greenberg et al., 1993). People with core shame also rarely experience positive emotions to their full intensity. They may feel too vulnerable to feel joy or interest because of the fear that good feelings will be taken away as soon as they start to enjoy them. Individuals who have experienced repeated core shame may also feel unworthy of experiencing positive emotions. Therapy can help these clients access joy and pride in self and open up to the therapist.

Work with core shame involves restructuring the shame-based emotion scheme by accessing and supporting the emergence of internal healthy resources via self-soothing and self-validation. Shame often is transformed by accessing primary adaptive empowering anger in therapy to assert oneself, to stand up to abusers in imaginal confrontations, and to empower oneself and challenge self-blame and contempt (Paivio, Hall, Holowaty, Jellis, & Tran, 2001). This form of imaginal confrontation, using gestalt empty chair work for resolving unfinished business, often is an important intervention for maladaptive shame (Greenberg et al., 1993). In working with the expression of anger to undo shame, adaptive, empowering anger at maltreatment needs to be distinguished from maladaptive rage associated with narcissistic slights and reactions to humiliation. Maladaptive rage is overly intense, chronic, destructive, and/or inappropriate and is often in reaction to minor insults or failure experiences. The EFT therapist helps clients attend to and intensify the experience of adaptive anger, which is empowering. The focus of such work is on asserting the self rather than destroying the other. In contrast, maladaptive rage, which is aimed at destroying the other, is bypassed, not intensified. Once anger is validated, clients generally shift their focus to their internal experience of being wounded and hurt.

When clients access introjected shaming messages associated with their core maladaptive shame, such as "You're so selfish" or "Homosexuality is deviant," which originated with significant others (e.g., parents, those in authority positions in society), therapists need to clarify the interpersonal origins of such messages and not reinforce self-blame. Once clients feel validated, they are encouraged to own that they are agents in the construction of their own misfortune by having internalized these shaming messages. As the client understands that shame is internally generated, the target problem becomes an intrapsychic struggle for self-acceptance.

Overcoming Secondary Shame Generated by Self-Criticism

Self-criticism is one of the most commonly occurring dysfunctional processes associated with secondary shame. People harshly judge themselves for their mistakes, flaws, or shortcomings and feel shame. This cognitive–affective process generates feelings of worthlessness or inferiority, damages self-esteem, and often leads to depression. The self-critical process differs from maladaptive shame in that the shame is activated periodically and in specific situations. If it is pervasive and occurs chronically across situations, it is a more central self-organization and then is symptomatic of primary maladaptive shame.

Secondary shame is evident in therapy when one part of the self is the harsh critic and judge, a part that rejects certain behaviors or characteristics of another part of the self; at the same time, the accused part of the self feels like a failure and feels ashamed but may react defensively or with hostility. The therapeutic objective in working with secondary shame generated by self-criticism is to access the underlying primary emotional experience of which the person feels ashamed. This is accomplished by bypassing the secondary shame. Rather than focusing on it, the therapist focuses on the person's underlying feeling of, say, anger or sadness of which the person feels ashamed. If that is not possible, the therapist works with the shame-producing self-criticism until a shift to the more primary experience occurs. Two-chair dialogue for self-criticisms is the intervention of choice for this form of shame (Greenberg et al., 1993).

In secondary shame one also can be ashamed of particular emotions or self-experiences, such as feeling ashamed of feeling hurt, weak, or needy or feeling ashamed of feeling sexual or angry. Feeling fearful that these internal experiences will emerge leads to shame anxiety, a feeling often indistinguishable from feelings of vulnerability. Shame anxiety is associated with fear of revealing internal experiences and fear of being judged. At moments of shame anxiety, clients may interrupt their emotional expression by tensing their muscles, holding their breath, and becoming silent.

Empathic attunement, support, and affirmation of the need to protect oneself are the most appropriate interventions for this form of shame. Provision of safety and empathic affirmation of vulnerability reduce interpersonal anxiety and allow the person to take the risk of accessing and disclosing the hidden aspects of self so that they can be exposed to new disconfirming information in the therapy session.

Another form of secondary shame is societal shame. In contrast to core maladaptive shame, which involves a chronic and pervasive sense of worthlessness, societal shame tends to occur as a result of perceived life failures such as getting divorced or losing a high-paying job that the person fears reflects defeat, poor judgment, immaturity, and so on. Clients with societal shame feel humiliated and ashamed in the eyes of others. Although societal shame is often situational due to loss of social position, sense of identity, and one's public image, it often evokes past trauma and unresolved conflicts in the area of confidence, self-worth, and efficacy. People who experience societal shame also feel isolated and alienated because societal shame blocks them from seeking others with whom to share their sense of loss and sadness and to rebuild their interpersonal network. The internal experience of societal shame often is associated with disappointment, exploitation, or traumatic loss. Therapy here involves dealing with the loss.

Two-chair dialogue for splits is frequently used to work with shame-producing self-criticism (Greenberg et al., 1993). This involves encouraging a client to engage in a dialogue between two aspects of the self; one aspect is expressed while sitting in one chair, and the other is expressed while sitting in the other chair. In therapy, markers of shame are obvious or implied self-critical statements accompanied by harsh vocal quality and facial expressions, such as a curled lip or sneer, that indicate feelings of contempt and disgust toward the self. When people engage in shame-producing dialogue, part of the self negatively evaluates, and expresses contempt or disgust toward, another part of the self. Here, intervention involves highlighting or analyzing the expressive quality of contempt, specifying the shame-producing cognitions, heightening awareness of agency in the shame-producing process, and countering shame by supporting the emergence of the healthy part of self with feelings of pride. An example of the contempt expressed from the Critic's chair (i.e., the self's critical voice) might be "You're pathetic," and this will evoke shame expressed from the other aspect of self: "I feel so worthless, like curling up into a ball and hiding." In this dialogue, people come to see that by denigrating themselves, they are agents in the production of their experience of shame and that they can change how they relate to themselves. People resolve this split as more adaptive feelings such as anger and sadness and later more self-assertion such as "Leave me alone; stop attacking me like that" evolve to counteract the shame. Resolution of the split is seen when the Critic softens into compassion, saying, "I don't want to make you suffer; I do care about you." An integration of the two aspects can then occur, resulting in self-acceptance and a stronger sense of self.

Two-chair dialogue highlights not only the cognitive content of the critical message but also the contempt and disgust directed at self along with the painful reaction of the self to this harshly negative self-evaluation. As we said, an important step in this intervention is that the person's awareness of agency in producing feelings of shame is heightened: He or she realizes that shame-producing messages are internally generated and, therefore, that he or she can change them. The tendency to protect the self from the criticism and to protest and challenge the shaming message spontaneously occurs in the other chair. The negotiation between the two sides of the self leads to a more self-accepting and self-soothing attitude, which weakens the negative evaluations and allows positive emotions such as pride and love to emerge.

CULTURAL ISSUES IN WORKING WITH SHAME IN EFT

In Asian collectivist cultures in which group harmony, social hierarchy, and the interdependence of individuals are socially emphasized, the sense of self is more closely related to one's membership in groups and fulfilling one's obligations to others. In Western cultures, autonomy, independence, and the uniqueness of each individual are prized (Markus & Kitayama, 1991). It is often argued that shame has a more primary role in regulating social roles and behaviors in collectivist cultures. In addition, the expression of negative emotions such as anger and sadness is apt to be suppressed, whereas nonindividualistic positive emotions such as joy and interest (as contrasted with pride and contentment) are used instrumentally to maintain and strengthen ties among group members (Doi, 1973).

In collectivist cultures, an emphasis on social hierarchy based on seniority contributes to the instrumental use of certain shame-related emotional expressions for role management. Being humble and acting with reserve are considered virtuous and respectful, whereas the expression of negative emotions is viewed as showing disrespect and disloyalty rather than as a spontaneous and direct expression of internal experience. Public humiliation and other forms of shaming are often used in child rearing and education.

Owing to its prevalence in Asian cultures, shame plays a prominent role in a variety of types of psychological dysfunction. For example, *taijin kyofusho* (anthropophobia or interpersonal phobia) in Japan refers to a class of phobic disorders associated with fear of a potential shaming experience in public such as interpersonal shaming, others' gaze, humiliation, exposure, and inappropriate behaviors, and is one of the most typical forms of neurosis (Morita, Kondo, & Levine, 1998). In collectivist cultures, clients often present problems related to maladaptive shame such as societal shame as well as secondary shame generated by self-criticism.

Although the main principles of EFT treatment with shame remain the same in therapeutic work with clients from a collectivist cultural group, therapists are advised to make sure that such clients understand the rationales behind accessing, tolerating the experience of, expressing, and understanding shame and other related emotions in therapy. In particular, they need to know that expression of negative emotions in front of the therapist is not only allowed but also is essential to therapeutic work. Clients from a collectivist culture may be under the assumption that they need to behave in ways that show respect to the therapist, who is in a position of authority. They may put on a social face, inhibiting themselves from experiencing and showing negative emotions such as anger and sadness while more frequently expressing instrumental emotions (Greenberg, 2002), which are emotions expressed for their effect on others. Particularly problematic is that the expression of positive emotions such as pride and contentment that counteract shame may be prohibited. Sometimes a client's inability to access immediate emotional experience in the presence of the therapist may be reflective of underlying shame anxiety that inhibits more spontaneous emotional reactions in interpersonal situations that would otherwise provide crucial experiential input to guide judgment and action. This disconnection from feelings, aimed at maintaining group harmony and a sense of belonging, unwittingly causes a sense of isolation and alienation because the person's own idiosyncratic experience is kept hidden behind the mask of instrumental emotions; thus, it is rarely known, validated, or understood by others. Exploration of the interruption and blocking of emotional experience can be a powerful intervention. It is also important to help clients become aware that emotional expression is being used to achieve an aim and to illuminate its function as well as its negative consequences.

CASE ILLUSTRATION

A male client in his 30s sought therapy for depression. He exhibited a number of shame-related issues. He had been diagnosed with attention-deficit/hyperactivity disorder as a child, was cruelly teased in school, and had developed a core sense of himself as a "loser." He learned to act like a clown by intentionally making "silly" mistakes and comments that were out of place and that invited others' laughter. His classmates were laughing at the mask that he created, catching his deliberate mistakes and failures but not his core shameful self. He was able to control and avoid the experience of deeper and more painful primary maladaptive shame by this deliberate instrumental shame; however, his sense of isolation grew as this maneuver became more refined and adept. His feeling of shame also grew deeper.

Facing his core sense of shame in therapy was excruciatingly painful for this client. Therapy then involved accessing strengths and anger at unfair treatment to help restructure his sense of himself. First, the therapist validated the client's need to hide and protect his vulnerable self and also emphasized his longing and his adaptive need to belong that lay beneath his acting like a clown. The therapist then empathically highlighted the underlying pain of the wounds to his self-esteem and the pain of being an outcast as a child. This evoked tears and activated the client's core shame-related emotion scheme. He disclosed how alone and lonely he had felt even when he was with other children. He lived with intense shame anxiety, always fearing he would be exposed as inadequate because he couldn't keep up with his classmates in academic work no matter how hard he tried. The therapist helped him acknowledge his core feelings of inferiority and his constant struggle with feelings of "falling behind" and "falling short" by responding, "All you wanted was to be like the other kids. You weren't asking for much: You didn't need to excel in anything. You just wanted to get along and be like everyone else instead of always being the one the other kids pointed a finger at." In an imaginal confrontation with the other children using an empty chair dialogue, he accessed and expressed his primary adaptive sadness and his need to feel emotionally connected, and he began to feel he deserved more. This led him to access primary adaptive anger, and he asserted, "I deserved to be treated as a worthwhile person and to be protected." The therapist supported and validated this stronger sense of self.

Therapeutic work also involved a series of self-soothing dialogues in which the client talked to his lonely and depressed child self, saying, "You're not bad at all. There is nothing wrong with you. I know it hurts. I know that it kills you when other kids laugh at you. You are a sweet kid. Everything will be all right. I am with you." The therapist had him repeat these phrases and pay attention to how he felt inside as he was saying and listening to these words. This work helped him look at himself with compassion. Two-chair dialogues were occasionally introduced to examine his self-critical processes that occurred in response to challenging situations in which he questioned his ability and his confidence and became shaky when the feeling of shame was evoked. Chair work that facilitated exploration and meaning creation, as well as the unfailing validating and empathic relationship with the therapist, helped him access a sense of worth and work through shame at multiple levels.

CONCLUSION

EFT recognizes both adaptive and maladaptive roles that shame may play in psychological well-being. Identification of different classes of shame allows for more differentiated intervention strategies specifically dealing with complex cognitive–affective processes involving the combination of self-critical processes, self-contempt, shame anxiety, and sense of worthlessness. EFT therapists can help clients achieve experiential mastery over this most painful emotion by helping them develop the capacity to regulate the intensity and distress of shame experience by self-soothing and self-compassion and helping them transform it by gaining access to more adaptive emotional experiences.

REFERENCES

Doi, T. (1973). *The anatomy of dependence*. Tokyo, Japan: Kodansha.

Elliott, R., Watson, J., Goldman, R. N., & Greenberg, L. S. (2004). *Learning emotion-focused therapy: The process-experiential approach to change*. Washington, DC: American Psychological Association Press. doi:10.1037/10725-000

Frijda, N. H. (1986). *The emotions*. Cambridge, England: Cambridge University Press.

Frijda, N. H. (2007). *The laws of emotion*. Mahwah, NJ: Erlbaum.

Gilbert, P. (1997). *Overcoming depression: A self-help guide using cognitive behavioural techniques*. London, England: Robinson.

Gilbert, P., & McGuire, M. T. (1998). Shame, status, and social roles: Psychobiology and evolution. In P. Gilbert & B. Andrews (Eds.), *Shame: Interpersonal behavior, psychopathology, and culture* (pp. 99–125). New York, NY: Oxford University Press.

Gilbert, P., & Procter, S. (2006). Compassionate mind training for people with high shame and self-criticism: Overview and pilot study of a group therapy approach. *Clinical Psychology & Psychotherapy, 13*, 353–379. doi:10.1002/cpp.507

Goldman, R., Greenberg, L., & Angus, L. (2006). The effects of adding emotion-focused interventions to the therapeutic relationship in the treatment of depression. *Psychotherapy Research, 16*, 537–549. doi:10.1080/10503300600589456

Greenberg, L. S. (2002). *Emotion-focused therapy: Coaching clients to work through their feelings*. Washington, DC: American Psychological Association. doi:10.1037/10447-000

Greenberg, L. S. (2007). A guide to conducting a task analysis of psychotherapeutic change. *Psychotherapy Research, 17*, 15–30. doi:10.1080/10503300600720390

Greenberg, L. S., & Angus, L. (2004). The contributions of emotion processes to narrative change in psychotherapy: A dialectical constructivist approach. In L. Angus & J. McLeod (Eds.), *Handbook of narrative psychotherapy* (pp. 331–349). Thousand Oaks, CA: Sage.

Greenberg, L. S., & Goldman, R. N. (2008). *Emotion-focused couples therapy: The dynamics of emotion, love, and power.* Washington, DC: American Psychological Association. doi:10.1037/11750-000

Greenberg, L. S., & Paivio, S. C. (1997). *Working with emotions in psychotherapy.* New York, NY: Guilford Press.

Greenberg, L. S., & Pascual-Leone, J. (2001). A dialectical constructivist view of the creation of personal meaning. *Journal of Constructivist Psychology, 14,* 165–186. doi:10.1080/10720530151143539

Greenberg, L. S., Rice, L. N., & Elliott, R. (1993). *Facilitating emotional change: The moment by moment process.* New York, NY: Guilford Press.

Greenberg, L., Warwar, S., & Malcolm, W. (2010). Emotion-focused couples therapy and the facilitation of forgiveness. *Journal of Marital and Family Therapy, 36,* 28–42.

Greenberg, L. S., & Watson, J. (1998). Experiential therapy of depression: Differential effects of client-centered relationship conditions and process experiential interventions. *Psychotherapy Research, 8,* 210–224. doi:10.1093/ptr/8.2.210

Greenberg, L. S., & Watson, J. (2006). *Emotion-focused therapy for depression.* Washington, DC: American Psychological Association. doi:10.1037/11286-000

Gross, J. J. (2002). Emotion regulation: Affective, cognitive, and social consequences. *Psychophysiology, 39,* 281–291. doi:10.1017/S0048577201393198

Horvath, A. O., & Bedi, R. P. (2005). The alliance. In J. C. Norcross (Ed.), *Psychotherapy relationships that work: Therapist contributions and responsiveness to patients* (pp. 37–70). New York, NY: Oxford University Press.

Johnson, S., Hunsley, J., Greenberg, L. S., & Schindler, D. (1999). Emotionally focused couples therapy: Status and challenges. *Clinical Psychology: Science and Practice, 6,* 69–79. doi:10.1093/clipsy/6.1.67

Keltner, D., & Harker, L. A. (1998). The forms and functions of the nonverbal signal of shame. In P. Gilbert & B. Andrews (Eds.), *Shame: Interpersonal behavior, psychopathology, and culture* (pp. 78–98). New York, NY: Oxford University Press.

Kohut, H. (1977). *The restoration of the self.* New York, NY: International Universities Press.

Lewis, H. B. (1971). *Shame and guilt in neurosis.* New York, NY: International Universities Press.

Linehan, M. M., Dimeff, L. A., Reynolds, S. K., Comtois, K. A., Shaw Welch, S., Heagerty, P., & Kivlahan, D. R. (2002). Dialectical behavior therapy versus comprehensive validation plus 12 step for the treatment of opioid dependent women meeting criteria for borderline personality disorder. *Drug and Alcohol Dependence, 67,* 13–26. doi:10.1016/S0376-8716(02)00011-X

Markus, H. R., & Kitayama, S. (1991). Culture and the self: Implications for cognition, emotion, and motivation. *Psychological Review, 98,* 224–253. doi:10.1037/0033-295X.98.2.224

Morita, S., & Kondo, A. (Trans.), & LeVine, P. (Ed.). (1998). *Morita therapy and the true nature of anxiety-based disorders* (shinkeishitsu). Albany, NY: State University of New York Press.

Nathanson, D. L. (1992). *Shame and pride: Affect, sex, and the birth of the self.* New York, NY: Norton.

Paivio, S. C. (2001). Stability of retrospective self-reports of abuse and neglect before and after therapy for child abuse issues. *Child Abuse and Neglect, 25,* 1053–1068.

Paivio, S. C., Hall, I. E., Holowaty, K. A. M., Jellis, J. B., & Tran, N. (2001). Imaginal confrontation for resolving child abuse issues. *Psychotherapy Research, 11,* 433–453. doi:10.1093/ptr/11.4.433

Rhodes, R. H., Hill, C. E., Thompson, B. J., & Elliott, R. (1994). Client retrospective recall of resolved and unresolved misunderstanding events. *Journal of Counseling Psychology, 41,* 473–483. doi:10.1037/0022-0167.41.4.473

Schore, A. N. (2003). *Affect dysregulation and disorders of the self.* New York, NY: Norton.

Tangney, J. P., & Dearing, R. L. (2002). *Shame and guilt.* New York, NY: Guilford Press.

Tomkins, S. S. (1987). Shame. In D. L. Nathanson (Ed.), *The many faces of shame* (pp. 133–161). New York, NY: Guilford Press.

Watson, J., & Greenberg, L. S. (1995). Alliance ruptures and repairs in experiential therapy. *In Session: Psychotherapy in Practice, 1,* 19–31.

Watson, J. C., Gordon, L. B., Stermac, L., Kalogerakos, F., & Steckley, P. (2003). Comparing the effectiveness of process-experiential with cognitive-behavioral psychotherapy in the treatment of depression. *Journal of Consulting and Clinical Psychology, 71,* 773–781. doi:10.1037/0022-006X.71.4.773

4

TREATING SHAME: A FUNCTIONAL ANALYTIC APPROACH

KELLY KOERNER, MAVIS TSAI, AND ELIZABETH SIMPSON

Shame evolved to sustain close connection to others; yet when gone awry, shame becomes the source of deepest alienation and pain. We the authors, as therapists and clinical supervisors, are motivated to find pragmatic ways to understand and help our clients and trainees work with shame. Functional analysis offers a conceptual platform to understand behavior in terms of its antecedents and consequences and ties directly to principle-based intervention. In our functional analytic approach to treating maladaptive shame, we first consider how emotion may have evolved as a rapid response system. Next, we provide a functional analysis of how shame may have evolved and how it is adaptive and maladaptive in particular contexts. Finally, we examine shame in psychotherapy and discuss how a functional analytic therapist can work with shame in terms of doing assessment, focusing on clinically relevant behaviors, creating conditions that evoke and reinforce improvement, observing his or her own impact, and exploring his or her personal shame.

EMOTION AS A RAPID RESPONSE SYSTEM

Like many emotion theorists and researchers (e.g., Fridja, 1986; Izard, 1991; Tomkins, 1963, 1984), we believe that emotion evolved as a rapid whole-body response: Our physiology, perception, actions, and cognitive processes coherently fire together to orient and organize adaptation to the continual changes in the environment and ourselves. During evolution, the challenges that our ancestors frequently encountered shaped neural circuits within the mammalian brain, wiring us for adaptive action to address triggering events (Panksepp, 1998). Consequently, various external stimuli have the capacity to arouse specific emotions.

When the environment changes, our emotions fire. A wail of pain from a child, and instantly you drop what you were doing and sprint down the stairs. At work, you listen attentively on a conference call until an e-mail notification pops into your field of vision. You open it to find that a coworker has unfairly criticized you to your supervisor (and copied everyone in your department). You are emotionally aroused, and the conference call instantly becomes irrelevant; you are consumed by the new situation. Emotions disrupt ongoing activity and rapidly reorganize us to respond to the changed situation.

When basic emotions (e.g., fear, anger, interest, shame) fire, the associated action urge may be clear. Complex blends of emotion, however, convey information more than they indicate a course of action (L. S. Greenberg, 2002). For example, imagine you received the e-mail just described. You might feel angry or ashamed at being criticized publicly, confused about the coworker's motives, sorry that your own decisions have left you vulnerable to such criticism, afraid that any response will make you look defensive, and sad and resentful that staying late to defend yourself will entail missing your child's soccer game. What, if any, course of action is motivated that fits or expresses the complexity of this situation? Successful navigation is not always straightforward.

Yet an optimal environment for emotional development does teach us how to navigate by using emotional experience, like echolocation, to notice what is happening within and outside our skin. Emotional experience provides a moment-to-moment readout of our own state and our needs with respect to the environment and goal attainment. The emotions that accompany a bad outcome prompt reflection on what went wrong. Even if it is too late to change the current situation, emotion can be used to make sense of events, and we may learn how to adjust behavior to avoid such problems in the future (Baumeister, Vohs, DeWall, & Zhang, 2007).

Emotional responding not only orients and mobilizes us, but it also communicates information to others. A colleague pokes his head into your office just after you read the critical e-mail and sees you are on the phone but also perceptively registers subtleties of your facial expression and body language—these prompt him to approach with a look of questioning and concern. You point to the screen. He reads the e-mail, rolls his eyes, shakes his head, and puts a kind hand on your shoulder, mouthing silently, "Find me when you finish your call." When we express emotion, we affect others and create conditions for others to affect us (L. S. Greenberg, 2002). If, when we display emotions in ways that fit the environmental cues and social situation, our caregivers provide contingent and appropriate soothing and respond positively, they strengthen and help us refine the naturally adaptive organizing and communicative functions of emotion (cf. M. T. Greenberg, Kusche, & Speltz, 1991).

A FUNCTIONAL ANALYSIS OF SHAME

Our functional analytic approach to shame, therefore, comes from a theory of how shame evolved in our species as well as an analysis of how individual learning history shapes the organizing and communicating functions of shame. Functional analysis identifies the controlling variables (i.e., the conditions that give rise to and maintain shame), problem behaviors, and improvements. From both the species and individual perspectives, shame occurs in particular contexts and "works," in the sense that it is maintained (reinforced) when it adapts us to survive in those contexts. In this view, shame can be said to be adaptive and maladaptive only relative to a particular context.

Because humans are a profoundly social species, one critical adaptive context or problem for the individual is to detect the danger of demotion or exclusion from beneficial social groups or dyadic relationships. Our access to vital resources depends on continued membership in specific groups and improves with higher rank. It is critical, therefore, that we can detect when our behavior is likely to elicit a demotion in status or exclusion from desirable relationships. We must inhibit the offending behavior, strive to correct it, or at least manage to keep it private. Indeed, a considerable amount of theory and research has shown that humans are strongly motivated to avoid social demotions and exclusions and that social exclusion is associated with aversive emotional reactions (cf. Allen & Knight, 2005).

In the work of Paul Gilbert (2004; Gilbert & Irons, 2005; Gilbert & Procter, 2006), shame is proposed to be the aversive emotional response to loss of rank and rejection by others. When we experience shame, we yield to the power, control, or demands of the other, inhibiting behavior that is unacceptable to them. We cast our eyes downward, our skin blushes or pales, we freeze. The felt sense of shame is one of vulnerability, of being looked at by others in a threatening manner. We typically feel contracted and small. Our action urge is to disappear, hide, or avoid notice. The fear of rejection and attendant shame motivate us to avoid behaviors that elicit shame by monitoring social comparisons, by striving to be valued by others, and by seeking status.

In its natural and most functional form, shame is cued by minor fluctuations in our readings of social success to motivate adjustments of our behavior for a smoother fit. Continuing our earlier example, imagine you find your colleague after the call ends, and in describing your reaction to the e-mail, you curse the coworker who sent it. As you notice your colleague's slight frown and withdrawal, you feel a twinge of shame and correct yourself by describing the situation in a less heated manner. By signaling untoward exposure, shame provides a means by which behavioral repertoires of individuals can be shaped to ensure acceptance by the group and to fit local custom, values, and rules (Gilbert, 2004).

As a species, then, we come wired with the capacity to be sensitive in general to contexts in which social rejection may occur and to use shame to reorganize us to reduce the threat of rejection. As individuals, we learn to experience or express shame in particular contexts because of the way others in our reference group respond. The consequences provided by important others shape the adaptive and maladaptive experience and expression of shame. For example, a parent walks into the bedroom to find her 6-year-old son destroying his 2-year-old sister's toy in retaliation for some offense. The parent's demeanor and comments set off shame. The son's display of shame softens the parent, and together they find ways for the son to make things right through apology, replacing the toy, and so on. This strengthens the whole sequence; the experience and expression of shame facilitate the boy's adaptation. Let's say, instead, that the parent does not walk in but later finds the demolished toy, inexpertly hidden. The parent berates the son, and when he shows shame, she continues on and on, citing other examples of the son's failures, and then gives him the silent treatment the entire next day. In that sequence, very different responses are learned, or arousal may be too high to allow much learning at all. Here the child's initial experience and expression of shame did nothing to reduce the parent's rejecting response. In such a context, he is likely to try many responses to reduce the threat (e.g., pleading, denying, being overly compliant, blaming others, withdrawing, joking).

Many different idiosyncratic learning histories are possible for this boy: He hides the toy and is never found out; he clowns around and the parent, charmed, softens and backs down, requiring no repair to the sister; he is flooded with shame and is unable to repair the rejection; and so on. Although the specifics may vary, we are hardwired to respond to rejection or demotion with shame. When what we express, say, or do evokes a rejecting response from another, shame fires. Shame reorganizes us to reduce the threat of rejection. If what we do reduces the threat, shame has been adaptive in that moment. From such an interaction, we learn that this context holds a threat of rejection and that certain actions reduce the risk. The next time we are in a similar context, actions that reduce the risk become stronger or more likely and our old responses weaker or less likely.

Simultaneously, we learn through classical conditioning. Just as getting sick after eating spoiled fish often results in feeling nausea at the next sight or even thought of fish, the same happens with shame. These painful responses result in shame even when thinking about the shameful behavior or having the shameful thought. Through the pairing of classical conditioning, the next time we are in similar contexts, then, the meaning has changed, and we more rapidly perceive cues of threat. Shame colors our experience in that context. Our own natural responses evoke a sense of embarrassment or shame even without an audience, even if there is nothing intrinsically unacceptable about our responses, and even if there are other contexts in which such responses would be acceptable. We become more likely to do what is required to reduce the threat of rejection.

To a great degree, without awareness, we all continuously analyze and respond to these implicit social signals. When cues indicate a risk of demotion or exclusion, a variety of responses may be evoked to escape the threat of rejection such that we act automatically in ways that have worked in the past to reduce the threat. For example, we may stop talking about the offensive subject, we may withdraw, we may strive harder to be pleasing, we may let go of a goal that seems unacceptable, or we may blow up at the person criticizing us. Through such events, our experiences and expressions of shame either facilitate or fail to facilitate adaptation to the changed environment or create or fail to create circumstances for others to affect us.

What becomes problematic is when these patterns of response become fixed and inflexible, tightly under control of the antecedents in the context, and thereby relatively insensitive to the consequences (Wilson & DuFrene, 2008). Such response patterns block new learning. It is as if we were a rat in a two-chamber cage: Each time we go to the left, the electrified grid comes on and we get shocked. In no time, we learn not to go to the left: We never go to the left, and we never get shocked. If the grid, however, becomes safe, we never notice—we are busy avoiding contact with the grid, which prevents learning about the change. Avoiding works 100% of the time, but it simultaneously blocks learning that conditions have changed. In this way, escape conditioning is pernicious and dangerous. Once we learn that rejection is contingent upon our behaviors, we typically avoid doing them again—we don't go to the left—even if there is nothing intrinsically unacceptable about our responses and even if there are other contexts in which such responses would be acceptable. If these behaviors are pertinent to getting our needs met, feeling loved, taking risks to achieve goals, or living our values, then this rigid, inflexible escape pattern destroys quality of life.

For example, a client was raised by a mother who seldom expressed interest in him. He remembers shyly attempting to share what mattered to him, only to have his mother, oblivious, change the topic. Although the boy was a talented athlete and student, his mother never went to his sports games, never asked about his grades. But she took an interest in his early talent with the piano. He remembers that when he was 7 years old she asked him to play piano before her girlfriends. He lost himself in the music, finished the piece, and then heard his mother stage whisper, "So . . . *passionate*." Her mocking tone and disinterest continued to pervasively influence him. Expecting that others wouldn't be interested or that hard work or passion would be mocked affected everything from work memos to personal relationships. He found it difficult to make eye contact when he spoke about himself. Despite being an exemplary employee, his boss had no sense of his true interests and accomplishments, and he was repeatedly bypassed for promotion. He was known as a great listener, but in fact this ability functioned mostly as skillful avoidance; by habitually focusing the conversation on the other, he avoided having to talk about himself. Avoiding any behavior that might provoke others' shaming responses left the client deeply lonely—no one knew him.

This core problem of escape conditioning is made yet worse because multiple, idiosyncratic cues may come to evoke this fixed, inflexible escape pattern. The escape pattern can be highly automatic, restricting the development of more adaptive responses to the cue that might elicit different consequences. We lack the ability to assess cues accurately (Am I actually being threatened?). These processes train us to be negatively aroused and hypervigilant in social contexts, interfering with noticing and being influenced by other aspects that might be reinforcing. For example, the client above was extremely sensitive to the therapist's quality of attention—when she shifted positions in her chair while he spoke, he subtly changed the topic, assuming he had lost her interest. The client was so attuned to threat that he failed to register that she continued to ask questions that indicated genuine interest and that, in fact, shifting positions was in the service of being able to pay better attention. When we have such histories, we might avoid situations in which evaluation is highly likely (e.g., ones in which there is competition for prizes, promotions, or acceptance). Proneness to such maladaptive experiences and expressions of shame increase vulnerability to various disorders, including depression and social phobia (Gilbert, 2004).

SHAME IN PSYCHOTHERAPY

In psychotherapy, either client or therapist may feel shame. Although evolution has hardwired shame to be adaptive, life experiences may or may not have shaped adaptive experiences and expressions of shame, and what may have been adaptive initially may be maladaptive in a different context. When the client experiences or expresses shame in ways that are maladaptive, the functional analytic therapist first assesses what triggers and maintains the problematic responses. Then the therapist creates conditions that help the client respond more adaptively. Depending on the circumstance, "responding more adaptively" may mean experiencing and expressing shame with better emotion regulation or learning to respond to the context without shame. It could mean responding with more skill and flexibility in contexts that evoke problematic shame even while feeling intense shame. When therapists' shame is problematic, the same change processes can be applied (therapist shame is discussed in the final section of this chapter).

HOW A FUNCTIONAL ANALYTIC THERAPIST WORKS

We turn now to describing a functional analytic approach to assessment and intervention with problematic shame. Our work grows from the general tradition of clinical behavior analysis (Dougher, 2000), alternatively called *functional contextualism* (Biglan & Hayes, 1996) or *radical behaviorism* (Leigland, 1992). Here we draw extensively on the principles articulated in one particular approach from this tradition, functional analytic psychotherapy (Kohlenberg & Tsai, 1991, 1994; Tsai et al., 2008). Functional analytic psychotherapy is an integrative therapy that provides a unifying theory within which we use many different methods of therapy. Other models either have grown from this same tradition (acceptance and commitment therapy, Hayes, Strosahl, & Wilson, 2003) or can be used in ways that are compatible with functional contextualism (dialectical behavior therapy, Linehan, 1993; mindfulness-based cognitive therapy, Segal, Williams, & Teasdale, 2002). Our particular interest in this chapter, however, is to show how we work with instances of problematic shame that occur in session that mirror the problems experienced in daily life.

Doing Assessment

As you listen to your client, you may note changes in voice, posture, or facial expression that show or hint of a problematic experience or expression of shame; you may note inflexible responding that seems to function to reduce the risk of rejection. At times, clients' problems with shame are glaring. For example, after a client raged at a roommate on their apartment's front lawn, she felt intense shame and reported repeatedly cutting her arms to escape the feeling and get relief.

At times, however, shame responses may be subtle. For example, you ask a question to clarify how a therapy homework assignment went. As your client answers, his voice gets tight, and he breaks eye contact for an instant. Then he makes a self-deprecating comment that expands into a hilarious monologue. He responds similarly at work and with his wife, creating the sense that he never takes others seriously. When you ask what he felt as you asked about the homework before his self-deprecating comment, he said he felt embarrassed—he was surprised it was difficult and expected you to think he was "stupid" for having a difficult time completing it.

You ask a different client the same question about homework. You see an infinitesimal flash of irritation before she apologizes to you for failing to complete the entire assignment but then details how she worked diligently with the ideas in the homework. In her daily life, she feels dissatisfied in her relationships but unsure what to do to change them. When you ask her what it felt like as you asked about the homework, she says, "fine." You say you thought she felt a flash of irritation. She freezes and stammers. With gentle, persistent questioning, she admits that the assignment was inconvenient to do. As you talk, she realizes she feels ashamed to feel and especially to express irritation or to come across as ungrateful. She habitually fails to notice the feeling of irritation that signals she or others are crossing her limits, the cues that would tell her she is overextended. Consequently, others seldom get accurate feedback about how their behavior inconveniences or irritates her.

These examples illustrate how when a functional analytic therapist notices problematic behavior, it prompts him or her to assess controlling variables, the conditions that give rise to and maintain the response. What sets this off? How does the experience or expression of shame help the client adapt? How is the shame no longer adaptive in this client's life?

Sometimes the private experience of shame is painfully intense, but shame-related problems can be nearly invisible to others, including the therapist. Some of us learn to mask the expression of shame completely even though the internal experience is excruciating. In our clinical experience, this is particularly true of people who have survived trauma, neglect, and abuse as children. These individuals may develop competence and outward accomplishment yet privately struggle with chronic suicidality. The discrepancy between the person's internal experiences versus what the therapist sees is vast. For example, a well-loved, successful, articulate man, seemingly fully engaged in therapy, says in a matter-of-fact voice that simply sitting in your office evokes the feeling that he does not deserve to "take up space." He can barely stand to exist. L. S. Greenberg's (e.g., Elliott, Watson, Goldman, & Greenberg, 2003; see also Chapter 3, this volume) description of *primary maladaptive shame* fits this client's experience of a pervasive sense of himself as worthless, inferior, and unlovable, of "shame that sticks" (L. S. Greenberg, 2002). See also Linehan (1993), who referred to this discrepancy between internal experience and the observer's perspective as *apparent competence*.

Whether obvious or subtle, we view these in-session maladaptive shame responses as instances of problematic clinically relevant behavior, behaviors that occur in the therapy relationship that are similar to problematic behaviors in daily life outside therapy (Kohlenberg & Tsai, 1991). When a functional analytic therapist notices problematic behavior, it prompts him or her to ask, What evokes this behavior? What function has this behavior served for the client in previous contexts? How does this behavior work for the client? How does this behavior interfere with the client's current life?

As we have argued, applying Gilbert's (2004) analysis of shame, we view it as essential for therapists to be particularly sensitive to how the therapist or the psychotherapy context presents risks of rejection or demotion and to be particularly aware that the client may act to reduce these risks in ways that are problematic. Because it is often difficult to see shame responses, it can help to be familiar with theories of common sets of cues or behaviors about which people learn to feel shame. For example, Kaufman (1989) described four common themes that help the therapist anticipate where problematic shame responses may occur in therapy that relate to clients' daily lives:

1. *Shame related to purpose:* When ridiculed during childhood for imaginative play or for daydreams or fantasies related to what we want to be when we grow up, we may find it difficult or impossible to talk about desires, dreams, fantasies, or our sense of purpose.

2. *Shame related to affect:* Many of us have been shamed for having certain types of feelings. For example, our culture typically shames distress affect and fear affect in men and boys and anger and power affect in women and girls. Many clients have been shamed or otherwise punished for expressing enjoyment, excitement, or pride. Others have been shamed for the intensity with which they experience or express emotion. Clinically relevant problem behaviors may include difficulty identifying feelings, intentional hiding of feelings, negative self-talk when feeling emotions, flat or distant emotional expression, difficulty feeling or expressing certain emotions (positive or negative), difficulty receiving positive feedback, difficulty receiving negative feedback, or difficulty tolerating conflict or disagreement.

3. *Shame related to sexual drives and hunger drives:* Some of us have felt shame for having sexual feelings (e.g., punished for masturbating or for playing doctor) or because unwanted attention was focused on our bodies (e.g., in normal adolescent development, for being overweight), both of which contribute to body image shame. Problematic clinically relevant behaviors may include

avoiding telling the therapist about sexual experiences and feelings or avoiding talking about body image and food issues.

4. *Shame related to interpersonal needs:* If our caregivers had a difficult time meeting our relational needs, we tend to feel shame around having these needs. Clinically relevant problem behaviors may include difficulty identifying or expressing needs or type of help wanted from one's therapist, fear of closeness or attachment, difficulty expressing closeness and caring, difficulty receiving closeness and caring, or reluctance to let one's true self be seen or heard.

The functional analytic therapist may use any theory or research that helps to recognize or anticipate shame-related problems. To identify what is relevant to a specific client's experience or expression of problematic shame, however, the therapist must analyze how shame functions for that person (i.e., the therapist should consider questions such as, "What evokes it? How does this function or work?" or "What purposes does the behavior serve? How is it currently adaptive or maladaptive?").

As we look for controlling variables in a functional analysis, we work from assumption of the behavior analytic tradition (e.g., Hayes & Brownstein, 1986; Skinner, 1953). For example, in everyday language one might say, "She cut herself *because* she was so ashamed" or "She felt so ashamed *because* she has deep beliefs about being worthless." In everyday language, this may feel like explanation enough. From our perspective, however, we prefer explanations that do not explain one behavior (cutting) with another behavior (feeling shame) or one behavior (feeling shame) as causing another behavior (thinking, "I'm worthless"). At times when she has felt more ashamed, she has not cut herself; sometimes she experiences thoughts as just thoughts that do not elicit much emotion. Everyday ways of explaining behavior leave out what is most relevant—why did feeling shame and cutting go together this time? Why is having the thought "I'm worthless" sometimes evocative and other times not? Thinking, feeling, and overt behaviors sometimes co-occur, but not always. To us, it is most useful to ask, Under what conditions do wanting, thinking, remembering, acting, feeling, and so on go together? In other words, we prefer explanations that describe how the context affects probabilities of various behavior–behavior relationships in terms of reinforcement contingencies. We use the term *reinforcement* in its technical, generic sense, referring to all consequences or contingencies that strengthen behavior (i.e., influence its future probability). The definition of reinforcement is a functional one; that is, something can be defined as a reinforcer (or punisher) only after it has shown an effect in increasing (or decreasing) the strength of a behavior.

Focusing on Clinically Relevant Behaviors

A functional analysis, then, typically begins by selecting a particular instance of a problem behavior and then analyzing the context that sets off and maintains the problem behavior (i.e., if–then contingencies between the response and its antecedents and consequences). The client and therapist work together to identify the sequence of events—including both private experiences and environmental events—that led to and followed the target behavior. For example, Lori came from a family of origin in which even the smallest mistake was scorned, teaching her to strive for perfection and to be constantly vigilant for criticism. As she began a session, she reported she felt "really bad." She and her therapist looked closely at her feelings to understand the controlling variables. At her new job, Lori made a small mistake, felt ashamed, and then automatically hid it from her supervisor rather than ask for help. Covering up the mistake provided a momentary reduction in shame. She worried all night, making plans to escape: "I'll quit and get a different job; I'll move away; I'll go back to school." Worrying functioned as cognitive distraction (Borkovec, Alcaine, & Behar, 2004), and it, too, provided relief from shame, at least while she engaged in worrying. Lori slept terribly. Exhausted the next day, she called in sick from work, exaggerating the hoarseness of her voice. This lie violated her values. As she fitfully lay in bed, she felt shame and remembered mood-congruent failures—past times she was fired or kicked out of school and relationships in which she was rejected. All afternoon and into the night, she drank, alone in her apartment. Eventually, she took several of her roommate's sleeping pills and passed out.

Many behaviors in this example served the same function: They worked (i.e., were maintained) because they reduced the experience of shame. Said differently, the reduction in the aversive state of shame reinforced hiding mistakes, worrying, drinking, and the potentially lethal overuse of medication. Much of Lori's life was organized to avoid or reduce shame; she habitually and automatically inhibited or quickly hid much of what she felt and needed in order to avoid rejection. She experienced intense shame but learned to mask its expression. Her shame-related behavior was largely maladaptive, particularly because her avoidance behaviors prevented her from learning more adaptive responses (e.g., sharing a mistake on a new job and finding her supervisor helpful and understanding).

Creating Conditions That Evoke and Reinforce Improvement

A functional analytic therapist intervenes by creating conditions that evoke and reinforce improvements. The therapist might do this in one of three general ways: by (a) helping the client remedy skills deficits by teaching or strengthening new adaptive responses, (b) helping the client change antecedents to shame-related problems or change how the client relates to the antecedents, or (c) helping the client change the consequences to decrease clinically relevant behaviors or strengthen clinically relevant improvements.

The first general strategy is used when shame-related problems arise in part because the client lacks needed skills. For example, Lori lacked the ability to differentiate emotion—sadness, fear, and shame were literally indistinguishable to her; she described all three emotions as "feeling bad." The therapist might remedy this skills deficit through psychoeducation about emotion and mindfulness practice to teach Lori to discriminate the physical sensations, action urges, and predictable patterns and processes of responding that go with the different emotion labels. Lori also lacked the ability to tolerate and soothe her experiences of shame. Through mindfulness practice, Lori became able to watch the unfolding responses in her mind and body and to experience the strands of sensation arising and passing away rather than experiencing a solid block of pain that must be escaped. Broad deficits in soothing and self-compassion might be best addressed using Gilbert and Procter's (2006) compassionate mind training (see also Chapter 14, this volume). Lori also lacked basic interpersonal skills of discussing mistakes and asking for help. Specific interpersonal skills training and practice were needed before others could have an opportunity to respond appropriately to her. When skills deficits are part of the client's shame-related problems, the therapist teaches and strengthens needed skills so that the client has more adaptive responses in his or her repertoire.

Second, when problematic responses seem primarily under the control of antecedent stimuli, then the functional analytic therapist works to change the antecedents or the client's relationship to the antecedents. Here the therapist may be guided by principles of exposure. Rizvi and colleagues (Chapter 10, this volume) describe in detail how formal exposure procedures can be applied to shame.

Principles of exposure can also be used informally to change antecedents. For example, Marvin was a polysubstance user who was reticent about reporting urges to use, making it hard to help him avoid slips. In session, this took the form of a failure to complete self-monitoring assignments and frequent, blank-faced answers of "I don't know." Upon analysis, shame appeared related to the difficulty reporting urges. As the therapist probed what it was like for Marvin to discuss urges, he said he felt ashamed that he could not control his use (like nonaddicted people) and shame that he still had urges ("Shouldn't I be over that by now?"). He felt shame that he had a vulnerability to addiction (i.e., that he wasn't "normal"). He felt shame at the things that he had done while under the influence (some of which were pretty awful). He felt shame at how much he enjoyed drugs ("I know they are bad."). He felt shame that he couldn't stop using.

When the therapist asked how intensely Marvin felt shame, as they talked, on a scale from 0 to 100, he reported an 85. This prompted the therapist to use informal exposure. Rather than go with the action urge of shame (in this case, to hide or avoid), he asked if Marvin would be willing to go against the action urge and, in fact, do its opposite. The therapist asked him to adopt a calm, upright posture and to use a matter-of-fact voice as he repeated, over and over, "I have a vulnerability to addiction, and when I use, I do things that I am not proud of." When his shame came down to 40 (i.e., the point at which he could again flexibly perceive and be influenced by more than shame and shame cues), they continued the conversation. Marvin decided that it was his intoxicated behavior that he was (not unreasonably) ashamed of, that the avoidance of intoxication seemed to be necessary for avoidance of intoxicated behaviors, and that the avoidance of intoxication required monitoring his urges so that he could act opposite to them. In this instance, treating shame via informal exposure allowed greater collaboration on Marvin's most important goal in therapy.

More generally, the therapist might change the relationship to antecedent triggers of shame using any number of interventions that help the client experience thoughts, feelings, and sensations as ongoing behavioral processes to shape the discrimination of "having a thought" or "having a feeling" in the presence of the cue. So, for example, rather than helping Lori counter the literal truth of the thought "I am worthless" through cognitive restructuring, mindfulness practices might be used to help her directly experience the thought as just a thought (Teasdale et al., 2002). Just as conditions arise that cause us to smell, see, hear, taste, or touch, so too conditions arise that cause the sensations we call "thinking." We can notice and label the direct experience ("I am having the thought that I am worthless") just as we can notice and label the direct experience of smelling a flower. Through the deliberate practice of observing, Lori noticed that certain cues simply set off self-criticism and shame, just as leaning toward a rose caused her to smell a rose scent—the cue became predictable, even boring, so that she changed her relationship to the antecedent triggers. This approach is emphasized in treatments that integrate mindfulness (e.g., dialectical behavior therapy, mindfulness-based cognitive therapy). Of course, straightforward changes in the environment to reduce the occurrence of cues may also help. For instance, Lori had an older female friend who was extremely critical and unforgiving, and when direct requests to reduce criticism had no effect, Lori ended that destructive, shaming relationship.

Finally, a third general approach is to change the consequences that maintain problematic behavior or prevent clinically relevant improvement. So, for example, Lori and her therapist designed a series of behavioral activation activities (Jacobson, Martell, & Dimidjian, 2001) in which she deliberately practiced making mistakes and talking about mistakes and imperfections with kind people who were likely to reinforce vulnerability and offer help or reassurance. Lori decided to take these weekly risks after she made a mistake in therapy. The therapist had recently raised her fee, and Lori mistakenly wrote the check for the old amount. When the therapist commented that the amount was wrong, Lori caught herself, blocked her old overly apologetic behavior in midsentence, and instead shifted her body from a shameful posture to say in a nonchalant tone, "Oh, I made a mistake. Here, let me fix that." Then, unprompted, she asked for reassurance: "Of course, I worry that you'll think it's a Freudian slip and I'm against paying your new fee. Do you think that?" When the therapist noted this improvement, it led to a moving, tender discussion of Lori's wish to be a "good auntie" to her niece and the powerful motivation to change that arose after seeing her niece mimic her overly apologetic, shame-based responses with a playmate. This discussion was consistent with acceptance and commitment therapy and with functional analytic psychotherapy's strong emphasis on explicit work related to values clarification as a method of strengthening motivation.

Consider another example of the importance of changing the consequences of client behavior to block problematic behavior and to reinforce clinical improvement. Maya was a client who sought therapy for depression and a sense of worthlessness and feeling "shut down." During a session, the therapist saw Maya "shutting down" as she felt ashamed of needing therapy. The therapist questioned Maya, who confirmed that this feeling was similar to what happened in her daily life. The therapist then oriented her like this:

> The most effective way for you to become less shut down and to develop into a more expressive person is to start right here, right now, with me, to tell me what you are thinking, feeling, and needing, even if it feels scary or risky. If you can bring forth your best self with me, then you can transfer these behaviors to other people in your life. Therapy has a greater impact when you talk about your experience of shame in the present moment. When we look at something that is happening right now, we can experience and understand it more fully, and therapeutic change is stronger and more immediate.

Because the structure and process of therapy often naturally evoke problems with shame, the therapist must pay close attention to managing contingencies occurring in therapy to ensure they strengthen improvements. In a later session, Maya experienced a wave of intense shame as she spoke about a disappointing interaction with a friend. In her daily life, if she expressed an interpersonal need that the other person did not meet, then she felt intense shame and withdrew, berating herself for being "needy." At moments like these in her daily life, Maya closed in on herself, losing contact with the broader context of care and affection others feel for her, feeling increasingly alone and full of self-loathing. When this seemed to happen in session, the therapist noted that Maya looked disgusted with herself, and Maya confirmed she was feeling "shut down" and "embarrassed at being so needy." On the basis of their prior discussions of this pattern, the therapist viewed this as an opportunity to block problematic behavior and pull for clinically relevant improvement:

Therapist: Let's focus right on this moment. Basically, in any moment, you can choose to open into a feeling of worthiness and caring that others feel toward you, or you can shut down and dislike yourself. Are you open to my caring for you right now?

Maya: I want to be.

Therapist: Be tuned in to how you feel with me right now. What are you picking up from me?

Maya: There's like a fight going on in my head. There's a warmth coming from you, but there's an underlying fear of accepting it. If I open up to your caring, I have to feel all of this pain over here with it, the loss of when I didn't receive caring from others. If I open up, I'll feel this huge tidal wave of pain.

Therapist: So you have this feeling that if you let in my caring, you're going to get a tidal wave of pain. Can you sit with that contradiction, can you just be loving with yourself around it? 'Cause what I'm feeling isn't that you have to accept my caring. What I'm feeling is simply caring; it's like caring for the contradiction that you are feeling for this intense dilemma you're in and being with you. Can you be with yourself around it? . . . that it's quite a dilemma, really, really anguishing.

Maya: And admitting not only my pain, but also my sisters' and brothers' in their 30s and 40s, and seeing the pain on my brothers' and sisters' faces, and seeing the pain in their lives.

Therapist: There's way, way too much. All I'm asking is for you to breathe and be with me in this moment.

Maya: There's one thing that's helped the last couple of days.

Therapist: Maya, Maya. [blocking her clinically relevant problem behavior of avoidance]

Maya: OK.

Therapist: You don't want to do this, do you? You want to talk, and you want to be with the last few days and be with your brothers and sisters. You don't want to breathe and be with me in this moment? [said in a gentle tone of voice]

Maya: Yeah, it's tough to be in this moment.

Therapist: Just feel your breath.

Maya:	[cries]
Therapist:	It's OK. You can make sounds; you don't have to be quiet.
Maya:	[cries for a couple of minutes] There's so much pain; I'm scared of opening the door too far.
Therapist:	Is it OK to open it a little just by feeling your breath? What was it like to open the door a tiny bit?
Maya:	It was OK.
Therapist:	So there's the pain, then there's also the exhilaration and the freedom to let yourself feel whatever is there. I feel really blessed that you allow yourself to be fully yourself, in your vulnerability, and in your trust of me. [attempting to reinforce her clinically relevant improvement]
Maya:	Well, this has been one of the few really safe places in my life.

In a final client example, we highlight the difficulty therapists may have when their clients are highly dysregulated by shame. In this case, the therapist asked Billie a routine follow-up question to learn more about something that had happened that week. As the therapist reflected what she'd heard to check her understanding, Billie began to feel anxious, breathing rapidly and soon sobbing uncontrollably. The therapist's questions to try to understand what had provoked the sobbing further exacerbated her response, and she became argumentative and verbally attacking. Only over several sessions could the therapist and client identify what had happened. For Billie, the therapist's neutral expression and matter-of-fact tone were experienced as interpersonal rejection. The therapist failed to read that Billie felt extremely vulnerable and ashamed to be asked about the topic. Being misread, along with a lack of warmth from the therapist, prompted a frantic and overwhelming sense of abandonment: Billie felt desperate for help, and nothing she could do seemed to reduce the threat of rejection she perceived.

For this therapist–client dyad, the therapist's usual style evoked shame-related problems of such intensity that no further work was possible. The therapist needed to increase her expression of warmth and direct validation in order to communicate explicitly that there was no threat of rejection or demotion. At times, Billie's shame and panic were so heightened that it was as if nothing the therapist said could penetrate the client's perception. For this reason, therapist and client both audiotaped subsequent therapy sessions so each could make sense of and give the other feedback about a process that was as fast as lightning in session. It would have been quite easy to dismiss and pathologize the client rather than see the mutuality of the interaction and take needed steps to remedy this major shame-related problem in the therapy.

The adoption of particular techniques depends on the therapist's judgment of what will evoke client issues and what will be naturally reinforcing of client target behaviors. Any activities that help clients contact and express to the therapist avoided thoughts and feelings may be used (e.g., free association, writing exercises, empty chair work, evoking emotion by focusing on bodily sensations, evoking a client's best self). The choice of using evocative strategies depends on how well regulated the client is in general. As therapists, we are more willing to be evocative when clients are well regulated.

Observing One's Own Impact

Therapists should observe the potentially reinforcing effects of their own behavior in relation to client in-session problems and improvements—in other words, one must be aware of one's own impact. From a functional analytic perspective, regular monitoring of one's effect on the client is essential: "An intervention (a 'process') can have various outcomes ranging from its immediate impact within the session (a 'process-outcome'), to its longer-term impact after the session (a 'little o'), to its even longer-term impact after termination (a 'Big O')" (L. S. Greenberg & Pinsof, 1986, pp. 7–8). The only way to know that a response that was intended to be reinforcing actually was reinforcing is by observing a change in the frequency or intensity of the target behavior (process outcome, or little o). Explicit process questions, however, can serve to give clues about the reinforcing effects of the therapist's responses. These questions can be straightforward and often occur after interactions in which the therapist attempted to strengthen improvement. For example, the therapist may simply ask, "How was that for you?" or "When I responded to you in that way, how did you feel?" or "Do you think my response made it more likely for you to do what you did again, or less likely?" Postsession questionnaires that ask about the client's experience of the session may also be particularly useful for shame-related problems; see Exhibit 4.1 for an example of a postsession questionnaire.

In sum, from a functional analytic perspective, the therapy relationship is a microcosm of a client's daily life relationships, and it provides an opportunity to explore the context of shame feelings—what precipitates them, what maintains the shame, how to tolerate and experience it, and how to build in positive behaviors that can be translated into relationships with others. Consequently, the therapist and client identify ways clients' outside life problems emerge within the therapy relationship, because such an in vivo focus facilitates the most powerful change.

EXHIBIT 4.1
Functional Analytic Psychotherapy Session Bridging Questions

Name: Date:

Part A (to be completed shortly after therapy session):
1. What stands out to you about our last session? Thoughts, feelings, insights?

2. On a 10-point scale, how would you rate the four items below?

Not at all		A little bit		Moderate		Substantial		Very Substantial	
1	2	3	4	5	6	7	8	9	10

    a. How helpful or effective the session was: _____
       What was helpful?
       What was not helpful?
    b. How connected you felt to your therapist: _____
    c. How engaged or involved you felt with the topics being discussed: _____
    d. How present you were in the session: _____

3. What would have made the session more helpful or a better experience? Is there anything you are reluctant to say or ask for?

4. What issues came up for you in the session or with your therapist that are similar to your daily life problems?

5. What risks did you take in the session or with your therapist, or what progress did you make that can translate into your outside life?

Part B (to be completed just prior to next therapy session):
6. What were the high and low points of your week?

7. What items, issues, challenges, or positive changes do you want to put on the agenda for our next session?

8. How open were you in answering Questions 1 through 7 above (0% to 100%)?

9. Anything else you'd like to add?

Note. From *A Guide to Functional Analytic Psychotherapy* (p. 215), by M. Tsai, R. Kohlenberg, J. Kanter, B. Kohlenberg, W. Follette, and G. Callaghan, 2009, New York, NY: Springer Science+Business Media. Copyright 2009 Springer Science+Business Media. All rights reserved. Reprinted with permission.

Exploring Therapist Shame

All of the above applies to us as therapists. We have intentionally used "we" throughout this chapter to emphasize that therapists share the common human nature of shame and that we may be in the client role ourselves. We also experience and express shame in the context of our work as therapists in ways that can be problematic for ourselves and for our clients. As for our clients, what we feel shame about is idiosyncratic depending on our histories and our training. Examples include when client shame experiences evoke similar shame issues within ourselves (e.g., addictive behaviors, body issues, shame about affect or interpersonal needs), when we make mistakes, when we avoid dealing with problematic client behaviors like chronic lateness or not paying therapy bills, when we don't observe our limits (e.g., answering client phone calls after bedtime), when we worry about being labeled unprofessional by other therapists, or when we feel unsure how to best treat our clients. We use all of the above general strategies to treat our own problematic shame. Seeking consultation from a trusted colleague when one's own shame issues interfere with treatment is both courageous and ethical.

The same sensitivity extended to clients is needed as we consult with each other. For example, in a consultation team meeting, a therapist shared an incident about a new client, recently transferred to her care. Before the transfer, the client had been working with a therapist with whom the client experienced unprecedented levels of disclosure and closeness. When that therapist had to leave the agency abruptly, the client was devastated. In session, the client expressed this devastation and her intense fear that her new therapist would also abandon her. After the session, the client called the new therapist to ask for support. The therapist viewed this as progress. In team, the therapist summarized the key moment of the next session:

> My client announced that she is "better" now, and that all that "weepy bullshit" is over. I said that I was glad that she felt less distressed, but that I had on some level enjoyed the greater intimacy afforded by her vulnerability. I said, in a gentle tone with some warmth, that, in fact, I felt privileged that she had trusted me enough to share it with me. Then she drew herself upright and snapped, "But I am 59 years old. Surely I should be over all that sort of foolishness by now!"

A colleague on the consultation team then commented that it was obvious that the client had a history of abuse (absolutely correct) and that the client experienced the therapist's warmth as an intrusion, that she probably feared that the therapist might try to hurt her. The treating therapist felt a wave of shame that she might have been harmful when she meant to be kind. The therapist also had viewed it as progress for herself to be more expressive of warmth in her therapeutic work. Rather than going with the action urge to withdraw or be defensive in the consultation meeting, she instead further articulated her interpretation that in this case the client's rejection of warm validation of her need for the therapist was problematic and similar to the shame reactions that interfered with closeness with others in her daily life. She further clarified the worry that her colleague had about the interaction. Then, in her next session, when the moment was right, the therapist asked process questions about the client's responses to the earlier interaction. She learned that, in fact, she had read her client correctly—the client felt embarrassed to be seen as needy in this new relationship, but the therapist's response had soothed and reassured her that her disclosures would not result in rejection.

There are times when disclosing to clients one's own thoughts, reactions, and personal experiences regarding shame is helpful to the therapeutic process. A major factor to take into account in making a decision to disclose is whether such disclosure will facilitate clients having greater contact with their shame issues or whether it will take them away from their own focus. Other considerations include whether the disclosure will engender more closeness from the client and whether the disclosure is a problem behavior for the therapist (e.g., when the therapist discloses to meet his or her own needs rather than the client's). Strategic disclosures can enhance the therapeutic relationship, normalize clients' experiences, model adaptive and intimacy-building behavior (Goldfried, Burckell, & Eubanks-Carter, 2003), demonstrate genuineness (Robitschek & McCarthy, 1991), and equalize power in the therapeutic relationship (Mahalik, VanOrmer, & Simi, 2000), establishing it as similar to outside relationships and thus facilitating generalization (Tsai et al., 2008). Disclosures should be titrated to what the client can handle and should almost always include a discussion of how the client is reacting to the disclosure and why the disclosure was offered. The thoughtful use of oneself as a therapeutic instrument of change within the context of a client's case conceptualization can provide an exploration of emotions, themes, and relationship factors that can help to heal client shame.

CONCLUSION

We have illustrated our current thinking about the pragmatic ways we use a functional analytic perspective to work with shame. Integrative, principle-based models such as this can help use changes in science and theory on treatment of shame while remaining tied to idiographic analysis. Throughout, we have pointed toward exemplars and resources from contemporary clinical behavior analysis, and we hope the reader will find these of benefit.

REFERENCES

Allen, N. B., & Knight, W. E. J. (2005). Mindfulness, compassion for self, and compassion for others: Implications for understanding the psychopathology and treatment of depression. In P. Gilbert (Ed.), *Compassion: Conceptualisations, research and use in psychotherapy* (pp. 239–262). London, England: Routledge.

Baumeister, R. F., Vohs, K. D., DeWall, C. N., & Zhang, L. (2007). How emotion shapes behavior: Feedback, anticipation, and reflection, rather than direct causation. *Personality and Social Psychology Review, 11,* 167–203. doi:10.1177/1088868307301033

Biglan, A., & Hayes, S. C. (1996). Should the behavioral sciences become more pragmatic? The case for functional contextualism in research on human behavior. *Applied & Preventive Psychology: Current Scientific Perspectives, 5,* 47–57.

Borkovec, T. D., Alcaine, O. M., & Behar, E. (2004). Avoidance theory of worry in generalized anxiety disorder. In R. G. Heimberg, C. L. Turk, & D. S. Mennin (Eds.), *Generalized anxiety disorder: Advances in research and practice* (pp. 77–108). New York, NY: Guilford Press.

Dougher, M. J. (2000). *Clinical behavior analysis.* Reno, NV: Context Press.

Elliott, R., Watson, J. C., Goldman, R. N., & Greenberg, L. S. (2003). *Learning emotion-focused therapy: The process-experiential approach to change.* Washington, DC: American Psychological Association.

Fridja, N. H. (1986). *The emotions.* Cambridge, England: Cambridge University Press.

Gilbert, P. (2004). Depression: A biopsychosocial, integrative and evolutionary approach. In M. Power (Ed.), *Mood disorder: A handbook of science and practice* (pp. 99–142). Chichester, England: Wiley.

Gilbert, P., & Irons, C. (2005). Focused therapies and compassionate mind training for shame and self-attacking. In P. Gilbert (Ed.), *Compassion: Conceptualizations, research and use in psychotherapy* (pp. 263–299). East Sussex, England: Routledge.

Gilbert, P., & Procter, S. (2006). Compassionate mind training for people with high shame and self-criticism: Overview and pilot study of a group therapy approach. *Clinical Psychology & Psychotherapy, 13,* 353–379. doi:10.1002/cpp.507

Goldfried, M. R., Burckell, L. A., & Eubanks-Carter, C. (2003). Therapist self-disclosure in cognitive-behavior therapy. *Journal of Clinical Psychology, 59,* 555–568. doi:10.1002/jclp.10159

Greenberg, L. S. (2002). *Emotion-focused therapy: Coaching clients to work through their feelings.* Washington, DC: American Psychological Association. doi:10.1037/10447-000

Greenberg, L. S., & Pinsof, W. (1986). *The psychotherapeutic process: A research handbook.* New York, NY: Guilford Press.

Greenberg, M. T., Kusche, C. A., & Speltz, M. (1991). Emotional regulation, self-control and psychopathology: The role of relationships in early childhood. In

D. Cicchetti & S. L. Toth (Eds.), *Internalizing and externalizing expressions of dysfunction* (Vol. 2, pp. 21–55). Hillsdale, NJ: Erlbaum.

Hayes, S. C., & Brownstein, A. J. (1986). Mentalism, behavior–behavior relations, and a behavior analytic view of the purpose of science. *Behavior Analyst, 9,* 175–190.

Hayes, S. C., Strosahl, K. D., & Wilson, K. (2003). *Acceptance and commitment therapy: An experiential approach to behavior change.* New York, NY: Guilford Press.

Izard, C. E. (1991). *The psychology of emotions.* New York, NY: Plenum Press.

Jacobson, N. S., Martell, C. R., & Dimidjian, S. (2001). Behavioral activation therapy for depression: Returning to contextual roots. *Clinical Psychology: Science and Practice, 8,* 255–270. doi:10.1093/clipsy/8.3.255

Kaufman, G. (1989). *The psychology of shame: Theory and treatment of shame-based syndromes.* New York, NY: Springer.

Kohlenberg, R. J., & Tsai, M. (1991). *Functional analytic psychotherapy: Creating intense and curative therapeutic relationships.* New York, NY: Plenum Press.

Kohlenberg, R. J., & Tsai, M. (1994). Functional analytic psychotherapy: A behavioral approach to treatment and integration. *Journal of Psychotherapy Integration, 4,* 175–201.

Leigland, S. (1992). *Radical behaviorism: Willard Day on psychology and philosophy.* Reno, NV: Context Press.

Linehan, M. M. (1993). *Cognitive behavior therapy for borderline personality disorder.* New York, NY: Guilford Press.

Mahalik, J. R., Van Ormer, E. A., & Simi, N. L. (2000). Ethical issues in using self-disclosure in feminist therapy. In M. Brabeck (Ed.), *Practicing feminist ethics in psychology* (pp. 189–201). Washington, DC: American Psychological Association. doi:10.1037/10343-009

Panksepp, J. (1998). *Affective neuroscience: The foundation of human and animal emotions* (pp. 47–56). New York, NY: Oxford University Press.

Robitschek, C. G., & McCarthy, P. R. (1991). Prevalence of counselor self-reference in the therapeutic dyad. *Journal of Counseling and Development, 69,* 218–221.

Segal, Z. V., Williams, J. M. G., & Teasdale, J. D. (2002). *Mindfulness-based therapy for depression: A new approach to preventing relapse.* New York, NY: Guilford Press.

Skinner, B. F. (1953). *Science and human behavior.* New York, NY: Macmillan.

Teasdale, J. D., Moore, R. G., Hayhurst, H., Pope, M., Williams, S., & Segal, Z. V. (2002). Metacognitive awareness and prevention of relapse in depression: Empirical evidence. *Journal of Consulting and Clinical Psychology, 70,* 275–287. doi:10.1037/0022-006X.70.2.275

Tomkins, S. S. (1963). *Affect, imagery, consciousness* (Vol. 2). New York, NY: Springer.

Tomkins, S. S. (1984). Affect theory. In K. R. Scherer & P. Ekman (Eds.), *Approaches to emotion* (pp. 163–195). Hillsdale, NJ: Erlbaum.

Tsai, M., Kohlenberg, R. J., Kanter, J., Kohlenberg, B., Follette, W., & Callaghan, G. (2008). *A guide to functional analytic psychotherapy: Awareness, courage, love and behaviorism.* New York, NY: Springer.

Wilson, K. G., & Dufrene, T. (2008). *Mindfulness for two: An acceptance and commitment approach to mindfulness in psychotherapy.* Oakland, CA: New Harbinger Press.

5

SHAME AND THE PARADOX OF GROUP THERAPY

ELIZABETH L. SHAPIRO AND THEODORE A. POWERS

Most of us have had the experience, so well captured by the Southwest Airlines "Want to Get Away?" television commercials (featuring painfully uncomfortable social situations), of wishing that we could escape the horrible, raw sting of the shameful moment. Yet despite the ubiquity of the experience, shame remains a hidden reality of much of psychotherapy, in particular group therapy. Gans and Weber (2000) pointed out the dearth of consideration of shame in the group therapy literature. Perhaps this paucity reflects the avoidance of shame found in the therapy process itself. As Lewis (1987) pointed out, shame is often a hidden emotion. Both patients and therapists have a tendency to look away in response to shame, either consciously or, more likely, unconsciously. Alonso and Rutan (1988) alluded to the fundamental paradox of shame in group therapy when they considered that being in a group acutely arouses the experience of shame while simultaneously providing particular advantages for the resolution of that shame.

In this chapter, we review shame as seen through the lens of the group therapy literature, and we elucidate the particular ways that group therapy provides the ideal opportunity to resolve the experience of shame. We use clinical examples to highlight the specific ways that shame is evidenced in the group therapy setting and that therapists might recognize and help resolve members' experiences of shame. Attention is paid to some of the typical ways that shame erupts and can be worked with through the various phases of group development. We also address the group leader's experience of shame and ways to identify and work with this phenomenon.

WANT TO GET AWAY? GROUP MEMBERS' EXPERIENCE OF SHAME

On the face of it, the experience of being in a group stimulates a heightened sense of shame. This is evidenced by the often-horrified looks received by therapists who raise the possibility of group treatment to their individual patients, especially those particularly vulnerable to shame. "Thanks, but no thanks," is not an uncommon retort, with patients often citing such concerns as having to share the group time with too many other people. Upon further inspection, many patients admit that they are afraid of revealing themselves to so many people, especially simultaneously. So why does even the specter of group therapy, not to mention the actual experience, so readily stimulate shame?

There are many reasons why group therapy easily stimulates the experience of shame, some obvious and others more subtle. To begin with the obvious, one is far more exposed in a group than in individual therapy. All that one is and does is exposed not just to a single other but to a seeming crowd of onlookers. Mere exposure can reawaken earlier moments when such exposure was accompanied by embarrassment, humiliation, rejection, or loss. Gans and Weber (2000) indicated two conditions of group therapy that can exacerbate the feeling of shame: heightened self-consciousness and the presence of others. Certainly most forms of therapy heighten self-awareness, but in group therapy there is a perceived pressure to become aware of oneself that stems not only from the therapist and from the nature of the therapeutic process but from the other members as well. This pressure can also be felt as it is generated by the norm of self-disclosure that develops in group therapy. This group expectation to reveal one's inner experience can be a powerful force that may elicit feelings of shame accompanied by urges to flee. The presence of others contributes to a heightened self-consciousness and can also provoke a tendency toward social comparison. The group members compare themselves with one another, often unfavorably judging the self as less important, less attractive, less intelligent, and even less self-aware (Gans & Weber, 2000). The group setting provides multiple opportunities for these unfavorable comparisons.

Morrison (1990) delineated several "explicit precipitants of shame" in group therapy. The group, he suggested, provides a multiplicity of *self-objects* (i.e., the internalized experience of another as part of the self, insofar as this "other" provides necessary functions for the self) and therefore a multiplicity of potential self-object failures. The experiences of injuries, real or perceived, increase as the number of potential perpetrators increases. For many group members, avoidance of intimacy has provided the best bulwark against repeated experiences of shame. This avoidance works, to a point; that is to say, the loneliness and longing for intimacy can never trail far behind. Being thrust into the group therapy situation may stimulate this longing and the chronically unmet dependency needs. The activation of these dependency needs can then engender the very shame in the face of vulnerability, weakness, and inferiority that these group members have been desperately trying to avoid.

A precipitant of shame that is particular to group treatment is the nature of group-level interventions and interpretations (Morrison, 1990). The group therapist often uses material gathered from one or perhaps a few members to make general statements about the group as a whole. Each individual's need to be "special," to have his or her offerings responded to in particular, is sacrificed for the group theme and focus. This sacrifice can be experienced as an empathic failure on the part of the group leader and can ultimately lead to attendant shame. Especially in the early phase of a group's development, there is an inherent tension in group therapy between a member's desire to become part of the whole (i.e., "merger fantasy") and a need to preserve a sense of distinctness and specialness. For some, this unconscious merger fantasy may conflict with a very real terror of engulfment and loss of self or self-annihilation. Both the awareness of this merger fantasy and the terror of engulfment may easily evoke shame in the group patient.

In addition to the presence of others, heightened self-awareness, norms of self-disclosure, social comparisons, group focus, and multiplicity of potential perceived injuries and empathic failures, there is the powerful and acute potential for object loss, both real and imagined, in group therapy. Surrounded by potential attachments, the group member is also surrounded by potential loss. The belief that "if they really knew me, they would want nothing to do with me" means that "when they do know me, they will reject or abandon me." It is difficult to really trust that the other members will stay once the toxicity is revealed. Even if one manages to convince oneself that a therapist will remain, if only because "it's her job," the belief that others will have any reason to stay is harder to muster. However, precisely because the other group members are less likely to embody the altruism found in the group leader, the group's acceptance of a member's imperfect self can have more believability and staying power than the therapist's acceptance of a member's imperfect self.

Another way in which group members are surrounded by potential loss is as a result of the very structure of the group norms. Although within-group relationships can be profoundly meaningful and useful (and hopefully translate to improved outside-group relationships), it is also true that the prohibition around extragroup relationships can be experienced as a deprivation that reevokes the very neglect and/or loss group members have already experienced as shaming and have been struggling to cope with since early on in their lives.

The group setting powerfully recapitulates the early family experience with all the longings, unmet needs, regressive dependency, urges to belong, rivalries, and conflicts that family dynamics entail. This recapitulation of the family reawakens memories and stimulates primal affects and impulses that can exacerbate the experience of shame. For example, the experience of being the "black sheep" or the less-cherished member of one's family can be painfully reawakened in the group setting. Most patients would rather avoid any situation that evokes these conscious and unconscious memories and the threat of shame they evoke. However, this set of similarities between the group and one's family sets the stage for a powerful reworking of early conflicts and developmental arrests.

WHAT YOU DON'T KNOW CAN HURT YOU: GROUP MEMBERS' DEFENSES AGAINST SHAME

All of the aforementioned factors can contribute to the way that the group experience particularly evokes shame in the group members. These factors, and probably others that we have neglected, indicate how difficult it can be to treat shame in group therapy. There are powerful forces to overcome, which naturally lean toward avoidance, withdrawal, and secretiveness. These patterns of avoidance, withdrawal, and secretiveness can lead to ever-larger problems in people's lives, including social isolation and compulsive behaviors, but because the source of these patterns (i.e., shame) often operates unconsciously, patients may be unaware of the connection between the affective experience and the destructive behavioral patterns.

Gans and Weber (2000) highlighted the group defenses used in reaction to the experience of shame and emphasized how the desire to hide from this universally painful affect hinders its detection. A fundamental belief accompanying the experience of shame is that "if other people *really* knew me, they would reject me." This belief understandably results in the profound motivation to conceal. The tendency toward concealment can create major problems for the therapeutic process, especially when the discomfort of facing shame directly evokes unresolved shame in the therapist and results in a collusion to avoid such areas (Morrison, 1990). The group experience provides multiple opportunities for the evocation of shame. Gans and Weber (2000) discussed group-level defenses used to avoid shame and the topics that elicit it, including the following:

- As a way to avoid painful differences and comparisons, the group may focus on themes that stress similarities among members, such as loss or failure.

- Fear and self-reproach can be masked by generating scorn and disdain for the therapist.
- Avoiding here-and-now material can be used to minimize the painful sting that the immediacy of the present moment generates, and so the group may opt to remain in the "there and then" rather than the "here and now".
- Guilt induction can at times serve to defend against shame in the perpetrator while simultaneously inducing shame in the recipient. For example, when a group member's shame makes him or her feel not entitled to consolation from others, that group member may cause others to feel guilty that their attempts to console him or her are inept.
- Shame may be embedded in certain types of transference reactions, mostly involving the projection of feelings of unacceptability. These reactions may take many forms—for example, expressions of self-sufficiency (e.g., "I don't need anything") or futility (e.g., "I have no one in my life who really cares, so there is no sense in asking").
- Finally, the group may work to preserve the illusion of the leader's infallibility in order to avoid feelings of disappointment and embarrassment over the leader's inevitable mistakes and limitations.

By using these and other defensive maneuvers, group members implicitly collude to avoid the experience and the discussion of shame and shame-related material. The group leader must be able to recognize and successfully navigate the furtive and dangerous shoals that these defenses pose. We argue, however, that despite these exacerbating factors, group therapy can still be a particularly powerful antidote to shame and can provide advantages for its treatment.

Group therapists such as Hahn (1994) specified that from an object relations point of view, the experience of shame results from the activation of "devaluing and devalued introjects" in both the shamer and the shamed. *Introjects* refers to the enduring relationship patterns initially established in early interactions with primary caregivers. The experience of shame and the attendant disruption in self-cohesion and feelings of abandonment and emptiness lead to a myriad of mostly primitive defensive responses. The re-experiencing of shame is primarily defended against through repression, denial, and projection (Alonso & Rutan, 1988). Projection of the devaluing introject leads to the perception of the other as critical and condemning and can lead to the ubiquitous desire to hide, withdraw, and isolate.

For example, a woman who was once repeatedly shamed by her father may internalize an image of her father, or men in general, as shaming and herself as the one who is shamed. This woman projects the shaming father onto her male professors and then feels ashamed and unworthy. Projection of the devalued self can lead to the perception of the other as defective, thus justifying contempt for the other (Hahn, 1994). This same woman projects the shamed self-image onto women around her and then perceives them as worthless. Morrison (1990) suggested that shame often hides behind the rage, envy, and contempt seen in group members. Likewise, the depression, indifference, and apparent amotivation witnessed in group members leading to minimal group participation may conceal group members' shame or fear of shame beneath their apathetic behavior.

Hahn (1990) also highlighted the importance of projective identification in understanding reactions to shame, especially in groups. Projective identification allows for the depositing of an unwanted part of oneself while maintaining a connection to the other and thus attenuating the experience of emptiness and aloneness. In projective identification, the extruded part of oneself (the projected introject) is taken up by an available other, and so a compromise can be reached between the desire to destroy and the need to preserve some connection. Naturally, the group setting allows a myriad of potential repositories for any given group member's projected introjects. For example, in the case of the woman described above, one can easily imagine that this group patient may experience comments from the men in the group as critical and devaluing and/or may criticize and devalue the women in the group. When projective identification occurs, the men and the women in the group would actually begin to feel devaluing or devalued. The group leader and the members then have the opportunity to explore this experience so that it can be reowned in a less toxic manner by the group member to whom it "belongs."

The following cases provide examples of the way that shame is manifested in group therapy. We give the barest outlines of the cases here and then return to them later in this chapter when we describe the attempt to resolve the group members' shame. Although the experience of shame erupts at many different moments in the life of a group, one way for the clinician to remain alert to its many forms and permutations is to pay attention to some of the typical ways shame manifests itself at different junctures in the group's development, for both the members and the leader. Authors have sliced the group developmental pie in different ways, but most often there are four stages noted in the course of the group's life: the group formation phase, the reactive phase, the mature phase, and the termination phase. We chose to use these phases outlined by Rutan and Stone (1993) because they represent a commonly accepted developmental framework.

Group Formation Phase: Alice

Alice was a 55-year-old divorced woman referred for group treatment by her psychiatrist because of chronic anxiety and depression. Alice was hoping to join the group in order to combat a pervasive feeling of loneliness in her life. She saw her grown children on occasion and infrequently socialized with coworkers at the company where she had held a job for 22 years, but she claimed no close friends and had not dated since her divorce nearly a decade ago. Her psychiatrist, Dr. Wallace, placed her in a five-member group he led that had been in existence for 2 years. On her first night, Alice entered the group 2 minutes late and sat with her arms crossed and her lips pursed, responding to the group's questions with minimal data and an attitude that suggested irritation and superiority. Finally, Cecilia, a group member generally known to be reticent, confronted Alice by saying, "Don't you think that blowing off our questions kind of defeats the purpose of your being here?" Alice responded by rising halfway up out of her chair, leaning over into Cecilia's face, and barking, "Don't you tell me what I can and can't do. I don't need your damn group."

The group formation phase is marked by anxiety around belonging, trust, and safety, with both conscious and unconscious experiences of dependency, helplessness, fear, and confusion. Members tend to be preoccupied with joining the group and finding similarities among themselves or with resisting these crucial tasks. Although in the above example it was not technically a new group, every time a new member is added to a preexisting group, a new group is formed, and the new member, the old members, and the leader must all endure a reawakening of old anxieties set off by the experience of joining or leading a newly configured group and the new dynamics that might emerge. The group therapist is wise to be on the lookout for members' shame regarding their dependency, as the example of Alice so poignantly illustrates.

The discrepancy between her initial stated objectives for joining a group (to combat her loneliness) and her statement to Cecilia, "I don't need your damn group," highlights Alice's dilemma: She was coming to group to face the very things (intimate relationships) she had assiduously avoided. Given the unrealized longing evident in her presenting problem, one can assume she had avoided relationships because of some very painful early and subsequent experiences. Both the evocation of those experiences and the very fact of her solitary life were exposed to this group of strangers by whom she both desperately wanted to be accepted and with whom she was terrified of repeating the same early experiences. Unfortunately for Alice, she did indeed need this "damn group."

Reactive Phase: Jeremy

Jeremy was a 34-year-old man with a new marriage and a newly pregnant wife. He was working as a research assistant in a pharmaceutical company after dropping out of school just short of his master's degree. Jeremy stated that his wife complained of his lack of ambition, his unwillingness to help out around the house, and her fears that he would become even less involved and helpful once the baby was born. He acknowledged feeling depressed and occasionally disappointed that he had not finished his master's degree. Upon further questioning, Jeremy reported the fear that his wife would leave him if he did not "shape up."

Jeremy was quite engaged and engaging in Dr. Wallace's group—playful, funny, and impressively articulate. The other members enjoyed his insightful perspective on group members' problems, but it was not until approximately 18 months into treatment that they began to seriously question him about why he was in the group and what he was or was not doing to accomplish his goals. Shortly thereafter he began coming just a few minutes late to each group. He usually had a very good "reason" for his tardiness, and, anyway, the group was inclined to give him the benefit of the doubt because he was so likable and because he was never more than a few minutes late.

The second phase of group development is the reactive phase. Some authors have labeled this the *storming* phase (Tuckman, 1965), capturing the highly charged nature of members' attempts to assert their individuality and unconsciously bring forth into view the very reasons for their decision to seek group treatment in the first place. This is the phase during which most of the testing around group norms occurs. Members may push or outright violate the boundaries established by the group contract (e.g., agree to be on time for the whole time, agree to be responsible for the fee each week the group is session, agree to keep the relationships therapeutic and not social) during the reactive phase. Jeremy's characterological stance in the world was revealed, as it often is during this phase. He got by on his charm until the group (or, presumably, his wife) confronted him, and then he reverted to a passive aggressive style that was sure to eventually annoy the group as it annoyed his wife.

Mature Phase: Fran

Fran was a very attractive 42-year-old woman who had been divorced multiple times. She joined the group to better understand these repeated failures. According to Fran, she was surprised every time each successive husband left her for another woman. Fran had a noticeable habit of wearing sexy clothes to group each week. One night, the week after a particularly tense but productive group session in which several members had confronted each other on some especially deep and painful issues, Fran showed up in an especially revealing dress. The leader noticed that the group seemed embarrassed by her outfit and responded by being more anxious and giggly than usual. The leader surmised that Fran was avoiding the shame of revealing her inner self—as many members had done in the previous week— by being ever more revealing of her outer self—that is, by getting others to focus on her body as a way to deflect attention from her insecure sense of self.

The third phase of group development is the mature phase. In this phase, the group members are deeply involved in working on the problems that brought them into treatment. A sense of safety abounds in the group, and members are thereby able to begin to discard old interactional patterns in favor of new ways of being in the world. Metaphorically speaking, the members maintain one foot in the transference (to the leader and the other members) and one foot out, so that a dialectical tension of rootedness in one's typical experience and the ability to be mindful of one's experience provoke a capacity to entertain how one's life might be different if one were to abandon old ways of being in the world. In this mature phase, the group cycles back to shameful aspects of the self hinted at in earlier phases. The group work intensifies, and therefore the opportunity arises to more deeply and comprehensively address the members' shame. For Fran, watching the other group members work deeply in this mature phase of their group was profoundly shame inducing, as it highlighted her own attempts to keep interactions with others on a more surface level. The intensification of Fran's characteristic seductiveness presented a difficult-to-ignore opportunity for her to join the other group members in their newly deepening capacity to work on the problems that brought them to treatment.

Termination Phase: George

George was a 62-year-old lawyer and widower who came to treatment when he became socially isolated after the sudden death of his wife 5 years earlier. Group treatment allowed him to discover his lifelong pattern of becoming enraged with others for perceived slights and managing always to drive them away with his anger. He became gradually more aware of his inability to tolerate what he saw as weakness in himself or others. George was well on his way to reestablishing a vital life for himself when he decided to terminate the group. A few weeks into the process of his 3-month-long termination, he became furious with another and fairly new member, Jim, who began to describe his meekness with his wife. When Jim did not show up to the next week's group session, George became severely anxious. George was confronted by other group members for his harsh reaction to Jim. He felt very bad for his behavior but was unclear about what fueled it. The group leader wondered if the specter of termination combined with the discussion of weakness evoked shameful feelings in George about his own neediness that in turn sparked a defensive rage reaction, characteristic of George's earlier interpersonal relationships.

Terminations in long-term groups can occur because individual members leave, the leader leaves (more common in clinic settings), or the entire group ends. They may occur prematurely or as the result of a unanimous agreement. In the case of the individual member's planned termination, many opportunities occur to address unresolved shame. Although group therapy had been enormously helpful to George, he was not conscious of his behavior in response to separations until he began to say goodbye to the group. Just as in individual treatment, terminations allow members to rework on a deeper level the conflicts they have been struggling with since entering group. In particular, termination often evokes shame because it highlights the experience of abandonment that itself was often the spur to members' original experience of shame early on in their lives. It is an axiom of psychodynamic treatment that every current loss echoes past losses and gives rise to an opportunity to rework those losses. The shame of abandonment caused by a departing member and the revelation of one's continuing dependence on the group can also be evoked in the members who are left behind. Questions may surface such as "Will I ever be able to leave, or am I so damaged that I will be in this group for the rest of my life?" or "Did I do something to make [this departing member] leave?"

LETTING THE AIR GET AT IT:
RESOLVING SHAME IN GROUP TREATMENT

If group therapy so readily evokes the experience of shame in patients and therapists, then how can it be a recommended treatment, let alone a treatment of choice, for the resolution of shame? The irony that Alonso and Rutan (1988) illuminated is that as painful as the presence of others may be, it is precisely the exposing of shame in the community of others that is "the ticket" out of that shame. A related discussion can be found in Chapter 15 of this volume. So, as with any avoidance, that which is most feared most needs to be faced. The most natural response to the experience of shame (i.e., to hide) is the most toxic, whereas the least automatic or natural (i.e., to expose the source of the shame) is the most healing. As the old adage goes, one needs to "let the air get at it." It is only when shame reaches the light of day that the healing process can begin. The presence of others allows in that light of day. Despite the intrapsychic origin of shame, the characterological problems it engenders and the internal healing it requires are best addressed in the interpersonal arena (Alonso & Rutan, 1988).

The group therapy experience offers several potential advantages for the treatment of shame (Alonso & Rutan, 1988; Hahn, 1994; Lear, 1990; Tantam, 1990). Several of the curative factors presented by Yalom (1985) and others address the resolution of shame provided by the group experience. For example, an advantage of group treatment is the possibility of vicarious experience—that is, experiencing or learning through another (Alonso & Rutan, 1988; Hahn,

1994). Although a group member may not be able to face an issue or feeling directly, the experience of another less-defended member may provide an indirect detoxification and/or new learning. Repeated exposure in this way may ease the stranglehold of shame over the individual. Universality is another factor that may ease the shame of group members. The sense of similarity and shared experience can mitigate the feeling of aloneness and individual corruptness that often accompanies shame. Group contagion or, in a more benign form, group norming tends to bring individual members along to places that they might not otherwise go on their own. For example, the norm of self-disclosure or risk taking can serve to grease the path for more reluctant members to follow. Altruism, or helping others, can also ease the grip of shame as it allows the group member to engage in building self-esteem by assuming a helping posture vis-à-vis the other members.

The case of Alice illustrates some of these curative factors. When Alice retorted to Cecilia, "I don't need your damn group," the group leader replied, "I think Alice is letting the group know just how scary it is to join this group." He surmised that Alice's angry behavior hid her fear, which hid her shame. He did not initially address the underlying shame, as he surmised that doing so at this early juncture might in itself be too shaming for Alice. Sensing that the group may be put off by Alice and need to not scapegoat her and/or push her right back out of the group, he soon asked the members directly, "I wonder who is remembering their own scary experiences of joining the group." Indeed, Edward acknowledged to Alice that he was so terrified that instead of attending his first day of group, he went out and had a few drinks after being sober for 4 years! Luckily, he called his AA sponsor, received the support he needed, and delayed entering the group until the following week. Bill revealed to the group that he didn't even tell his own wife he was joining the group until 5 months after his first session. He said he was so ashamed because he thought his individual therapist's referral to a group signaled her belief that he was hopelessly sick and a "failure" at individual therapy. Alice didn't say much that evening, or even for the first several months, but her body language showed she was beginning to relax a bit, and she even joined in the laughter when one of the members made fun of himself for his behavior around the time of his initial joining of the group. Vicarious experience, repeated exposure, universality, group contagion, and altruism all helped play a role in Alice's move from a defensive, angry posture to a more curious and relaxed position.

Alonso and Rutan (1988) pointed out how the group contract can serve as a powerful force, providing a safe container for the painful and frightening experiences of shame. Among other things, the contract is an explicit agreement among the members not to flee in the face of the unbearable. The profound fear of object loss accompanying shame is thus mitigated by the external boundary provided by the contract. This contract allows for the reestablishment of bonds that may be disrupted or that may be perceived as precarious or vulnerable. This constancy is enormously important, and it provides for the possibility of a corrective emotional experience that is "not contrived but negotiated and maintained by the good will of the group and the group ego as evidenced in the group contract" (Alonso & Rutan, 1988, p. 10). This contract allows for a face-saving way to return to the group after the inevitable empathic breach occurs.

In the case of Jeremy, working with the group contract proved invaluable in confronting what later turned out to be his overwhelming shame. Jeremy had indeed violated at least two of the leader's stated group agreements: (a) to be at every meeting, on time, for the whole time, as much as is humanly possible; and (b) to talk about the problems that bring you to therapy and to communicate in words as many aspects of those problems as you can. In retrospect, it would have been helpful if the leader had not been as charmed by Jeremy as the group and had confronted him earlier than she did. It is always useful for the group leader to attend to the ways that each member relates to the group agreements because this offers information that is often only unconsciously communicated and may encapsulate the group member's most shameful and hidden internal dynamics.

When confronted first by the group and later by the leader, Jeremy revealed that he had spent a lifetime making others feel good about themselves and felt woefully inadequate when it came to knowing who he was, what he wanted, or what he was feeling. He was painfully embarrassed by the fact that he was in his mid-30s, now with a young child, and had no idea what he wanted to do "when he grew up." It wasn't until even later on in his work in the group that he revealed he had secretly hoped that by being such a "good" group member and then by coming late to group, he could finally garner the attention he had so craved all his life and yet was also afraid of receiving for fear of what he would reveal about himself.

Hahn (1994), citing Tantam (1990) and Lear (1990), emphasized the importance of disclosing one's shame to an accepting audience and the need to create a safe therapeutic environment in which that is possible. Lear suggested that group preparation and the exploration of fantasies about group therapy along with the establishment of ground rules (the group contract) help to build that safe environment. Pointing out similarities between members' experiences and making group-as-a-whole interventions also contributes to establishing a safe environment that decreases defensiveness around shame and shame-related topics. Self-acceptance is increased by internalizing the acceptance provided by the group. Morrison (1990) indicated that secrets must be respected until trust develops. The group and leader provide the reparative self-object functions for the members by accepting the mirroring, idealizing, and twinship transferences (their needs to have experiences accurately reflected and to attach to others they perceive as valuable or similar to them) and by empathically identifying and accepting shame. In the natural progression of group development, there is a movement from the need to be special to the desire to be one of the group.

Indeed, it turned out that Fran's desire to be one of the group led her to "up the ante" by walking into group in an especially revealing dress. In the face of the group's anxiety in response to Fran's dress, the leader said to the group, "How hard does poor Fran have to work before the group will see beneath her artful distraction?" This led to a discussion of Fran's seductiveness that stirred up many powerful feelings in the other members. Cecilia chastised Fran for her "shameless seductiveness of the men in the group." It took several weeks before Cecilia could acknowledge, with the group's help, that she, too, wanted the attention of the men in the group but was too ashamed to be seen as seeking it. Fran timidly revealed that she had no confidence in her ability to engage others except in a sexual way and that she felt horribly inferior in the face of the group's growing capacity for intimacy in the form of confrontation and honesty. Perhaps not surprisingly, Fran admitted that she had never enjoyed sex and only engaged in sex to keep her partner happy. In the process, Cecilia began to realize that Fran was not "shameless" at all. Nate boldly acknowledged that he had—initially unconsciously—encouraged Fran's seductiveness and desperately wanted to be seen as desirable by her. Plentiful shameful memories emerged from each member of painful rejections, both real and imagined, in middle and high school years. Nervous laughter and a palpable sense of relief ensued.

Hahn (1994) acknowledged that the disclosure of shame to an accepting audience is vital to the resolution of shame, but he emphasized the need to understand and work through the projections and projective identifications that occur within a group. He pointed out that, as Alonso and Rutan (1988) indicated, group members "need" each other to contain disavowed parts of the self. Projective identifications serve a necessary function by allowing the maintenance of object ties while projecting unacceptable parts of the self. The leader must therefore "allow" them, observe them, and "intervene by fostering an analytic attitude of self-reflective curiosity" (Hahn, 1994, p. 452), as the leader of Fran's group was able to do. This helped Fran and each of the other members to own disavowed parts of themselves that could then be observed, internalized, and contained within the self. The key is for group members to expose their shame without receiving the anticipated condemnation or rejection.

The case of George also illustrates the way that projection works as a defense against shame. The group members confronted George when Jim did not return to group that night. Rebecca told George that he had been unnecessarily hard on Jim and that she was feeling guilty for not intervening on Jim's behalf the prior week; others chimed in with similar feelings. This group input enabled George to examine the connection between his rage at others for a perceived weakness and his intolerance of his own perceived weakness. Furthermore, the group leader pointed out the inescapable truth that this rage was occurring as he was saying goodbye and that it was easier for George to be angry at some relatively new and unsuspecting member than to confront his own deep sadness at the loss of the group. This comment finally provoked George to see on a much deeper level just how ashamed he was of his need for connection and his sadness in the face of the impending loss of connection with the group. Not surprisingly, the process of termination reawakened George's discomfort with his dependence on the group. He uncharacteristically shed tears as he realized that he had frequently pushed his wife away and that these behaviors usually coincided with an impending separation from her.

The leader's decision to call Jim the next day after the missed group and urge him to return to the following group gave Jim an opportunity to work on the meekness that was compromising his intimate relationships and gave George an opportunity to apologize to Jim and expose the roots of his behavior in Jim's presence. George's revealing his shame about both being a bully and his underlying neediness encouraged several other members to similarly explore hidden and shameful aspects of themselves.

WHAT GOES AROUND COMES AROUND: THE LEADER'S EXPERIENCE OF SHAME

The heightened experience of shame in group therapy is by no means confined to the group members. Weber and Gans (2003) argued that above and beyond personal vulnerabilities, there are factors inherent in group leadership that particularly evoke shame in the leader. To be sure, the leader's unresolved shame, both conscious and unconscious, is likely to be stimulated by much of what transpires in the therapy experience, and there is a natural tendency to avoid this discomfort. But in addition to the natural proclivity to avoid shame, there is in the professional therapist a tendency to "feel ashamed of feeling ashamed" (Weber & Gans, 2003, p. 396). A therapist's professional identity is often tied to a grandiose ego ideal that includes omniscience, omnipotence, and total benevolence (Brightman, 1984). This type of perfectionism results in shame when the therapist inevitably falls short of the ideal. In addition, this self-evaluation demands not only that we not make mistakes but also that we not feel ashamed when we do. This tendency can be compounded by additional factors present in the group setting. For example, group therapists are not immune to members' unconscious fantasies of merging with them as with the mother very early on in life, but they may be defended against such a fantasy. Part of this defensive maneuvering may include a wish to see ourselves as healthier than the group members we treat and thus separate from the group. Nonetheless, group therapists are likely to want to be liked by the group members or at least perceived as helpful to the group, and they are likely to often view themselves as falling short of this goal. Livingston (2006) cogently summarized some of these factors, observing that "a group leader is frequently at risk of having shame evoked through revived trauma, barrages of criticism, the emergence of taboo topics, high expectations for oneself, and an exposure to internal as well as external audiences" (p. 321).

When the individual therapist makes a mistake, there is only one person to witness it, but when a group leader fails, there is a crowd of witnesses. The same increased exposure that can exacerbate shame in the group members is equally true for the leader. Many therapists in training remark that group therapy feels much scarier to them because of this increased exposure and the potential audience to their mistakes. Especially when one is new to the work, one is vulnerable to such shame-inducing events as the scorn of one's patients. Therefore, the idea of the simultaneous scorn of multiple patients is potentially overwhelming. We know of no studies to this effect, but one could certainly hypothesize that many individual therapists avoid training in group therapy because of this very same fear.

Therapists often struggle with questions of adequacy and competence. Particularly when they are novices, group therapists may struggle with their identity as a group leader. As with group members, social comparison can contribute to shame in the leader as well. In this case, the reference group for the comparison may be the group members, coleaders, supervisors, and conjoint individual therapists or other colleagues such as referral sources, all of whom might scrutinize and judge the work of the group leader (Lazare, 1997; Weber & Gans, 2003). This additional potential scrutiny adds to the self-scrutiny already imposed by the harsh comparison with the ego ideal. As with the group members, there are also increased opportunities to take on the projections of the group participants by becoming the shamer or the shamed (Hahn, 1990). In the case of projective identification, the leader may become the shamed projection and begin to experience the disturbing and disorienting affective experience of the group members' projected part objects. Conversely, the leader may become the projected shamer and enact the felt contempt and/or rejection of the members. As MacNab (1995) described it, this too may ultimately result in shame for the leader who is caught in this dynamic but is unable to extract himself or herself.

Weber and Gans (2003) identified a number of particular areas that the group therapist is called upon to address that can elicit shame in the leader, such as finances and professional devaluation. Dealing with money is an area fraught with potential shame-provoking content for patient and therapist (Gans, 1992; Shapiro & Ginzberg, 2006). This can be especially true when deciding how to address finances with a group. Setting fee policies, dealing with cancellations and missed sessions, and addressing late payments or failure to pay may all stir up discomfort for the group and the therapist, and both the group and the therapist are often unaware of the potential meanings that underlie the decisions that are made and the actions taken. Facing these meanings in the public forum with the entire group can further stimulate the experience of shame. Feelings of vulnerability, dependency, and entitlement are evoked and exacerbated by the increased exposure of the group.

Group members often disparage and devalue the leader. Group members are emboldened to confront the group therapist to an extent not as commonly seen in individual therapy. There is comfort and protection in numbers. Disparaging the leader may be an attempt to distract the group or to avoid more difficult material, or it may evidence the projections of unacceptable parts of the self as discussed earlier in this chapter. The leader must anticipate these reactions and be prepared to respond effectively in the face of the personal sense of inadequacy they may provoke.

Weber and Gans (2003) suggested that the professional is also often devalued both by the community at large and at times from within our own ranks. This is evidenced by popular media portrayals of therapists, by the increased "shopping around" by prospective group members who will not settle for the word of the referral source, and by the pecking order within the mental health profession. The experience of being disparaged, even if misplaced or specious, and the experience of being passed over for another group or of being relegated to a lower position in the professional pecking order can all leave the therapist feeling vulnerable and devalued and thus more prone to shame. We would add that for many years, group therapy has been perceived as occupying a lower position in the constellation of therapeutic modalities despite empirical evidence to the contrary, and this may add to a particular sense of vulnerability in the group therapist in response to the members' devaluation.

GROUP THERAPIST CASE EXAMPLE: DR. WELLBORN

Dr. Wellborn was a man in his late 60s who had been practicing for more than 30 years. His strong build and white hair made others view him as commanding and potent. This paternal transference was quite comfortable and served as a valuable source of self-esteem for him. However, this particular group began to criticize Dr. Wellborn for his being late with handing out monthly patient bills. Once while returning to his chair after opening the door and ushering in the members for the group session, Dr. Wellborn tripped and bounced awkwardly into his chair. When he looked up, all of the members who had already entered the room had their eyes averted. No one made mention of the incident for the first 30 minutes of the group.

The reader will note that once again we have presented an example involving the body. Earlier it was Fran's sexuality, and this time it is Dr. Wellborn's tripping and nearly falling. This is not a coincidence. Of the many shame-prone topics that can emerge in therapy, Weber and Gans (2003) highlighted two: sexuality and nonsexual body activities. Insofar as shame relates to deeply held evaluative experiences of the self, it is clear why the body evokes such acute shame. Whether it is sexual arousal, flatulence, or the loss of hearing, there is something deeply personal about bodily functions. A primitive vulnerability is awakened by these situations, and a profound threat to one's sense of bodily integrity and personal cohesion can be experienced, especially for the more narcissistically compromised. These topics naturally provoke a desire to hide on the part of both members and the leader. Avoidance of these topics will of course lead to greater shame, especially for the leader who has hopefully been trained to attend to such issues and may therefore become even more ashamed of yielding to the impulse to hide. It is important to note, however, that in addition to the body revealing essential and often shameful aspects of the self, experiences of the body can also be used to disguise more profound and troubling aspects of the self, as in the case of Fran. In either case, the group leader's attention to the body—his or her own, as well as that of each of the group members—will often create opportunities to significantly deepen the work.

In discussing the dynamics that evoke shame in the group leader, Weber and Gans (2003) suggested two sources stemming from the leader: erroneous notions about leadership tasks and countertransference. The former include being more invested in patients' progress than the patients and believing it is the therapist's job to keep the patient alive. This sense of inappropriate hyper-responsibility creates a dynamic whereby the therapist loses leverage and can be rendered impotent, leaving the therapist more vulnerable to shame and the group vulnerable to stagnation and failure. Countertransference difficulties can of course range from the common and temporary to the profound and pervasive. Weber and Gans chose to focus on the more commonplace in an effort to normalize the shame experience while acknowledging the possibility of a leader with more pronounced pathology. They identified four common countertransference challenges that may elicit shame in the leader: (a) collusion with scapegoating and role lock (i.e., the effort to bring forth one aspect of a group member's personality or behavior to the relative exclusion of another aspect), (b) containing and detoxifying noxious projective identifications, (c) negative transference, and (d) idealization of the therapist (p. 407).

In the first case, the leader may experience shame to the extent that he or she or the group recognizes the collusion to put the unwanted feelings of the many onto the convenient one. The failure to contain and metabolize projective identifications limits the capacity of the members to reown the projections and thereby to heal (Alonso & Rutan, 1988; Hahn, 1994). The therapist's own vulnerability to these projections can lead to this therapeutic "failure" and can be a resulting source of shame for the therapist. If the group leader is knocked off track by negative transference reactions that provoke self-protective countermaneuvers, then the leader can feel shame for failing to respond effectively.

Finally, Weber and Gans (2003) seemed to suggest that the group leader need not collude with the group's desire to idealize the leader. Although some authors have noted that there are times when the group may need to idealize the leader (e.g., Morrison, 1990), the leader must remain aware of his or her own desire to be idealized. Sometimes this powerful wish to be seen as perfect can prevent the leader from allowing the group to begin to relinquish its need to idealize him or her and to express anger and disappointment about the therapist's imperfections. Both the need to be idealized and the exposure of one's imperfections can lead to the therapist's shame or defensive avoidance of shame. The case of Dr. Wellborn occurred during the group's mature phase in which the

> therapist is viewed as an authority and expert, but he is demystified and not imbued with magical powers. In other words, a therapeutic alliance has been established that allows for a more complete conviction that he or she is an ally in the therapeutic venture. (Rutan & Stone, 1993, p. 44)

Because of this timing, Dr. Wellborn—once he had regained his composure—was able to confront the group on its silence in regard to his awkward movements. He led with the simple statement, "I noticed that no one made mention of my nearly falling on the floor." Several members laughed nervously but then silence ensued again, so Dr. Wellborn responded, "It can't be easy to let me know you see that sometimes the emperor has no clothes!" This comment turned out to be the cause of the dam breaking and the group allowing itself to discuss with some timidity, but also relief, the mixed feelings that were stirred up by Dr. Wellborn's frailties. The members acknowledged their wish for him to be invincible and their increasing awareness that he was not. They experienced sadness as they felt themselves relinquishing the fantasy that he could care for them forever and completely. However, they were also surprised by an increased sense of self-worth stemming from their ability to "take him on" without anyone being damaged in the process. The way that Dr. Wellborn was able to face his shame in front of the group members is a profound example of Weber and Gans's (2003) observation that "we can best overcome our patients' resistance to dealing with their shame through our willingness to acknowledge, bear with, and work through our own" (p. 396).

CONCLUSION

The power of group therapy to induce shame is directly proportional to its power to heal the wounds of shame. As represented in the iconic dream of being naked in front of a group of people, shame is the sense of oneself as defective in one's eyes as well as the eyes of others. If one can bear the experience of shame in the presence of others, one can confront this aspect of oneself and the consequent self-reflections as they are mirrored by the other group members.

Group therapy provides a unique environment for the resolution of shame because of the power of the community. As Alonso and Rutan (1988) suggested, the group setting forces an individual to necessarily live out his or her life problems as they are in the real world. The group is truly a "social microcosm" (Yalom, 1985). One must be oneself and expose that self to others in this context. One's worldview, no matter how distorted, is also exposed in this setting. The opportunity then exists in this context for tremendous growth. The group forces engagement with disavowed parts of the self. The consistent and continuous presence of others decreases the withdrawal into self-evaluation and reproach. The group provides empathic mirroring, understanding, and acceptance that can heal the chasm between the real and the ideal self. Self-esteem can increase as one becomes a valued member of a valued community, and in the search for self-acceptance, there are few substitutes for the power of community acceptance and forgiveness.

Many of the curative factors of group therapy as delineated by Yalom (1985)—including instillation of hope, universality, catharsis, imitative behavior, and interpersonal learning—allow for the gradual detoxification of the painful affect of shame. One group member is exposed, and the other group members observe that he or she is still accepted by the group. This then encourages other group members to expose the hateful parts of themselves. A member experiences the intensity of the shame in the context of the safety of the group and learns new ways of viewing himself or herself—for example, "I am brave because I took the risk of sharing this shameful part of myself" or "I am not the only one who has this ugly side."

Because shame is indeed the "hidden emotion" (Gans & Weber, 2000), as well as profoundly unsettling and deeply evocative for patients and group therapists alike, consultation is highly recommended. Consultation or supervision can be immensely useful not just in instances of already perceived shame experiences but when group therapists find themselves confused, stymied, or deskilled. It is useful to suspect shame as the culprit and valuable to allow another set of eyes to ferret out the potential manifestations of shame and the defenses aroused in response to its presence.

As Livingston (2006) wrote, "Becoming aware of shame gives us an opportunity to transform archaic grandiosity into a more solid sense of well-being by gradually discovering and integrating aspects of ourselves" (p. 321). Many patients who join therapy groups express the view that they simply cannot do what they want to do or know they should do for fear of exposing themselves to humiliation, but they discover that there is no substitute for the slow but rewarding journey of painstaking attention to the experience of shame. This journey entails the fight against the impulse to crawl into the corner and hide, and efforts to continually expose one's thoughts and feelings to others, and the salutary effects of an accepting audience.

REFERENCES

Alonso, A., & Rutan, J. S. (1988). The experience of shame and the restoration of self-respect in group therapy. *International Journal of Group Psychotherapy, 38*, 3–14.

Brightman, B. K. (1984). Narcissistic issues in the training experience of the psychotherapist. *International Journal of Psychoanalytic Psychotherapy, 10*, 293–317.

Gans, J. S. (1992). Money and psychodynamic group psychotherapy. *International Journal of Group Psychotherapy, 42*, 133–152.

Gans, J. S., & Weber, R. (2000). The detection of shame in group psychotherapy: Uncovering the hidden emotion. *International Journal of Group Psychotherapy, 50*, 381–396.

Hahn, W. (1994). Resolving shame in group psychotherapy. *International Journal of Group Therapy, 44*, 449–461.

Lazare, A. (1997). Shame, humiliation, and stigma in the medical interview. In M. R. Lansky & A. P. Morrison (Eds.), *The widening scope of shame* (pp. 383–396). Hillsdale, NJ: Analytic Press.

Lear, T. E. (1990). Shameful encounters, alienation, and healing restitution in the group. *Group Analysis, 23*, 155–161. doi:10.1177/0533316490232007

Lewis, H. B. (1987). *The role of shame in symptom formation*. Hillsdale, NJ: Erlbaum.

Livingston, L. R. (2006). No place to hide: The group leader's moments of shame. *International Journal of Group Psychotherapy, 56*, 307–323. doi:10.1521/ijgp.2006.56.3.307

MacNab, R. T. (1995). Public exposure of shame in the group leader. In M. B. Sussman (Ed.), *A perilous calling: The hazards of psychotherapy practice* (pp. 115–124). New York, NY: Wiley.

Morrison, A. P. (1990). Secrets: A self-psychological view of shame in group therapy. In W. N. Stone, B. E. Roth, & H. D. Kibel (Eds.), *The difficult patient in group: Group psychotherapy with borderline and narcissistic disorders* (pp. 175–189). Madison, CT: International Universities Press.

Rutan, J. S., & Stone, W. N. (1993). *Psychodynamic group therapy*. New York, NY: Guilford Press.

Shapiro, E. L., & Ginzberg, R. (2006). Buried treasure: Money, ethics and counter-transference in group therapy. *International Journal of Group Psychotherapy, 56,* 477–494. doi:10.1521/ijgp.2006.56.4.477

Tantam, D. (1990). Shame and groups. *Group Analysis, 23,* 31–43. doi:10.1177/0533316490231003

Tuckman, B. W. (1965). Developmental sequence in small groups. *Psychological Bulletin, 63,* 384–399. doi:10.1037/h0022100

Weber, R., & Gans, J. S. (2003). The group therapist's shame: A much undiscussed topic. *International Journal of Group Psychotherapy, 53,* 395–416. doi:10.1521/ijgp.53.4.395.42833

Yalom, I. (1985). *The theory and practice of group psychotherapy.* New York, NY: Basic Books.

6

SHAME IN FAMILIES: TRANSMISSION ACROSS GENERATIONS

EDWARD TEYBER, FAITH H. McCLURE, AND ROBERT WEATHERS

There is a well-developed literature about the role of parental rejection, excessive criticism, denigration, persistent and attacking invalidation, perfectionistic standards, and the development of a toxic, shame-based sense of self. We believe toxic shame, or a shame-prone sense of self, is interpersonally derived. More specifically, children develop a shame-based sense of self when their attachment figure communicates contempt for them, overtly or covertly. With great appreciation of this rich literature, we wish to draw on the attachment and intersubjective traditions (Beebe & Lachman, 2002; Holmes, 2001; Kohut, 1977; Mahler, Pine, & Bergman, 1975; Schore, 2001, 2003; Slade, 2000; Stern, 1985, 2004; Stolorow, 2007) to further highlight aspects of shame dynamics using an extended family case study.

Our clinical vignette provides a framework for illustrating how to work with shame in a family context. First, we show the shame dynamics that become evident during the initial family interview. We then use a relational perspective to explore how attachment and attunement influence the development of shame. Using the case study, we demonstrate how an empathic, compassionate therapeutic stance is essential to establishing a strong working relationship. We illustrate how to uncover the early origins of shame and the potential for shame to be perpetuated within families. Finally, we provide specific techniques for healing individual and family-based shame, such as providing general psychoeducation, teaching emotion regulation strategies, helping clients become more self-compassionate, and guiding clients to be more attuned to one another's emotions. The goal of these intervention strategies is to establish healthier family dynamics wherein each family member becomes more attentive and responsive to the needs of the individual members and to the family as a whole.

SHAME DYNAMICS IN THE INITIAL FAMILY INTERVIEW

Five-year-old Sam had come to therapy at our center after being expelled from his second kindergarten placement. Prior to kindergarten, Sam had attended and been expelled from numerous preschools. His adoptive parents had sought therapy in the past and reported seeing several previous therapists, all of whom had worked extensively on behavior management and parenting skills with the family. Despite these good interventions that would help many children, Sam's significant symptoms remained unchanged because his core, shame-based sense of self remained unaddressed and afire.

Sam's parents had little belief that therapy would be helpful, especially the father, Joe. However, the staff at the school district in which they were trying to get Sam placed wanted him and the family to be in treatment as part of Sam's school placement plan and indicated that they had worked with our facility. Sam's mother, Jane, while also skeptical, seemed more receptive to therapy. During the initial assessment, Joe indicated that he simply *made* Sam behave when he was at home. Although he denied using physical force, he clearly "had a temper" and said Sam just "knew" never to misbehave when he was home. He clearly expressed being furious that Sam kept acting out. Joe was exasperated that he was called to the school frequently about Sam's aggressive and defiant behavior.

Jane said she tried "so hard" to do the right things yet constantly felt blamed by teachers and others (including her mother and extended family) for Sam's acting out behavior. She felt that she was failing as a mother and was mortified by her own mother's injunctions that it was her job to just "make him behave." She said her mother would sometimes state, "What's wrong with you? Can't you see that he is embarrassing our entire family? Why can't you do anything with him?" Her mother's shaming evoked core messages she had heard as a girl and was compounded by Jane's own feeling that many of Sam's preschool teachers agreed with her mother that it was a "mother's job" to make a child behave. Jane clearly believed that she was failing as a mother and also expressed the feeling that she thought all the preschools Sam had attended had wanted their family to just "go away." She often felt overwhelmed, and although not actively suicidal, she often did just want to "go away" herself. She acknowledged a period earlier in life when she had struggled with suicidal ideation and had engaged in restrictive eating behavior and excessive concern about grooming and presentation. Now, her focus was on presentation as a mother, and she felt great shame that she was failing at this significant role.

Sam, a physically large boy, was frequently teased because he was often encopretic and enuretic. He also had not grasped basic academic skills, such as counting to 20 or reciting the alphabet, despite having an excellent spoken vocabulary. Sam was adopted at age 3 by Joe and Jane—they were unable to have children, and Sam was about to be removed permanently from his extremely neglectful, drug-involved mother when they decided to adopt him.

During the family portion of the therapy intake, Sam engaged in play until he was asked if he knew why he was at the center, at which time he stopped play, looked at his adoptive parents, put his thumb in his mouth, and began to rock back and forth. It was heartbreaking to feel the pain underlying this regressive behavior. The question might have inadvertently triggered Sam's shame. It is possible that coming to therapy had been presented as something the family was being forced to do because of Sam's "shameful" behavior—his fighting and rebellious conduct that had led to his frequent dismissals from previous school settings. After giving his parents the opportunity to respond should they wish to, the therapist acknowledged that this might be "hard and maybe even scary to talk about just now" and transitioned to an activity that was less threatening for Sam.

At this point, Joe said, "Tell him how bad you are at school so we have to come and take you home all the time; how you don't listen and get into trouble." Sam's rocking behavior escalated at this point, and the therapist, looking at Sam, said, "It has been hard to let others know what you need or what you feel without getting into trouble. Perhaps we can be partners and figure this out together so you can get into less trouble." Similarly, feeling empathy for the parents' potential shaming experiences at being called in to the school, the therapist said, "I'm sure this has been a challenging time. I hope we can find ways to help you and Sam be together as a family in the way you were hoping for, so you can each understand what the other is trying to communicate. You are here today, and I see that as hopeful. Let's partner together in working on a plan that will help Sam's school and home adjustment."

It appeared that this family had felt blamed for Sam's problems, felt that they had failed in their ability to effect lasting change, and would clearly need intervention in several modalities, including family therapy. Joe's anger and hostility were evident in his dismissive "Yeah, let's see if you can do any better than the others," and Jane's need to present well was echoed in her "We have tried our best, he just won't listen or try." The therapist, feeling empathy for all and wanting to acknowledge their discouragement, yet also wanting to instill some hope said, "This has not been easy. We do need a partnership to make progress. Let's agree to a limited number of sessions. If you do not find it helpful, I will be happy to meet with you and the principal to convey that information. I am also happy to go with you to your first scheduled IEP [individualized educational plan] meeting and join with you as you work on how to proceed with Sam's school plan if you like, regardless of whether you decide to continue with treatment after that IEP."

Addressing immediate concrete needs (while recognizing that deeper shame-based issues were central and in play for all) seemed to be an important place to form an initial alliance. This was especially urgent because this family had already felt ostracized by teachers and administrative personnel in other educational settings. The idea here was that, strategically, the family might benefit from initially building success experiences around concrete needs being met before delving any further into possible underlying family dynamics of shame, self-blame, and frustration. With this idea in mind, we agreed to an initial 8-week treatment phase that later was extended (at the time this case was written, Sam and his family had been seen in treatment for close to a year).

Thus, in the initial intake, it appeared that this was a family in turmoil with a deeply troubled child. Sam had overt behavioral problems, including bullying, temper tantrums, kicking, biting, refusing to follow directions, breaking toys, and sometimes breaking furniture. He was labeled "bad and disruptive" by teachers, his parents, and most adults he interacted with. Sam had no friends at school. It appeared likely that shame played a significant role in Sam's behavioral problems—his symptoms escalated significantly whenever he was criticized, chastised, or asked to complete a task that he felt was beyond his ability. He became emotionally and behaviorally volatile, often yelled profanity and threw things angrily when distressed, and now, sadly, was an ostracized and rejected child. Few kids wanted to play with him, and most adults were quick to find fault with him.

In addition to his emotional and behavioral problems, Sam was made fun of at school for being behind academically—he was laughed at for being "stupid." This often coincided with an episode of either enuresis or encopresis or both, which resulted in further ridicule and humiliation. The enuresis and encopresis were problems at home, too, and the family had been given guidance about dealing with them that had not been useful and had actually led to increasing distress. For example, they were told to show him how to clean up and then to ignore him when he had episodes of enuresis or encopresis and to instruct him to clean up on his own. Unfortunately, this dynamically replayed Sam's history of neglect. Because of prior severe maltreatment (including being ignored while soiled), Sam needed parental support as he cleaned up. His enuresis and encopresis typically escalated during times of distress and did abate when a new approach to cleaning up was designed. In the new approach, he was not shamed, and his mom simply focused on how well he was doing on cleanup and then quickly transitioned to a new activity so that time spent on cleanup was minimized (increasing the number of parent–child pleasant activities not focused on soiling). Given Sam's history of severe neglect and overt rejection, his problems (including his inability to modulate his affect or behavior, evidenced by his shame, rage, and aggressive behavior, for example) made sense, and it was clear that he and his family would need substantial intervention.

The family's relationships with each other also had elements of shame. Sam's acting out at school had led his father to begin telling him he was a "bad boy" and barking, "What's wrong with you?" His mother's pleas to Sam were, "Honey, why can't you just stop this; can't you see how you are embarrassing our family?" Their shame around Sam's behavior extended to their relationship with the school to the point that they did not want to return calls from the school. Clearly, shame dynamics were at play for all three members of this family, leaving them vulnerable and significantly at risk. As an alliance was established, therapy, strategically administered over time, would need to address shame dynamics as they affected the individuals, the family, and their relationships with each other and with the world at large.

HOW SHAME DEVELOPS: ATTACHMENT AND ATTUNEMENT

As noted by several prominent writers, children's sense of who they are—their "selves"—is embedded in the level of caregiver attunement or sensitivity (Beebe & Lachman, 2002; Kohut, 1977; Mahler et al., 1975; Schore, 2001, 2003; Stern, 1985, 2004). The match between the child's needs and the parents' perceptive and appropriate responses is critical not only to the child's sense of who he or she is, but also to the child's long-term ability to orient, organize, and engage in effective self-regulation (Lieberman & Van Horn, 2008; Putnam, 1995, 2005; Schore, 2003). Parents' sensitive, affectively attuned responses serve as orienting "compasses." That is, the compass provided by the parents' responses lets the child know what is appropriate and not appropriate. Importantly, it also conveys to the child that he or she is secure in the parents' love, is worthy of that love, will not be abandoned, and will be kept safe. This core communication is foundational to the child's sense of self, and without it children are at risk of negative outcomes, including a shame-prone self. That is, should children lack this secure and attuned foundation and then experience maltreatment in the form of abuse and ridicule, the trajectory to a shame-based self is set in motion (Stolorow, 2007). A pioneer in this field, Erik Erikson (1950), also identified shame as an outcome of parent–child problems in early life. According to Erikson, when primary, foundational trust between infant and caregiver is compromised, the developmental seeds of shame take root in that child's nascent sense of self.

Thus, when children experience trauma, chaos, and disorder, and when they lack responsiveness and consistent nurturing, this exacerbates the likelihood of shame proneness. In Sam's case, as an infant and toddler, he lacked safety and consistent nurturing. More bluntly, he experienced profound contempt, active hostility, and overt rejection. For the first 3 years of his life, he lived with an extremely neglectful biological mother who was addicted to methamphetamine; he never knew his biological father. Social worker reports indicated that on numerous occasions they were called to his home to find his mother in a drug-induced haze and Sam in feces-soaked diapers on the floor of a filthy trailer. He would be removed from the home and placed in foster care, and then his mother would "clean up" and present with a family member who would agree to help with Sam's care. Unfortunately, she often took Sam from the family member, and family members did not report this to the social worker, in part because they too were burdened with their own extensive child care responsibilities. It appears that despite the intervention by social services, Sam still lived a substantial portion of his first 3 years with his mother. She frequently had men in and out of the house who used drugs with her, so Sam may have experienced other types of abuse from these men, including physical abuse and possibly sexual violation.

As noted by many, early trauma has significant impact on attachment as well as on self-regulation (Fonagy & Target, 1997, 2002; Hofer, 2004; Putnam, 2005; Schore, 2003; Sroufe, 2005; see also Chapter 11, this volume). Sam's ability to self-organize (which is central to both affect and behavioral regulation) was greatly compromised and left him at great risk of acting out. In terms of regulating affect, Sam's problem was highly evidenced in his inability to regulate shame and rage. Sam often expressed deep and unrelenting shame. This painful affect, which can involve feelings of defectiveness, inferiority, emptiness, powerlessness, vulnerability, and painful exposure, is especially difficult for traumatized children like Sam. By virtue of both its affective intensity and its absolute unmanageability, there is simply no way for the child to "turn off the spigot" of overwhelming inner suffering. During outbursts, Sam would throw objects he had in his hand (a book, toy, mechanical tool, kitchen utensil, art object, anything within reach). His adoptive family soon learned not to have prized objects in plain view. The literature also suggests that shame can involve thoughts of being inadequate, incompetent, lacking in substance, and lacking in worth. Sam was especially volatile when told he was "dumb" or asked to engage in a task he felt he would fail at. The literature indicates further that these shame affects and cognitions, because they can become so intolerable, often evoke defensive reactions and can result in blaming or attacking someone or even hurting oneself. As described in more detail later, Sam's dysregulation was evident in his aggressive behavior when he was made to feel incompetent, inadequate, or worthless.

Schore (2003) suggested that abused children are so frequently recipients of humiliation and shame that "dissociated rage" and "shame–rage" are often associated outcomes. It seemed that Sam's core identity had been so gravely affected by his early abusive experiences that his ability to self-regulate was deeply damaged. This impaired ability to self-regulate emotionally and behaviorally was having disastrous effects on his relationships. Although he very much wanted to make friends, it was difficult for him to not engage in aggressive behavior when shamed by peers. His inner disruptedness and faulty attempts at "feeling better" poured involuntarily into most sustained interpersonal interactions, hence alienating him from the very experiences of being liked and cared for that might serve as healing balm for the pain flooding him within. For example, when teased or not included in an activity (e.g., not chosen as a player early in a game), Sam would explode verbally and/or lunge at whoever was around with whatever "instrument" he had in his hand (e.g., book, toy, pencil, scissors). Other studies have similarly noted that shame and shame proneness contribute to often profound interpersonal difficulties and myriad other psychological problems (Balcom, 1991; Cook, 1991; Gilbert, Pehl, & Allan, 1994; Gramzow & Tangney, 1992; Grosch, 1994; Murray & Waller, 2002; Wells, Bruss, & Katrin, 1998; Wong & Cook, 1992).

In addition to Sam's difficulties with shame, Joe and Jane came from families in which they had been expected, within chronically stressful family contexts, to behave in particular ways. Joe had been shamed by his frequently inebriated father, who physically abused him and was denigrating toward him. Jane had been shamed by her persistently critical and rejecting, emotionally unavailable mother. Sadly, the "cycle" of shame transmission was likely to be continued inadvertently unless they got help stepping back, looking more objectively on the process they were enacting with Sam, and thinking through how they wished to proceed. They needed help becoming "observers" or "witnesses" of the process that was unfolding in their family and understanding that they could prevent the shame legacy from being passed on.

WORKING WITH SHAME IN FAMILY THERAPY

Creating a Safe Environment and Connecting With the Client

Peter Fonagy and his colleagues (e.g., Allen, Fonagy, & Bateman, 2008) wrote eloquently about the importance of helping parents have the child's "mind in mind" (p. 7)—helping parents learn to be more reflective and think about the child and the child's mental state, experience, or intentions—what might be going on inside for the child. A parallel process is required from the therapist. The therapist must be able to "hold in mind" the individual and collective family members' experience, especially their shame, as fully as possible with understanding and great sensitivity. *Mentalization,* a term coined by Fonagy and colleagues to describe the experience of having the other's "mind in mind," thus involves entering the client's experience as fully as possible so the therapist can understand, empathize, and articulate for the client what that experience is, including the deeply felt shame experienced by the client. Stolorow, Brandchaft, and Atwood (2000) used and honed a similar clinical concept in their intersubjective focus—*sustained empathic inquiry*— whose one goal is to provide the client with an experience of being known radically and completely. One central aim, then, is for the therapist to constantly clarify with the client whether those thoughts, feelings, memories, impulses, and sensations that are being identified within therapy are indeed the very ones being experienced by the client.

One key corollary of this clinical approach, or better "posture" or "attitude," is that when shame is involved, the therapist needs to sustain inner, felt connection to himself or herself to ensure that he or she is not flooded with his or her own shame. The abiding aim here is for the therapist to be able to provide a safe environment in which the client can explore more fully and articulate more coherently his or her own shame. Thus, the therapist needs to be sensitively attuned (emotionally present, attending, tracking cues, listening actively, conveying empathy) and to help the client clarify what is going on regarding the client's own shame. If the therapist is activated and becomes preoccupied with his or her own shame, the therapist's own capacities to provide such nonimpositional attentiveness will be severely diminished. There are times when the behavior the client is exhibiting may on the surface *look* a certain way; however, an attuned therapist (attentive, responsive, tracking verbal and nonverbal cues) will help the client clarify what underlying shame-based issues might need to be addressed.

The following is an example from Sam's case illustrating the actual process of implementing such attuned therapy in the presence of family dynamics revolving around shame. Sam was in the playroom putting a puzzle together.

> Mom: Sam, pay attention; you keep making the same mistakes on that. I'm afraid for you—try to pay attention. *[Sam ignores mom and continues to play]* Sam, can't you even do a little puzzle right? I'm afraid for you, what will others think? *[starts to take over doing the puzzle]* Do it like this, Sam.
>
> Sam: Why?
>
> Mom: Because that's the right way.

Sam:	Why?
Mom:	Just do things right for once, Sam; just once!
Therapist:	Doing things right is really important to you—there's something really important about doing things wrong and being made to feel stupid that matters here. Can you tell me and Sam what is so important about that?
Mom:	People will judge you. People will say you are an idiot. You just always have to do things right!
Therapist:	Right now, in here, who will judge you and Sam if the puzzle is not just right?
Mom:	If he doesn't do it right, you will think I don't teach him very well, that I'm not a good mother, that I don't show him how to do things right.
Therapist:	So, you feel judged even in here by me—you feel on performance all the time?
Mom:	Yes! I'm always having to perform, always having to do it right!
Therapist:	What a huge burden you carry—and it sounds as though you have the same perfectly high standards for Sam.
Mom:	[crying] But shouldn't I always be making sure he is doing it right? Don't we always have to do things just right, or people will judge us badly?
Therapist:	Judgment by others is a big problem in your life.
Mom:	Yeah, I've always been judged. I'm always told I'm not doing it right, I'm a failure.
Therapist:	Judged as a failure by many people and made to feel inadequate.
Mom:	Yes, a failure . . . I just want to hide at times. My mother was always telling me that if I just tried harder, did more . . . I'd be a better daughter, a better wife, a better mother. As far as my mother is concerned, I am a failure . . . and everyone else probably thinks so, too.
Therapist:	Do you think that I believe you are a failure?
Mom:	How could you not?
Therapist:	So here, too, you feel you have to do things right for me?
Mom:	I have to correct Sam so . . . I guess . . . I can show you that I'm not a failure as a mother.

Therapist: Jane, how painful it must be in here, where you are trying so hard to learn how to listen to and respond to Sam's needs, that you are worried about my judgment of you. That I, like everyone else in your life, will shame you and judge you as a failing mother.

Mom: [sobbing] That's what it always is.

Therapist: I understand that and am sorry to see that you expect the same from me here.

Mom: Yes, you haven't done that yet, but you must be thinking that inside. I am trying the best I can.

Therapist: Yes, Jane, I see that you want to do the best you can, and I'm not thinking that inside. Actually, I'm thinking that it is your fear of failing with me and everyone else that is partly affecting your relationship with Sam.

Mom: Yes, I keep telling him to do things right because I'm afraid I will be judged if he fails.

Therapist: So you feel like you are failing . . . and it really is a big fear that *you* will be judged—so in turn, you keep telling Sam he has to do things right?

Mom: Yes, I hadn't thought of things like that before, but I get what you're suggesting. I'm trying to get him to do things right so I won't be told I'm failing and won't feel like a failure. I'm judging him like I've been judged. I'm asking him to perform like I'm performing.

Therapist: You are being insightful and just captured that so well. Why don't you sit with those thoughts for a while? Then we can spend some time thinking about how can you help Sam so he doesn't feel like you do—that he has to perform perfectly or he is a failure.

Mom: OK; I know what I'm doing isn't working. [after a few moments of reflective silence] I don't know where to start, but I don't want to do to him what was done to me.

Therapist: Great. Let him know that what you have done in correcting him so often is based on what you have had in the past—that you yell and get mad because that happened to you, and you want to learn to talk and teach him without yelling like you were yelled at.

Mom: Sam, I yell, I don't listen, I make you feel bad because that is how I was raised. I want to try to talk and teach you without yelling and calling you stupid or dumb.

Therapist:	Great, Jane. Sam, Mom grew up with people who made her feel bad, and she sometimes finds herself saying things that make you feel bad—she wants to change that. We are going to work together to change that.
Mom:	I feel like I'm a bad mother.
Sam:	I feel like I'm a bad boy.
Mom:	You aren't a bad boy.
Sam:	But that's what the teacher and you say when you get mad at me.
Mom:	Sam, I need to yell less. Nana [Sam's name for Jane's mother] yelled at me a lot. I want to yell less and listen more. [At this point, Sam takes the puzzle over to her and asks her to help him put it together.]

In this vignette, two issues became evident. One was the multigenerational transmission of shame—Jane's history of being judged was being repeated in her judging Sam. In this way, Sam was likely to develop a sense of "badness" very similar to that of his mother's. In fact, without intervention, this pattern of "handed-down" shame might very well continue on to "infecting" even future generations within the family. Second, although on the surface Jane expressed concern that Sam would be seen as stupid and a failure if he didn't do things right, what was most significant was *her* underlying feeling of being a failure as a mother. Via a process of projecting onto her son her own worst fears, she was perhaps attempting an antidote, though unsuccessfully, to resolve her own shame—something along the lines of, "If I can at least ensure that my son performs at such-and-such a standard of behavior, then that would surely mean I am a good mother, or even a good person."

A Note About Therapist Shame

As noted, it is extremely important that therapists working with individuals and families for whom shame is a primary affect be self-aware and possess a sufficient amount of psychological security (or support from a colleague or supervisor) that they do not become flooded with their own shame. Why? Because this therapeutic engagement around shame issues involves "being" with another in a nondefensive and fully present way. Therefore, it is indeed essential to connect with the client emotionally and to provide a consistent milieu of personal safety that allows the client to process his or her multiple layers of emotions in tolerable doses, "titrating" the shame, as it were. The therapist needs to be able to engage with the client fully and grasp the client's experience in a benevolent, caring, and accepting way so that the client can, with a connected and validating other, work through issues that have limited initiative and mastery in his or her life. Shame, because it goes to the core self, requires the ability to connect at a deep intersubjective level. Many relationally oriented, developmentally grounded theorists and therapists write eloquently about therapists' need to be able to self-regulate or tolerate their own affects, especially shame, that are routinely activated when therapists feel with and join clients in experiencing difficult emotions (Allen & Fonagy, 2006; Schore, 2003; Stern, 2004). The hope is that clients who have experienced the therapist's attuned presence and validation of their authentic self will be able to internalize the therapist's "regulatory" or "reorganizing" presence. This reparative experience, what self psychologists call *transmuting internalization*, provides clients over time with the ability to better tolerate stress, have greater emotional range, and be more cognitively and behaviorally flexible.

Helping the Client Feel Understood

Back then to our case. Late one morning, Jane called after a crisis at Sam's school and asked if the therapist had an opening to meet with her that afternoon, during which the following dialogue took place.

> *Jane:* I was called to the school today—Sam threw a book at the teacher and called her an f-ing bitch. He was trying to get her attention while they were getting ready to leave for a class outing, and she was busy attending to other things. He apparently yelled her name louder and louder because he said he needed to go to the bathroom and then threw the book. I don't know what to do. I haven't told Joe. They want a meeting tomorrow. I don't know if they will let him stay at the school.

> *Therapist:* You sound pretty upset right now; I'm glad you called. We'll figure this out together. Let's talk first about how you are feeling right now.

> *Jane:* I'm so mad at Sam—I don't know what Joe will say. I know my mom will tell me how useless I am at controlling Sam. The teacher already said I needed to do a better job of teaching Sam to restrain himself—that he's so disrespectful because I'm too easy on him. I feel so ashamed. And I'm sure Joe will say the same thing—that I'm not firm enough, and so I guess that's why I'm failing.

> *Therapist:* You keep coming back to "failing"—that's the theme for you. It sounds as though, when Sam acts out, you almost immediately take that as evidence that you are failing as a

	mom. And you mention feeling ashamed—how painful that must be for you right now.
Jane:	*[crying]* I feel so inadequate. I keep failing. My mom was probably right; I am just worthless. So, how do I make a 5-year-old behave? Tell me what I'm doing wrong.
Therapist:	It sounds like you feel responsible for all of it—that you alone are culpable, and you are responsible for making all the change happen. That's a pretty large burden.
Jane:	But it is my responsibility.
Therapist:	Yours alone? What a staggering responsibility for one person. Feeling that you *should* have the power to change it all, while at the same time feeling so powerless to actually change it all.
Jane:	Yes, it's driving me crazy.
Therapist:	It makes sense to me that you are feeling overwhelmed. I'm glad you are sharing these feelings with me, and maybe we can be partners in figuring out what to do next. It sure would be a lot to feel responsible for alone.
Jane:	I do feel overwhelmed, and alone; that's why I called you. But, yes, I see how I set unrealistic expectations, and doom myself to fail, and end up feeling like a failure.
Therapist:	I'm glad you came. Why don't you be with those expectations for a minute and think about how they affect how you interact with Sam.
Jane:	Because I feel like a failure as a mom, I either get harder on Sam and become more critical and harsher with him, or I feel overwhelmed and just withdraw from him. Like today—I just can't talk to him. I'll just scream if I talk to him. I could hardly listen to the teacher when she was telling me how awful Sam was today and that we needed to implement something or he would have to leave the school. I just can't keep hearing what a terrible mother I am.
Therapist:	I'm so glad you risked coming to talk with me. I think it is a way you are getting better and acting stronger. Is there anything I could do differently to make this easier, or feel safer, for you?
Jane:	You know, I called you because I thought you wouldn't tell me I was a bad mom. You didn't seem judgmental the time I was yelling at Sam about the puzzle, or the other times I yelled at him, so I thought it would be OK to tell you about something that went wrong.
Therapist:	Good, but let's keep working on safety here in our relationship. Is there anything else that might help?

Jane:	I don't know. I think you understand that I do want the best for Sam, so that helps.
Therapist:	Yes, Jane, I think you are trying very hard to figure out how to be a good mother. Your feelings of being overwhelmed suggest to me that you are taking your responsibility of being a parent very seriously. You feel like a failure when they call, but that is also in part because you so desperately want to do well by him. I do see how much you want to be the best parent you can be.
Jane:	Thank you for seeing that; I do want to be a good parent.
Therapist:	I see and hear that very clearly. *[after a while]* How are you feeling right now? Where have you landed?
Jane:	It helps to have you see that my overwhelmed response is partly because I care so much about being a good parent.
Therapist:	I'm glad we can share that together—I do see how much you care about being a good parent.
Jane:	I think I'd like to talk through with you a plan for talking to the school tomorrow. Can we do that?

In this session, Jane was able to begin to "reset her compass" in a way that gave her a better sense of direction, order, and organization. Being held in the mind of another (now, the therapist), one who grasped the core feelings at the root of her daily suffering as a mother, began to transform her deepest sense of who she is, as a mother, a wife, the individual human being she truly is. She began to gradually internalize the empathically attuned, nonjudgmental, encouraging stance of her therapist into her own recalibrating self-sense. She felt affirmed and more secure. The therapist hoped that this would allow her to have a more autonomously chosen voice and to become more connected to herself and to others.

Exploring the Origins of Client Shame

Several attachment researchers and relationally oriented clinicians have written powerfully about the significance of affect-filled attunement in helping children and others develop organization physiologically, emotionally, cognitively, and behaviorally (Greenspan & Wieder, 1998; Stern, 1985; Stolorow et al., 2000). Central to the phenomenology of shame is the way it overwhelms all other aspects of the self and "swamps out" self-organization and affect regulation. As clients resolve their shame proneness, self-organization reactivates, and the client's sense of personal ambition and vitality—what Heinz Kohut (1977) called one's *nuclear program*, or what James Masterson (1985, 1988) called *autonomy*—is manifested behaviorally in increased goal directedness, experienced self-congruence, and personal integrity. Family therapy is unique in that it provides the opportunity to work on misattunement and shame with parents, who themselves have become a source of affective misattunement (to their children and significant others), likely because they did not experience attuned responses in their families of origin.

In our clinical example, Sam's father Joe learned early to "behave or else." His often-inebriated father abused him and his mother both physically and emotionally. His father degraded him by calling him worthless, stupid, "a good for nothing weakling" as he shoved and hit him. Joe learned early to be "tough" and show few emotions. This sternness became a part of his persona, and he acknowledged having difficulty sustaining warmth and nurturance for fear that he would be caught "off guard and hurt." So he had difficulty sustaining warmth with Sam and thought that the strict "do as I say" was the right way to go. One can readily see how this posture may have served as an attempted antidote to Joe's fears of being further shamed (cf. Brandchaft, in press). Joe believed that this was the way to get and sustain his son's respect. He believed his job was to always be in charge and in control. The shame below his exterior of control was too threatening for him to risk having it emerge. In the playroom, for example, when Sam and Joe were interacting, Joe often gave Sam stern looks when he didn't follow directions, and Jane often intervened to mediate the play. An example of Joe's struggle with issues of "disrespect" was illustrated by an exchange that occurred as Jane and Joe observed Sam in the playroom. Sam was playing aggressively with "pirates" who were in a fierce battle, and swords were flying around the playroom.

> Joe: Sam, keep those more controlled. You almost hit me with that sword.
>
> Sam: [ignoring Joe] Shoosh! Watch out you one-eyed monster, here I come!
>
> Joe: Stop that right now. That sword hit my shoe!
>
> Jane: Play more carefully, Sam. Here, let's move more to this side.
>
> Sam: Yahoo! Come on, matey, let's get that one-eyed Andy! [Now the pirate is demolished, a familiar theme in Sam's play.]
>
> Joe: Start to put things away! If you can't be respectful and listen, you'll just have put everything away.
>
> Jane: Sam! Listen. Do what your Dad says.
>
> Joe: [his voice getting louder] See how disobedient he is? This just can't be allowed!

Jane quickly began to help Sam put things way. Joe glowered at Sam, who withdrew to a corner, picked up a toy, and put his thumb in his mouth.

In this interaction, Joe's activation around disrespect is quickly noted. We can see how shame, even if out of his conscious awareness, led him to react and dictate to Sam in order for Joe to self-regulate. Sam's play around the fight and pirate interaction likely was a form of communication that might have helped the family learn more about him. But Joe's own shame, and the anxiety that accompanied it, barred him from being able to empathically attune to Sam's symbolic communication. Rather, Joe got caught in a concrete battle of wills with his son, thereby missing an opportunity to connect with him and perhaps heal part of the son's own increasingly shame-based sense of self. Predictably, as Joe got angrier, Sam's regressive behavior became more marked.

Therapist: Sam, you look scared when Dad gets mad.

Joe: [bellowing] He has to listen! [At this point, Sam is rocking back and forth.]

Therapist: I agree. Respect is very important, but he seems more fearful than disrespectful to me right now.

Joe: So what? He's not being beaten. There's nothing to be fearful about! Fear is when a drunk dad beats the shit out of you. Stop being such a sissy.

Therapist: Joe, it seems like there is something really important that we need to hear here—about respect, and about fear. Can you tell us more so we can understand better?

Joe: My dad beat the shit out of me and told me that he was doing it so I would not be a little sissy. Well, he thinks he showed me who was the boss when he beat me. Sure, I feared him, but I'm damned if I would give that a-hole the pleasure of knowing that I was afraid. [turning to Sam] Do you hear that, boy?

Therapist: Joe, you are saying you became someone who hid your fear. Does that mean you hide other feelings too? Do you hide tenderness and loving feelings?

Joe: What do you mean?

Therapist: I'm just wondering, Joe, if needing to be tough makes it hard to be warm and affectionate also?

Joe: Well . . . maybe . . .

Therapist: So it might be hard to let anyone too close to love you?

Joe: [after a long silence] I guess.

Therapist: How does your dad's abuse of you continue to affect your relationship with Sam and Jane? What is the impact of living in the shadow of your dad's abuse?

Joe:	I want that bastard out of my life.
Therapist:	That makes sense. How is he influencing your life right now?
Joe:	Well, as we talk, I see that I act like him sometimes. I yell too much. I shut off feelings.
Therapist:	Those are big statements, Joe. You act like your dad sometimes. You yell too much. You shut off feelings.
Joe:	Yeah, like right now, I get so pissed off when I feel Sam doesn't respect me, and I yell, just like my dad. I don't beat him, but I easily could. I just hold back. I don't really want to scare the kid. I just want respect.
Therapist:	Does your dad have your respect?
Joe:	Hell, no!
Therapist:	You describe him as very abusive, Joe. I can see how you do not have respect for him.
Joe:	He was an abusive SOB. I was scared but never showed it.
Therapist:	Given how he abused and scared you as a child, it makes sense to me that he doesn't have your respect.
Joe:	Yeah, I was afraid of him as a child, really afraid.
Therapist:	That must have been hard, since you had to hide your fear.
Joe:	Yeah, but I managed. The SOB wanted me to be afraid and ashamed. I want Sam's respect, though, not his fear.
Therapist:	Yes, Joe, I hear that. You want respect, yet what I see is fear in Sam—he is scared when you yell. Let's first help Sam understand why you yell and together find a way to develop respect between the two of you—without the shame that has hurt both of you so much.
Joe:	[to Sam] I yell because that's how I was raised, and I suppose I don't know how to do it better. But I do want you to respect me. I hear that I make you scared instead. My dad made me scared, too. [Sam nods.]
Therapist:	Sam is hearing you better as you talk more calmly, gently— he is listening. [to Sam] Dad yells, and it scares you. Dad wants respect, and you want less yelling. Let's try to figure out how we can get Dad the respect he wants, and get you less yelling and maybe more fun playing with Dad. How would that be? [Sam nods.]

The therapist started slowly rolling one ball toward Sam and gestured that he roll it toward his Dad. As they continued talking and rolling the ball in a circle to each person in the playroom, they talked about "attunement" to each others' needs and how sensitivity to each others' needs is communicated and responded to, especially when shame dynamics are activated.

How Shame Can Be Passed on From One Generation to the Next

This vignette illustrates how easily behavior once experienced (here, the abuse and yelling Joe had experienced as a form of control) subsequently translates to the next generation and had great negative impact on Sam. If Sam's response in the playroom was to be so regressive (thumb sucking and rocking), it was no wonder that he had problems with enuresis and encopresis—he was clearly a shame-filled and often terrified young boy. Parents' ability to understand accurately children's signals and respond to these accurately is critical to children's appropriate development. Helping parents become more reflective and keep the children's needs in mind is a key goal here. Adults who have not been appropriately responded to in childhood are often also flooded with feelings and may need therapists to assist them in understanding their own "wounded" histories (i.e., by providing empathy). Further, therapists need to be a "secure base" for these parents, and from this space the parents can become a secure base for their children (Berlin, Ziv, Amaya-Jackson, & Greenberg, 2005).

The Importance of Not Ignoring Shame

Bromberg (2006) discussed the therapeutic value of processing relational experiences (especially with shame) with a receptive other in the present. He emphasized the importance of providing safety in the "here and now" of the therapeutic relationship. Bromberg noted that shame needs to be approached and addressed; otherwise, it is given "legitimacy." (One might say, colloquially, that we can't exorcise the demon shame until we can name it.) Therapists who comply with familial and cultural prescriptions to avoid shame inadvertently collude with the client's shame and make it seem reasonable and acceptable. Here it is evident how absolutely essential to effective, shame-ameliorating therapy it is that the therapist has worked through any significant shame-based psychological issues in his or her own life. Otherwise, the potential, and damaging, "blind spot" of not seeing, or not commenting upon, in vivo shame within the therapy hour is likely to play out unhelpfully or countertherapeutically with one client or family after another. It is essential that shame's validity or justification be challenged so that shamed clients can develop a nonshamed internal working model, one of themselves as worthy of being loved, cared about, and affirmed, in their imperfections. The therapist does this, in part, by being able to listen with compassion and to accept the client's shame without reassuring or trying to argue or explain away their pain.

As previously noted, Jane also came from a shaming background and had a very critical mother. Research suggests that criticism may be a far more central cause of shame than previously recognized (Gilbert & Procter, 2006). Jane's mother was frequently depressed, and Jane spent much of her childhood trying to please a mother who was never happy and whose standards she felt she could never meet, so she constantly felt she was failing. As an adult, she continued the people-pleasing style and often felt inadequate and took on blame. It was obvious how challenging it was for her to deal with the school system. It was also obvious how Joe's fear of showing warmth and nurturance made the family environment tense, in general, and more specifically exacerbated Jane's lifelong psychological vulnerabilities around people pleasing in a depressed and critical home environment.

In the context of play, Sam frequently revealed themes of defectiveness and inferiority. His characters were often bad guys, banished to the outskirts, often for damaging or hurtful "crimes" or behavior. In one play session, with his favorite pirates at hand, Sam yelled, "Show me your sword, Bozo! Where are your weapons? I'm going to slay the old drunkard and burn his medals."

Therapist: Oh, are the drunkard's medals getting melted today?

Sam: Hurry, if you don't rush, you'll be slashed too—that mean old fart.

Therapist: Which fart are we getting today?

Sam: The fart that gets drunk and sleeps all day, stinking Grandpa; when he starts snoring, we'll burn his army medals.

Therapist: Burn his medals—you sure are stinking mad!

Sam: Yeah. I wish he would just die, the fat slob.

Therapist: [grabs a character] Did you hear that?

Sam: [speaking to the character] Go to jail, mean slob. I'm going to get you! [grabs a sword and attacks, and then becomes anxious]

Therapist: [(using a calm voice] You are so mad and don't know what to do with your mad feelings right now?

Sam: I hate you, slob, I'm going to burn your medals! [hands the sword to the therapist]

Therapist: You're so, so mad, you could just burn something. It feels like too much. Let me help, I'll hold the sword.

Sam: Fat slob!

Therapist:	Mad feelings when someone hurts you make sense. Do you want to draw mad pictures or hit a baseball or kick the soccer ball?
Sam:	Go kick some butt!
Therapist:	Bash the baseball?
Sam:	Yeah.
Therapist:	OK, let's see how far you can bash those baseballs and let out those mad feelings—how would that be?
Sam:	Yeah, let's go smash those balls. You're on my team!
Therapist:	OK, I choose to be on your team!

The reality was that Sam and the therapist were the only players, but he often was reassured by having a partner or "friend," given his typical isolation in school and other play settings.

Sam often used "bathroom humor" with his characters, and they would get into awful trouble because they used all kinds of bad words. In the context of play, the initial affects were the profound anger ("I'm just going to leave you here to die because you are just a piece of caca") that masked this profound shame (defective, inferior, not worthy of being saved). At other times, the characters would be attacked by ferocious, huge creatures ("I'm going to crush you, you dingbat. Out of my way. Let me see you broken"). Often, as the play became too intense, Sam would hand over to the therapist the most ferocious character, and, as time went on, the crushed, attacked victim. He would say, "You hold him," as though needing containment for his overwhelming feelings. The therapist, in a quiet, calm way, would say, "Yes, let me keep him; he's just too mad and is being hurtful" (when it was the attacker) or "Yes, let me keep him safe" (when it was the victim). This seemed to calm him, as he would lean against the therapist's shoulder, initially for 30 seconds or so and for longer periods as therapy progressed. As time went on and they were more actively mutually engaged in the sessions, Sam became increasingly able to recognize agitation and escalating affect in the characters, and he became better able to talk through the feelings and what was going on for the characters.

Providing Psychoeducation and Feedback

When present, both parents were included and invited to participate; sometimes the sessions were with Sam alone, sometimes with Sam and both parents (when his father's schedule permitted, although often only his mother attended), and sometimes with the parents only. In the parents-only sessions, the therapist often focused on providing some basic child development information to assist Jane and Joe in engaging in developmentally appropriate practices and expectations given Sam's developmental level and early abusive life experiences. These sessions also provided parental guidance such as the importance of communicating with clarity, specificity, directness, warmth, and consistency—experiences that Sam had not received in his early years. Sam also needed his parents to see his behaviors, especially his aggression, as a form of communication and to try to understand what it was he was trying to communicate. The purpose here was aiding the parents to interpret many of Sam's "problem" behaviors as instead representing "protest" (or communicative) behaviors. Often what Sam was attempting to communicate was his profound sense of shame, his inability to express the need for help, his desperation not to be ignored and "unseen," his feeling of terror at being hurt, and so forth. That is, it became helpful to Joe and Jane to recognize that often Sam's acting out was about feelings that were not being appropriately expressed (or heard). They became less blaming and shaming of him, and they less frequently labeled him as "bad" or "stupid." They were less likely to accuse him of being intentionally disrespectful and making them feel like failures as parents. They learned to take far less personally his various ways of making contact and communicating, even when aggressive. Rather, they tried to adopt a more objective standpoint from which they might engage with him more compassionately and with greater empathic attunement.

It also helped to educate the parents about the impact of developmental trauma on brain development and attachment (Lieberman & Van Horn, 2008; Perry & Szalavitz, 2007; Putnam, 2005; Schore, 2003) so they could have greater empathy for his dysregulation—an outcome of feeling so scared and humiliated from being yelled at so frequently and intensely. In addition, they learned to use "I" messages and made sure Sam was being attentive (i.e., at eye level, listening, engaged) when they were interacting with him. Further, to the extent possible, they began providing him with choices (e.g., his clothes for school, one TV show for the day), redirection (e.g., aim the arrow at the tree rather than my shoe), explanations (e.g., if you play with the knife, you can get cut, and that will hurt you), and praise for specific behaviors (e.g., thank you for helping me set the table). The importance of helping Sam learn to reregulate (calm down, soothe) was always stressed. For example, Sam was easily disrupted or activated by noise and did not do well on school outings. Playing ball or engaging in one-on-one activities that had a rhythmic quality were useful in calming him down, and they quickly learned to implement this in their routines (cf. Beebe et al., 2000; Beebe, Stern, & Jaffe, 1979; Condon, 1980; Jaffe & Feldstein, 1970 on the crucial nature of rhythmic, parent–child communicative matching and the gradual internalization of affective self-regulation on the part of the previously dysregulated child).

Sam was also a child who benefited greatly from "when–then" sequences (e.g., "When you are done with your math homework, then we'll go to the park"). He also very much needed routines, needed to be given transitional warnings, and benefited from having his own timer ("In 5 minutes, it will be time to take a bath"). His previous experiences of emotional trauma and shameful interactions with parents left him in a hypervigilant and/or avoidant mental state, one that was positively responsive to sensitively and consistently communicated temporal sequences and predictable, nonshaming routines or transitions (Herman, 1997).

The sessions were also videotaped so that, as needed, we could selectively review the play segments as learning opportunities to further understand Sam's needs, what his behavior was communicating, and how to best respond. There were many examples of situations in which Sam became activated (anxious— "mad" was his word—or, in truth, shamed by something someone had said or done), such as being called "bad," "stinky," or "stupid," or when he was asked to do something that was beyond his ability. His activation could be recognized by his facial expressions and hand gestures, and he frequently moved his body in ways that foreshadowed his distress and often impending rage: a kind of "prodromal" phase prior to the fully visible, shame-based behavioral response. As his parents observed this, they became more sensitive and responsive to these cues and were able to respond and help him manage his distress from escalating, at least in the home environment. Learning from the video playback how to better read his cues helped the parents recognize what evoked Sam's shame-based affect and behavioral acting out and how their own shame-based behavior (i.e., shaming him in response to their own feelings of shame, fear of vulnerability, fear of failing, and so on) often escalated his unwanted behavior, bringing further chaos to their family emotional environment. The use of video feedback to enhance effective parenting has received increasing empirical support in the literature (see Juffer, Bakermans-Kranenburg, & van IJzendoorn, 2008) and was very useful with this family.

Exploring and Accepting the Various Parts and Complexities of the Self

In this case example, the inferior, defective qualities of the play characters were revealed in counseling sessions and noted with interest. As Sam grew in awareness that his therapist's reflections of these defective characters was not shaming but rather empathic ("Nobody wants to play with Stinky." "Stinky, what a name!"), he began to share his feelings of shame (Sam: "He doesn't like being called Stinky." Therapist: "No, it is not a kind name."). Later, the therapist began to demonstrate to Sam the fact that individuals have different parts of the self (Therapist: "You know, this guy they call Stinky, he's a pretty good soccer player"; soccer was something Sam was quite skilled at). Thus, as time went on, the differentiation of varying strengths and weaknesses within the same character—rather than good–bad polarities—became extremely important as a way to manage shame and talk more directly about Sam's struggles. In fact, shame—whether interpersonally or intrapsychically mediated—characteristically labels the individual in drastic, either/or language. Reclaiming the client's identity as being a complex pattern of assets and liabilities, inextricably woven together to form his or her essential uniqueness, is therefore one of the most powerful interventions on the way back to a more balanced and inclusive, non-shame-based sense of self.

The issue of "complexity" existing in an individual was also part of parental guidance and family therapy. For example, although Sam struggled with reading, he had an excellent vocabulary. We began to note that weaknesses in some areas were not defining, and in this way being unable to do something did not make someone stupid, dumb, or bad; it simply was a skill or arena yet to be learned. Similarly, in Jane's case, being called to the school because Sam did something that warranted being sent home did not define her "total mothering," and Sam's toileting accidents did not mean that they were failures as parents. In this way, the parents became more accepting of their own strengths and limitations and were able to use a scaffolding approach with Sam (i.e., building on what he knew, on his strengths and abilities) that was affirming rather than shame based.

Over time, Sam became willing to have a tutor for his academic skills deficits. He also worked with an occupational therapist on identifying sensory and motor sensitivities such as his difficulties with sequencing, managing sounds that disturbed him, and so on. Significantly, Sam indicated that he was no longer being called "Stinky" (other factors contributed to this, as discussed below) and that he had made a friend at school. Although he had a few notes sent home from school for "talking back" to the teacher, he had maintained more than an 8-month period of consistent enrollment—a record for Sam!

Establishing New, Healthier Family Patterns

Several features in the treatment of this family were significant. It was important for the therapist to model attunement for the parents and help them recognize how overwhelming and painful it is for a child to feel shamed. Following the guidance on parenting, the therapist recognized the parents' own experiences with being shamed, which was critical in helping the parents to see Sam's behavior as a form of communication about his needs. Also, the therapist recognized how their inadvertent shaming behaviors in the form of yelling and asking him to "just do it right" and stop being "bad" were indeed a repetition of what they had experienced growing up. In addition, it was important to assist the parents in understanding that there are multiple or different aspects to Sam and themselves—no one is just good or bad. Thus, we worked to differentiate and validate the different parts each possessed (both strengths and weaknesses), and this was significant in reducing the shame proneness each held. In particular, both Joe and Jane seemed reassured by the acknowledgment that none of us contain perfection.

In this vein, the important lessons included times when the therapist would reflect questions such as "Tiger sounds scared," and Sam would correct the therapist—"No, he's sad." The therapist's ability to say "I made a mistake; I'd like to hear what makes him sad" provided safety. Similarly, when Joe said, "You can't help," the therapist replied, "I might not be able to help, but I would like to see if we can try working together," and when Joe said, "You don't know everything," the response was, "True, Joe, I don't know everything." When Joe challenged, "You didn't have my son-of-a-bitch father. Who are you to think you can help me?" the therapist was nondefensive and said, "Yes, I didn't have your abusive father, and you are the expert on what was so terribly wrong in your life; I'd like to partner with your family to see if we can figure out how to have things work better for you now." For Joe, because of his experiences with his father, it seemed important not to feel "dominated" or shamed as being "one-down" by a therapist in a "superior" role. Once that was acknowledged, the working alliance was solidified. See Stolorow, Brandchaft, and Atwood (1994) for an excellent exploration of the clinical leverage to be found in the therapist's maintaining a consistent stance of nondefensive, human "fallibilism."

In terms of toileting accidents, Sam made significant progress in asking Jane for help in cleaning up, and she made progress in helping without shaming him (instead of saying, "You are a big boy and should be able to do it on your own," she now said, "Sure, we'll do it together" and talked him through the process). This notion of client response specificity (McClure & Teyber, 2003; Teyber & McClure, 2011) involves responding in such a way that a particular individual will feel cared about (i.e., Sam grew up with a neglectful and unresponsive biological mother, and now having one who joined him made a huge difference and made him feel cared about). Although other therapists had indicated that helping him clean up would simply continue his "acting out" behavior, it was clear that over time, his primary need—and the real issue at play—was whether he was going to be ignored (neglected) or be attended to. Here is another example, then, of the importance of both therapist and parents being able to "see" the symbolic, communicative underpinnings of a child's concrete, "problem" behavior. Focusing only on overt, observable behaviors and what is to be done about them risks missing the child's inner experience of shame and vulnerability and likely perpetuates the various behaviors parents wish to be "fixed" or "eliminated." A present-moment empathic connection between parent and "offending" child paves the way for lasting, long-term change, first emotionally, then behaviorally. Psycholinguist Noam Chomsky's key distinction between "surface" and "deep" structure pertains, and the sensitively attuned therapist wants to avoid unwittingly committing or colluding with "category error" in mistaking one for the other (see Anbar, 2009). Stated another way, the current approach to addressing parent–child interactions, as they are informed and shaped by shame dynamics, focuses on the relational underpinnings of the child's behavior. Understanding the emotional context or relational embeddedness of a child's "misbehavior" is the first, and most critical, step toward its eventual resolution and healing.

Indeed, as Sam felt responded to, learned that his mother was not agitated by his needs, and found that he could ask for attention in appropriate ways (i.e., ask if she would play, read, or watch a TV program with him), his symptoms, such as his soiling, did in fact subside. Over time, as mother and son developed other shared activities, such as gardening, going to the park, and swimming at the YMCA together, toileting accidents ceased completely. Again, the relational context and meaning are given priority over any individual, isolated act. (See Stolorow et al., 1994, 2000, on the isolated mind fallacy.)

SUMMING UP THE PROCESS

It is clearly important to understand shame in a way that puts it into historical context so that there is empathy, kindness, and compassion for how it developed. Bromberg (2006) emphasized that it is essential to watch for and bring into the "here and now" signs of "dissociated shame" that may be present in both client and therapist in order for treatment to progress. Thus, unless historical shame can be processed in the present, which means it is named overtly and addressed directly but sensitively in the therapy relationship, it will continue to fester within the client. The importance of the therapist's ability to approach his or her own shame in order to be able to provide safety for the client to increasingly approach and process his or her shame is imperative. Further, working to increase compassion for failings and inadequacies—often by helping with developing a realistic self-appraisal that encompasses mistakes, failings, and human imperfections—is very important. Bromberg insightfully stated that clients surrender "self-state coherence to protect continuity" (p. 68). In this way, a coherent, authentic, and flexible self is sacrificed, lost to the urgency to ward off being flooded by intolerable and all-encompassing feelings of being bad, worthless, unwanted, and so forth. Thus, the ability to acknowledge, accept, and integrate all aspects of self (the good, bad, strong, weak, powerful, vulnerable, joyful, sad, competent, dependent, and so on) is essential to coherence, yet is relinquished in deeply traumatized children and adults for the sake of existence, preserving some ongoing sense of self that is necessary for survival. Put differently, psychological integrity is sacrificed for the sake of emotional (or, sometimes, physical) survival. While the trade-off is understandable, its long-term effects are no less crippling. Here then enters the work of the therapist aware of, and sensitized to, the devastating impact of unhealed shame dynamics within the family.

Shame is often felt globally, so identifying specific areas of strength and weakness is useful. By doing so, weaknesses do not become all defining, and strengths and resources can be affirmed as part of a fuller and more coherent self-definition. When the self is more integrated and coherent, acknowledging and processing shame are less threatening. Then it is possible to work on the shame-ful feelings in a "mindful" way, with an awareness that does not let such feelings predominate or become overwhelming or lead to an overidentification with them. It is a huge first step for the client, and for each family member, to be able to observe, rather than be completely identified with, various shaming self-statements or self-perceptions. They may note, "If I can see my shame in oper-ation, mindfully, then perhaps I am something other than that emotion which I'm observing." Or they may ask, "Who is it that is actually watching this shame in action? Could it be that I am the 'witness' of the shame, rather than simply its passive victim?" Such mindfulness, even in the face of potentially undermining shame-rooted affect, provides a deeper foundation for self-coherence and per-sonal integrity. Self-coherence, because it allows for holding in mind disparate parts of self with acceptance, makes it possible to face criticisms and not be undone by them, to be more flexible in responding to oneself and others, to be more able to tolerate disagreements or disappointments, and to be more grounded in self-appraisals. It also makes developing social relationships and choosing extracurricular activities easier—the "menu" of options is infinitely larger. Why? Because the client is no longer on constant "red alert," vigilantly scanning the environment in hopes of avoiding further interpersonal activation of internal shame. The truth of oneself—that each of us is a "perfect" mix of "imperfect" ingredients and that, "No, we won't allow ourselves to be shamed today"—truly does set us free to live a broader, more life-engaged, more robust human existence. Thus, treatment goals for this family included the following:

1. naming shaming feelings, symptoms, and experiences;
2. encouraging the parents to refute Sam's "badness" so the shame he felt was diminished or moderated;
3. helping the parents recognize their own shame dynamics, pro-viding empathy for them and the wounding they experienced, and helping them have empathy for each other;
4. helping each find ways to evaluate shaming experiences as episodes that did not define them so they were not overwhelmed by those experiences and could continue to function effectively and flexibly;

5. helping them find ways they could reregulate or soothe themselves (e.g., meditating, listening to music, talking to friends, taking walks, taking warm showers, being held, and so on) when they felt deeply shamed; and, importantly,

6. using their relationship with the therapist as the place where shame in the here and now could be addressed as it was enacted.

CONCLUSION

In this case, the therapist's intersubjective attunement was critical (and often healing) given the lack of attunement the parents had experienced in their early years and how it contributed to the shame proneness that had resulted for each of them. It is essential to help family members have empathy for their own woundedness—modeled first by the therapist's affirming and compassionate response to shame that is experienced in the session—and to educate them about the potential generational transmission of wounding shame dynamics. It is useful to help them understand that although the defensive coping mechanisms they originally developed as children were once adaptive (e.g., pleasing, complying), they become maladaptive and cost much more than they provide at a later point in life (Teyber & McClure, 2011). For example, Joe's defensive coping in response to his father's abuse was to become tough and minimize warm feelings, but it translated into intolerance of "disobedience" and a harsh approach to Sam. The need no longer existed for a tough exterior and fear of warm, "vulnerable" feelings that were reality based for Joe as a child. Now, in Joe's current adult life, sadly, the coping strategy that once allowed him to physically survive an abusive father worked against him and kept him from an authentic and warm connection with his wife and son.

Similarly, as Jane's drive for perfection was relaxed, she became more playful, and the tension both in her marriage and in her parenting diminished significantly—she learned that "perfection" didn't preclude being playful and that making errors was "perfectly human!" Her empathy for both her husband and her son translated into greater warmth and increased positive family time. It appeared that for this family, as often occurs for distressed families, providing them with compassion for their own, often unseen needs, which they experienced as shamefully weak, demanding, needy, or simply unacceptable—allowed them to be able to provide the same empathy for each other. They began to change as the contagious shame proneness in the family system abated, along with mutual acknowledgement that the ways of relating that had been shame engendering could be modified. As they began to make these changes in small but significant ways, they felt rewarded for the changes seen in Sam and in each other.

REFERENCES

Allen, J. G., & Fonagy, P. (2006). (Eds). *Handbook of mentalization-based treatment*. West Sussex, England: Wiley.

Allen, J. G., Fonagy, P., & Bateman, A. W. (2008). *Mentalizing in clinical practice*. Washington, DC: American Psychiatric Press.

Anbar, A. (2009). Generative transformational theory: Between competence and linguistic performance. *Educational Sciences, 36*, 410–434.

Balcom, D. (1991). Shame and violence: Considerations in couples' treatment. *Journal of Independent Social Work, 5*, 165–181.

Beebe, B., Jaffe, J., Lachmann, F., Feldstein, F., Crown, C., & Jasnow, M. (2000). System models in development and psychoanalysis: Case of vocal rhythm coordination and attachment. *Infant Mental Health Journal, 21*, 99–122.

Beebe, B., & Lachman, F. (2002). *Infant research and adult treatment: Co-constructing interactions*. Hillsdale, NJ: Analytic Press.

Beebe, B., Stern, D., & Jaffe, J. (1979). The kinesic rhythm of mother–infant interactions. In A. W. Siegman & S. Feldstein (Eds.), *Of speech and time: Temporal patterns in interpersonal contexts* (pp. 119–134). Hillsdale, NJ: Erlbaum.

Berlin, L. J., Ziv, Y., Amaya-Jackson, L., & Greenberg, M. T. (Eds.). (2005). *Enhancing early attachments*. New York, NY: Guilford Press.

Brandchaft, B. (in press). *The self in developmental trauma: Attachment and pathological accommodation*. Mahwah, NJ: Analytic Press.

Bromberg, P. (2006). *Awakening the dreamer*. Mahwah, NJ: Analytic Press.

Condon, W. S. (1980). The relation of interactional synchrony to cognitive and emotional processes. In M. R. Key (Ed.), *The relationship of verbal and nonverbal communication* (pp. 51–64). New York, NY: Mouton.

Cook, D. R. (1991). Shame, attachment, and addictions: Implications for family therapists. *Contemporary Family Therapy: An International Journal, 13*, 405–419. doi:10.1007/BF00890495

Erikson, E. (1950). *Childhood and society*. New York, NY: Norton.

Fonagy, P., & Target, M. (1997). Attachment and reflective function: Their role in self-organization. *Development and Psychopathology, 9*, 679–700. doi:10.1017/S0954579497001399

Fonagy, P., & Target, M. (2002). Early intervention and the development of self-regulation. *Psychoanalytic Inquiry, 22*, 307–335. doi:10.1080/07351692209348990

Gilbert, P., Pehl, J., & Allan, S. (1994). The phenomenology of shame and guilt: An empirical investigation. *British Journal of Medical Psychology, 67*, 23–36.

Gilbert, P., & Procter, S. (2006). Compassionate mind training for people with high shame and self criticism. *Clinical Psychology & Psychotherapy, 13*, 353–379. doi:10.1002/cpp.507

Gramzow, R., & Tangney, J. P. (1992). Proneness to shame and the narcissistic personality. *Personality and Social Psychology Bulletin, 18*, 369–376. doi:10.1177/0146167292183014

Greenspan, S. I., & Wieder, S. (1998). *The child with special needs*. Cambridge, MA: Da Capo Press.

Grosch, W. N. (1994). Narcissism, shame, rage, and addiction. *Psychiatric Quarterly, 65*, 49–63. doi:10.1007/BF02354331

Herman, J. (1997). *Trauma and recovery*. New York, NY: Basic Books.

Hofer, M. A. (2004). Developmental psychopathology of early attachment. In B. J. Casey (Ed.), *Developmental psychobiology* (pp. 1–28). Arlington, VA: American Psychiatric Publishing.

Holmes, J. (2001). *The search for the secure base: Attachment theory and psychotherapy*. New York, NY: Brunner-Routledge.

Jaffe, J., & Feldstein, S. (1970). *Rhythms in dialogue*. New York, NY: Academic Press.

Juffer, F., Bakersmans-Kranenburg, M. J., & van IJzendoorn, M. H. (Eds.). (2008). *Promoting positive parenting*. New York, NY: Psychology Press.

Kohut, H. (1977). *The restoration of the self*. Madison, CT: International Universities Press.

Lieberman, A. F., & Van Horn, P. (2008). *Psychotherapy with infants and young children*. New York, NY: Guilford Press.

Mahler, M. S., Pine, F., & Bergman, A. (1975). *The psychological birth of the human infant: Symbiosis and individuation*. New York, NY: Basic Books.

Masterson, J. F. (1985). *The real self: A developmental, self, and object relations approach*. New York, NY: Brunner/Mazel.

Masterson, J. F. (1988). *The search for the real self: Unmasking the personality disorders of our age*. New York, NY: Free Press.

McClure, F. H., & Teyber, E. (2003). *Casebook in child and adolescent treatment*. Pacific Grove, CA: Brooks/Cole.

Murray, C., & Waller, G. (2002). Reported sexual abuse and bulimic psychopathology among nonclinical women: The mediating role of shame. *International Journal of Eating Disorders, 32*, 186–191. doi:10.1002/eat.10062

Perry, B., & Szalavitz, M. (2007). *The boy who was raised as a dog*. New York, NY: Basic Books.

Putnam, F. W. (1995). Development of dissociative disorders. In D. Cicchetti & D. J. Cohen (Eds.). *Developmental psychopathology: Vol. 2. Risk, disorder, and adaptation* (pp. 581–608). New York, NY: Wiley.

Putnam, F. W. (2005). The developmental neurobiology of disrupted attachment: Lessons from animal models and child abuse research. In L. J. Berlin, Y. Ziv, L. Amaya-Jackson, L., & M. T. Greenberg (Eds.), *Enhancing early attachments* (pp. 79–99). New York, NY: Guilford Press.

Schore, A. N. (2001). The effects of relational trauma on right brain development, affect regulation, and infant mental health. *Infant Mental Health Journal, 22,* 201–269. doi:10.1002/1097-0355(200101/04)22:1<201::AID-IMHJ8>3.0.CO;2-9

Schore, A. N. (2003). *Affect regulation and disorders of the self.* New York, NY: Norton.

Slade, A. (2000). The development and organization of attachment: Implications for psychoanalysis. *Journal of the American Psychoanalytic Association, 48,* 1147–1174. doi:10.1177/00030651000480042301

Sroufe, L. A. (2005). Attachment and development: A prospective, longitudinal study from birth to adulthood. *Attachment & Human Development, 7,* 349–367. doi:10.1080/14616730500365928

Stern, D. N. (1985). *The interpersonal world of the infant.* New York, NY: Basic Books.

Stern, D. N. (2004). *The present moment in psychotherapy & everyday life.* New York, NY: Norton.

Stolorow, R. D. (2007). *Trauma and human existence: Autobiographical, psychoanalytic, and philosophical reflections.* Mahwah, NJ: Analytic Press.

Stolorow, R. D., Brandchaft, B., & Atwood, G. E. (1994). *The intersubjective perspective.* Northvale, NJ: Jason Aronson.

Stolorow, R. D., Brandchaft, B., & Atwood, G. E. (2000). *Psychoanalytic treatment: An intersubjective approach.* Mahwah, NJ: Analytic Press.

Teyber, E., & McClure, F. (2011). Interpersonal process in therapy: An integrative model. Belmont, CA: Brooks/Cole.

Wells, M., Bruss, K. V., & Katrin, S. (1998). Abuse and addiction: Expressions of a wounded self and internalized shame. *Psychology: A Journal of Human Behavior, 35,* 11–14.

Wong, M. R., & Cook, D. R. (1992). Shame and its contribution to PTSD. *Journal of Traumatic Stress, 5,* 557–562. doi:10.1002/jts.2490050405

7

SHAME IN COUPLE THERAPY: HELPING TO HEAL THE INTIMACY BOND

NORMAN B. EPSTEIN AND MARIANA K. FALCONIER

Couple therapists and researchers have devoted considerable attention to ways in which negative emotions such as anger, depression, and anxiety influence, and are influenced by, the quality of couples' relationships (Beach, 2001; Epstein & Baucom, 2002; Snyder, Simpson, & Hughes, 2006). Less attention has been paid to shame, a powerful emotion that can have a negative influence on partners' behavior toward each other and their individual experiences in the relationship. Shame involves an individual's negative appraisal of core characteristics of the self as diminished, flawed, and worthless, often paired with depressed emotion (for a review, see Tangney & Dearing, 2002).

Romantic relationships involve a variety of roles within which partners' performance can elicit shame. Every culture holds prescribed standards for partners' roles and ways of relating to each other. These standards involve definitions for being a good wife, good husband, good lover, good listener, good provider, good friend, good communicator, and good parent, among others (Baucom & Epstein, 1990; Baucom, Epstein, Rankin, & Burnett, 1996; Dattilio, 2010). Even when individuals are unaware of their partners' shame issues, or when they are aware of these issues but do not intend to cause their partners to experience further shame, their actions still may inadvertently have that negative effect. For example, a man's casual critical remark to his wife about her clothes may elicit her long-held feelings of shame regarding her body.

This chapter describes how couple relationships are one of the major interpersonal contexts in which individuals experience shame. It addresses how partners' communication quality, level of mutual trust, and intimacy, as well as aspects of each person's history, cognitive style, and affect regulation, play major roles not only in the likelihood of experiencing shame but also in the degree to which shame can be resolved. We emphasize the importance of understanding shame experiences in relationships and intervening with couple dynamics to reduce negative impacts of shame. The chapter provides guidelines for assessing and treating shame in the couple context. Our cognitive–behavioral concepts and methods should be applicable for couple therapists with a variety of theoretical orientations.

SHAME VERSUS GUILT

Although some situations may trigger feelings of both shame and guilt (Menesini & Camodeca, 2008), it is important to differentiate between these two self-conscious emotions due to significant implications for assessment and therapeutic intervention. Shame involves a negative evaluation of the entire self, whereas guilt is linked to negative evaluation of a specific behavior (Tangney & Dearing, 2002). An individual may feel guilty about lying to a partner because he or she considers that lying is morally wrong but still have a positive overall self-concept ("I'm a good person who did something inappropriate"). However, an individual who feels shame about lying condemns himself or herself as a person (e.g., "I'm no good"). For many people, the experience of shame is more painful and devastating than that of guilt, because shame involves a judgment that one has failed to live up to one's personal standards. As such, shame is difficult to tolerate and, therefore, to reveal if the individual does not feel safe from condemnation by others. Shame also poses more challenges for change than guilt, because changing a specific behavior seems far more attainable than changing one's core self.

It is possible for an individual to experience shame and guilt concurrently or independently, depending on the meanings that the individual attaches to his or her behavior. These meanings can be shaped by the person's preexisting proneness to shame or guilt, a personal history of perceived transgressions, and perception of the current circumstances associated with the behavior. For example, an individual who reveals or is discovered to be having an extramarital affair may feel guilt to the extent that he or she evaluates the affair simply as an action that should not have been taken because it means a violation of the marital vows. Alternatively, the individual may feel shame to the degree that he or she interprets the infidelity as an indication of being a bad person. Understanding the distinction between shame and guilt is particularly important when an individual is experiencing both emotions, so that each can be targeted in therapy to the extent that it is affecting the individual and relationship negatively. As we discuss in more detail later, in some cases an individual's guilt regarding a particular action that negatively affected a partner may be considered appropriate and provide motivation for constructive change, but there is greater danger that shame involving self-condemnation will lead the person to cope in negative ways such as being critical toward the partner or withdrawing.

SITUATIONAL SHAME VERSUS PRONENESS TO SHAME

As described elsewhere in this book, the literature on shame has differentiated between individuals who may experience shame from time to time as a common reaction to specific situations and those who have a tendency to react with feelings of shame consistently regarding a particular area (e.g., body image) or across a range of different areas of life (Tangney, 1990). For example, situational shame is likely to occur in specific contexts in which an individual is aware that he or she has violated social norms for appropriate treatment of others. In contrast, generalized proneness to shame tends to develop in early childhood on the basis of experiences with adult caretakers (for a review, see Mills, Imm, Walling, & Weiler, 2008) and persists through life as the individual experiences shame across a variety of situations that may not elicit shame in many other people. Shame proneness has been described by cognitive therapists as a traitlike cognitive style involving self-blame, an expectancy that other people will condemn and reject oneself as a person, and/or a general negative self-concept (A. T. Beck, Rush, Shaw, & Emery, 1979). In clinical assessment it is important to distinguish between, on the one hand, situational shame that has been triggered by specific interactions between the partners and may be best treated through dyadic interventions and, on the other hand, shame proneness that may call for individual therapy in conjunction with (or occasionally instead of) couple therapy.

SHAME IN COUPLES' RELATIONSHIPS

Although some people may be more prone than others to experience shame, moments of shame are likely to occur in any couple's relationship. Shame originates interpersonally (Kaufman, 1989), most often in significant relationships in which individuals are particularly attentive to what other people (e.g., parents, partners, friends) may think about them and to how they evaluate themselves in relation to the others. An intimate partner's evaluation that leads a person to feel inadequate or uncomfortable about who he or she is has the potential to trigger feelings of shame. The more a situation within a relationship connects the person to an "unwanted identity" in areas such as physical attributes or skills, cognitive abilities, interpersonal and intimacy issues, and personal preferences (Ferguson, Eyre, & Ashbaker, 2000), the more shame the person is likely to experience.

Occasional experiences of shame are normal and not necessarily dysfunctional, and they may motivate an individual to make changes in his or her behavior to benefit a relationship. However, shame responses have the potential to become detrimental for the partners individually and for the couple's relationship when they are pervasive, persistent, or severe. The potential for shame experiences to become dysfunctional depends to a large extent on the shamed partner's individual characteristics (e.g., tendency toward self-blame, capacity for regulating his or her emotional responses), the non-shamed partner's response to the other's shame reaction (e.g., a belief that people should be punished for wrongdoing, a tendency to reinforce the other's shame in order to increase his or her own power in the relationship), and the couple's ability to interact in ways that keep them communicating effectively and connected emotionally. Consequently, clinicians need to assess these characteristics of the two partners and evaluate the couple's interaction pattern in order to understand the role that shame plays in their relationship.

Similar to the factors involved in eliciting shame within a couple's relationship, recovery from a shame experience depends on characteristics of the shamed individual, partner, and couple as a dyad. The person experiencing shame benefits from the capacity to identify the feeling, communicate it to the partner, and manage the intensity of his or her own response. A common barrier to self-disclosure of cognitions and emotions is limited self-awareness of subjective experiences, so therapists must assess the degree to which each person monitors inner experiences and considers them important. Epstein and Baucom (2002) described cognitive–behavioral interventions that can be used when deficits in self-awareness are identified; we provide an overview of these interventions in our discussion of treatment approaches.

When individuals have enough self-awareness to identify feelings of shame, two major pathways for resolving them are individual coping and interactions with the partner. Regarding individual coping, one may use coping strategies such as cognitive restructuring or reframing of the experience (e.g., telling oneself "It was not so bad; other people go through the same situation" or concluding that one's sense of shame is a positive quality that reflects caring about another person) or a variety of other self-soothing strategies. In some instances these affect regulation mechanisms may prove to be sufficient, particularly for mild shame. A man may become aware that he feels ashamed of his clumsiness in a social situation with which he is unfamiliar (e.g., a cocktail party), share his feeling with his partner, and overcome the shame when his partner responds supportively. However, in other cases shame may lead to negative coping responses of anger, defensiveness, withdrawal, or other vivid responses that hide the sentiment of shame from the person and/or the partner (Retzinger, 1995). It is precisely in situations of covert shame that the ability to identify and disclose shame becomes a critical factor in recovering from it. Thus, the man who feels shame regarding social ineptness at a party may deflect his shame experience by criticizing his wife for putting him in such an uncomfortable situation, leading to an argument and reducing the wife's empathic response.

In order for couple interactions to help an individual recover from shame experiences, the person who is aware of his or her shame feelings must share that information clearly and constructively with the partner. Deficits in communication can be based on a limited vocabulary for describing thoughts and emotions; a lack of skills for phrasing self-disclosures; habitual negative forms of communication (e.g., criticizing the partner, withdrawing); difficulty regulating emotions, such as anxiety, that inhibit interaction with the partner; and cognitions, such as a belief that revealing shame is a sign of weakness (Epstein & Baucom, 2002). Barriers to communication about shame must be evaluated during the clinical assessment of the couple.

A couple's constructive coping with one member's shame experience also depends on the nonshamed partner's responses. The partner's emotional attunement and ability to read the other's emotional cues can assist him or her in identifying the emotion. If partners can listen and validate uncomfortable feelings instead of avoiding the topic or condemning the person for experiencing shame, the couple is more likely to recover from shame. When a shamed individual responds by withdrawing, the partner's ability to help the person reengage is important for the couple to be able to process the shame and its causes. At other times, the partner's ability to provide the person some time to cope individually with shame before discussing the experience or the eliciting event becomes a key aspect of successful communication. However, some supportive partners may unwittingly maintain the other's shame if they protect the person from feeling the pain of shame by colluding to avoid the topic. Thus, a constructive response from a partner involves finding an appropriate time to discuss the shame experience.

Even more challenging, the person feeling shame may blame the partner, and a constructive response from the partner may require identifying the underlying shame, remaining nonreactive, and encouraging the individual to disclose feelings further to uncover the shame feelings. The partner's ability to provide such facilitative responses depends on his or her emotional sensitivity, capacity to constructively ask the person about what was noticed, personal standards for what types of behavior are shameful, personal tolerance for the experience of shame, and the couple's tendency to be collaborative versus adversarial with each other.

Unfortunately, some individuals may use knowledge of a partner's areas of shame purposefully to gain more power in the relationship, punish the partner, or boost their own self-esteem. The person may attack the partner's areas of vulnerability by diminishing or devaluing him or her, thus making shame experiences part of the couple's negative pattern of interactions. For example, when discussing financial difficulties, a wife who is aware of her husband's sense of failure in his breadwinning role may express her disappointment with him and reinforce his shame for not being a good provider and competent man. Similarly, one parent might remind the other of the things that the other has done that may have contributed to a child's behavior problem, reinforcing the partner's sense of shame as a parent. Thus, the couple's interactions exacerbate an individual's tendency to experience shame, with both partners blaming the individual for personal flaws and shortcomings. Such blaming has been linked in research studies to individuals experiencing hopelessness and depression and to members of couples feeling hopeless and distressed about their relationship (Abramson, Metalsky, & Alloy, 1989; Bradbury & Fincham, 1990; Karney & Bradbury, 2000). When one member of a couple exploits the other's shame-inducing issues, this is likely to reduce the quality of the relationship and also to exacerbate the other's low self-esteem and sense of incompetence. Therefore, it is important for the therapist to identify and intervene with any factors that interfere with the partner's ability to be supportive of the shamed person or that lead him or her to elicit and reinforce shame responses. The processes involved in assessing these characteristics of the partner are described in the assessment section of this chapter.

When shame-eliciting situations occur for couples with low intimacy or whose communication tends to be destructive, psychological and/or physical aggression and emotional distancing are likely results. For example, a man may note to his wife that a person she was talking about in derogatory terms was sitting behind her and might have overheard her comments. The wife may protect herself from the uncomfortable feeling of shame by redirecting the blame by becoming angry and blaming the husband for failing to warn her that the person was sitting behind her. In response, the husband may then defend himself, and a negative cycle of mutual blaming and defending may occur that obscures the underlying shame experience:

> Wife: You could have told me that she was sitting next to us! [redirecting blame]

> Husband: If I had noticed, I would have told you. [defending himself]

> *Wife:* How come you just realized it after I've already made a fool of myself? *[accusing]*
>
> *Husband:* Here we go again, with you blaming me for things and not taking responsibility for your own problems, like speaking so loud and not checking to see who is nearby! *[attacking]*

Unfortunately, this negative reciprocity has three major harmful consequences for the couple's relationship. First, once the cycle is initiated, it may escalate to psychological and/or physical aggression, particularly given the intense emotion commonly involved in experiences of shame. Second, both partners remain unaware of the role that shame has played in their interaction. Third, both partners may perceive their relationship as less safe and become more fearful of revealing vulnerability to each other, reducing their capacity for intimacy.

In contrast, couples in which partners trust each other, feel intimately connected, and have developed constructive ways of communicating may be better equipped to process experiences of shame and reestablish a shamed individual's positive evaluation of the self. Partners act as coaches or support figures who assist each other in counteracting shame instead of exploiting the situation or exacerbating it. They allow themselves to be vulnerable in front of each other, facilitating the identification and access of painful emotions and negative self-evaluations. Couples who are able to respond to shame in such constructive ways seem to have advantages in maintaining both partners' self-esteem as well as the quality of their relationship. These couple resources are especially valuable when both members of a couple experience shame, such as a couple who both feel that they have failed as parents when they learn that their child attempted suicide. These situations are especially challenging because each partner is dealing simultaneously with his or her own and the other's negative self-evaluations and intense emotions. When partners feel safe with each other and communicate well, experiences of mutual shame may actually strengthen the couple's intimate connection and their belief that their relationship can survive major life stressors.

In summary, shame-eliciting situations can occur even in well-functioning relationships. Successful resolution of shame experiences within the couple's relationship depends on a number of factors, including each person's capacity to access and identify his or her feelings of shame, the non-shamed partner's intentions and behavior regarding supporting the individual versus reinforcing the shame, the couple's overall levels of intimacy and trust, and their communication and conflict resolution skills. The risks are likely to be even greater for couples in which one or both partners have a trait-like proneness to shame. The extent to which shame occurs in the context of intimate relationships and the degree to which couple dynamics influence how well it is resolved suggest that couple therapy should be a significant component of treatment. This chapter describes the application of a cognitive–behavioral approach to the assessment and treatment of shame within couple relationships.

A COGNITIVE–BEHAVIORAL APPROACH TO TREATING SHAME IN COUPLE RELATIONSHIPS

The most common theoretical orientations to couple therapy for shame are emotion-focused therapy (Greenberg & Goldman, 2008; see also Chapter 3, this volume) and cognitive–behavioral couple therapy (CBCT), although psychodynamic approaches also are common (e.g., Balcom, 1991). This chapter focuses on CBCT, which is well suited to address the intra- and interpersonal aspects of shame in the relationship context.

CBCT draws on principles of social learning theory, social exchange theory, cognitive psychology, and systems theory, examining interrelationships among (a) partners' cognitions about themselves, each other, and their relationship; (b) the two individuals' emotional responses to events occurring in the relationship; and (c) the behavioral interactions between partners (for detailed descriptions, see Baucom & Epstein, 1990; Dattilio, 2010; Epstein & Baucom, 2002; Rathus & Sanderson, 1999). Interventions for modifying negative behavioral interactions typically include training in communication and problem-solving skills, along with structured agreements or contracts between partners to enact particular types of behavior (e.g., forms of social support, intimate behavior). Because partners also provide reinforcement or punishment for each other's actions by the consequences that they provide for them (e.g., reinforcing the other's nagging behavior by ignoring simple requests but paying attention when the partner nags), therapists also identify such sequences in a couple's interactions, point them out to the couple, and coach them in altering the stimuli and consequences that they create for each other.

Despite the direct influence that each partner's behavior has on the other, CBCT also is based on an assumption, which has received empirical support, that subjective cognitions and emotional responses mediate the impact of one partner's behavior on the other (Epstein & Baucom, 2002). Five types of cognition that have been found to affect couple relationships include:

1. each individual's *selective perception* (i.e., noticing only a subset of information available in a situation while not attending to other data),

2. *attributions* (i.e., inferences about the determinants of a partner's behavior, such as attributing a hurtful remark to malicious intent),
3. *expectancies* (i.e., inferences about future relationship events and partner behaviors, such as predicting that shaming a partner will lead to the partner being very compliant),
4. *assumptions* (i.e., beliefs that each person holds about the characteristics of intimate relationships and the partners who comprise them, such as an assumption that a person who feels shame must have a valid reason for feeling that way), and
5. *standards* (i.e., beliefs about the characteristics that partners and their relationships *should* have, such as a standard that an individual who hurts their partner's feelings should be punished for it; Epstein & Baucom, 2002).

Although the interventions for modifying the cognitive, affective, and behavioral components of shame often overlap, we present them separately in this chapter for the sake of clarity. Before providing details about interventions, we discuss cognitive–behavioral assessment issues and methods in the next section.

COGNITIVE–BEHAVIORAL ASSESSMENT OF SHAME IN COUPLE RELATIONSHIPS

In this section, we describe methods for assessing aspects of the shamed person, the nonshamed partner, and the couple's interaction patterns that can affect the elicitation of shame as well as the degree to which it is resolved. Cognitive–behavioral assessment of a couple commonly begins with one or more joint interviews with the couple to identify presenting concerns and relationship strengths, take a relationship history, and observe the couple's interaction patterns. An individual interview with each partner is used to assess individual functioning and screen for substance abuse and partner violence. Questionnaires also may be administered to tap shame experiences. Before describing the assessment of shame within this context, we discuss some characteristics of shame that can serve as barriers to its assessment.

Aspects of Shame That Can Affect Assessment

A number of characteristics of shame responses within couple relationships (and in general) can pose challenges for assessment. First, for many clients it is easier to self-disclose feelings of anger, depression, or anxiety spontaneously or in response to a clinician's questions than it is to reveal shame, because the individual is likely to view those other negative feelings as less socially undesirable than shame. As noted earlier, people commonly protect themselves from experiencing shame by using a variety of strategies such as avoidance, blaming and shaming the partner, and expressing anger or rage. When clients exhibit only the anger and other defensive responses during sessions, it may be easy for clinicians to overlook the potential for underlying shame unless they are aware of the dynamics of shame. Therapists need to be aware of defensive strategies and create an atmosphere of safety and acceptance in the therapy room to facilitate emergence of shame issues.

Second, although defensive avoidance of shame may occur in individual therapy when clients are uneasy about the therapist's evaluation, it is likely to be more challenging to create conditions during couple therapy in which shamed clients will feel comfortable being vulnerable enough to self-disclose in the presence of their partner. No matter how empathic and accepting a couple therapist may be, an individual's partner may respond in a critical and rejecting way when the person self-discloses regarding experiences that have caused him or her shame. In addition, an individual may experience shame during a couple therapy session when the partner alludes to one of his or her undesirable characteristics. The exposure to the therapist of the negative characteristic may intensify the shame and lead the shamed individual to withdraw during the session and afterward or to an angry defensive response that leads the couple into an argument.

Interventions During Assessment to Reduce Barriers to Disclosure of Shame

The therapist must intervene immediately during initial assessment sessions to establish a structure and ground rules for the couple to interact in constructive ways and to block partners from eliciting or exacerbating each other's shame experiences during and between sessions. The therapist may allow a couple to interact relatively freely initially during an assessment session in order to determine how the partners tend to express a variety of thoughts and emotions, as well as to observe how they respond to each other's disclosures. However, it is important to limit partners' shaming behaviors toward each other, or else there is a risk that a shamed individual will either drop out of therapy or respond in a highly guarded manner in future sessions.

Cognitive–behavioral strategies for limiting shame experiences during assessment are for the most part the same as those used during subsequent treatment sessions for moderating clients' aversive experiences (Epstein & Baucom, 2002, 2003). Given the importance of minimizing shaming during assessment, we describe these strategies here and refer back to them in the section on treatment interventions.

First, early in an initial joint assessment session, the therapist should state a goal of creating a safe, collaborative atmosphere in therapy. He or she should discuss how couple therapy can be a significant opportunity to improve the quality of a relationship through building on existing strengths and making changes in patterns that have been distressing to the partners. One can explain that in order for the therapist and couple to work together as a team toward goals of overcoming difficulties and producing more satisfying interactions in the relationship, it is crucial that the partners approach the sessions in a spirit of collaboration. The therapist notes that one important time for collaboration occurs when he or she is collecting information from the couple regarding their concerns, because they may be tempted to criticize each other for past behavior. Whereas the therapist needs to know about past events that have been upsetting, verbally attacking one's partner and making him or her feel publicly shamed is likely to create more distance within the couple and lowered motivation to come to therapy sessions. The therapist then can provide a few brief guidelines for expressing one's concerns about a partner's past or current behavior (e.g., no yelling, no threats, descriptions of a partner's behavior in objective rather than judgmental terms, no name-calling or labeling each other with derogatory traits; Epstein & Baucom, 2002, 2003).

In addition to describing prohibited negative behaviors, the therapist can role-play concise examples of them and of more constructive alternative behavior. He or she also can emphasize resisting the urge to criticize and denigrate one's partner. The therapist can explain that even when one partner feels an urge to punish the other for his or her behavior, retaliating by attempting to shame the person during sessions may feel good in the short term but is likely to create an adversarial atmosphere in therapy and decrease the probability that the couple will experience closeness, affection, and mutual support. Furthermore, the therapist can normalize the experience of negative emotions such as shame, guilt, and sadness, emphasizing that such feelings commonly arise during sessions and explaining that therapy provides good opportunities to understand and deal with these emotions.

Throughout assessment and subsequent treatment sessions, the therapist must be prepared to interrupt the couple's interactions whenever one or both partners violate the ground rules for constructive discussion (Epstein & Baucom, 2002, 2003). However, it also is important to express empathy for the distress experienced by the individual who has engaged in critical and shaming behavior toward the partner. The therapist can validate the person's desire for change but stress that punitive approaches have not worked in the past and will not work now. After blocking a partner's shaming behavior, the therapist can coach the client to express concerns and dissatisfaction in a more constructive way, especially by describing a request for positive change rather than complaining about and denigrating the other person's behavior.

Another factor that the therapist should assess that may contribute to a partner engaging in shaming behavior during sessions is the individual's difficulty in regulating his or her emotional experience and expression. The client's tendency to vent upset feelings and denigrate the other person may reflect his or her experience of being flooded by strong feelings and having seemingly irresistible urges to express them. The therapist can inquire about such subjective experiences and ask how much personal control the individual feels over emotional responses. When the individual perceives little control over experiencing and venting negative thoughts and emotions to the partner, the therapist can coach both partners in anger management and other emotion regulation skills, including self-talk to counteract "hot cognitions," self-soothing activities such as muscle relaxation, and use of time-outs to block negative expression (Deffenbacher, 1996; Epstein & Baucom, 2002; Meichenbaum, 1985).

Thus, both a shamed individual's own defensive responses and the other partner's negative responses to the individual's past or current behavior may interfere with self-disclosure of shame. The couple therapist who is assessing for shame experiences must probe for both types of inhibiting factors and be prepared to intervene to create safe conditions for the individual to discuss negative self-evaluation regarding his or her thoughts or behavior.

Interview Assessment of Individual and Dyadic Factors in Shame Experiences

Cognitive–behavioral therapists commonly begin their assessment with joint interviews with the two partners to collect information about the relationship's history and current functioning, often followed by an individual interview with each partner regarding past experiences and current personal functioning (Epstein & Baucom, 2002). During joint and individual interviews, partners may report past shame experiences in their relationship spontaneously or in response to probes by the therapist, or the therapist may uncover shame that is elicited in the moment during the interviews, such as when a person feels shamed as the partner reveals the person's socially undesirable personal characteristic or behavior to the therapist.

Because clients are unlikely to consult with clinicians specifically about issues of shame, these responses typically will be revealed during discussions of other presenting concerns. On the one hand, shame may be implicit when a couple describes particular presenting problems such as infidelity and a perpetrator describes feeling that he or she is "an awful person" for being disloyal. On the other hand, shame can be triggered by the therapy process itself. For example, when treating a couple for partner abuse, an abuser may begin to experience shame when the partner vividly expresses the emotional and/or physical pain that he or she has endured and the perpetrator begins to engage in very negative self-evaluation.

In general, as the members of a couple describe the concerns that brought them to therapy, the therapist can probe for shame through questions asking about how the events in the relationship have affected each person, followed by listening for self-evaluative statements and asking follow-up questions to specify the cognitions, emotions, and behavioral components of the person's response. Thus, when a wife said that she felt "terrible" about her infidelity, the therapist asked her to describe what feeling terrible was like. She replied, "It's something I never thought I'd do. He trusted me, and I wasn't loyal." The therapist probed further, "So, how have you been feeling about not being loyal?" The wife responded, "I feel like I've been an awful wife . . . an awful person. I wish I could just disappear." It is not necessary for either the client or therapist to label the feelings specifically as shame, as long as the negative self-evaluation and sense of worthlessness associated with violation of personal values and ethical standards are identified.

The wife's comment that she wished she could disappear is consistent with the common withdrawal aspect of shame responses, which interferes with active problem-solving behavior. However, her language also raises the possibility that she views her situation as hopeless and is having suicidal thoughts, and as with any distraught client it is essential that the therapist conduct a careful inquiry to assess suicidal risk. In cases where there is significant suicidal risk, couple therapy must be supplemented with individual therapy to address the shame and other factors contributing to the suicidal ideation. Nevertheless, to the extent that the person's partner is fueling the suicidal risk (e.g., through punitive denigrating comments), couple therapy that addresses the partner's responses may be an important component of treating the danger.

Even when shame is not associated with suicidal risk, it is important to assess how often and intensely each partner experiences shame and the degree to which shame is related to depression, lowered self-esteem, a tendency to avoid situations that elicit shame, and limited initiative toward problem solving. In a cognitive–behavioral assessment, the therapist asks a series of questions to identify links between shame responses and these other difficulties, for example, by looking for patterns in which an individual tends to experience depressed mood states and has limited ability to regulate the intense emotion whenever reminded of personal actions that he or she considers shameful and identifying how the person withdraws cognitively and physically whenever his or her partner makes any comments regarding the shame-related behavior. For example, a therapist can ask an individual who frequently experiences intense shame when thinking about the couple's relationship to describe whatever strategies he or she uses to reduce the emotional stress—what the person thinks or does and how effective these strategies tend to be in reducing shame experiences. Furthermore, the therapist can ask about the person's ability to moderate other types of strong emotions in daily life, such as anger and anxiety, both in the couple relationship and with other people. The goal of this assessment is to identify the range and effectiveness of the individual's emotion regulation skills.

During the individual interviews with the two partners, the therapist can obtain information regarding each person's history, particularly in the family of origin and prior significant friendships and romantic relationships (for detailed interview guidelines, see Dattilio, 2010; Epstein & Baucom, 2002). To what degree did the individual's parents use shaming as a means for disciplining and socializing him or her? Did parents or others express contempt for the child, which may have become internalized as a negative self-concept associated with shame? Did the individual experience painful shaming by a close friend or romantic partner? (For example, a male client may have painful memories of his first sexual partner laughing at him when he experienced erectile dysfunction.) To what degree is there evidence that the individual is shame prone, needing attention to this vulnerability in couple and perhaps individual therapy?

On the basis of the assessment of the breadth and severity of negative effects that an individual's shame responses have on personal functioning, a clinical decision must be made regarding a recommendation that the individual receive some individual therapy to reduce these consequences. If the personal difficulty with shame is severe, it may be necessary to postpone couple therapy sessions while the person receives assistance in individual therapy, but our experience suggests that most often couple therapy is an important component for addressing shame proneness because ongoing negative interactions between partners that continue to elicit shame will undermine progress in individual therapy. In such cases, active intervention in the couple's relationship, concurrent with individual treatment, is needed.

Assessing Positive Consequences of Shame for the Shamed Individual and Relationship

Although we have focused on negative effects of shame experiences, it is important to note that there are circumstances in which a mild to moderate level of shame can motivate an individual to make positive changes in his or her role in a couple relationship. Shame experiences that involve broad condemnation of the self often are tied to an individual's violations of standards for behavior that are widely shared in society, and they involve patterns of behavior that must be addressed if the couple's relationship is to improve. The actions that have triggered shame commonly involve violations of safety, trust, and other core qualities of a mutually satisfying intimate relationship, so the therapist needs to evaluate what violations have occurred and help the couple identify changes that may be required on their parts in order to behave as partners who are safe, trustworthy, and so forth. Thus, guilt may be sufficient to motivate an individual to change a behavior that hurt a partner, but shame may initiate an individual's broader examination and modification of the ways that he or she has functioned in the role of an intimate partner.

For example, a physically abusive individual may become motivated to enter individual anger management treatment, as well as to make specific efforts to create a safe environment for the partner at home, based on feeling shame at being a person who has been willing to inflict emotional and physical pain on a partner. In such a case, a therapist may emphasize the positive motivating function of the shame, as long as its intensity does not lead the individual to "shut down" and avoid constructive problem-solving behavior. During assessment the therapist also differentiates between partners holding a belief that individuals should take personal responsibility for their hurtful actions toward others versus holding a retaliation-oriented belief that a person who behaves negatively toward a loved one deserves to be punished severely. As we noted earlier, when a nonshamed partner holds such a retaliation belief, it may lead him or her to attempt to elicit and reinforce the other's shame responses.

Identifying the Topics Associated With Shame

The assessment of shame should include a survey of the topics that elicit partners' shame responses. Not only does this help the therapist develop a treatment plan that will meet each couple's needs, it also helps determine the degree to which a partner tends to be shame prone in general rather than responding to a specific situation in the relationship. For example, a male client reported shame that was triggered by being fired from his job for underperformance and his resultant conclusion that he was a failure as a provider for his family. Upon inquiry by the therapist, he reported similar shame experiences over the course of his life whenever he failed to live up to his personal expectations of himself or those of his parents (e.g., regarding his grades in school, when he was a substitute rather than a starting player on his high school basketball team). Consequently, the therapist encouraged the client to seek individual therapy to assist him with his apparent vulnerability to shame in addition to continuing couple therapy to work jointly with the partners on how they were adapting to their financial stressors and to the husband's depressive withdrawal.

Among the areas that may elicit shame, the therapist should be aware of those that involve an individual's evaluation of his or her personal characteristics (e.g., negative body image, self-appraisal as being of relatively low intelligence or incompetent) and those that involve negative evaluations of the self as a partner (e.g., belief that one does not adequately satisfy the partner sexually, violation of one's standards for appropriate behavior in the role of a caring partner). The therapist can inquire about what qualities the person believes he or she should have and the extent to which the person's perceived qualities meet the personal standards. Whenever an unmet standard is identified, the therapist inquires about the thoughts and emotions that the person experiences about it, searching for the person's self-evaluation in this area and the associated mood states. Here the distinction between guilt and shame becomes important because in some cases an individual may feel guilt over a specific behavior toward a partner, being disappointed in his or her performance and making a commitment to improve the behavior, but without experiencing the self-condemnation involved in shame.

Culture and Shame Experiences

Assessment of an individual's shame experiences, including past experiences in the family of origin, must take into account cultural variations in child-rearing techniques and beliefs about proper behavior. For example, Lewis (1992) noted that Western views of child rearing have focused on developing the individuality and self-concept of the child. However, because the individual has great freedom, he or she is responsible for negative consequences of his or her actions, creating a risk of experiences of shame. Furthermore, Lewis suggested that decreased reliance on religious institutions to help people achieve forgiveness leaves many people vulnerable to experiencing shame. Also, many Asian cultures with collectivist values place importance on not losing face through one's public actions and not shaming one's family. Children are raised to engage in indirect forms of communication that avoid confrontation with others and the potential for either party losing face (Lau & Yeung, 1996). Therefore, when interviewing couples regarding sources of shame in their family histories as well as in their current relationships, one should inquire about cultural standards for behavior and child-rearing practices. Such beliefs are likely to influence not only the intensity of one partner's shame but also whether or not the other partner is empathic and supportive versus punitive.

Assessment of Couple Interaction Patterns Associated With Shame

In addition to relying on partners' reports during interviews regarding shame experiences, couple therapists directly observe dyadic interaction patterns associated with each individual's shame responses because these specific interactions often elicit and maintain shame. In their emotion-focused therapy approach, Greenberg and Goldman (2008) proposed that in long-term couple relationships, partners commonly elicit each other's preexisting core shame schemas and can reinforce the shamed person's negative view of the self, thereby increasing the person's self-blame. Greenberg and Goldman's assumption is very similar to a core concept in cognitive–behavioral therapy that current life situations, including interactions between significant others, trigger an individual's underlying schemas about the self and world (A. T. Beck et al., 1979; J. S. Beck, 1995; Dattilio, 2010).

Epstein and Baucom (2002) described how joint sessions with a couple provide a therapist in vivo opportunities to observe how one person's actions trigger responses in the other partner. For example, when one member of a couple describes how his or her partner's past actions were very hurtful, the therapist can ask the partner what he or she was thinking and feeling upon hearing this (especially if the therapist noticed nonverbal cues that the partner was having a reaction). It is important to assess the partner's cognitive evaluations of both the hurt partner (e.g., "She is unreasonable, too sensitive," etc., versus "She is a caring partner and did not deserve to be treated poorly") and the self ("I only behaved that way because I was lonely, I did not realize that my behavior would hurt her," etc., versus "I am a terrible person for treating her that way"). In addition, the therapist should assess the type (e.g., anger, anxiety, depression) and intensity of the person's emotional responses to the other's description of being hurt by his or her behavior. Within a cognitive–behavioral model (A. T. Beck et al., 1979; J. S. Beck, 1995), the individual's emotions are likely to be consistent with the cognitive theme; for example, anger would be associated with evaluating the partner's expression of hurt as unfair and manipulative, whereas shame and depression would be associated with a negative self-evaluation.

Observation of couple interactions also may reveal circumstances under which shame responses appear to serve functions that may not be constructive for the couple. For example, a therapist observed that whenever a husband in one couple described being hurt by his wife's revealing problems in the couple's sexual relationship to members of her family, the wife immediately expressed self-condemnation and shame and then became silent. Although there was a positive aspect to her expressing regret at her violation of the couple's privacy, her response usually led her husband to soothe her, and no further actions were taken to improve their relationship. In another couple, a woman who had been hurt by her male partner's secretive excessive spending brought up this behavior whenever the partner voiced disagreement with her regarding child-rearing approaches, relationships with in-laws, and so forth. Her comments would shift his attention to his feelings of shame regarding his violation of her trust, and there would be no further problem-solving discussion of their areas of conflict. Based on observing this interaction pattern, the therapist formed a hypothesis that the woman's triggering of her partner's shame allowed her to avoid negotiating with him about other issues in their relationship. Thus, direct observation of couple interactions during sessions may reveal patterns in which the elicitation of shame (or guilt) responses detracts from the couple's ability to resolve issues in their relationship. During treatment sessions, the therapist can intervene to block those patterns and help the couple develop more constructive ones using cognitive–behavioral approaches for improving partners' communication and problem-solving skills.

Self-Report Questionnaires for Assessing Shame

If a clinician wants to use standardized self-report questionnaires to assess each partner's proneness to shame or current feeling of shame, a variety of instruments are available for such purposes (for a review, see Robins, Noftle, & Tracy, 2007). The selection of a particular measure will depend mostly on whether the therapist wants to evaluate the clients' proneness to shame or recent shame states and whether a longer or a shorter instrument is needed. Clinicians interested in assessing partners' proneness to shame could use self-report instruments such as the Harder Personal Feelings Questionnaire (PFQ2; Harder & Zalma, 1990) or the Test of Self-Conscious Affect—3 (TOSCA–3; Tangney, Dearing, Wagner, & Gramzow, 2000). The PFQ2 includes a 10-item shame subscale and a six-item guilt subscale, with a 5-point Likert-type response format. The longer TOSCA–3 asks the respondent to rate his or her affective tendencies (proneness to guilt, proneness to shame, externalization, pride in one's self, pride in one's behavior, and detachment) in particular scenarios using a 5-point Likert-type response scale. If clinicians want to assess only a client's level of internalized shame, they can rely on the Internalized Shame Scale (Cook, 1994), which includes a 24-item internalized shame subscale.

To assess an individual's current state of shame, clinicians can use the State Shame and Guilt Scale (SSGS; Marschall, Sanftner, & Tangney, 1994). The SSGS is a brief measure with three subscales (shame, guilt, and pride) of five items each that asks respondents to indicate on a 5-point Likert response scale the extent to which each statement describes the feeling they experience (e.g., "I want to sink in the floor and disappear").

COUPLE INTERVENTIONS FOR SHAME PRONENESS

When the assessment of a couple indicates that one or both partners have a tendency to respond with shame, a number of interventions have the potential to reduce this tendency while minimizing the singling out of either partner as the identified patient. Some interventions focus on cognitive restructuring or modifying each individual's ways of thinking that contribute to feeling shame in a variety of situations. Other interventions target the shame-prone individual's difficulty in regulating his or her emotional responses. Finally, behavioral interventions focus on altering both partners' actions toward each other that either elicit or reinforce shame responses.

Modification of Cognitions Involved in Shame

Because negative self-evaluation is at the core of shame, interventions to modify cognitions are a crucial component of treatment. Key targets for cognitive restructuring include beliefs regarding violation of personal standards and punishment for doing so, a tendency to be perfectionistic and highly critical of oneself, failure to differentiate between a person's behavior and the broader traitlike characteristics of the person as a human being, and an exaggerated concern about other people's evaluations of oneself. A full overview of interventions for these types of cognitions is beyond the scope of this chapter, but we describe representative examples.

Modification of Unrealistic Standards

Concerning violation of personal standards (e.g., regarding a desirable body image, how one should treat one's partner, performance of a role such as provider for the family), first it is important to guide the shamed individual in specifying the characteristics required by his or her standards, as well as in identifying how much (if any) flexibility exists in the standard. Next, the therapist asks the individual to make separate lists of the advantages and disadvantages of living according to the standard, conveying to the client that he or she would not have adhered to the belief for so long if it did not have some significant positive consequences (Epstein & Baucom, 2002). For example, a common advantage of holding a high standard for one's physical appearance is that it motivates the person to be well groomed and to engage in exercise that may enhance health. Sometimes it may take coaching from the therapist for the individual to identify significant disadvantages of a standard (e.g., frequent unhappiness and even shame from comparing one's body with others' unfavorably, excessive exercise and dieting that may be unhealthy), and the therapist may enlist the nonshamed partner in thinking of other disadvantages of the standard as a way of providing support for the shame-prone person. In addition, having the couple work together in considering advantages and disadvantages can help reduce a nonshamed partner's own unrealistic standards for the other's characteristics, thereby decreasing the partner's reinforcement of the other's shame.

Given that many unrealistic standards have their roots in an individual's family of origin, another useful intervention is to explore the shame-prone person's family experiences (e.g., being criticized strongly by parents for having a particular characteristic) that may have shaped his or her beliefs.

Merely focusing on this insight is unlikely to dispel long-standing shame-inducing standards, but it may motivate the individual to make efforts to "break free" of early influences that continue to cause emotional pain. Again, engaging the nonshamed partner as an ally in counteracting the other's distressing standards can strengthen his or her support for the shame-prone person, and during daily interactions the partner may help the other notice when he or she is applying the standard unreasonably. To minimize focusing on the shame-prone individual as the identified patient in the couple, therapists commonly spend time exploring the nonshamed partner's own personal standards and coaching him or her in challenging those that at times cause stress. This procedure normalizes the existence of unrealistic standards (the idea that most people have developed some and can benefit from modifying them).

One standard that some nonshamed partners may become defensive about modifying is the belief that some forms of behavior are truly shameful, and if one's partner has engaged in them he or she deserves to be reminded of it, made to feel awful, and be punished for it. An individual who adheres to this standard is likely to attempt to elicit and reinforce the other's shame, perhaps increasing the other's shame proneness. A therapist can coach the individual in examining advantages and disadvantages of the standard, emphasizing that any advantage associated with having the partner feel bad is likely to be outweighed by the degree to which punishment and an adversarial atmosphere damage the relationship. In addition, both partners are more likely to benefit if the therapist shifts the meaning of the event from shame (in which the perpetrator is evaluated negatively as a person) to guilt (in which the perpetrator's actions are evaluated negatively). Key advantages of this reconceptualization that the therapist can emphasize are that a guilty party can apologize and make amends, and a hurt partner then has an opportunity to forgive him or her, resulting in healing of their relationship.

Modification of Negative Attributions Associated With Shame

A cognitive–behavioral approach to shame also includes modification of negative attributions that both members of a couple make regarding the characteristics of a shamed individual. An individual who is shame prone tends to attribute his or her negative behavior to stable undesirable traits (e.g., "I am a selfish person") rather than to potentially controllable situational conditions, and the individual's partner may share and reinforce this view. To reduce shame proneness, a therapist can coach both members of the couple in considering alternative attributions for the individual's distressing behavior and in conducting a functional analysis of specific occurrences of negative acts (conditions in which they occurred and consequences that followed them; for detailed intervention procedures, see Epstein & Baucom, 2002). One result of undermining negative trait attributions may be that instead of feeling shame and hopelessness regarding his or her actions, based on believing that such actions are due to stable negative traits, the individual experiences guilt about specific acts and feels motivated to behave differently in the future.

In addition, the nonshamed partner's relationship distress will be less to the extent that he or she avoids attributing the other's acts to negative motives or intent or a lack of love (Pretzer, Epstein, & Fleming, 1991). Consequently, it is important to coach the couple in exploring evidence regarding more benign explanations for the negative behavior. For example, a man who had a brief affair with a coworker described how his actions had occurred during a period in his life when his self-esteem was low due to career failures and noted that the affair was a means of making himself feel better temporarily. He stressed that he never felt a decrease in his love for his wife and that it was selfish behavior, rather than a lack of love or an attempt to hurt his wife. Although his wife still was very hurt and angry, his self-disclosure shifted her attributions regarding the cause of his infidelity, leading her to tell him, "I do believe you love me, but your love won't be sufficient to save our marriage if you don't learn to deal with your personal problems."

Addressing Forgiveness

Cognitive–behavioral therapists also address the cognitive barrier to resolution of shame that exists as long as one or both members of the couple fail to forgive an individual for the shame-related behavior or characteristic. Shame responses persist as long as the shamed partner cannot reach a level of self-acceptance and the other partner cannot forgive the individual. By *forgiveness*, we are referring to (a) acknowledgement that an individual behaved in a negative way, (b) the individual's acceptance of responsibility for his or her actions and expression of regret for the negative impact on the partner, (c) acceptance that the negative events did occur but that the couple's relationship can survive in spite of it, (d) identification of the vulnerability characteristics within the two partners and their relationship that contributed to the individual's negative behavior, and (e) a commitment to make concerted efforts to improve the individual's behavior and the relationship (Baucom, Snyder, & Gordon, 2009). Forgiveness involves accepting rather than forgetting or excusing negative behavior.

Baucom et al.'s (2009) cognitive–behavioral approach to treating couples that have experienced infidelity includes guidelines for helping partners explore what it would mean to forgive an individual who has engaged in hurtful behavior, and it is well suited to working with couples that have experienced shame over a variety of distressing experiences. It involves a major cognitive component of discussing definitions of forgiveness and exploring and addressing concerns that either partner may have about granting forgiveness to the self or partner. For example, a man feared that if he forgave his wife for sharing intimate details about their relationship with her family, she would interpret it as permission to violate that boundary in the future. The therapist guided the man in expressing his concerns and the wife in listening empathically. Next, the therapist guided the wife in expressing her regret that her behavior had been hurtful to her husband and guided the husband in responding empathically. Finally, the therapist coached the couple in problem solving to devise guidelines for keeping information private. Thus, the wife's initial shame regarding her behavior and the husband's hurt and anger motivated the couple to change the boundary between the marriage and the wife's family of origin. The therapist guided the couple toward accepting what had occurred and understanding vulnerabilities within each individual and in their relationship that had been risk factors for the violation of privacy and trust. This, in turn, created the level of forgiveness that was needed for them to work on reducing the vulnerabilities and strengthening their relationship.

Reducing Excessive Emotional Responses Associated With Shame

Because an individual's shame responses and the partner's negative responses to the individual's negative actions or characteristics can be exacerbated when either or both members of the couple have difficulty regulating their emotions, therapists can coach couples in self-soothing and other strategies for emotion regulation. Interventions include providing brief psychoeducational presentations regarding the impact of emotions on behavior, coaching partners in tracking their own emotional responses and the conditions eliciting them (the behavior of one partner and the interpretations of the other), establishing guidelines for safe expression of emotions during sessions, exploring vulnerable feelings (e.g., loneliness) and underlying expressions of anger, compartmentalizing the time and place for expression of strong emotions, and practicing distress tolerance (Meichenbaum, 1985) and self-soothing strategies such as muscle relaxation and time-outs (Epstein & Baucom, 2002).

Modification of Couple Interaction Patterns

Some behavioral interventions focus on reducing interaction patterns between partners that elicit or exacerbate shame responses, whereas other interventions are intended to build constructive communication and problem solving. The following are brief descriptions of these behavioral interventions, and the reader can consult CBCT texts (Baucom & Epstein, 1990; Epstein & Baucom, 2002; Rathus & Sanderson, 1999) for more detailed procedures. Overall, a goal of these interventions is to help the couple shift from shame-focused interactions to solutions and behavior that enhance both part-ners' self-esteem and relationship satisfaction.

Reducing Excessive Focus on Shame

Although it can be constructive for an individual to express feelings of shame to a partner regarding his or her actions toward the partner, repeated self-denigration can interfere with the couple's constructive resolution of problems in their relationship. Consequently, a therapist can commend an individual for taking responsibility for addressing actions or personal charac-teristics that he or she regrets but then should encourage the client to take steps toward more positive behavior rather than perseverating on problems.

In contrast, when an individual responds to feeling shame by withdraw-ing from interacting with the partner (and even the therapist) during sessions, the therapist needs to intervene to reengage him or her. The therapist can dis-cuss the signs that the individual is feeling uncomfortable, praise him or her for the efforts made to improve the couple's relationship, and explore the distress-ing shame thoughts and emotions that the person is experiencing. Through gentle encouragement, the therapist can coach the withdrawn individual to participate in constructive communication and problem-solving skills.

The therapist also may need to interrupt or block the nonshamed part-ner from making critical and contemptuous remarks that elicit shame in the other person. The therapist can note that it is legitimate for the hurt partner to describe the negative effects that the shamed partner's actions have pro-duced, but the therapist should also underscore that attacks on the other's self-esteem are destructive and unlikely to contribute to more positive cou-ple interactions. Cognitive–behavioral therapists stop negative interactions as often as necessary and redirect the couple toward more positive forms of behavior toward each other (Epstein & Baucom, 2002).

Building Positive Communication Skills

Shame can be reduced when both members of a couple use skills for expressing thoughts and emotions clearly and constructively and skills for empathic listening. Detailed descriptions of procedures used in communica-tion skills training can be found in texts such as those by Baucom and Epstein (1990), Epstein and Baucom (2002), and Rathus and Sanderson (1999). These interventions typically include psychoeducation regarding goals and guidelines for expressive and listening skills, modeling of skills by the thera-pist, and repeated practice by the couple with specific coaching by the ther-apist. An individual can express feelings of shame to his or her partner in concise terms, and the partner can reflect those feelings back to the individ-ual without blaming or criticizing. These skills are used to increase mutual understanding, validation, and support. However, it is important that the therapist monitor the degree to which an individual is devaluing the self when expressing shame, because it may be necessary to interrupt this process and guide the individual in challenging his or her self-denigration. Similarly, the therapist may need to challenge a nonshamed partner's negative cognitions that are interfering with his or her ability to respond empathically when the other person expresses shame. These are examples of a therapist integrating interventions targeting negative cognitions with those focused on modifying behavioral interactions.

Enhancing Problem-Solving Skills

Problem-solving skills are often useful in resolving issues associated with shame. For example, if an individual experiences shame after secret excessive spending, the couple may benefit from identifying a problematic pattern in their joint handling of their finances and from generating a new plan for saving and spending. Detailed procedures for teaching couples problem-solving skills for resolving issues in their relationship can be found in CBCT texts. The components of the training (psychoeducation, instructions, modeling by the therapist, practice by the couple with coaching by the therapist) are the same as those for communication training. The couple is taught the stages of problem solving, which include identifying a problem in observable behavioral terms, brainstorming possible solutions without evaluating them, evaluating pros and cons of each potential solution, selecting a solution that is acceptable to both partners, and attempting to carry out the solution on a trial basis. The therapist monitors and intervenes with obstacles to the partners' problem-solving interaction. For example, a partner of an individual who feels shame over secretive excessive spending may believe that adequate punishment should involve the shamed person having no say in decisions regarding the couple's finances for the foreseeable future. This punitive stance is likely to block collaborative problem solving, so the therapist may need to use cognitive interventions to reduce the partner's belief.

CONCLUSION

Couple relationships are a prime context for individuals to experience shame due to the strong emotional bonds that exist between intimate partners and the high standards that many people set for their own and their partner's ways of conducting themselves within the relationship. Consequently, focusing solely on the individual who experiences shame risks overlooking powerful interpersonal forces that must be addressed for effective treatment.

Understanding and treating shame in the couple context requires assessment of each partner as well as of the couple's interaction patterns. Shame responses can be situation specific or can occur broadly in a relationship, depending on each individual's shame proneness (related to personal history of shame experiences in prior relationships and/or his or her current emotion regulation ability) and each person's tendency to elicit and reinforce shame in the other. A couple's ability to resolve conditions that have elicited shame depends on the quality of their communication and problem-solving skills and on their ability to support each other and achieve conditions of acceptance and forgiveness for shame-related behavior. A cognitive–behavioral approach to assessment and treatment of distressed couples provides a framework for individual and dyadic assessment and intervention with shame.

REFERENCES

Abramson, L. Y., Metalsky, G. I., & Alloy, L. B. (1989). Hopelessness depression: A theory-based subtype of depression. *Psychological Review, 96,* 358–372. doi:10.1037/0033-295X.96.2.358

Balcom, D. (1991). Shame and violence: Considerations in couples' treatment. *Journal of Independent Social Work, 5,* 165–181.

Baucom, D. H., & Epstein, N. (1990). *Cognitive-behavioral marital therapy.* New York, NY: Brunner/Mazel.

Baucom, D. H., Epstein, N., Rankin, L. A., & Burnett, C. K. (1996). Assessing relationship standards: The Inventory of Specific Relationship Standards. *Journal of Family Psychology, 10,* 72–88.

Baucom, D. H., Snyder, D. K., & Gordon, K. C. (2009). *Helping couples get past the affair: A clinician's guide.* New York, NY: Guilford Press.

Beach, S. R. H. (Ed.). (2001). *Marital and family processes in depression: A scientific foundation for clinical practice.* Washington, DC: American Psychological Association. doi:10.1037/10350-000

Beck, A. T., Rush, A. J., Shaw, B. F., & Emery, G. (1979). *Cognitive therapy of depression.* New York, NY: Guilford Press.

Beck, J. S. (1995). *Cognitive therapy: Basics and beyond.* New York, NY: Guilford Press.

Bradbury, T. N., & Fincham, F. D. (1990). Attributions in marriage: Review and critique. *Psychological Bulletin, 107,* 3–33. doi:10.1037/0033-2909.107.1.3

Cook, D. R. (1994). *Internalized Shame Scale: Professional manual.* Menomonie, WI: Channel Press.

Dattilio, F. M. (2010). *Cognitive-behavioral therapy with couples and families: A comprehensive guide for clinicians.* New York, NY: Guilford Press.

Deffenbacher, J. L. (1996). Cognitive-behavioral approaches to anger reduction. In K. S. Dobson & K. D. Craig (Eds.), *Advances in cognitive-behavioral therapy* (pp. 31–62). Thousand Oaks, CA: Sage.

Epstein, N. B., & Baucom, D. H. (2002). *Enhanced cognitive-behavioral therapy for couples: A contextual approach.* Washington, DC: American Psychological Association. doi:10.1037/10481-000

Epstein, N. B., & Baucom, D. H. (2003). Couple therapy. In R. L. Leahy (Ed.), *Roadblocks in cognitive-behavioral therapy* (pp. 217–235). New York, NY: Guilford Press.

Ferguson, T. J., Eyre, H. L., & Ashbaker, M. (2000). Unwanted identities: A key variable in shame–anger links and gender differences in shame. *Sex Roles, 42,* 133–157. doi:10.1023/A:1007061505251

Greenberg, L., & Goldman, R. (2008). *Emotion-focused couples therapy: The dynamics of emotion, love, and power.* Washington, DC: American Psychological Association. doi:10.1037/11750-000

Harder, D. W., & Zalma, A. (1990). Two promising shame and guilt scales: A construct validity comparison. *Journal of Personality Assessment, 55,* 729–745. doi:10.1207/s15327752jpa5503&4_30

Karney, B. R., & Bradbury, T. N. (2000). Attributions in marriage: State or trait? A growth curve analysis. *Journal of Personality and Social Psychology, 78,* 295–309. doi:10.1037/0022-3514.78.2.295

Kaufman, G. (1989). *The psychology of shame.* New York, NY: Springer.

Lau, S., & Yeung, P. P. W. (1996). Understanding Chinese child development: The role of culture in socialization. In S. Lau (Ed.), *Growing up the Chinese way: Chinese child and adolescent development* (pp. 29–44). Hong Kong: Chinese University Press.

Lewis, M. (1992). *Shame: The exposed self.* New York, NY: Free Press.

Marschall, D., Sanftner, J., & Tangney, J. P. (1994). *The State Shame and Guilt Scale.* Fairfax, VA: George Mason University.

Meichenbaum, D. (1985). *Stress inoculation training.* New York, NY: Pergamon Press.

Menesini, E., & Camodeca, M. (2008). Shame and guilt as behavior regulators: Relationships with bullying, victimization and prosocial behavior. *British Journal of Developmental Psychology, 26,* 183–196. doi:10.1348/026151007X205281

Mills, R. S. L., Imm, G. P., Walling, B. R., & Weiler, H. A. (2008). Cortisol reactivity and regulation associated with shame responding in early childhood. *Developmental Psychology, 44,* 1369–1380. doi:10.1037/a0013150

Pretzer, J. L., Epstein, N., & Fleming, B. (1991). Marital Attitude Survey: A measure of dysfunctional attributions and expectancies. *Journal of Cognitive Psychotherapy: An International Quarterly, 5,* 131–148.

Rathus, J. H., & Sanderson, W. C. (1999). *Marital distress: Cognitive behavioral interventions for couples.* Northvale, NJ: Jason Aronson.

Retzinger, S. (1995). Identifying shame and anger in discourse. *American Behavioral Scientist, 38,* 1104–1113. doi:10.1177/0002764295038008006

Robins, R. W., Noftle, E. E., & Tracy, J. L. (2007). Assessing self-conscious emotions: A review of self-report and non-verbal measures. In J. L. Tracy, R. W. Robins, & J. P. Tangney (Eds.), *The self-conscious emotions: Theory and research* (pp. 443–467). New York, NY: Guilford Press.

Snyder, D. K., Simpson, J. A., & Hughes, J. N. (2006). *Emotion regulation in couples and families: Pathways to dysfunction and health.* Washington, DC: American Psychological Association. doi:10.1037/11468-000

Tangney, J. P. (1990). Assessing individual differences in proneness to shame and guilt: Development of the Self-Conscious Affect and Attribution Inventory. *Journal of Personality and Social Psychology, 59,* 102–111. doi:10.1037/0022-3514.59.1.102

Tangney, J. P., & Dearing, R. L. (2002). *Shame and guilt.* New York, NY: Guilford Press.

Tangney, J. P., Dearing, R. L., Wagner, P. E., & Gramzow, R. (2000). *The Test of Self-Conscious Affect—3 (TOSCA–3).* Fairfax, VA: George Mason University.

8

THERAPY WITH REFUGEES AND OTHER IMMIGRANTS EXPERIENCING SHAME: A MULTICULTURAL PERSPECTIVE

EMI FURUKAWA AND DENNIS J. HUNT

Shame that challenges the value of self seems equally painful for people of all cultures. The fundamental experience of moral emotions such as shame appears to be universal, although there may be variations in the frequency, intensity, expression, or implications of such emotions across cultures (Furukawa, 2005; Matsumoto, Kudoh, Scherer, & Wallbott, 1988; Tracy & Robins, 2004, 2007; Wallbott & Scherer, 1988, 1995). One way to examine cultural continuity and discontinuity of shame may be to study the psychological adjustment of refugees and other immigrants who have come to the United States from diverse lands. It is well documented that many refugees and other immigrants suffer unspeakable traumas and multiple losses that complicate their adjustment (e.g., Davis, 2000; Fox, Burns, Popovich, & Ilg, 2001; Gold, 1992; Goldfeld, Mollica, Pesavento, & Faraone, 1988; Hunt, 1989; Kandula, Kersey, & Lurie, 2004; Locke, Southwick, McCloskey, & Fernandez-Esquer, 1996; Steel, Silove, Phan, & Bauman, 2002). Intense feelings of shame often accompany their memories of these traumatizing events, though very little systematic research has been conducted on shame among refugees and other immigrants. As shame is strongly associated with negative psychological and behavioral outcomes, including withdrawal, depression, anger, and sometimes aggression (e.g., Ashby, Rice, & Martin, 2006; Crossley & Rockett, 2005; Feiring, Taska, & Lewis, 2002; Harper & Arias, 2004; Henderson & Zimbardo, 2001; Stuewig, Tangney, Heigel, Harty, & McCloskey, 2010; Tangney & Dearing, 2002), addressing shame and its consequences in a therapeutic way can help refugee and other immigrant clients heal from past trauma and rebuild their lives.

The material that follows is based on the clinical experience of the authors, who worked for many years at the Center for Multicultural Human Services, a mental health and social service organization serving refugees and other immigrants in the Washington, DC, area. The unique experiences and worldviews of recent refugees and other immigrants are discussed. We focus on the issues of shame commonly presented by refugee and other immigrant clients in therapy, which include shame associated with past traumas as well as shame triggered by adjustment challenges. We also provide an overview of therapeutic approaches that we have identified over the years to help these clients deal with the emotion of shame. Throughout the chapter, we frame our experiences with refugee and other immigrant clients using the definition of *shame* as a negative evaluation of the global self, as opposed to *guilt*, which is a negative evaluation of specific behavior as conceptualized by Lewis (1971) and Tangney and Dearing (2002). We provide case studies and examples to illustrate how shame is demonstrated and approached in therapy with refugee and other immigrant clients.

SHAME FROM THE PAST

The stories of rape, torture, deprivation, and death of loved ones that refugee and other immigrant clients tell may surprise and even shock many therapists who have lived and trained in the United States. When treating these clients, it is essential to understand their perspectives, beliefs, and core values. It is especially important to examine an emotion like shame, which is strongly associated with one's morality and one's judgment about the self, within the contexts of clients' experiences.

Most disaster or war situations that many refugee and other immigrant clients experience do not give them the time or psychological space to make complex moral choices. In the face of life-threatening situations, primitive survival instincts often take over, causing the individual to freeze or flee. These instinctual responses leave the person incapable of rationally assessing his or her options. Yet in retrospect, he or she may feel paralyzing guilt for not having chosen an alternative course of action that could have prevented the harm suffered by friends or loved ones. It is common for these individuals to fantasize about reliving the experience in a way that would produce a more positive outcome.

For example, one Ethiopian man believed that he could have turned to fight off two soldiers with machine guns who threatened his family and killed his son. His belief that he could have changed the situation was not grounded in reality. If he had tried, it is likely that he and all of his family members would have been killed. Initially, he experienced guilt over his actions or inactions. When he still could not make sense of the event after thinking about it and reliving it many times over, he started to question his value as a person. When he came to realize that he could not undo what had happened, guilt seemed to turn into shame. He started thinking that he must have deserved this tragedy. In situations in which no real alternatives exist, when there is no specific behavior to contemplate or regret, the self—one's core identity and value— can easily become the focus of one's own psychological scrutiny.

Feelings of shame associated with extreme trauma may come from an exaggerated sense of responsibility and a distorted sense of one's power to challenge violence and force. Thanh, a 30-year-old Vietnamese refugee, also believed that he had a choice and did not take action to protect his wife and son. Thanh, his wife, and his two young sons escaped Vietnam in an old, overcrowded fishing boat. After days at sea, the boat was attacked by Thai pirates who threw Thahn's youngest son into the sea and raped his wife. Thahn watched helplessly, holding his 3-year-old son protectively against his chest. He felt a deep sense of shame and worthlessness as a father and husband for not being able to protect his children and wife.

Even though he was psychologically immobilized and physically incapacitated (a normal reaction to such an extreme event), he believed that he had been too weak and cowardly to save his family. He experienced intrusive thoughts of the event and had vivid revenge fantasies. His shame was accompanied by feelings of rage. Being yelled at by his boss in a job training program was all that was needed for him to explode in rage. He felt humiliated in front of his coworkers, exacerbating his already paralyzing feelings of shame. Because of this violent outburst, he was forced into counseling as a condition of remaining in the training program, a requirement to receive ongoing refugee cash assistance. Of course, this further compounded his sense of shame.

Another client, a Kurdish man from a small village, had made a choice to give police the name of his neighbor who distributed flyers against the current government. He knew that his neighbor would be killed. If he had refused to turn in his neighbor, he would have had his finger cut off, and his daughter would have been kidnapped. He felt an overwhelming need to protect himself and his daughter. In retrospect, he felt great regret and shame that he had made a choice that resulted in the death of his neighbor.

Among many refugee and immigrant groups, shame can also result when there is a failure to live up to cultural role expectations. In many cultures, one's roles in the family and community are an important part of one's self-identity.

People define themselves using concrete role categories, such as being a good mother or a village leader, rather than abstract values, such as being smart or kind, as do many people in Western societies (Markus & Kitayama, 1991). Thus, failing to fulfill role responsibilities, even when largely due to external circumstances, can be extremely shameful. It is not a consolation to know that you are still a good person when your child dies—your value as a human is measured by being a good father, and you failed. A Mexican woman felt that she failed in her role as a mother because she could not protect her children from witnessing her being raped in the desert after they crossed the U.S. border. Many Sierra Leonean men took a very long time to acknowledge that anything had happened to their families—not being able to live up to their role as a protector was so shameful that they avoided discussion of what they had been through.

Most people's reactions to such painful emotions of shame are unproductive and maladaptive (Tangney & Dearing, 2002). Refugee and other immigrant clients who experience shame associated with extreme trauma are no exception. A client with political asylum talked obsessively about going back to his country to kill his daughter's rapist. The father's focus on revenge distracted the family from the real challenge of making a living to provide a new start for the family, in particular the daughter, who may have been experiencing adjustment difficulties because of her past trauma. Because the father's fantasies were never achieved, his feelings of inadequacy were exacerbated. He started to drink heavily, he was unable to hold a job, and verbal and physical conflicts in the family increased. Overwhelmed by shame, his attempts to reclaim a sense of pride were unsuccessful. Shame can significantly undermine the efforts of refugees and other immigrants to rebuild their lives in a new environment.

SHAME AFTER RESETTLEMENT

In addition to the shame triggered by past trauma, many refugee and other immigrant clients experience shame as they build a life in a new land (Eisenbruch, 1988; Phan, 2000; Sam & Berry, 1995). They must develop new sources of self-worth. When refugees and other immigrants come to a new country, many of them give up the prestige, status, and money they had in their home country and accept jobs, such as taxi drivers and maintenance workers that would be viewed as lower-status positions in their homeland. This often leads to feelings of shame and a loss of pride. Some people who had a high social status and were wealthy in their homeland go to extraordinary lengths to maintain appearances of prosperity and elite status in the immigrant community. Some work several jobs to hold on to the trappings of their previous identity.

The novel and film *The House of Sand and Fog* deftly portrayed such an Iranian family (Dubus, 1999; Perelman & London, 2003). The father, who used to be a high-ranking military officer, changes from his road maintenance clothes to a suit after work. He returns to his wife and children every day with a leather briefcase in hand. He drives an expensive car and comes home to their upscale apartment, which he works nights and weekends to pay the rent for. His children have no idea about the financial situation of the family and the father's real work. His daughter has a lavish wedding to which the father invites hundreds of members of the Iranian community. As the novel shows, such behavior driven by shame easily translates to bitterness, resentment, and anger that diminish the capacity of the person to function in a healthy way.

On a daily basis, many immigrants experience shame from appearing incompetent because of their limited language skills, lack of education or job skills, or unfamiliarity with the host country's cultural practices (Aronowitz, 1984; D'Avanzo, Frye, & Froman, 1994; Dhooper & Tran, 1998; Kinzie, Tran, Breckenridge, & Bloom, 1980; Miller, Chambers, & Coleman, 1981; Yeh, 2003). Not being able to negotiate even simple transactions is frustrating. Shopping, ordering food at restaurants, taking public transportation, and reading bills are challenges. When they go to a doctor, they may need to ask their children to translate in examination rooms. They cannot help their children with their homework. These situations threaten their roles as parents, providers, and protectors and can lead to feelings of worthlessness. In addition, some may feel unwelcome in the community and experience shame because of their ethnic or religious identity or newcomer status.

Feelings of shame can also be triggered by rejection and negative evaluation from one's compatriots in the community. Threats to one's support network are frightening for anyone, but for refugees and other immigrants who have been cut off from their natural support systems back home, being accepted by compatriots in the community is critical. Regrettably, some refugees and other immigrants are shunned by their compatriots because their names are associated with a political group or individual or family linked to negative events in their homeland. In the 1980s, many unmarried Vietnamese women with Amerasian children were resettled in the United States. The children were looked down on by the rest of the Vietnamese refugee community, who assumed that their mothers had been "bar girls," which was not true in most cases. The shame associated with such rejection by one's compatriots can significantly interfere with successful adjustment.

For Cristina, a 25-year-old woman from Guatemala, painful feelings of shame from multiple sources presented in acute somatic symptoms. One weekend, she weakly stumbled into a hospital emergency room saying that her heart hurt. She appeared to be having a heart attack, but doctors found no medical explanation for her pain. They concluded that she was experiencing a panic attack and should seek mental health assistance. Earlier in the week, there was a violent robbery at the McDonald's where she worked, and she was held hostage for a few hours, with the assailant at one point putting the barrel of the gun into her mouth. Two weeks prior to the incident, she had been raped on the way home from work. She did see a mental health counselor and told him that what had happened to her caused her to feel great shame, which she experienced as a pain in her heart. These incidents significantly diminished Cristina's sense of self-worth. She felt that she deserved to be a victim and that she must be a bad person. After all, bad things cannot happen twice to a good person. She did not tell friends or family members about these incidents because she was ashamed and afraid that she would be looked upon as a person to be avoided. In her community, there was a strong belief that some people have bad spirits around them and that these spirits bring misfortune. Once a person is labeled as having bad spirits, that person can become an outcast from the community. Cristina had limited language skills, and she did not have any friends outside her community. She could not afford to become an outcast, and so she felt that she had to live in silence with the pain.

The stigma and shame associated with mental health problems are universal, but they are particularly extreme in certain cultures. Mr. and Mrs. Nguyen, a Vietnamese couple in their 60s, were too ashamed of their 30-year-old mentally retarded daughter to get her the help she needed. They kept the young woman isolated in their home, but she had begun sneaking out of the home and drawing the attention of neighbors as she walked in their yards and the street and tried to play with their children. The couple experienced an emotional crisis when Adult Protective Services were called in to address the needs of their daughter. They were humiliated in front of their neighbors and hardly able to function when they were called to court for a hearing on the case. Their worst fear was that news of their treatment of their daughter would become known in the Vietnamese immigrant community, which of course it eventually did. The couple needed significant mental health support to get through the ordeal. A caseworker helped educate them about mental retardation and explained how it was viewed in the United States and what resources were available to help them give their daughter a fuller life. They were introduced to a support group of other parents with older mentally retarded children. They were surprised to see how many other families, even in the Vietnamese community, had a mentally retarded or mentally ill child. They also felt less shame when they came to understand that others did not blame them for their daughter's mental retardation.

Refugees and other immigrants often struggle with the shame of not being able to meet the expectations for support of family members left behind. Relatives and communities in their homeland may be expecting them to send money, medicine, and other vital goods to help them survive. Some mothers and fathers immigrate first, leaving all or some children behind. They have high expectations and make this choice as a way to provide a better life for their family over the long term. However, when they encounter the harsh economic realities of life in the United States, they are often unable to send the support they had promised their families in their home country. Sometimes they raise expectations by sending money regularly when times are good but must suddenly stop their support when they lose their jobs. Many start to question their choices, abilities, values, and worth as human beings. Many who are at this stage of adjustment report wanting to escape and hide, so overwhelmed are they by their feelings of inadequacy and shame.

SHAME AND INTERGENERATIONAL ISSUES

Immigrant parents often put exceedingly high expectations on their children to achieve (Zhou & Bankston, 1994). They strive to make up for all they gave up to come to the United States. They work multiple jobs to earn enough money for their children to have opportunities. They push their children to go to college and become doctors or engineers. But not all children are suited to attending college or want to be a doctor or engineer. They may have different dreams and aspirations. Many children feel pressure from their parents and experience shame when they are not able to achieve the dreams their parents have for them.

Children, more than parents, are forced to blend into mainstream culture (Kwak, 2003; Liebkind & Jasinskaja-Lahti, 2000; Zhou, 1997; Zuniga, 2002). At school, things like dressing differently, wearing a head scarf, having an accent, and using free lunch tickets can induce shameful feelings. These immigrant children may not understand their teachers or be able to answer questions in class when called on. For students from some cultures, this form of public humiliation is very shame inducing. Their education system back home may not have prepared them to perform as expected in the American classroom. They may perceive U.S. classrooms as less structured and may be unaccustomed to the level of class participation expected. They may not be used to exercises in which they are expected to express their own views; they may be unfamiliar with test formats such as multiple choice or filling in the blank. Male immigrant high school students may feel a sense of inadequacy when they are threatened and demeaned in words and actions by mainstream American students. One way of responding to their feelings has been through organized gang violence (Esbensen, 2000; Snyder & Sickmund, 2006). By belonging to a gang of their ethnic group, these students feel less vulnerable and regain a sense of acceptance and power (Egley, 2000; Katz, 1996).

Romantic relationships are also often a source of conflict in refugee and other immigrant families. Interracial relationships and romantic relationships at a younger age are fairly well accepted by American culture, but not by most refugee and other immigrant families. It is easy for adolescents and young adults who grow up in the United States to lose touch with their parents' traditional perspective. They do not understand why their parents would consider some behaviors shameful. In these cases, they no longer have a shared code of shame because theirs has been altered by acculturation. Behaviors, attire, relationships, friendships, academic achievement, and so forth are all potential sources of shame and conflict as young people begin to develop perspectives and values that are different from their refugee and other immigrant parents.

For example, Preti was a 15-year-old Pakistani girl whose parents listened in on her phone calls, limited her contact with female peers, and prohibited any contact with boys. Under pressure to be accepted by her American peers, Preti had been engaging in behaviors that her parents found unacceptable. They were terrified of losing their daughter to drug use, sex, and other "corrupting behaviors of American youth culture." They threatened to send her back to Pakistan to be married rather than risk having her shame the family by becoming like "other American girls." One day their worst fears came true. Preti became pregnant from her African American boyfriend. Her mother and father felt great shame and believed they had failed as parents. They could not now send her back to Pakistan because the shame might be even greater and could result in violence against her. Her parents allowed Preti and her baby to live in the house but withdrew from involvement in the Pakistani immigrant community.

For Arian, a 15-year-old Afghan girl, a similar situation played out somewhat differently. In this case, the shame of their daughter's pregnancy was so great for the family that they disowned their daughter, telling her that she was no longer a member of the family and was to never contact them again. For this family who had struggled to rebuild their lives in the United States, their reputation in the tight-knit refugee community was of critical importance. The girl and her baby were welcomed into the family of her Hispanic boyfriend. In their home country, El Salvador, having a child at a young age and not being married are not uncommon and not a source of shame; they do not diminish the whole person's value or the family's integrity.

Caring for elderly parents can also be a source of conflict arising from intergenerational differences in the perception of what is shameful and what is not. In many cultures, children are expected to take care of their parents. Failing to do so can be shameful for individuals but also for their families. However, second- and third-generation immigrants may not feel that taking care of their parents is their responsibility. In some instances, taking care of elderly parents is a practical matter. An unmarried son or daughter may find it more cost-effective to stay in the family home. A struggling young family may find it difficult to house parents and decide instead to place them in a home for older adults. However, immigrant parents may view the failure of their children to take care of them as shameful. Their children may feel guilty about the decision, but they may not understand that caring for elderly parents is a moral choice and that the choice reflects the children's view of their parents' value or decency as a person. Failure to provide for elderly parents is seen as an unforgivable act in some cultural codes. In Japan and other Asian cultures, it is the obligation of the oldest son to take care of his aging parents. This son also is the heir to all of the parents' property when they die. For an oldest son to ignore this responsibility is seen as a very shameful choice.

BRIDGING GAPS, IDENTIFYING SHAME, AND ESTABLISHING RAPPORT WITH IMMIGRANT CLIENTS

Engaging refugees and other immigrants in therapy entails many challenges. Language and other cultural barriers make it difficult to gain access to mental health services (Cheung & Snowden, 1990; Hu, Snowden, Jerrell, & Kang, 1993; Koppelman, 2005; Lefley, 1990; Vega, Kolody, Aguilar-Gaxiola, & Catalano, 1999; Wasserman et al., 2003). It is difficult for many in this population to share sensitive issues and emotions with professionals who come from different cultural backgrounds and have difficulty relating to their experiences. Others, however, may feel ashamed to share their traumatic experience with a professional from the same culture, especially if he or she represents an opposing political or ethnic group in their homeland. In refugee and other immigrant communities, gossip travels fast. So even though a trained therapist or an interpreter must respect the client's confidentiality, many refugees and other immigrants do not understand this and fear that their problems will become known in the community.

For example, a man and his brother walked into the Center. They did not have an appointment but told the receptionist it was an emergency. The brother appeared to be in the midst of a psychotic episode. There was a Turkish therapist on the staff, and she spoke the same language. However, the client refused to work with her. The brothers were ethnic Kurds who lived in Turkey, and the therapist was ethnic Turkish. Historically, the Kurds have felt demeaned by the Turks. The Kurdish brothers may have felt shame at having to get help for a mental health problem from a Turkish therapist. The therapist did not have strong political affiliations and she was a very kind person, but that did not matter. The brothers did not trust her. They became upset, and the client's agitation and paranoia increased dramatically. They spoke the same language as the therapist, but there was a great divide of ethnicity, culture, and politics, and the shame that would result from accepting Turkish help was not worth it.

It is important, therefore, for therapists not to make assumptions when we see clients from a particular culture, ethnicity, or background. To work successfully across cultures involves an ongoing questioning of our assumptions about other cultures and our own reactions to them. It requires therapists to be humble. Working with people from cultures unlike our own sometimes has a tendency to make us feel less competent and less sure of ourselves. For example, it may be difficult for a Western-trained female therapist to work with a traditional Afghan couple. The Afghan woman may be covered from head to toe in a burka, with a mesh screen over her face. If a therapist asks the wife a question, the husband is likely to answer. The wife may not say a word during the entire session. This could trigger uneasy feelings or anger in a therapist who believes in having equal power in relationships and wants to empower the wife. Responding appropriately within the framework of an unfamiliar culture is difficult. Recognizing these challenges can help us feel less self-conscious about ourselves as therapists and be more attuned to how the clients want us to relate to them. In fact, therapists should look to the client for cues regarding direct eye contact, direct questioning, sharing of personal information, handshakes, and the power relations within families.

Finally, therapists need to understand the role that shame may play in the development of certain psychological disorders. For example, among Vietnamese, shame appears to be a key element in depression. Kinzie et al. (1982) developed a depression scale to screen the flood of Vietnamese refugees arriving on American shores. Rather than translate one of the many English-language depression scales, Kinzie's research team worked with a group of Vietnamese professionals to generate a list of depression-related concepts in Vietnamese. The resulting scale included such culturally specific items as "sad and bothered," "angry," and "shameful and dishonored." In a sample of 1,998 Vietnamese refugees, 7% endorsed the "shameful and dishonored" item, and compared with those scoring below the clinical cutoff point, the depressed group endorsed all of the culture-specific symptoms at a significantly higher rate (Buchwald et al., 1995).

REMOVING THE SHAME OF RECEIVING PROFESSIONAL HELP

For refugees and other immigrants, seeking professional mental health services can create feelings of shame because of pervasive negative attitudes toward the mentally ill population in their homelands. Many refugees and other immigrants are also unfamiliar with the social service system in the United States. They do not know what services are available. They do not know what to expect from a therapist. Therefore, it is important for therapists to take extra time to explain confidentiality, clinic policies, and our role—what we can and cannot do. In their homeland, these clients might have sought help from other healers such as herbalists, religious leaders, or indigenous healers. A therapist may need to explain how he or she is similar to or different from these other types of helpers. It may help to talk about the kind of training a therapist goes through and the limitations in the kind of help they can give. Similarly, antidepressant and antianxiety medication may be unfamiliar to foreign-born clients, and such medication may carry a heavy stigma. Although many American-born clients also experience stigma when seeking mental health services, this reluctance is often magnified among foreign-born clients. For refugees and other immigrants, community-based mental health centers or private clinics may also be unfamiliar concepts because in their homelands mental health treatment may be limited to the services provided in hospitals by physicians and psychiatrists. It may be important to emphasize how common and acceptable it is to seek help from psychologists and other mental health professionals who are trained to help them with challenges they are facing.

The shame of being seen at a mental health clinic may be compounded by the shame of not speaking English well. We need to reassure clients that English is difficult to learn and acknowledge that they know English much better than we know their language. Ask for their forgiveness when you ask them to repeat themselves, and assure them that you are willing to work hard to communicate with them. This can greatly reduce the anxiety and feelings of incompetence and shame.

When refugees and other immigrants seek professional help, the presenting problem is usually a reason other than psychological issues. They may be having problems at work; a child may be demonstrating behavioral or academic problems; child protective services may have called because parents left their children home alone at night while they worked; the family may need financial assistance; or the family may have come to the attention of authorities because of an incident of domestic violence. A child may come in for therapy presenting a wide range of behavioral and psychological symptoms. However, the parents may take up most of the sessions asking where to get food, how to find an apartment or a job, or how to obtain help with their legal issues. Practical survival problems may be associated with feelings of incompetence, worthlessness, and shame and cannot be ignored.

The challenge for the therapist is to deal with these superficial but serious case management problems that clients face while being aware of and addressing underlying psychological issues. When working with refugee and other immigrant clients, it is important for therapists to be flexible and accommodating. The clients may not have reliable transportation to come to therapy on time. Having adequate housing and shelter is essential before beginning to work on psychological issues. If they do not feel confident in their ability to provide for their family, they may not be able to face the underlying issue of shame associated with their past traumas.

How can therapists help clients like Thanh, the Vietnamese father who was forced to witness his wife being raped and his son thrown out of a refugee boat? Thanh was probably not ready to talk about his feelings of shame. Others perceived him as having anger or self-control problems. For his part, he just wanted the therapist to help him get back on the job or find a new job. For an insight-oriented therapist, this may be frustrating. However, it is important to understand that Thanh sees his primary concern as figuring out how to support his family. This is a real problem for him; fulfilling his responsibility as a father is crucial for him to maintain his dignity and sense of pride. Unless Thanh feels that his therapist understands his urgent need, he will not come back for another therapy session. As with any client, the main goal of the early stage of treatment is to establish rapport and keep him coming back to subsequent appointments.

METHODS FOR HEALING SHAME IN DIFFERENT CULTURAL TRADITIONS AND PRACTICES

For many multicultural clients, religious or spiritual beliefs and practices are essential parts of their lives. A strong belief system can also act as a guiding force that helps make sense of tragic events and diminish shame and guilt. This belief system is often a helpful coping mechanism and a powerful healing tool, especially when working with clients who have experienced unimaginable events that are difficult for anyone to make sense of. A therapist and client can explore together and identify cultural traditions and religious activities, rituals, sacrifices, offerings, or cleansings that offset shame and reestablish equilibrium. Consultation with a religious leader from the client's faith community may provide valuable ideas for rituals that are appropriate to and build on a client's cultural traditions. Clients from traditional Eastern cultures may draw strength from a belief in karma or in the idea of a soul having many lives to live. Some may find peace in surrender and acceptance. Others may find hope in the ultimate triumph of justice or the will of God. Although many Western psychological theories and training for therapists do not incorporate religious and spiritual practices, these traditional beliefs may have the potential to help some clients by creating a starting point for healing and by preparing them for further introspection.

Therapists should not make assumptions about clients' belief systems and core values on the basis of ethnicity or dress. Instead, therapists should ask clients about their religious, spiritual, and folk beliefs and practices and try to understand their views of the world and life. For many clients, Westernized beliefs about autonomy, independence, achievement, or control over one's life are foreign and may even be threatening. Some clients may turn to herbs, balms, acupuncture, and patent medicines as remedies. Others may be inclined to seek relief from depression by consulting traditional healers or through religious rituals (Rodriguez, Lessinger, & Guarnaccia, 1992). Although some therapists may feel uncomfortable about clients seeking help from other sources, it is often beneficial for individuals to receive services from multiple sources. One of the therapist's roles is to understand the potentially valuable roles of other professionals, identify potential conflicts, if any, and make sure that everyone is working as a team toward the common goal of enhancing client well-being.

Using Rituals to Ease the Burden of Shame

Some cultural and religious practices allow the client to pay for sins, which may be closely associated with feelings of shame. In Christian tradition, Christ is thought of as the sacrificial lamb—"*Agnus Dei, qui tollis peccata mundi,*" or "Lamb of God, who takes away the sins of the world." One of the major tenets of Christianity is that God is infinitely forgiving and by acknowledging one's sins and performing acts of penance, one can have a fresh start. The notion of compensation is also a tradition in many Middle Eastern cultures. The individual who offends or kills a member of another family must make some form of reparation to compensate for the offense. Shame in immigrant clients may be lessened by helping them find some way to compensate for the responsibility they feel for a negative outcome and to forgive themselves. By helping the clients engage in prayers or rituals that they are accustomed to, therapists can help them cope with the shame that they feel, even though they may not be able to eliminate the feelings of shame entirely or face and resolve their negative evaluation of the self.

In many cultures of Central and South America, a "sweeping" ritual helps free individuals from the shame and other negative emotional consequences of past traumatic events. These rituals typically involve brushing the body from top to bottom with special herbal branches, removing one layer at a time of the painful emotional residue of negative past events. These rituals often also involve pouring milk, perfume, water, or other liquids over the individual's head to aid in the cleansing process. Sometimes, scented smoke is also used to drive away negative forces. Often supporters sing or chant during the ceremony. Following the ritual, the individual feels free of the past and negative sentiments and is ready for a renewed life.

Because of the focus on survival needs before coming to the United States and the resettlement challenges after arrival, many immigrants cannot properly mourn the death of a loved one. There may be obligatory culture-specific rituals that an individual has been unable to carry out in relation to the departed loved one. This can result in intense shame and guilt that may be alleviated by carrying out traditional mourning rituals. Immigrant clients can often benefit from carrying out symbolic mourning rituals even when they are not part of their cultural tradition. For example, a therapist can help the client put objects, notes, or pictures in a paper boat to release into the ocean or into the sky attached to a helium balloon or wrap them in a special cloth and bury them. These closure rituals can be carried out individually but can be very powerful when performed publicly with families, friends, and fellow clients. Such powerful symbolic rituals can be a way to begin to accept the terrible things that have transpired and move on with life.

As therapists, we may feel that a client's feeling of shame is a distortion in thinking or is being used as a defense. However, we need to work within the client's belief system. Their view of the world has worked for them—it has helped them get through the survival phase. Furthermore, denying their world-view will be seen as disrespectful of their values. Shame might have been helping clients create a coherent way of understanding what happened to them, but at the same time, it may be inaccurate or maladaptive. However, even at the cost of shame, it may be easier to blame themselves for what happened than to accept the reality that they were powerless at a time when others needed them to help. In addition, accepting the reality that innocent people can be victimized may undermine one's belief that the world is a fair place and may destroy one's sense of security and control over life events.

Challenging beliefs that are dysfunctional can occur only after establishing a sense of trust within the therapy relationship. Of course, this principle applies when working with all clients. For many refugees and other immigrants, the reality of life is defined as a string of survival events. Coping skills that are now maladaptive and are tied to a sense of shame may have worked while the client was fighting to survive. Shutting off one's emotions may have protected against sadness and anger, and self-blame may have been the only way to make sense of what happened. Naturally, a therapist would want to help the client move on, but it must be at a pace the client can manage. Regardless of the therapeutic orientation or methods a therapist may use, it is important to stabilize the client first. With some clients, medications may be necessary, and skill building may be useful. When working with refugee and other immigrant clients, therapists may have to approach this initial phase of the therapeutic process in more creative and culturally appropriate ways. Reinforcing the client's value as a human being and recognizing the amazing internal strengths that have allowed him or her to survive will help build his or her capacity to let go of maladaptive feelings of shame. At the same time, by helping clients engage in cultural or religious rituals that are important and meaningful, therapists can gradually shift their focus from feeling shameful about the self to dealing effectively with regret and guilt about past events.

Facing Shame

Unfortunately, many refugee and other immigrant clients end therapy at the point when they find they are minimally functional in day-to-day life without moving on to more introspective psychological work. It is gratifying when a therapist can work with immigrant or refugee clients to come to terms with profound and devastating feelings of shame. For example, a Salvadoran immigrant was referred by the court after incidents of domestic violence. He was previously a solider and was engaging in violent behavior at home but didn't understand why. He loved his wife and children and did not know why he was so angry at them. He wanted to change. With the therapist's help, he was able to work through his thoughts and understand the connection between past events and his mood and behavior. He came to understand how his violent behavior at home helped him avoid the feelings of shame he felt about things he had done as a soldier. He realized that the domestic violence he was engaging in helped him maintain a sense of power and control and warded off feelings of helplessness and shame.

Although it may take some time before refugees and other immigrants will talk openly with others about the shame-inducing experiences of their past, group work can provide opportunities for these clients to explore feelings of shame in a safe environment. It can be powerful even just to educate the client and normalize the experiences by showing that others are dealing with the same or similar issues (Kataoka et al., 2003). Sharing a shameful act publicly is also a way to normalize it and to get recognition from others who have been through similar experiences and share the same cultural background. Group members are like a jury of peers that declares that the fault is not the client's. In sharing similar experiences, they form a safe and credible body of fellow humans who allow a client to forgive himself or herself. Clients can accept what happened as an event over which they had very little control and perhaps as an event with some kind of divine purpose. It is easier for people to look objectively at the experience of others than it is to evaluate their own situation. Group members can jointly move to understand that the forces they faced were so overwhelming that there was no reasonable way that they could have changed the outcome. Individuals can then cease to devalue themselves and start solving problems more effectively.

Another powerful way to shift immigrant clients' perspectives and help them forgive themselves is to ask them to give advice or comfort to a real or imaginary friend who has been through a similar shame-inducing experience. Individuals are usually much better at comforting others who are experiencing shame than they are at forgiving themselves. In a group setting, clients can also be asked to tell stories not of themselves but of a third person. By removing the self from the event, clients can remove the shame attached to the event and gradually see how shame is distorting their understanding of the event.

For some clients, it may also be that it is culturally inappropriate, insensitive, or callous not to express sentiments of shame. It may be reasonable, just, or even noble to acknowledge some responsibility for what has happened. In these instances, the therapist's role may be to help clients identify an act that will compensate for and reduce the shame they feel. Perhaps clients can engage in some generous or selfless act, such as volunteering in the community. Such activity allows clients to feel empowered by helping others who are struggling with their own challenges. It helps them feel better about themselves and see themselves as righting some of the wrong that results when bad things happen to innocent people.

When dealing with shame-related intergenerational conflicts, it is helpful to have a parallel process aimed at helping parents and children see each other's perspectives. It is important for parents to understand how they may be misinterpreting their child's behavior as a rejection of traditional values. For example, a female adolescent dressing like other American girls in a short skirt is not trying to look like a prostitute or sleep around; she is just trying to fit in. She may feel shame or even experience ridicule if she wears traditional dress to school. However, her parents may see her style of dress as bringing shame to the family and react punitively, even threatening to send her back to their homeland. The role of the therapist is to help parents and children each understand and respect their different views of what is shameful and find a middle ground. A young person may respect the parents and understand the difference but not know in practical terms how to find a solution that will maintain harmony. The therapist needs to ask both sides to tolerate, but not necessarily accept, some behaviors while showing respect for each other's values and empathizing with their difficulties. This may be challenging for many Western therapists, who may see the parents' expectations as unrealistic and strongly believe in individualism, empowerment, and independent thinking.

Huy was a 17-year-old Vietnamese boy who was gay. He had accepted his sexual identity, but his mother could not. For her it was morally wrong and would bring great shame to the family. She was not going to change her conviction. However, a therapist worked with her to examine her own reactions. She was encouraged to talk with some of her Vietnamese friends, who did not reject her as she feared—her friends did not see her son's sexual identity as a reflection of her parenting. She still could not accept her son being gay. However, in time she realized that it was a reality, and she was able to work on how to cope with the situation. She and her son learned to talk with each other and set rules in the house so that they were less likely to irritate each other in relation to this issue. When a parent is rigid and unwilling to let in new ideas because such ideas challenge traditional values, the only choice may be to focus on helping the child learn how to relate to the parent and present himself or herself in a way that will be least shameful to both of them.

CONCLUSION

Training to enhance therapists' multicultural knowledge is invaluable when working with refugees and other immigrants. Throughout this chapter we have emphasized the importance of taking clients' unique cultural perspectives into account. As Western-trained therapists, it is important to acknowledge that we try to solve the problems triggered by shame based on training that reflects a very limited worldview. Research conducted mostly in Western cultures reflects a belief that shame is a bad thing that needs to be reduced or eliminated because it often leads to psychological maladjustment and maladaptive behavior. Like grief, shame is often especially problematic when it persists. However, we need to recognize that shame serves an important function in certain cultures (Fessler, 2007) and is a common consequence of traumatic experiences (Budden, 2009). As mental health professionals, the task before us is to determine how to help refugees and other immigrants address shame therapeutically in a culturally appropriate way when it interferes with their ability to successfully adjust to their new lives. To help rebuild the lives of refugee and immigrant clients, we must be open to alternative perspectives on the role of shame in the lives of highly traumatized, culturally diverse populations and be flexible in our therapeutic approaches to identifying and working with the feelings of shame.

REFERENCES

Aronowitz, M. (1984). The social and emotional adjustment of immigrant children: A review of the literature. *International Migration Review, 18*, 237–257. doi:10. 2307/2545949

Ashby, J. S., Rice, K. G., & Martin, J. L. (2006). Perfectionism, shame, and depressive symptoms. *Journal of Counseling and Development, 84*, 148–156.

Buchwald, D., Manson, S. M., Brenneman, D. L., Dinges, N. G., Keane, E. M., Beals, J., & Kinzie, J. D. (1995). Screening for depression among newly arrived Vietnamese refugees in primary care settings. *Journal of Western Medicine, 163*, 341–345.

Budden, A. (2009). The role of shame in posttraumatic stress disorder: A proposal for a socio-emotional model for DSM—V. *Social Science & Medicine, 69,* 1032–1039. doi:10.1016/j.socscimed.2009.07.032

Cheung, F. K., & Snowden, L. R. (1990). Community mental health and ethnic minority populations. *Community Mental Health Journal, 26,* 277–291. doi:10.1007/BF00752778

Crossley, D., & Rockett, K. (2005). The experience of shame in older psychiatric patients: A preliminary enquiry. *Aging & Mental Health, 9,* 368–373. doi:10.1080/13607860500131252

D'Avanzo, C. E., Frye, B., & Froman, R. (1994). Stress in Cambodian refugee families. *Journal of Nursing Scholarship, 26,* 101–106. doi:10.1111/j.1547-5069.1994.tb00926.x

Davis, R. E. (2000). Refugee experiences and Southeast Asian women's mental health. *Western Journal of Nursing Research, 22,* 144–168. doi:10.1177/01939450022044331

Dhooper, S. S., & Tran, T. V. (1998). Understanding and responding to the health needs of Asian refugees. *Social Work in Health Care, 27,* 65–82. doi:10.1300/J010v27n04_05

Dubus, A. (1999). *The house of sand and fog.* New York, NY: Norton.

Egley, A. (2000). *Highlights of the 1999 National Youth Gang Survey: OJJDP fact sheet.* Washington, DC: U.S. Department of Justice, Office of Justice Programs, Office of Juvenile Justice and Delinquency Prevention.

Eisenbruch, M. (1988). The mental health of refugee children and their cultural development. *International Migration Review, 22,* 282–300. doi:10.2307/2546651

Esbenson, F. (2000). *Preventing adolescent gang involvement.* Rockville, MD: Juvenile Justice Clearinghouse.

Feiring, C., Taska, L., & Lewis, M. (2002). Adjustment following sexual abuse discovery: The role of shame and attributional style. *Developmental Psychology, 38,* 79–92.

Fessler, D. M. T. (2007). From appeasement to conformity: Evolutionary and cultural perspectives on shame, competition, and cooperation. In J. L. Tracy, R. W. Robins, & J. P. Tangney (Eds.), *The self-conscious emotions: Theory and research* (pp. 174–193). New York, NY: Guilford Press.

Fox, P. G., Burns, K. R., Popovich, J. M., & Ilg, M. M. (2001). Depression among immigrant Mexican women and Southeast Asian refugee women in the U.S. *International Journal of Psychiatric Nursing Research, 4,* 778–792.

Furukawa, E. (2005). Cross-cultural differences in self-conscious emotions. *Dissertation Abstracts International: Section B: The Sciences and Engineering, 65,* 4869.

Gold, S. J. (1992). Mental health and illness in Vietnamese refugees. *Western Journal of Medicine, 157,* 290–294.

Goldfeld, A. E., Mollica, R., Pesavento, B., & Faraone, S. (1988). The physical and psychological sequelae of torture. *JAMA, 259,* 2725–2729. doi:10.1001/jama. 259.18.2725

Harper, F., & Arias, I. (2004). The role of shame in predicting adult anger and depressive symptoms among victims of child psychological maltreatment. *Journal of Family Violence, 19,* 359–367. doi:10.1007/s10896-004-0681-x

Henderson, L., & Zimbardo, P. (2001). Shyness, social anxiety, and social phobia. In S. G. Hofmann & P. M. DiBartolo (Eds.), *From social anxiety to social phobia: Multiple perspectives* (pp. 46–85). Needham Heights, MA: Allyn & Bacon.

Hu, T. W., Snowden, L. R., Jerrell, J. M., & Kang, S. H. (1993). Public mental health services to Asian American ethnic groups in two California countries. *Asian American and Pacific Islander Journal of Health, 1,* 79–90.

Hunt, D. J. (1989). Issues in working with Southeast Asian refugees. In D. R. Koslow & E. P. Salett (Eds.), *Crossing cultures in mental health* (pp. 49–63). Washington, DC: SIETAR International.

Kandula, N. R., Kersey, M., & Lurie, N. (2004). Assuring the health of immigrants: What the leading health indicators tell us. *Annual Review of Public Health, 25,* 357–376. doi:10.1146/annurev.publhealth.25.101802.123107

Kataoka, S. H., Stein, B. D., Jaycox, L. H., . . . Fink, A. (2003). A school-based mental health program for traumatized Latino immigrant children. *Journal of the American Academy of Child and Adolescent Psychiatry, 42,* 311–318. doi:10.1097/00004583-200303000-00011

Katz, S. R. (1996). Where the streets cross the classroom: A study of Latino students' perspectives on cultural identity in city schools and neighborhood gangs. *Bilingual Research Journal, 20,* 603–631.

Kinzie, J. D., Manson, S. M., Vinh, D. T., Tolan, N. T., Anh, B., & Ngog, T. (1982). Development and validation of a Vietnamese-language depression rating scale. *American Journal of Psychiatry, 139,* 1276–1281.

Kinzie, J. D., Tran, K. A., Breckenridge, A., & Bloom, J. (1980). An Indochinese refugee psychiatric clinic: Culturally accepted treatment approaches. *American Journal of Psychiatry, 137,* 1429–1432.

Koppelman, J. (2005, July). *Mental health and juvenile justice: Moving toward more effective systems of care* (Issue Brief No. 805). Washington, DC: National Health Policy Forum.

Kwak, K. (2003). Adolescents and their parents: A review of intergenerational family relations for immigrant and non-immigrant families. *Human Development, 46,* 115–136. doi:10.1159/000068581

Lefley, H. P. (1990). Culture and chronic mental illness. *Hospital & Community Psychiatry, 41,* 277–286.

Lewis, H. B. (1971). *Shame and guilt in neurosis.* New York, NY: International Universities Press.

Liebkind, K., & Jasinskaja-Lahti, I. (2000). Acculturation and psychological well-being among immigrant adolescents in Finland. *Journal of Adolescent Research, 15,* 446–469. doi:10.1177/0743558400154002

Locke, C. J., Southwick, K., McCloskey, L. A., & Fernandez-Esquer, M. E. (1996). The psychological and medical sequelae of war in Central American refugee mothers and children. *Archives of Pediatrics & Adolescent Medicine, 150,* 822–828.

Markus, H. R., & Kitayama, S. (1991). Culture and the self: Implications for cognition, emotion, and motivation. *Psychological Review, 98,* 224–253. doi:10.1037/0033-295X.98.2.224

Matsumoto, D., Kudoh, T., Scherer, K., & Wallbott, H. (1988). Antecedents of and reactions to emotions in the United States and Japan. *Journal of Cross-Cultural Psychology, 19,* 267–286. doi:10.1177/0022022188193001

Miller, B., Chambers, E. B., & Coleman, C. M. (1981). Indo-Chinese refugees: A national mental health needs assessment. *Migration Today, 9,* 26–31.

Perelman, V. (Producer/Director), & London, M. (Producer). (2003). *The house of sand and fog* [Motion picture]. United States: DreamWorks.

Phan, T. (2000). Investigating the use of services for Vietnamese with mental illness. *Journal of Community Health, 25,* 411–425. doi:10.1023/A:1005184002101

Rodriguez, O., Lessinger, J., & Guarnaccia, P. (1992). The societal and organizational contexts of culturally sensitive mental health services: Findings from an evaluation of bilingual/bicultural psychiatric programs. *Journal of Mental Health Administration, 19,* 213–223. doi:10.1007/BF02518987

Sam, D., & Berry, J. (1995). Acculturative stress among young immigrants in Norway. *Scandinavian Journal of Psychology, 36,* 10–24. doi:10.1111/j.1467-9450.1995.tb00964.x

Snyder, H. N., & Sickmund, M. (2006). *Juvenile offenders and victims: 2006 national report.* Washington, DC: U.S. Office of Juvenile Justice and Delinquency Prevention.

Steel, Z., Silove, D., Phan, T., & Bauman, A. (2002). Long-term effect of psychological trauma on the mental health of Vietnamese refugees resettled in Australia: A population-based study. *The Lancet, 360,* 1056–1062. doi:10.1016/S0140-6736(02)11142-1

Stuewig, J., Tangney, J. P., Heigel, C., Harty, L., & McCloskey, L. A. (2010). Shaming, blaming, and maiming: Functional links among the moral emotions, externalization of blame, and aggression. *Journal of Research in Personality, 44,* 91–102.

Tangney, J. P., & Dearing, R. (2002). *Shame and guilt.* New York, NY: Guilford Press.

Tracy, J. L., & Robins, R. W. (2004). Show your pride: Evidence for a discrete emotion expression. *Psychological Science, 15,* 194–197. doi:10.1111/j.0956-7976.2004.01503008.x

Tracy, J. L., & Robins, R. W. (2007). The nature of pride. In J. L. Tracy, R. W. Robins, & J. P. Tangney (Eds.), *The self-conscious emotions: Theory and research* (pp. 263–282). New York, NY: Guilford Press.

Vega, W. A., Kolody, B., Aguilar-Gaxiola, S., & Catalano, R. (1999). Gaps in service utilization by Mexican Americans with mental health problems. *American Journal of Psychiatry, 156*, 928–934.

Wallbott, H. G., & Scherer, K. R. (1988). How universal and specific is emotional experience? Evidence from 27 countries and five continents. In K. R. Scherer (Ed.), *Facets of emotion: Recent research* (pp. 31–56). Hillsdale, NJ: Erlbaum.

Wallbott, H. G., & Scherer, K. R. (1995). Cultural determinants in experiencing shame and guilt. In J. P. Tangney & K. W. Fischer (Eds.), *Self-conscious emotions: The psychology of shame, guilt, embarrassment, and pride* (pp. 465–487). New York, NY: Guilford Press.

Wasserman, G. A., Jensen, P. S., Ko, S. J., Cocozza, J., Trupin, E., Angold, A., . . . Grisso, T. (2003). Mental health assessments in juvenile justice: Report on the consensus conference. *Journal of the American Academy of Child and Adolescent Psychiatry, 42*, 752–761.

Yeh, C. J. (2003). Age, acculturation, cultural adjustment, and mental health symptoms of Chinese, Korean, and Japanese immigrant youths. *Cultural Diversity & Ethnic Minority Psychology, 9*, 34–48. doi:10.1037/1099-9809.9.1.34

Zhou, M. (1997). Growing up American: The challenge confronting immigrant children and children of immigrants. *Annual Review of Sociology, 23*, 63–95. doi:10.1146/annurev.soc.23.1.63

Zhou, M., & Bankston, C. L. (1994). Social capital and the adaptation of the second generation: The case of Vietnamese youth in New Orleans. *International Migration Review, 28*, 821–845. doi:10.2307/2547159

Zuniga, M. (2002). Latino immigrations: Patterns of survival. *Journal of Human Behavior in the Social Environment, 5*, 137–155. doi:10.1300/J137v05n03_08

II

CHALLENGING PROBLEMS IN THERAPY: SHAME-BASED CLINICAL DISORDERS

9

THERAPY WITH SHAME-PRONE ALCOHOLIC AND DRUG-DEPENDENT CLIENTS

RONALD T. POTTER-EFRON

It might seem obvious that shame is strongly related to addiction. After all, what could be more shameful than waking up one morning not remembering what you did the evening before, where you are, or who that person is lying next to you? Indeed, the evidence is strong, both anecdotal and through scientific research, that there is a pronounced interrelationship between shame and addiction.

One study of the moral emotional style of public school children indicated that "shame-proneness assessed in the fifth grade predicted later high school suspension, drug use of various kinds (amphetamines, depressants, hallucinogens, heroin), and suicide attempts" (Tangney & Dearing, 2002, p. 134). Dearing, Steuwig, and Tangney (2005) studied substance use patterns among both college students and jail inmates. They reported a positive link between shame proneness and problematic alcohol and drug use in both groups. Of particular interest is their finding that shame proneness was not powerfully linked with frequency of use of these substances but with dependency and other problems and consequences related to substance use. They also noted, as would be predicted by their general model of the differences between shame and guilt, that guilt proneness seemed to provide a protective effect

219

against the development of alcohol or substance abuse problems in these two groups of people.

Two additional research studies compared individuals in recovery from drug and alcohol problems with a community sample of adults (Meehan et al., 1996; O'Connor, Berry, Inaba, Weiss, & Morrison, 1994). Both studies found that individuals in recovery scored higher on shame proneness and lower on guilt proneness compared with individuals recruited from the community. These results suggest that shame proneness may continue to be a problem for individuals with a history of substance abuse problems even when they are not actively using alcohol or other substances. Shame proneness may also be a risk factor for relapse, as demonstrated by a retrospective study of women in alcohol recovery that found that women with higher levels of shame reported more occurrences of prior relapse (Wiechelt & Sales, 2001). These research findings point to an inextricable link between shame and addictive behaviors.

The goal of this chapter is to help the reader better understand and treat clients with shame and addiction issues. I discuss the primary conceptual linkages between shame and addiction, provide two key concepts that organize treatment (deficiency statements and the four spheres of self), and suggest additional treatment guidelines.

SHAME AND ADDICTION: CONCEPTUAL LINKAGES

The interrelationship between shame and addiction can take many forms. The specific connections for any particular individual must be evaluated on a case-by-case basis. Several shame–addiction interrelationships commonly observed during treatment are addiction as an escape from shame, addiction as a substitute for interpersonal relationships, the shame–addiction spiral, addiction as a distraction from core self-shame issues, addiction as a source of pride and belonging, and addiction as proof of one's intrinsic shamefulness.

Addiction as an Escape From Shame

The most evident connection between the addictive process and shame is that some individuals, in particular shame-prone persons, discover that alcohol, other substances, or compulsive behaviors help them feel less shameful about themselves, at least in the short run. Affect theorists (Kaufman, 1996) have argued that addictions begin as "sedative scripts" that buffer people from their shame and other negative feelings. Under the influence of alcohol or drugs, the user gains either the relief of feeling "normal" or the euphoria of exchanging his or her usual sense of inferiority for a brief period of dominance and superiority (what is termed *grandiosity* in the vocabulary of Alcoholics Anonymous [AA]). These sedative scripts eventually can develop into "addictive scripts" in which the greatest emotional distress becomes linked with the possible loss of the sedating substance. In other words, the individual now fears the loss of the substance even more than he or she fears the shame, practically guaranteeing the development and continuation of shame-producing behaviors.

In treating shame-prone addicts, it is critical to realize that their behavior did work at some time in the past and perhaps is still occasionally effective in the present. Drinking or drug use did and can still alleviate shame, but only temporarily.

Addiction as a Substitute for Interpersonal Relationships

Human relationships can be painful, clumsy, and difficult. All too often, especially for the shame-prone individual, interpersonal contacts become a series of dangerous encounters. There is always the possibility of saying or doing something that will beget criticism from others and trigger a shameful sense of inadequacy from within. What if you could find something better, something that seemed always to affirm your existence? Some persons find that mood-altering substances fit that role. After a while, it's easy for "Al" or "Alice" (alcohol) to become their best and only friend. Drinking or using alone becomes all too easy. The addict's isolation becomes the price he or she pays to avoid potentially shameful encounters in the real world.

The Shame–Addiction Spiral

It is important to consider the possible causal links between shame and addiction. For example, the concept of shame proneness implies that shame could be the causal agent, leading potential addicts into physical and psychological dependence as they desperately attempt to escape their shameful sense of self. However, it is equally possible that addictive events increase the experience of shame even in non-shame-prone individuals. Already shame-prone people who have lost control of their drinking or drug use are likely to have their shame magnified by the effects of their addictive behaviors to the point where their shame becomes the characterological center of their psychological identities.

The term *shame–addiction spiral* labels this reciprocal and interdependent process (Potter-Efron, 2002, p. 39). The spiral begins with a possibly shame-prone person's vague sense of defectiveness. That individual feels a need to escape this unpleasant sensation and discovers, accidentally or with intent, that alcohol or drugs (or some other compulsive behavior, including gambling, pornography, etc.) accomplishes that purpose. Gradually that person's use of the substance or behavior increases in an attempt to further reduce the bad feelings. Eventually he or she goes a little overboard, such as drinking too much. This person then suffers an "embarrassing" incident, perhaps speaking too loudly or insulting the host at a party. Now the developing addict feels worse than before, besieged by his or her original feelings of inadequacy, plus the shame of this newly unacceptable performance, plus the shame of having lost control.

This individual needs solace, but by now it's become hard to gain comfort from anything but the substance itself because other possible comforting sources, such as nondrinking friends, have been left behind. That means the only refuge left is the addicting substance, and so the shamed user turns more and more frequently to it. Now the loss of control increases, the embarrassing incidents become shaming and then humiliating, and the individual develops a true physiological and psychological dependence. Shame leads to more shame in a deepening spiral. In the words of Craig Nakken (1996), a family therapist specializing in addictions, "the more addicts seek relief through addiction, the more shame they'll start to experience and the more they will feel a need to justify the addictive relationship to themselves" (p. 29).

Addiction as a Distraction From Core Self-Shame Issues

Preoccupation with the need to obtain a drug, use that drug, and recover from the effects of the drug is a common development in addiction. Certainly such preoccupation serves as yet another way for shame-prone individuals to run from their shame. By this I mean that some persons can become so excessively attentive to the need to obtain and use their addictive substances that they can effectively bypass the shame that might normally accompany this loss of control. If all you can think about is your addiction, then the shame about having an addiction can be escaped, if only temporarily.

However, another aspect of preoccupation must also be recognized in counseling. Some persons with an addictive disorder can become intensely preoccupied with the shame that surrounds their addictions. Many addicts feel intensely shameful about their physical and emotional dependency on an external substance or compulsive process. Indeed, they can go through long periods of counseling and treatment detailing their shame related to dependency. However, in so doing they avoid dealing with their core shame issues that affect them at the deepest levels of their being. Oddly, their very shame about their addiction serves to defend them against their awareness of a sensed defectiveness as a human being. They confuse "I am ashamed of being addicted" with "I am ashamed of who I am." This cognitive error implies to them that they should feel normal or good once they curtail their addictive behavior. But since they fail to address their underlying shame issues, these persons are likely to relapse when they discover that they still feel inadequate, worthless, defective, and diminished even when sober.

Addiction as a Source of Pride and Belonging

"I can drink anyone under the table." "I feel right at home down at my favorite bar." These two statements serve as a reminder that addictive behavior can help some shame-prone individuals lessen two great shame-related problems: their sense of defectiveness and their feeling of not belonging. Instead, these persons might discover that they are really good at drinking or drugging and feel a sense of pride in their accomplishments. This pride is just as real as anything else one does that brings with it the conviction that "I can do this, and I can do it well." In essence, these users become local stars who come to epitomize such traits as aggressiveness, sexuality, and risk taking. Their status assures them a warm welcome at the bar, free drugs from their friends, and, most important from a shame perspective, a "place where everyone knows their name."

It may be difficult for people recovering from addiction to admit or discuss this "junkie pride" phenomenon in treatment, much less for them to let go of their pride related to using and the accompanying sense of belonging. These issues must be addressed carefully during treatment, and counselors must empathically understand the addict's desire to feel pride and connection. It then becomes important to guide these individuals toward socially acceptable ways to meet their need for belonging. AA and other 12-step programs seem explicitly designed to fill these needs.

Addiction as Proof of One's Intrinsic Shamefulness

Although some individuals use addictions as a way to escape their shame, others seem to embrace their dependencies and compulsions as undeniable validation of their worthlessness. "You see," they announce, "I told you I'm garbage. What more proof do you need?" These individuals are not saying their shame comes from their addiction. Instead, they believe they are so damaged, useless, worthless, and flawed that they are shameful to the core of their being. Addiction, to them, is more an advertisement of their shame than a causal agent.

These clients certainly need help in addressing their belief that they are essentially shameful. Although their addictive behaviors can never be ignored, it is also true that merely achieving abstinence will have little effect on their self-esteem. In addition to addiction treatment, they will almost certainly require long-term therapy that helps them reconstruct their self-concept.

Unfortunately, standard treatment programs seldom address this issue, and the kind of longer-term therapy needed for effective shame work may be unavailable to the newly recovering individual with addiction problems.

CLINICAL INTERVENTIONS WITH SHAME-PRONE AND ADDICTED CLIENTS

Several clinical interventions are recommended in work with shame-prone and addicted clients: respond to deficiency statements, intervene in all four spheres of self, regularly attend to the therapeutic relationship during counseling, accept the client's shame rather than try to argue it away, and listen and watch carefully for subtle signs of shame.

Respond to Deficiency Statements

Many shame-prone clients have difficulty expressing their shame in a coherent manner. This is partly because shame remains a half-hidden emotion in American society. Although there are a few words and phrases that convey this feeling (e.g., *embarrassment, chagrin, diminishment, humiliation, mortification, loss of face*), the vocabulary of shame is sparse compared with the set of words describing fear, anger, sadness, and other negative emotions. For example, just a sample of words and phrases reflecting various states of anger includes *annoyed, irritated, resentful, furious, enraged, pissed off, melting down, ticked, incensed, riled, exasperated, maddened, seeing red, infuriated, short-fused, explosive,* and *irate.*

Consequently, it can be very helpful to provide clients with ways to describe their shame experiences. Five deficiency statements essentially serve this task: (a) "I am not good," (b) "I am not good enough," (c) "I do not belong," (d) "I am unlovable," and (e) "I should not be." Each of these phrases reflects one core aspect of the shame experience. Any particular client may identify with one or two phrases or with all of them. It is usually possible, however, to identify which phrase or phrases most need to be addressed and disputed during treatment. These statements serve as entrées into cognitive therapy approaches.

"I am not good" is a damaging generic shame statement that reflects the belief that the individual is doomed to fail at everything he or she does, whether that is relationships, work, or maintaining abstinence from alcohol or drugs. Failure seems inevitable, leading to avoidance of opportunities for success and classic addictive escape behavior. Cognitive treatment begins with exploring "exceptions" to the rule in which the client succeeded at some important task ("Well, I did win an athletic scholarship to the university") or relationship ("Even though it's been tough since the divorce, I've maintained regular visitations with my kids").

"I am not good enough" recognizes that the social emotions often involve comparative evaluations. Shame, guilt, embarrassment, and pride all involve contrasting one's personal performance with the behavior of others or with one's own idealized expectations. That means that an initial question the therapist might ask when a client endorses this statement is "compared with whom?" This question may reveal that a client compares his or her real self with idealized versions of parents, peers, neighbors, or recovering addicts. The client may also be comparing his or her real self with an idealized, perfect self-image that is likely unattainable. The gap between the actual and idealized self may feel so tremendous that the individual is tempted to give up in despair. Addiction then becomes a concession, a statement of failure compared with others or one's own ideal.

"I do not belong" is a reminder that the central fear related to shame is that of being abandoned or cast out because of one's deficiencies. Clients who identify strongly with this belief are likely to take extreme measures to hide their addictive behaviors from others. For instance, an Internet pornography addict might spend hours late at night on the computer, continually vigilant so as to be ready to press the escape key immediately if any family members happen to enter the room. These clients might recoil from accepting any label that identifies them as addicted because of their conviction (sometimes correct) that significant others will reject them for that flaw. They need help separating their unacceptable behavior from their core self-identities. Any movement they can make from a shame focus toward a guilt focus will help them feel more acceptable in the world.

Membership in AA represents one way this transformation occurs. People who wholeheartedly join this group find a place where they can belong not only despite but actually because of their addictive behaviors. Once they belong, they are encouraged to separate their character flaws from their core selves (Step 4) and to make amends for what they have done wrong during their addictions (Steps 8 and 9). Thus, gradually they move from a shame to a guilt focus.

Clients who agree with "I am unlovable" basically sense that they have long ago and irretrievably been rejected by their families and loved ones. Of note here is one study (Dutton, 1998) that revealed that the most shame-prone (and shame–rage-prone) children were those whose core personality traits were rejected by their parents. This sense of rejection then becomes a template for all future relationships, predicting that such relationships are bound to fail and that the individual's fate is to go through life alone and lonely. Addiction, then, is likely to provide the user with the best friend and lover he or she never will find in real life. Clients with this pattern probably need longer term therapy as opposed to straightforward addiction treatment in order to challenge this sense of unlovability.

"I should not be" is the ultimate suicide/annihilating shame belief. Clients who develop addictions around this belief are likely to both actively and passively demonstrate self-destructive behaviors, including outright suicide attempts, high-risk-taking actions, and consumption of unknown substances. For example, I was once asked to make a call on a hospitalized patient. This woman had been injured in a fall from a horse, the last of a long list of accidents and injuries, all of which occurred during bouts of severe inebriation. Not knowing how to approach her, I brought her entire set of hospital records with me to her room in an attempt to impress her with the seriousness of her behavior. Throwing the records on her bed, I dramatically intoned that she was killing herself with her drinking. Her reply was "I know that, sonny. Now leave me alone."

Clients who endorse the belief that they should not exist need help at a deep existential/spiritual level. The emphasis in AA on recovering addicts developing a strong relationship with their Higher Power certainly relates to this theme. Clients who identify with a relatively standard version of God/Higher Power may eventually come to believe that God has a purpose for them in this universe, indicating that their very existence is not a mistake. Agnostic clients, spiritually but not religiously focused individuals, and persons who have an antagonistic relationship to God (e.g., "I cannot forgive God for letting my daughter die") will need help crafting a more individualized path to feeling that they truly belong in the world. Mindfulness training and positive psychology can be useful adjuncts to therapy for this purpose. For example, the Values in Action—Inventory of Strengths (Peterson & Seligman, 2001; see also Park, Peterson, & Seligman, 2004) helps clients identify their most significant character strengths.

Intervene in All Four Spheres of Self

Shame and addiction concerns can be addressed at many levels of existential awareness. One model I use to portray these options is the four spheres of self. These spheres are imagined as a set of spheres set inside each other. The outermost sphere is labeled the presentation sphere, followed in turn by the defensive sphere, the flawed sphere, and the core sphere.

The *presentation sphere of self* is a label for the parts of the self that each person readily allows others to see. Primacy here goes to appearance, publicly played roles, and our known values and beliefs. From a shame perspective, the primary purpose of the presentation sphere of self is to publicly display evidence that the person fits into society and therefore should not be rejected or abandoned. Shame-prone individuals are likely to spend much energy propping up this aspect of their being, sometimes to the relative exclusion of the other spheres. Image becomes more important than reality. Because maintaining a positive outward image is all important, evidence of addictions must be hidden along with anything else that conceivably triggers exclusion.

Treatment here can take on two forms. First, clients can be presented with hope that they can really clean up their image by sobering up and maintaining abstinence or some acceptable level of alcohol or drug use. In other words, there could be less of a gap between image and reality and therefore less potential opportunity for shameful exposure. Second, clients can be helped to question how much energy they need to devote to image affirmation. Instead, they could choose to develop greater interest in self-affirmation (which is explored in the other spheres of self).

The main function of the *defensive sphere of self* is to protect and preserve the claimed (presentation) self from scrutiny and attack. Shame-prone individuals with addiction issues commonly use such defenses as denial, minimization, rationalization, and justification for this purpose. They may also become highly aggressive in response to a perceived attack, developing a shame–rage pattern that can be highly dangerous to anyone who intentionally or unintentionally triggers their internal shame alarm (Potter-Efron, 2007). They may also develop addictive patterns to keep themselves from noticing or questioning the gap between their image and reality. It is at the point at which these defenses become habituated and virtually unconscious that they can be said to become the second sphere of self. In other words, it could be said that the person becomes his or her defenses and that these defenses come to define an important part of the self.

Shamelessness and exhibitionism are two defenses against shame that addictive individuals sometimes demonstrate. One such person, Dave, would get drunk in a tavern and then loudly announce that he was illiterate, a fact he claimed to be proud of. Indeed, he was so proud of his illiteracy that he'd be delighted to discuss the matter (with his fists) if any so-called educated person would care to debate it. It is of great interest that after Dave quit drinking, he admitted he was actually tremendously ashamed of his inability to read. He then enrolled in an adult literacy program and eventually served on his community's literacy programs board. As this example illustrates, treatment for shame-prone clients in recovery from addiction around defensive sphere issues should focus on helping them identify their defenses against shame, understand how their use of these defenses only perpetuates their shame in the long run, and move toward being more honest both with others and with themselves.

The *flawed self* is the name for the third sphere of self. The bulk of the client's sensed weaknesses, deficiencies, character flaws, and shameful secrets reside here. The shame-prone client is convinced that exposure of these flaws would result in instant rejection. Depending on the nature of that individual's secrets, of course, he or she could be correct in that prediction. However, shame-prone people tend to believe their flaws are far more socially fatal than they really are and fail to realize that everyone has similar flaws. One job during treatment is to help clients expose some of these unnecessary secrets in a safe and accepting environment.

I reside in Wisconsin, a state popularly recognized for its relatively high number of problem drinkers. It is important to note that, at least in this part of the country, quitting drinking may be as much a cause for family disenfranchisement as excessive drinking. Practically speaking, this means that counselors must be careful to discuss with their recovering clients which individuals they will disclose their new sobriety status to.

Finally, clients reach the *core sphere of self* when they begin to address questions like "What gives your life meaning?" and "Who are you when you let go of your roles and defenses?" Although with most clients shame is primarily addressed when dealing with the flawed sphere of self, some clients are so "shame bound" (Kaufman, 1996) that their shame has invaded their core sense of self. These are the clients who mostly or fully agree that that they are fatally flawed and should not even exist. It is as if their souls have been steeped in shame for so long that the stain of shame can no longer be separated from their being. Their addictive behavior can be exceptionally self-punishing as they confirm and reaffirm their intrinsic defectiveness through acts of increasing depravity.

Clients in early recovery programs must be handled carefully when dealing with the core sphere of self. A few may be able to plunge into this terrain immediately but will need a great deal of support while doing so. Others might fare better if they are just introduced to the concept of the shame-bound core sphere of self while being steered toward concentrating upon more immediate issues of recovery. However, such individuals will need long-term therapy in addition to alcohol and drug treatment to harbor any real long-term hopes for recovery. Therapists for such individuals who can develop a deeply trusting relationship with them may be able to use this connection to gently encourage them to explore their shame further while not shaming them in the process. The core sphere of self may also be addressed from a positive perspective. Here again I use material from positive psychology to help clients identify their signature strengths (Seligman, 2002) and central values to help them recognize their intrinsic worthiness.

Regularly Attend to the Therapeutic Relationship During Counseling

Evans (1988) stated that the "main element in healing a shame-based identity is developing a caring relationship with someone trustable" (p. 175).

This means that the interactive process between therapist and client is more important than the actual content discussed in resolving the client's shame concerns. The reason for this, of course, is that shamed individuals almost inevitably fear that even their counselors will eventually summarily dismiss them from treatment (and, by implication, from the human race). The relationship between client and therapist can become a new template that the client can then use as a guide to restructure other relationships.

Shamed clients have a specific hope, not necessarily stated, within the counseling relationship. They desire to reveal everything within them that feels dirty, disgusting, and defective. They seldom reveal all this material immediately and may never be able to share some of it. Practically speaking, clients tend to reveal their shame in layers, from least personally revolting to most. Each layer of revelation represents a test of their helpers. Can the therapist handle the current revelation without becoming disgusted? If so, then it's likely that clients will continue in this process throughout therapy. Sometimes clients return to outpatient therapy months or years later, leading off with this statement: "I liked what we did the last time I counseled with you, but I never told you about something I felt really bad about. I'm ready to do that now."

Clients like this need counselors who are willing to become deeply engaged with them, not individuals who use their professional status to remain emotionally sheltered behind their roles of therapist or counselor. Clients who share their shame need to do so with a human being, not a role player, no matter how well someone may play that part. Only a whole therapist can reasonably expect clients to work past their presentation layer of self and into the defensive, flawed, and core spheres of self.

Clients need to see that their counselors are human. How can helpers demonstrate their humanity, however, while maintaining proper boundaries? One approach is to share small daily experiences with shame that highlight the universal absurdity of the human condition. One example I've used is the time I was dressed up in my best suit on my way to an important meeting. Walking up the stairs I was so busy appreciating my appearance that I failed to watch my step and fell flat on my face. As I stumbled, I noticed that my thoughts changed instantly from "Look at me now!" to "I hope nobody's watching." This transition from vanity to embarrassment is a common shame experience but at a low enough level that most people can laugh at themselves when it happens. Let me note that although embarrassment can be viewed as an emotion distinct from shame (Miller, 1996), many shame-prone clients cannot and do not initially recognize the differences, so that what seems to an observer to be an experience that should trigger only a moderate amount of embarrassment may trigger in the shame-prone person devastating feelings of shamefulness. Additionally, the specific situation encountered by the client alone does not completely predict that individual's emotional reaction. That situation, the person's particular vulnerability in that area, and that person's more general level of shame proneness all interact to produce the final response.

Accept the Client's Shame Rather Than Try to Argue It Away

It is often painful to bear witness when clients reveal their shame during treatment. For example, a woman who lost her children because of neglect due to addiction may sob uncontrollably with shame and grief. Her emotional despair is palpable and seemingly eternal as she claims she'll never be able to forgive herself (an indicator that this person has at least as much shame about her behavior as guilt, as guilty infractions are usually self-forgivable). Certainly many therapists have never experienced shame at this level. They may be sorely tempted to avoid the issue completely, perhaps by diverting the client's attention to another subject (thus subliminally giving the message that the client's shame is beyond repair) or by issuing facile reassurances that surely this pain will go away after a period of abstinence. But this kind of pain does not always heal over time. If anything, this newly sober woman is now relatively undefended against her pain. Relapse and/or suicidal ideation can often accompany this profound shame experience.

The therapist's task here is to stay with the client, metaphorically to step inside the client's circle of shame. This client, and every client who reveals shame at this deep level, needs to believe that he or she does not have to suffer alone. The counselor must accompany clients into this encounter, giving comfort and hope when needed. Above all, therapists must be willing to coencounter this shame while maintaining a strong enough boundary so as not to be engulfed by it.

Listen and Watch Carefully for Subtle Signs of Shame

Clients do not always directly communicate their experience of shame with their counselors. Rather, they may hint at their shame through relatively subtle cues: downcast eyes, sudden speech stoppages, avoidance of an apparently innocuous topic, unusual phrasings, and so forth. They may also speak at length about other emotions they feel regarding a particular experience without adding that they also or even primarily feel shame about it. Helpers who recognize these signs may immediately attend to them. Alternatively, they may allow them to go unchallenged but come back to them later ("John, I noticed before when you started to talk about your mother's death, you hesitated a little when you mentioned that you were too stoned to visit her on her death bed. Did you stop yourself from dealing with something there?"), perhaps in a safer setting such as during individual rather than group counseling.

TREATING FAMILY SYSTEMS WITH SHAME
AND ADDICTION PROBLEMS

Addiction compounded by shame is seen not only in individuals but also within family systems. Treating the shame-bound family system creates an additional layer of complexity for the addictions therapist. The defining characteristics of this system are that at least one member has an addiction that seriously affects the entire family and that at least one person, not necessarily the same individual, has a significant shame proneness that also causes difficulty within the family. One example of how the interactions between shame and addiction might play out in this situation is if one or more members of the family becomes extremely ashamed of the addicted family member, even if that member appears to act shamelessly. What follows are recommendations drawn from the author's experience with treating these impaired family systems.

Attend to Attempts by Family Members to Protect the Family Image

Shame-prone family members are quite sensitive to the threat of family dishonor caused by the addict's careless, irresponsible, or dangerous behaviors. Thus, they may take pains to protect that image by denying, minimizing, or justifying the actions of the individual with addictive concerns. Thus develops the classic "elephant in the living room" problem in which everybody pretends not to see any problem with the addict and/or refuses to discuss the problem even in the face of serious familial disruption. Loyalty is usually highly valued in these families, far more appreciated than honesty, since honesty can challenge the family's image-guarding blindness to reality. Indeed, someone who does try to call attention to the addiction problem risks being shamed and blamed, accused of betraying the family, shamed for these indiscretions, and ultimately banished from the family circle.

Therapists must be sensitive to family honor concerns while simultaneously attempting to help all members recognize and deal with the addiction problems of one or more members. It is particularly important not to place only one person in the role of family truth teller, lest that individual get sacrificed on the altar of family image preservation. Instead, the therapist should attempt gradually to have at least two or three members take responsibility together to deal with the issue. Hopefully, these individuals can become convinced that honesty about the real problems the family faces is actually a form of loyalty rather than betrayal and a first step toward healing.

Families that fail to acknowledge addiction problems because of shame are also less likely to express positive feelings about a member's journey into treatment or commitment to abstinence or more moderate substance use.

Demonstrating pride creates more exposure risks. Consequently, clients undergoing outpatient treatment while living at home or who return from inpatient treatment elsewhere are often virtually ignored. "Don't ask, don't tell" becomes the family theme. Unfortunately, this form of neglect can increase the likelihood of the addict's relapse. Families need to take pride in their member's recovery rather than ignore or penalize it. Therapists should be alert to transferred shame within the client's entire family system.

Shame is a slippery emotion at all times, half hidden as it is behind a screen of avoidant and defensive tactics. As mentioned previously, some individuals and families don't even possess the word *shame* in their vocabularies. That means that shame can stealthily infiltrate the family system without family members being able to name it, much less reduce it. The therapist's task is to help the family as a whole identify the shame issues related to one or more members' problems with addiction.

Shame can also be transferred within the family system from the identified patient to other members. In rural Wisconsin, for example, that can literally mean that an adult family member refuses to visit his hometown because as soon as anybody hears his last name, they will know he's related to the town drunk. Meanwhile, the addicted individual proceeds through life as if he or she has no shame, engaging in unabated drinking and carousing around town.

Another useful term for transferred shame is *borrowed* shame. This word carries with it several implications: (a) the shame actually belongs to someone else, not the carrier; (b) family members unconsciously acquired this shame in response to their innate sense that the addict's behavior was unacceptable to society; and (c) because the shame rightfully belongs to the addict, it makes sense to let go of it and return it to the addict. If and when family members accept this reframing of the situation, they begin to feel free from the burden of shame they've been carrying for years.

Help Recovering Individuals Rejoin Their Families

One characteristic of addiction is that dependent individuals often become isolated from their families of origin as well as from their nuclear units. They separate themselves voluntarily and involuntarily from their families (to ensure maintaining proximity to their drug), but also their families may also ostracize them because of their addictions. How better to validate the unworthiness of an already shame-prone person than to ban that individual from family functions such as Christmas gatherings, visitations with the children after a divorce, and so forth? Marginalization of the addict certainly serves to preserve the family system from chaos. However, the cost of forbidding a father from attending his daughter's wedding can be devastating not only to the addict but also to other family members.

Newly abstinent or moderating users are frequently eager to have their previous family roles restored. They want desperately to belong somewhere again. They sense, correctly, that regaining their place in the family would help them lessen their shame. However, their families may be less than excited about this prospect for several reasons. First, in most cases, they may have lingering doubt that the straying member will stay sober. This may be a realistic fear, especially if that person has a long history of failed recoveries. Second, even when addicted individuals maintain sobriety, they may not be ready to assume the ongoing responsibilities of their previous roles. "What good is it," a husband may ask, "for my wife to come home when she is still so damaged from drug use that I wouldn't dare leave the kids alone with her?" Besides, by now someone else in the family, perhaps an oldest daughter, has taken on the roles abandoned by the user. That individual cannot be counted on to relinquish those roles, and the rewards accompanying them, merely because the previous role holder has returned. Finally, some members of the family may feel tremendous resentment toward the addict. They want the addict to suffer, and not allowing that individual back into the family is one form of punishment.

The counselor's job under these circumstances is to patiently advocate for the recovering client while staying responsive to the family's doubts, fears, resentments, and hesitations. The hope is that eventually the former addict will be able to recover some or all of his or her former roles and responsibilities, especially those vital to that person's sense of self-worth. It certainly helps, I would add, for the client to admit fault and to make amends whenever possible. Dealing with these guilt issues prepares the ground for dealing with the family's more difficult shame concerns. The therapist can guide the client toward making amends as a form of self-healing, knowing that these acts of restitution will help begin a process of reconciliation.

Help Shame-Prone Families Develop Nonshaming Communication Patterns

Some recovering alcoholics can stay abstinent even when every other family member drinks, and some shame-prone people may be able to maintain positive self-regard even in the face of continually shaming family members. Obviously, though, a nonsupportive family increases the likelihood for relapse in either situation. It is wise to identify family shaming during treatment. If possible, the next step is to target that behavior for change during follow-up couples or family counseling. Family members need to learn to replace shaming statements with supportive ones, personality attacks with specific grievances, criticism with praise, and disinterest with interest.

One approach I use is to teach shame-prone families the "Five As" of positive interactions: attention, approval, acceptance, admiration, and affirmation. Each message can be stated in one brief sentence:

- Attention: I have time for you.
- Approval: I like what you do.
- Acceptance: It's OK for you to be you.
- Admiration: I can learn from you.
- Affirmation: I celebrate your existence.

The goal is to help families actually put these concepts into practice. They may very well need guidance in the form of role-playing, repeated communication practice, and so forth. It may be most realistic to aim simply to increase the ratio of positive versus negative interactions within the family rather than to expect the absolute elimination of shame-inducing statements. The stakes are significant, though, because shame-prone addicts who reside in nonshaming households seem least likely to relapse.

It should be noted that many clients must deal with family shame issues without family members present or with family members who continue unabatedly to shame them. Nevertheless, they can be educated with regard to family therapy concepts. They can also be encouraged to maximize their interactions with less-shaming family members while minimizing contact with more shaming persons.

CONCLUSION

I once ran a seminar titled "Shame and Blame Is the Name of the Game." Certainly this is true for persons who become mired in shame-based addictive patterns. These individuals continually play games around their own shame by avoiding it on many occasions, only to embrace it at other times. Their shame facilitates addiction while their addiction furthers their shame in deepening downward spirals. Family members frequently get caught up in these patterns, adding their own shame and their shaming of the addict to the mix. Fortunately, appropriate treatment can at least begin a healing process in which the recovering person and, hopefully, that individual's family can leave behind both shame and addiction.

REFERENCES

Dearing, R. L., Steuwig, J., & Tangney, J. (2005). On the importance of distinguishing shame from guilt: Relations to problematic alcohol and drug use. *Addictive Behaviors, 30,* 1392–1404. doi:10.1016/j.addbch.2005.02.002

Dutton, D. (1998). *The abusive personality*. New York, NY: Guilford Press.

Evans, S. (1988). Shame, boundaries, and dissociation in chemically dependent, abusive, and incestuous families. In R. Potter-Efron & P. Potter-Efron (Eds.), *The treatment of shame and guilt in alcoholism counseling* (pp. 157–180). Binghamton, NY: Haworth Press.

Kaufman, G. (1996). *The psychology of shame* (2nd ed.). New York, NY: Springer.

Meehan, W., O'Connor, L. E., Berry, J. W., Weiss, J., Morrison, A., & Acampora, A. (1996). Guilt, shame, and depression in clients in recovery from addiction. *Journal of Psychoactive Drugs, 28*, 125–134.

Miller, R. (1996). *Embarrassment*. New York, NY: Guilford Press.

Nakken, C. (1996). *The addictive personality* (2nd ed.). Center City, MN: Hazelden.

O'Connor, L. E., Berry, J. W., Inaba, D., Weiss, J., & Morrison, A. (1994). Shame, guilt, and depression in men and women in recovery from addiction. *Journal of Substance Abuse Treatment, 11*, 503–510. doi:10.1016/0740-5472(94)90001-9

Park, N., Peterson, C., & Seligman, M. E. P. (2004). Strengths of character and well-being. *Journal of Social and Clinical Psychology, 23*, 603–619. doi:10.1521/jscp.23.5.603.50748

Peterson, C., & Seligman, M. E. P. (2001). *VIA Survey of Character Strengths*. Retrieved from http://www.authentichappiness.sas.upenn.edu/Default.aspx

Potter-Efron, R. (2002). *Shame, guilt and alcoholism* (2nd ed.). New York, NY: Haworth Press.

Potter-Efron, R. (2007). *Rage*. Oakland, CA: New Harbinger.

Seligman, M. (2002). *Authentic happiness*. New York, NY: Free Press.

Tangney, J., & Dearing, R. (2002). *Shame and guilt*. New York, NY: Guilford Press.

Wiechelt, S. A., & Sales, E. (2001). The role of shame in women's recovery from alcoholism: The impact of childhood sexual abuse. *Journal of Social Work Practice in the Addictions, 1*, 101–116. doi:10.1300/J160v01n04_07

10

THE ROLE OF SHAME IN THE DEVELOPMENT AND TREATMENT OF BORDERLINE PERSONALITY DISORDER

SHIREEN L. RIZVI, MILTON Z. BROWN, MARTIN BOHUS,
AND MARSHA M. LINEHAN

Borderline personality disorder (BPD) is a psychological disorder involving severe, pervasive, and chronic dysregulation of emotion, behavior, and cognition. Diagnostic criteria include volatile interpersonal relationships, affective instability, anger problems, unstable self-identity, destructive impulsive behaviors, frantic efforts to avoid abandonment, chronic feelings of emptiness, transient dissociative symptoms or paranoid ideation, and suicidal and self-injurious behaviors (American Psychiatric Association, 2000). Individuals with BPD use many forms of mental health treatment at exceptionally high rates, and the costs of such services are high (Bender et al., 2001). BPD is one of the most challenging psychological disorders to treat in part because of numerous and severe self-destructive and avoidant behaviors.

There are mixed findings regarding the long-term course of BPD, both with and without treatment. Recent large studies suggest that about one third of clients with BPD initially admitted to a short-term treatment in a psychiatric hospital no longer met criteria for BPD 2 years later, and about 88% achieved remission after 10 years (Zanarini, Frankenburg, Hennen, Reich, & Silk, 2006). Results indicate that impulsive behaviors improved the quickest over time, whereas problems with emotion dysregulation were the most chronic. Thus, many individuals with BPD still experience substantial emotional suffering long after diagnostic criteria are no longer met (Skodol et al., 2002).

Self-inflicted injury (SII; both suicide attempts and other intentional, nonfatal, self-injurious behaviors) is often considered one of the defining features of BPD. BPD is the only disorder in the *Diagnostic and Statistical Manual of Mental Disorders* (American Psychiatric Association, 2000) for which SII is included as a diagnostic criterion. A majority of treatment-seeking individuals diagnosed with BPD engage in SII (e.g., Soloff, Lis, Kelly, Cornelius, & Ulrich, 1994), with up to 8% of individuals ultimately committing suicide (see Linehan, Rizvi, Shaw Welch, & Page, 2000, for a review). Furthermore, individuals with BPD engage in more repetitive SII than individuals with other diagnoses (e.g., Links, Heslegrave, Mitton, van Reekum, & Patrick, 1995).

BPD is one of the most challenging disorders to treat for several reasons. First, many client behaviors are exceptionally stressful for therapists, including dysfunctional interpersonal behaviors (e.g., criticizing or getting angry at the therapist) and serious impulsive behaviors, such as dangerous substance abuse, suicidal behaviors, and serious self-mutilation, all of which can contribute to therapist burnout. Second, the long-standing patterns of emotional sensitivity and dysfunctional behaviors found in BPD are often slow to change, which can lead therapists to become frustrated or hopeless. Third, individuals with BPD engage in many behaviors that interfere with receiving therapy, such as missing sessions, arriving at sessions late, leaving early, not doing assigned tasks, or becoming passive or emotionally shut down within session (Linehan, 1993a; Stone, 2000).

We propose that shame is an especially insidious problem in therapy with individuals with BPD because it has a major role in the most serious behaviors, such as suicidal behavior and self-injury, and at the same time interferes with efforts to solve problems effectively. Shame is associated with a variety of avoidant behaviors that can impede therapeutic progress. Successful therapy relies on the detailed discussion of one's life, problems, and behaviors that are in need of changing. However, by its very nature, shame hinders such discussion because it evokes hiding and concealing and various other avoidant behaviors (e.g., criticism or anger toward the therapist to divert attention away from an uncomfortable self-focus). Moreover, the experience of shame is often so aversive that clients may avoid shame altogether by missing therapy sessions or leaving sessions early or by failing to think about problems between sessions and thereby not practicing new, more effective responses when they are most needed. The end result of all of these avoidant shame responses is that the problems remain unsolved. If these behaviors occur repeatedly, it is easy to see how treatment can fail.

In this chapter, the relationship between shame and BPD is examined from a developmental and behavioral perspective. The biosocial theory is put forth to explain the association between BPD and the presence of frequent and intense episodes of shame. Existing research on shame and BPD is summarized. Next, clinical applications are discussed and a behavioral treatment approach, based on a behavioral skill taught in dialectical behavior therapy (DBT), is suggested as an empirically driven method for reducing maladaptive shame. Finally, a case example is presented to demonstrate the use of these behavioral principles to treat shame in session with a BPD client.

BPD, EMOTION DYSREGULATION, AND SHAME: LINEHAN'S BIOSOCIAL THEORY

Linehan's (1993a) biosocial theory of BPD posits that the disorder is primarily a dysfunction of the emotion regulation system. From this perspective, most dysfunctional BPD behaviors are seen as either attempts to regulate negative emotions or direct consequences of dysregulated emotions. For example, self-injury may persist over time because it effectively alleviates emotional distress in the short term (Welch, Linehan, Sylvers, Chittams, & Rizvi, 2008). Unstable and explosive relationships with others may directly result from out-of-control shame, anger, and fear triggered by real or perceived criticism. Furthermore, the theory states that chronic emotion regulation difficulties develop over time as a result of reciprocal influence between a biologically influenced emotional temperament—characterized by emotions that are easily triggered, highly intense, and slow to subside—and environments that punish, correct, trivialize, or ignore the individual's behavior and emotional responses regardless of whether they are normal or understandable. Thus, the biosocial theory suggests that individuals with BPD are both biologically more prone to experience negative emotions, including shame, than individuals without BPD and also more likely to develop shame responses through interactions with this invalidating environment, in which individuals learn to regard their own experiences, emotions, and behaviors in a similar invalidating manner. It is through this process of increasing self-invalidation, in combination with the biological predisposition, that chronic feelings of shame develop.

Some of the most invalidating environmental interactions during childhood are experiences of sexual abuse, persistent physical abuse, emotional neglect, and humiliation. Biographical interviews with adult individuals with BPD have revealed that about 65% report sexual traumatic experiences, 45% physical abuse, and almost 70% emotional neglect (Kleindienst et al., 2010; Zanarini et al., 1997). Furthermore, the majority of the clients report that these events were recurring. Although these estimates are based on retrospective reports of adult individuals with BPD and therefore subject to potential reporting biases, they are nevertheless important indications of perceived and/or actual experiences of invalidation. These types of experiences often persist during adulthood, and empirical data suggest that experience of adult abuse is strongly associated with a failure to remit from BPD (Zanarini, Frankenburg, Hennen, Reich, & Silk, 2005).

The biosocial theory also provides an explanation for SII in BPD and suggests a potential critical role of shame in the process. According to Linehan (1993a), SII is related to negative emotions in three specific ways expanded upon below: (a) high emotional arousal interferes with solving the problems that trigger SII, (b) SII regulates aversive emotional arousal in the short term, and (c) SII may be a form of self-invalidation or self-punishment triggered by feelings of shame.

Self-Inflicted Injury as a Primary Problem-Solving Strategy

Because of the reinforcing effects of SII, the behavior quickly becomes a primary form of problem solving. An individual learns over time to associate self-injury with a reduction in emotional distress, and thus when the "problem" of emotional distress appears, self-injury becomes a method to "solve" it. Further, SII may also be associated with influencing others in a way that is reinforcing to the individual (e.g., the SII is related to an increase in positive attention from a loved one). Because the SII is positively reinforced by both within-individual and environmental factors, it is likely to be strengthened as a response over time. Coupled with the fact that individuals with BPD have often not been taught effective emotion regulation strategies (a side effect of the invalidating environment), the individual thus fails to learn alternative problem solving strategies. Therefore, SII is more likely to repeatedly occur despite any intention to change it.

Self-Inflicted Injury as a Form of Emotion Regulation

Many experts in the field believe that suicidal acts are attempts to permanently escape from physical or emotional pain (Baumeister, 1990; Maris, 1981; Shneidman, 1993). Multiple studies have documented this intent for suicide attempts (e.g., Brown, Linehan, & Comtois, 2002; Kienhorst, De Wilde, Diekstra, & Wolters, 1995; Michel, Valach, & Waeber, 1994), and there is some evidence from both self-report studies and physiological studies that suicide attempts and nonsuicidal self-injury often temporarily reduce emotional pain in both BPD populations and populations not selected for BPD (e.g., Brown et al., 2002; Doron, Stein, Levine, Abramovitch, Eilat, & Neuman, 1998; Kienhorst et al., 1995; Kleindienst et al., 2008; Sachsse, von der Heyde, & Heuther, 2002; Welch et al., 2008). Because SII effectively reduces emotional distress, it is more likely to recur in similar circumstances (i.e., via negative reinforcement).

Self-Inflicted Injury as a Form of Self-Punishment

Linehan's (1993a) emphasis on self-invalidation suggests that SII may also be a form of self-punishment. *Self-punishment* is a broad category, including self-criticism, self-deprivation, self-contempt, overt self-injury, and other "deserved" negative consequences to perceived transgressions. Self-verification theory (Swann, Hixon, Stein-Seroussi, & Gilbert, 1990) posits that people behave in ways that are consistent with their self-concepts (Aronson & Mette, 1968). According to this theory, if shame triggers negative self-judgmental thoughts in BPD individuals, they will experience intense anxiety and an aversive feeling of being out of control until there is sufficient confirmation of their core negative self-beliefs. Inconsistencies between the cognitions "I am a bad person and deserve to be punished" and "I have not been punished" would create aversive affect and cognitive dissonance (Festinger, 1978). When this dissonance is experienced, individuals may engage in various behaviors to restore both their sense of control and their experience of the world as predictable. Thus, when BPD individuals think that they are bad or have committed some serious transgression, SII may be a way of reducing emotional arousal by confirming their belief that "I am a bad person and deserve to be punished." In support of this hypothesis, self-punishment is a common reason reported for engaging in SII (Brown et al., 2002; Gratz, 2000; Penn, Esposito, Schaeffer, Fritz, & Spirito, 2003).

RESEARCH ON SHAME AND BPD

It is difficult to evaluate the evidence for the relationship of shame to BPD, as there are many studies relevant to shame that do not use the term *shame,* and there are studies of "shame" that are based on poor definitions and measures (see Rizvi, 2010). Although the number of empirical studies on shame and psychopathology has grown exponentially in recent years, much of what is believed about the role of shame in psychological problems is based on clinical theories of shame and empirical studies of similar constructs like self-esteem. Psychologists usually regard self-esteem as an enduring personality trait that encompasses self-evaluative beliefs (e.g., generally believing "I am worthy/worthless") and proneness to emotional states such as pride versus shame. Some research focuses on short-term reductions in self-esteem states (i.e., increases in self-judgmental thoughts and associated dysphoric affect) that occur in specific circumstances (e.g., failure, criticism, rejection; see Kernis &

Goldman, 2005). Similarly, shame is defined as an aversive emotional state accompanied by negative self-judgment, perceived risk of rejection or loss of social attraction, and the urge to hide or disappear (Lewis, 2000; Tangney & Dearing, 2002). Thus, the construct of shame proneness may be similar to the notion of trait self-esteem, but more research is needed to clarify the relationship between these two constructs (see Tangney & Dearing, 2002, for a proposed model of this relationship).

There is an extensive body of literature showing that trait self-esteem predicts problems associated with BPD including suicidal behaviors. In populations not limited to BPD, many studies demonstrate that low self-esteem is associated with a history of suicidal behavior (e.g., Crook, Raskin, & Davis, 1975; Neuringer, 1974) and suicidal ideation (e.g., De Man & Leduc, 1995; Jin & Zhang, 1998; Shagle & Barber, 1993). Several prospective studies have shown that low self-esteem, independent of depression, predicts future suicidal ideation (Kaplan & Pokorny, 1976), suicide attempts (Lewinsohn, Rohde, & Seeley, 1994), and completed suicide (Beck & Stewart, 1989, cited in Weishaar & Beck, 1992). Presumably, these individuals with "low self-esteem" attempt suicide when adverse events trigger self-blame or self-contempt, thoughts of being inferior or worthless, and painful affect, such as shame and dysphoria, especially when they feel hopeless about ever improving their undesirable qualities or social acceptance.

Research on the states preceding SII and the reasons given for SII also implicate the role of shame. Most individuals report self-hatred, feeling lonely or unwanted (which suggests sadness and shame), or feelings of "rejection" or "failure" prior to their SII acts (Bancroft, Skrimshire, & Simkins, 1976; Hawton, Cole, O'Grady, & Osborn, 1982; Herpertz, 1995), and they commonly attribute their SII to these feelings (e.g., Bennum & Phil, 1983; Rosen, 1976; Roy, 1978). Feeling "like a failure" has been shown to be the aspect of depression that most strongly differentiates suicide attempters from individuals with recurrent depressive episodes who do not attempt suicide (Bulik, Carpenter, Kupfer, & Frank, 1990). Extensive analyses of suicide notes also suggest that most suicides are prompted by "feelings of failure" (Hassan, 1995).

Furthermore, studies that have separately assessed the hostility directed toward oneself versus others have found that both types of hostility are high among individuals who engage in SII (Brittlebank, Cole, Hassanyeh, & Kenny, 1990; Vinoda, 1966). However, individuals more often attribute their SII to anger at self rather than anger at others (Bennum & Phil, 1983; Roy, 1978), and only hostility toward oneself has been found to predict the suicide intent of SII (Farmer & Creed, 1986). Similarly, many individuals report that they self-injure to punish themselves (Briere & Gil, 1998; Favazza & Conterio, 1989; Herpertz, 1995).

Several studies using nonclinical samples have documented a link between shame and suicidal behaviors. Hastings, Northman, and Tangney (2000) found that proneness to shame, but not guilt, was associated with current suicide ideation in a sample of college students. In another study, college students who reported having ever considered, threatened, or attempted suicide reported higher levels of shame but not guilt (Lester, 1998). In a longitudinal study of fifth-grade children, shame proneness predicted later suicide attempts by young adulthood (Tangney & Dearing, 2002).

In addition to the studies of correlates of BPD reviewed above, a few recent studies have examined shame specifically and within the BPD diagnosis. For example, one study found that scores on an implicit measure of shame (the Implicit Association Test) were higher among individuals with BPD compared with clients with social phobia (Rüsch et al., 2007). Nonverbal shame behaviors while talking to a clinical interviewer about the triggers for a recent episode of SII predicted repeated SII in the following 12 months in a sample of treatment-seeking individuals with BPD (Brown, Comtois, Murray, Linehan, & Chapman, 2009). Furthermore, many individuals with BPD report that they engage in nonsuicidal self-injury to punish themselves (Brown, Comtois, & Linehan, 2002; Kleindienst et al., 2008). Thus, both self-report and indirect measures of shame suggest that shame is an important problem in BPD.

In summary, a growing body of research indicates that shame is associated with BPD and SII. More research, however, is needed to verify and better clarify the role shame plays in BPD. First, more BPD studies are needed that use psychometrically valid measures of shame and other emotions to verify that problems in BPD, such as SII, are primarily related to shame. Second, research needs to clarify the processes that explain the relationship between shame and both SII and therapy-interfering behaviors in BPD. Moving beyond correlational research will help elucidate whether a causal chain between shame and ineffective behaviors exists. This future research could help provide clearer targets for treatment of BPD.

SHAME IN THERAPY WITH INDIVIDUALS WITH BPD

Shame poses a unique problem in psychotherapy. All forms of psychotherapy serve as a forum for discussing intensely personal information with another person, thus exposing internal thoughts and feelings as well as current or past behaviors. As Greenberg and Paivio (1997) wrote, "Shame operates everywhere in therapy because clients are constantly concerned about what parts of their inner experience can be revealed and what parts must be hidden" (p. 235). The nonverbal responses that are associated with shame, such as decreased eye contact, slumped or rigid posture, and mental and physical withdrawal, can interfere with continued and fluid discussion of a topic in therapy.

As discussed previously, individuals with BPD are likely to have frequent and intense experiences of shame (Brown et al., 2002; Brown et al., 2009; Ebner-Priemer et al., 2008; Rizvi, 2010; Rosenthal, Cukrowicz, Cheavens, & Lynch, 2006; Rüsch et al., 2007). Any clinician working with this population can likely attest to the severity of the shame responses, and the associated avoidant behaviors, that occur in sessions. It is also quite possible that therapists often fail to identify shame responses or misinterpret them because of the many avoidant behaviors that effectively conceal the problems. If this happens repeatedly, the therapist ultimately is not working on the primary problem, and the client is likely to feel invalidated and misunderstood. For example, a client who experiences shame about an episode of SII that occurred during the week may think of herself as a failure and a terrible person. She may come to therapy worried that the therapist will ask about the incident and feel so ashamed that she responds by shutting down and not speaking for most of the session. The therapist, not knowing that SII behavior occurred, has no way of knowing what prompted this in-session behavior and may come up with many (inaccurate) interpretations. Moreover, because the SII episode does not get discussed, the therapist and client lose the opportunity to work together to solve the problem that prompted the self-harm, and therefore the likelihood that the behavior will occur again is high. Thus, more systematic work on shame and the reduction of shame is imperative within treatment-resistant populations such as clients with BPD. This can occur both formally (i.e., via a structured intervention designed specifically to target shame) and informally (i.e., when shame arises in any therapy session).

OPPOSITE ACTION AS A TREATMENT FOR SHAME IN BPD

The treatment of maladaptive shame has been largely overlooked in treatment models and manuals across all disorders, including BPD. There have been no randomized controlled trials conducted on interventions for shame specifically, and only one study has examined a structured intervention for shame within BPD. Using single-subject design methodology, Rizvi and Linehan (2005) presented and evaluated an 8- to 10-week cognitive–behavioral intervention based on an expansion of the DBT principle of opposite action for shame, as outlined by Linehan (1993b).

DBT (Linehan, 1993a, 1993b) is a comprehensive psychosocial treatment originally developed to treat suicidal individuals with BPD. DBT has been found to be an efficacious treatment for BPD in numerous studies (see Robins & Chapman, 2004, for a review). The model of DBT suggests that dysregulation across all emotions is the core feature of BPD, and specific aspects of DBT target shame in several ways. There are a number of emotion regulation skills designed to help clients prevent, tolerate, and modulate negative emotions. In addition, DBT has a strong emphasis on therapist validation of the client to reduce shame and enhance the quality of the therapeutic relationship. Therapists are encouraged to conceptualize core problems as related to self-invalidation and to look for and block avoidant and escape responses in order to promote more skillful behaviors. However, up to one quarter of individuals may continue to engage in seriously problematic behaviors following a year of DBT (Linehan et al., 2006), suggesting that further efforts must be made to better understand and treat the core problems in BPD. One such avenue may be to more explicitly target shame in this population through structured DBT-informed interventions (Rizvi & Linehan, 2005).

Opposite action as a treatment strategy is itself an expansion of evidence-based treatments of disorders of fear and anxiety. It extends the principles of exposure to feared stimuli (the opposite of fear responses) to a more general principle of opposite-to-emotion behavior. Although the term *opposite action* originated with Linehan (1993a, 1993b), the strategy itself has its origins in the earliest forms of behavior therapy. Barlow (1988) suggested that the crucial function of successful exposure therapy for anxiety disorders, such as specific and social phobias, is the prevention of natural action tendencies associated with anxiety and promotion of actions incompatible with anxiety. Other earlier emotion theorists had come to similar conclusions. Izard, for example, stated that treatment for anxiety disorders involves "the individual learn[ing] to act his way into a new feeling" (cited in Barlow, 1988, p. 410). Cognitive–behavioral interventions for anxiety disorders or fear include a common element: Individuals have to approach the object or situation that is fear provoking, thus acting counter to (and inhibiting) their prominent urges to avoid. Further, acting opposite often allows for corrective information about the situation. For instance, acting opposite by approaching a feared situation allows a phobic person to experience the true safety of the situation, a process often referred to as *emotional processing* (Foa & Kozak, 1986).

Successful treatments for other maladaptive affective responses common in major depression and anger disorders also encourage action that is incompatible with urges associated with the emotion. For example, treatments for depression, such as cognitive therapy (Beck, Rush, Shaw, & Emery, 1979) and behavioral activation (Martell, Addis, & Jacobson, 2001), often require that individuals engage in activities that give them a sense of mastery or pleasure and help them solve, rather than avoid, their problems—behaviors that are opposite to sadness, hopelessness, and fatigue. Similarly, effective treatments for anger (e.g., Kassinove & Tafrate, 2002) focus on getting the individual to increase empathy, gentleness, and forgiveness for the people or situations toward which they feel anger—behaviors that are opposite to the urges to attack. There are also hundreds of studies on *cognitive dissonance induction* that have shown that getting people to act contrary to their attitudes (when they believe they have freely chosen to do so) is a powerful way to change beliefs and attitudes, including low self-esteem (e.g., Zimbardo & Leippe, 1991).

In DBT, opposite action is a behavioral skill proposed to regulate emotions. The premise behind the skill is that one can change an unwanted emotion by identifying the current emotion, identifying the urges (action tendencies) associated with the emotion, determining the actions that are opposite to those urges, and then engaging in those opposite actions. The hypothesized agent of change is the integrated opposite action of the individual when faced with an emotion-eliciting cue. By preventing maladaptive action tendencies and generating new incompatible response patterns, the initial emotional response is weakened, and the incompatible response is strengthened. The application of opposite action to the emotion of shame specifically is described briefly in the DBT skills manual (Linehan, 1993b, p. 94) but was modified in two important ways in the Rizvi and Linehan (2005) pilot study. First, the notion of justified versus unjustified emotions, specifically as related to shame, was expanded upon. Second, the importance of determining opposite actions specific to individual clients was emphasized. Each of these exceptions is described below.

To treat shame effectively, it is important to conduct a behavioral (functional) analysis of an individual's various shame responses. A behavioral analysis is a step-by-step process that identifies the contextual, antecedent, organismic (i.e., thoughts, emotions, behavior), and consequent factors that are directly related to the maintenance of a problem behavior, as well as the functional relationships between problems. This level of detail is important for many reasons; primarily, it allows for an evaluation of all the various components of the shame response, which can highlight specific points of intervention. In addition, it allows for a more careful assessment of the causes of the shame response, the specific urges that accompany that cue, and the determination of whether the shame is "justified" by the events preceding it, all of which have implications for treatment.

This causal analysis leads to treatment plans tailored to individual clients rather than a "one size fits all" approach. For example, clients who are ashamed of, and thus avoid, their anger responses would be encouraged to approach situations that elicit anger while allowing and focusing on the internal experience of anger. In contrast, clients who get angry as a way to avoid shame and the triggering events would be encouraged to approach and focus on situations that elicit shame while simultaneously blocking angry responses. Key assessment questions are the following: What does the client not do because of his or her dysfunctional thoughts and emotions? and What would the client do if he or she did not have these dysfunctional thoughts and emotions?

The notion of justified versus unjustified emotions has been articulated by Linehan (1993a, 1993b) and is modeled on the notion that emotions evolved as effective responses to common problems in living. Justification of emotions, from this perspective, has to do ultimately with the survival value of the emotion broadly considered. It is similar to the notion of *context-appropriate emotion* or *context-inappropriate emotion* (Davidson, Jackson, & Kalin, 2000) in the larger emotion literature, which refers to whether the intensity of the emotion is effective, normal, or in proportion to the particular situation or context. For some emotions, it may be relatively easy to determine whether the situation warrants the emotion. For example, fear can be considered justified in situations in which one's life or well-being is truly threatened because it can motivate effective actions to escape or avoid the danger. In contrast, fear is unjustified when it is based on false beliefs about the likelihood of danger and the person needlessly avoids safe situations.

It is often more difficult to determine the extent to which shame responses are justified. Rizvi and Linehan (2005) suggested that shame can be justified for an individual in two ways: (a) if the action or characteristic of the individual would likely lead to rejection from an important individual or social group if revealed or known and (b) if the action or characteristic of the individual violates a personally held moral value. If neither of these conditions is met, then the shame is considered to be unjustified for that situation. To complicate the matter further, however, many shame responses are both justified and unjustified to some extent—for example, when the individual exaggerates the severity of social rejection (e.g., expecting total ostracism from everybody, when in truth the person would only be moderately criticized or teased by a few people).

It is important to note that justified versus unjustified is not the same as good versus bad, right versus wrong, complicated versus simple, or understandable versus incomprehensible. In fact, a DBT approach would include an assumption that all behavior makes sense given the causal factors leading up to it (see Linehan, 1993a, for a more thorough description of this philosophy). Rather, the discussion about justified versus unjustified is limited to an assessment of whether the criteria are met. However, even that evaluation can be difficult, as an event or characteristic can prompt justified shame in one context and unjustified shame in another or may provoke shame in one individual but not another. For example, an individual who experiences shame about being homosexual may have justified shame if he lives in a community that believes that homosexuality is a sin and a personal weakness. However, if he was part of a very progressive and gay-friendly community that would not reject him if he disclosed his sexual orientation, the shame could be considered unjustified. To complicate matters even further, an individual may be part of a community that will reject her if homosexuality is revealed (e.g., the U.S. military) and simultaneously be a valued member of an "underground" community of other homosexual soldiers. Shame is justified in one context but not in the other.

Other examples of situations or behaviors that may prompt justified shame could include a combat veteran having killed in war, a mother having physically abused her children, and a person receiving disability money from the government who believes it is a moral violation to accept money without making a greater contribution to society. Examples of unjustified shame could include an anorexic client's shame over her perceived fatness, a perfectionist client's shame over performing less than 100% on an exam, or a client's shame in disclosing something to a therapist whom she has seen for a year and who has expressed acceptance toward the client (i.e., is unlikely to reject the client on the basis of the disclosure). It is this last form of unjustified shame that may be most prominent in treatment with individuals with BPD. The treatment goal for unjustified shame is to attempt to eliminate shame altogether, whereas the treatment goal for justified shame is to reduce shame enough so that the person can actively work on solving the problem to avoid the future risk of social rejection. The therapist should never assume whether shame is justified or not and, instead, should make the determination in collaboration with the client only after a careful assessment.

Because of the complexity of shame, the emerging evidence that shame has more than one action tendency (e.g., withdraw, avoid, lash out), and the distinction between justified and unjustified shame, it is necessary that opposite action be based on the principles of cue exposure, response prevention, and opposite action using an idiographic plan rather than a one-size-fits-all approach. Thus, various opposite actions can be identified for an individual according to the specific context and his or her specific urges in that situation. The process then involves a series of five steps:

1. determine the relevant shame cues and urges for the individual,
2. appraise whether the shame is justified or unjustified,
3. expose the individual to the shame cue,
4. block maladaptive shame action tendencies or urges (including self-blame), and
5. elicit and reinforce actions that are in opposition to the shame urges.

In general, opposite actions for unjustified shame include behaviors such as making a detailed disclosure in a direct and nonjudgmental manner, maintaining eye contact and upright posture, repeating the avoided behaviors, and validating oneself. In essence, clients practice acting as if they are not ashamed even when fully revealing themselves. Common strategies for justified shame include apologizing and repairing the damage, committing to and implementing an effective plan to solve the problem (e.g., anger management therapy), accepting consequences, and accepting prior mistakes. This process may be similar to what others describe as shifting from shame to guilt (e.g., Tangney & Dearing, 2002). There also may be times when the client is encouraged to keep a behavior hidden if possible (to avoid rejection).

The therapist should be aware that habituation to shame-eliciting cues will likely take significantly more time than habituation to fear-related cues. It takes almost no time to verify that the assumed threat of fear-related cues is irrelevant in the current (therapeutic) context (i.e., you will not die from standing in a secure location high above the ground, you will not be bitten by a spider, and even hyperventilation will not kill you). With shame, however, the client cannot be sure prior to the disclosure that the therapist will not reject him or that the therapist is telling the truth if she says she will accept the client no matter what. Therefore, correction of dysfunctional shame-related assumptions requires an authentic therapeutic relationship that includes radical genuineness on the part of the therapist as well as appropriate self-disclosure. An example of this type of therapist behavior would be honestly telling the client the therapist's personal reaction to the client's disclosure—for example, "Hearing that story of your abuse makes me feel really sad for you, but it does not make me think you are a bad person" or "I want you to know that I would probably feel ashamed if I did that also, and we're going to work together to make sure that event doesn't happen again."

In DBT, mindfulness and acceptance are other primary interventions used to target shame in conjunction with opposite action (Linehan, Bohus, & Lynch, 2007). *Mindfulness* is a state of awareness in which people effectively focus their attention and get "unstuck" from internal experiences, including dysfunctional thinking and action urges. For example, a client working on shame can be mindful of negative judgments such as "I'm bad" by "stepping back from" and observing the thoughts or describing instead of judging (i.e., just sticking to the facts). In addition, clients in DBT use a mindfulness strategy originally developed by Marlatt (1985) called "urge surfing" in which they observe the urge as it rises, crests, and diminishes. This technique can help clients get "unstuck" from dysfunctional action urges, which facilitates acting contrary to the urges. Many clients who feel shame about their other emotions (e.g., sadness, anger) are encouraged to fully allow and experience the physical sensations associated with the emotions that they normally avoid (see Borkovec, Alcaine, & Behar, 2004).

In the Rizvi and Linehan (2005) study, five women with BPD were treated with a structured intervention of opposite action using a single-subject, multiple baseline design. The treatment was provided over eight to 10 weekly sessions each lasting 90 to 120 minutes. The first session consisted of an orientation to the treatment, provision of didactic information about the nature of shame, and attainment of commitment to the therapy using DBT commitment strategies (Linehan, 1993a). In addition, a measure called the Shame Inventory (Rizvi, 2010; available from the first author upon request) was developed and used to obtain information about the individual's personally relevant shame cues. The clinical version of the Shame Inventory consists of 98 situations or characteristics derived from both the literature on shame and clinicians' responses to a request for situations that have elicited shame in BPD clients. Examples include "a time when I was laughed at in front of others," "a time when I physically attacked someone," "being overweight," and "having a mental disorder." Individuals were asked to indicate items on the Inventory that they had experienced and then to rate these experiences on a scale of 0 to 100 to indicate their present level of shame about that situation. The therapist then used this measure to formulate a shame hierarchy of potential cues that might be used in subsequent sessions to which the treatment would be applied.

The subsequent sessions largely adhered to a standard protocol. Each week, the therapist asked about the client's experiences and reactions thus far. The opposite action procedure was initiated by having the client first provide as much detail as possible about the event from the shame inventory that was chosen for the session. The therapist used a writing pad to analyze the components of the shame experience, including prompting events, thoughts, emotions, behaviors, and urges. The therapist and client then determined collaboratively to what extent they considered the shame to be justified. Finally, the opposite action behaviors were determined and elicited from the client in session. This was largely done by having the client retell the story of the event over and over again while engaging in opposite behaviors, though this could vary depending on the situation (see the case example later in this chapter for some variations). Finally, the client was given homework assignments that usually involved listening to a recording of the session at least once and engaging in the opposite action protocol several times throughout the week. The therapist monitored the client's shame throughout by asking for ratings on a 0-to-100 scale and asked the client to engage in self-monitoring between sessions.

Results from the pilot study (Rizvi & Linehan, 2005) suggested that the intervention reduced shame about a specific event for some of the clients. An unintended finding from the study was the high degree of acceptability of the treatment and level of motivation on the part of the clients as indicated by the following: There were no treatment dropouts during the intervention, no sessions were missed unless previously planned, and there was high compliance with homework assignments. Most clinicians who treat individuals with BPD would recognize that this is noteworthy for a population that has long been associated with a number of therapy-interfering behaviors. Although the sample size was quite small and future research is needed to replicate the findings, the opposite action intervention appears to hold promise as a treatment for shame in the BPD population. Furthermore, because it is based on standard empirically based behavioral principles, it is likely that using opposite action in a less formal manner when shame arises in sessions may be a useful tool for reducing shame in the moment. This reduction could assist therapists and their clients with BPD in working toward active problem solving that is not interfered with by an extreme shame response, as demonstrated in the case example that follows.

CASE EXAMPLE

Sara was a 35-year-old White woman who met criteria for BPD, dysthymic disorder, social anxiety disorder, and avoidant personality disorder. She had a long history of self-injurious behavior since her teenage years, which included cutting her arms and legs, head banging, and overdosing on sleeping pills. She entered into the shame treatment pilot study because she reported that shame was such a prominent problem for her that it prevented her from working toward her goals and living up to her values. Sara was married, with one daughter, and she reported frequent disappointment in herself about being a bad mother and wife. She felt like she was more of a drain on her family than a source of loving support.

During the first session, Sara reported feeling shame at a high level of intensity on a daily basis. She also reported that she engaged in self-injury when she felt intense shame and wanted to punish herself (in the case of cutting and head banging) or to avoid the situation altogether (in the case of overdosing and sleeping for long periods). Sara could not recall an incident of self-harm that did not involve intense feelings of shame.

Sara completed the Shame Inventory. During the second session, the inventory was reviewed, and a situation that prompted a midlevel intensity of shame was chosen. Therapists are encouraged to start with a situation that is midlevel in intensity to increase the likelihood that it will be a success experience and to model the steps of the treatment without starting with the most difficult situations. For Sara, the situation chosen was telling her sister that she had a diagnosis of BPD (rated 45 on the Shame Inventory). Through assessment, it was determined that there was very little likelihood that her sister would reject her for such an admission. Thus, following the assessment, the in-session work consisted of practicing telling her sister about her BPD in a nonshameful manner (direct eye contact, forthcoming manner, upright posture, absence of fidgeting and long pauses, a clear and audible voice). Using monitoring of shame intensity throughout, this was continued until Sara reported a 50% reduction in her level of shame. For homework, she was assigned the task of having this conversation with her sister, which she accomplished effectively.

In other sessions, the shame cues explored included a previous therapist not showing up for a scheduled appointment, self-harm episodes, sexual attraction to women, and sexual fantasies and behaviors. As an example of opposite action for justified shame, Sara reported feeling intense shame following an episode of self-harm (thus indicating the cyclical nature of shame as it both led to and resulted from the behavior). This shame was considered justified both because it violated her personal values of not wanting to purposely cause harm to herself and also because it would likely lead some other people to reject her if they knew about her self-injurious behavior. Further, this behavior was not something the therapist wished for Sara to disclose to many other people, so the opposite action would not include talking about it in a nonshameful way with anyone other than the therapist. The action tendencies for Sara associated with the shame over self-harm included urges to attack herself through self-blame and more self-harm and to punish herself by removing sources of pleasure (i.e., "Because of what I do to myself, I don't deserve to do anything nice for myself"). The therapist worked with Sara to determine what some opposite behaviors might be for this experience. They "repaired" by working to identify and implement effective strategies for stopping all future intentional self-harm. For example, more adaptive ways of coping with negative emotions (e.g., distracting, self-soothing, other distress tolerance skills) were taught and their practice was reinforced. The therapist also had the client do as many pleasurable activities as possible that the client thought she did not "deserve" to do. It was determined that for any additional therapeutic work to be successful, Sara needed to accept the fact that the self-harm occurred while reducing judgment of herself as well.

Although the structured intervention was primarily used throughout the treatment, there were also opportunities for more informal use of opposite action for shame, as demonstrated by the following transcript segment. This type of work could also be done with a client who is not in a structured intervention. At the beginning of Session 6, Sara came into session appearing very withdrawn and tentative. When asked if she had any reaction to the previous week's session, she reported that something was weighing heavily on her mind but that she did not want to discuss it. However, it was clear to the therapist that avoiding the topic might interfere with Sara's ability to actively engage in the current session. The previous session had focused on Sara's shame surrounding her experience of being sexually abused by a neighbor when she was a small child (rated as a 90 on the Shame Inventory).

Therapist:	Is whatever's on your mind something that is interfering right now? Interfering with your ability to throw yourself into whatever we do?
Sara:	Yes.
Therapist:	Then I want to talk about this, because I see you now engaging in behaviors totally consistent with shame. Should I list them for you? The lack of eye contact, the withdrawing, spacing out, the fidgeting with your hair, other things. And I think you're shutting down.
Sara:	Yeah, I can tell I'm shutting down. I think part of what upset me from listening to the tape of last week's session is that, I guess, I assumed you didn't really believe me.
Therapist:	Oh, so this wasn't something that happened last week, but just in listening to the tape of last week's session? What did you think I didn't believe you about?
Sara:	*[long pause]* That you didn't believe I had been abused when I was little.
Therapist:	So that's preventing you from talking about it now, because you're worried that I won't believe you? I mean, frankly, that would stop me from telling somebody something. Is that it?
Sara:	Yes. I guess I'm mad at you for not believing me.
Therapist:	For the interpretation of that.
Sara:	Yes.
Therapist:	OK; so that's what it had to do with. As best you can tell, your shame ratings went up when you starting having the thought that I didn't believe you.
Sara:	Yes.
Therapist:	OK. So this is, by the way, opposite action—what you're doing right now, though you could do it a little more. Because the cue is the interpretation that I'm not believing you, and your urge is to withdraw.
Sara:	To withdraw from you.
Therapist:	Right! Because you're afraid I might reject you or think poorly of you. And that's a shame response, but what it's doing is functioning to shut you down entirely and not solve this problem. So you are doing opposite action because you're talking about it. You got to the point where you

explicitly said what the problem was in your mind, and that allows for a problem solution to start coming into play. But it's not until that point that we can actually talk about it. Do you see that?

Sara: Yes.

Therapist: And I try to read minds, but usually I'm not that successful! And this wouldn't have occurred to me. Because it didn't occur to me last week, and so I wouldn't have been able to figure it out. So how can you use opposite action in this moment to get your shame to go down and therefore get this problem to be solved?

Sara: I don't know.

Therapist: You don't know?

Sara: I suppose I could talk about it in a nonshameful way without fidgeting with my hair and while looking at you.

Therapist: That is so true! [moves to eliciting and reinforcing that behavior from the client]

This transcript of a brief few minutes in a therapy session highlights several important features of treating shame in BPD. First, experiences of shame in session are quite common and to be expected when discussing such personal information. Second, the therapy often benefits from direct attention to the shame when it arises, by labeling it as shame and discussing it openly as an obstacle to successful problem-solving efforts. Third, eliciting opposite action behaviors in session provides a ripe opportunity not only to show that it is effective for reducing shame in the moment but also to make it more likely that such behavior will generalize to other life contexts. Successful "anti-shame" experiences in therapy will promote less automatic reactions to shame when it occurs again and provide more effective options for responding.

CONCLUSION

BPD is notoriously difficult to treat and is associated with a number of life-threatening and therapy-interfering behaviors that further limit clinicians' willingness to treat it. It is suggested in this chapter that many problems that individuals with BPD experience are related to chronic and intense feelings of shame. This shame typically leads to more problematic behaviors as it appears to interfere with effective problem-solving methods. Thus, it is important that shame be identified and treated in therapy with BPD individuals. DBT is an effective treatment for BPD that includes principles and strategies for reducing emotion dysregulation, including dysregulated shame. One such strategy, opposite action, can be used in both formal and informal interventions to reduce shame as a means to create more effective behavior that ultimately will lead to a life worth living for individuals with BPD.

REFERENCES

American Psychiatric Association. (2000). *Diagnostic and statistical manual of mental disorders* (4th ed., text rev.). Washington, DC: Author.

Aronson, E., & Mette, D. K. (1968). Dishonest behavior as a function of differential levels of induced self-esteem. *Journal of Personality and Social Psychology, 9,* 121–127. doi:10.1037/h0025853

Bancroft, J. H., Skrimshire, A., & Simkins, S. (1976). The reasons people give for taking overdoses. *The British Journal of Psychiatry, 128,* 538–548. doi:10.1192/bjp. 128.6.538

Barlow, D. H. (1988). *Anxiety and its disorders.* New York, NY: Guilford Press.

Baumeister, R. F. (1990). Suicide as escape from self. *Psychological Review, 97,* 90–113. doi:10.1037/0033-295X.97.1.90

Beck, A. T., Rush, A. J., Shaw, B. F., & Emery, G. (1979). *Cognitive therapy of depression.* New York, NY: Guilford Press.

Bender, D. S., Dolan, R. T., Skodol, A. E., Sanislow, C. A., Dyck, I. R., McGlashan, T. H., . . . Gunderson, J. G. (2001). Treatment utilization by patients with personality disorders. *The American Journal of Psychiatry, 158,* 295–302. doi:10. 1176/appi.ajp.158.2.295

Bennum, I., & Phil, M. (1983). Depression and hostility in self-mutilation. *Suicide & Life-Threatening Behavior, 13,* 71–84.

Borkovec, T. D., Alcaine, O., & Behar, E. (2004). Avoidance theory of worry and generalized anxiety disorder. In R. G. Heimberg, C. L. Turk, & D. S. Mennin (Eds.), *Generalized anxiety disorder: Advances in research and practice* (pp. 77–108). New York, NY: Guilford Press.

Briere, J., & Gil, E. (1998). Self-mutilation in clinical and general population samples: Prevalence, correlates, and functions. *American Journal of Orthopsychiatry, 68,* 609–620. doi:10.1037/h0080369

Brittlebank, A. D., Cole, A., Hassanyeh, F., & Kenny, M. (1990). Hostility, hopelessness and deliberate self-harm: A prospective follow-up study. *Acta Psychiatrica Scandinavica, 81,* 280–283. doi:10.1111/j.1600-0447.1990.tb06497.x

Brown, M. Z., Comtois, K. A., & Linehan, M. M. (2002). Reasons for suicide attempts and nonsuicidal self-injury in women with borderline personality disorder. *Journal of Abnormal Psychology, 111,* 198–202. doi:10.1037/0021-843X.111.1.198

Brown, M. Z., Comtois, K., Murray, A., Linehan, M., & Chapman, A. L. (2009). Shame as a prospective predictor of self-inflicted injury in borderline personality disorder: A multi-modal analysis. *Behaviour Research and Therapy, 47*, 815–822. doi:10.1016/j.brat.2009.06.008

Brown, M., Linehan, M., & Comtois, K. (2002). Reasons for suicide attempts and non-suicidal self-injury in women with borderline personality disorder. *Journal of Abnormal Psychology, 111*, 198–202. doi:10.1037/0021-843X.111.1.198

Bulik, C. M., Carpenter, L. L., Kupfer, D. J., & Frank, E. (1990). Features associated with suicide attempts in recurrent major depression. *Journal of Affective Disorders, 18*, 29–37. doi:10.1016/0165-0327(90)90114-N

Crook, T., Raskin, A., & Davis, D. (1975). Factors associated with attempted suicide among hospitalized depressed patients. *Psychological Medicine, 5*, 381–388. doi:10.1017/S0033291700057007

Davidson, R. J., Jackson, D. C., & Kalin, N. H. (2000). Emotion, plasticity, context, and regulation: Perspectives from affective neuroscience. *Psychological Bulletin, 126*, 890–909. doi:10.1037/0033-2909.126.6.890

De Man, A. F., & Leduc, C. P. (1995). Suicidal ideation in high school students: Depression and other correlates. *Journal of Clinical Psychology, 51*, 173–181. doi:10.1002/1097-4679(199503)51:2<173::AID-JCLP2270510205>3.0.CO;2-R

Doron, A., Stein, D., Levine, Y., Abramovitch, Y., Eilat, E., & Neuman, M. (1998). Physiological reactions to a suicide film: Suicide attempters, suicide ideators, and nonsuicidal patients. *Suicide & Life-Threatening Behavior, 28*, 309–314.

Ebner-Priemer, U., Kuo, J., Wolff, M., Schlotz, P., Kleindienst, N., Rosenthal, Z., . . . Bohus, M. (2008). Distress and affective dysregulation in patients with borderline personality disorder: A psychophysiological ambulatory monitoring study. *Acta Psychiatrica Scandinavica, 96*, 314–320. doi:10.1097/NMD.0b013e31816a493f

Farmer, R., & Creed, F. (1986). Hostility and deliberate self-poisoning. *British Journal of Medical Psychology, 59*, 311–316.

Favazza, A. R., & Conterio, K. (1989). Female habitual self-mutilators. *Acta Psychiatrica Scandinavica, 79*, 283–289. doi:10.1111/j.1600-0447.1989.tb10259.x

Festinger, L. A. (1978). *Theory of cognition*. Evanston, IL: Row, Peterson.

Foa, E. B., & Kozak, M. J. (1986). Emotional processing of fear: Exposure to corrective information. *Psychological Bulletin, 99*, 20–35. doi:10.1037/0033-2909.99.1.20

Gratz, K. L. (2000). *The measurement, functions, and etiology of deliberate self-harm*. Unpublished master's thesis, University of Massachusetts Boston, Boston, MA.

Greenberg, L. S., & Paivio, S. C. (1997). *Working with emotions in psychotherapy*. New York, NY: Guilford Press.

Hassan, R. (1995). Effects of newspaper stories on the incidence of suicide in Australia. *Australian and New Zealand Journal of Psychiatry, 29*, 480–483. doi:10.3109/00048679509064957

Hastings, M. E., Northman, L. M., & Tangney, J. P. (2000). Shame, guilt, and suicide. In T. Joiner & M. D. Rudd (Eds.), *Suicide science: Expanding the boundaries* (pp. 67–79). Boston, MA: Kluwer Academic.

Hawton, K., Cole, D., O'Grady, J., & Osborn, M. (1982). Motivational aspects of deliberate self-poisoning in adolescents. *The British Journal of Psychiatry, 141*, 286–291. doi:10.1192/bjp.141.3.286

Herpertz, S. (1995). Self-injurious behavior: Psychopathological and nosological characteristics in subtypes of self-injurers. *Acta Psychiatrica Scandinavica, 91*, 57–68. doi:10.1111/j.1600-0447.1995.tb09743.x

Jin, S., & Zhang, J. (1998). The effects of physical and psychological well-being on suicidal ideation. *Journal of Clinical Psychology, 54*, 401–413. doi:10.1002/(SICI) 1097-4679(199806)54:4<401::AID-JCLP2>3.0.CO;2-Q

Kaplan, H. B., & Pokorny, A. D. (1976). Self-derogation and suicide: I. Self-derogation as an antecedent of suicidal responses. *Social Science & Medicine, 10*, 113–118. doi:10.1016/0037-7856(76)90062-7

Kassinove, H., & Tafrate, R. C. (2002). *Anger management*. Atascadero, CA: Impact Publishers.

Kernis, M., & Goldman, B. (2005). Stability and variability in self-concept and self-esteem. In M. R. Leary & J. P. Tangney (Eds.), *Handbook of self and identity* (pp. 106–127). New York, NY: Guilford Press.

Kienhorst, I. C. W. M., De Wilde, E. J., Diekstra, R. F. W., & Wolters, W. H. G. (1995). Adolescents' image of their suicide attempt. *Journal of the American Academy of Child and Adolescent Psychiatry, 34*, 623–628. doi:10.1097/00004583-199505000-00014

Kleindienst, N., Bohus, M., Ludascher, P., Limberger, M., Kuenkele, K., Ebner-Priemer, U., . . . Schmahl, C. (2008). Motives for nonsuicidal self-injury among women with borderline personality disorder. *Journal of Mental Disease, 196*, 230–236. doi:10.1097/NMD.0b013e3181663026

Kleindienst, N., Limberger, M., Dyer, A., & Bohus, M. (2010). *Biographic experience in female patients with borderline personality disorder in Germany*. Manuscript in preparation.

Lester, D. (1998). The association of shame and guilt with suicidality. *The Journal of Social Psychology, 138*, 535–536. doi:10.1080/00224549809600407

Lewinsohn, P. M., Rohde, P., & Seeley, J. R. (1994). Psychosocial risk factors for future adolescent suicide attempts. *Journal of Consulting and Clinical Psychology, 62*, 297–305. doi:10.1037/0022-006X.62.2.297

Lewis, M. (2000). Self-conscious emotions: Embarrassment, pride, shame, and guilt. In M. Lewis & J. M. Haviland-Jones (Eds.), *Handbook of emotions* (2nd ed., pp. 623–636). New York, NY: Guilford Press.

Linehan, M. M. (1993a). *Cognitive-behavioral treatment of borderline personality disorder*. New York, NY: Guilford Press.

Linehan, M. M. (1993b). *Skills training manual for treating borderline personality disorder*. New York, NY: Guilford Press.

Linehan, M. M., Bohus, M., & Lynch, T. R. (2007). *Dialectical behavior therapy for pervasive emotion dysregulation*. New York, NY: Guilford Press.

Linehan, M. M., Comtois, K. A., Murray, A. M., Brown, M. Z., Gallop, R. J., Heard, H. L., . . . Lindenboim, N. (2006). Two-year randomized trial and follow-up of dialectical behavior therapy vs. therapy by experts for suicidal behaviors and borderline personality disorder. *Archives of General Psychiatry, 63,* 757–766. doi:10.1001/archpsyc.63.7.757

Linehan, M. M., Rizvi, S. L., Shaw Welch, S., & Page, B. (2000). Psychiatric aspects of suicidal behaviour: Personality disorders. In K. Hawton & K. V. Heeringen (Eds.), *The international handbook of suicide and attempted suicide* (pp. 147–178). New York, NY: Wiley. doi:10.1002/9780470698976.ch10

Links, P. S., Heslegrave, R. J., Mitton, J. E., van Reekum, R., & Patrick, J. (1995). Borderline psychopathology and recurrences of clinical disorders. *Journal of Nervous and Mental Disease, 183,* 582–586. doi:10.1097/00005053-199509000-00004

Maris, R. (1981). *Pathways to suicide: A survey of self-destructive behaviors.* Baltimore, MD: Johns Hopkins University Press.

Marlatt, G. A. (1985). Lifestyle modification. In G. A. Martatt & J. R. Gordon (Eds.), *Relapse prevention* (pp. 280–348). New York, NY: Guilford Press.

Martell, C. R., Addis, M. E., & Jacobson, N. S. (2001). *Depression in context: Strategies for guided action.* New York, NY: Norton.

Michel, K., Valach, L., & Waeber, V. (1994). Understanding deliberate self-harm: The patients' views. *Crisis, 15,* 172–278.

Neuringer, C. (1974). Attitudes toward self in suicidal individuals. *Life-Threatening Behavior, 4,* 96–106.

Penn, J. V., Esposito, C. L., Schaeffer, L. E., Fritz, G. K., & Spirito, A. (2003). Suicide attempts and self-mutilative behavior in a juvenile correctional facility. *Journal of the American Academy of Child and Adolescent Psychiatry, 42,* 762–769. doi:10.1097/01.CHI.0000046869.56865.46

Rizvi, S. L. (2010). Development and preliminary validation of a new measure to assess shame: The Shame Inventory. *Journal of Psychopathology and Behavioral Assessment, 32,* 438–447. doi:10.1007/s10862-009-9172-y

Rizvi, S. L., & Linehan, M. M. (2005). The treatment of maladaptive shame in borderline personality disorder: A pilot study of "opposite action." *Cognitive and Behavioral Practice, 12,* 437–447. doi:10.1016/S1077-7229(05)80071-9

Robins, C. J., & Chapman, A. L. (2004). Dialectical behavior therapy: Current status, recent developments, and future directions. *Journal of Personality Disorders, 18,* 7–89. doi:10.1521/pedi.18.1.73.32771

Rosen, D. H. (1976). Suicide survivors: Psychotherapeutic implications of egocide. *Suicide & Life-Threatening Behavior, 6,* 209–215.

Rosenthal, M. Z., Cukrowicz, K. C., Cheavens, J. S., & Lynch, T. R. (2006). Self-punishment as a regulation strategy in borderline personality disorder. *Journal of Personality Disorders, 20,* 232–246. doi:10.1521/pedi.2006.20.3.232

Roy, A. (1978). Self-mutilation. *The British Journal of Medical Psychology, 51*, 201–203.

Rüsch, N., Lieb, K., Gottler, I., Hermann, C., Schramm, E., Richter, H., . . . Bohus, M. (2007). Shame and implicit self-concept in women with borderline personality disorder. *American Journal of Psychiatry, 164*, 500–508. doi:10.1176/appi.ajp.164.3.500

Sachsse, U., von der Heyde, S., & Huether, G. (2002). Stress regulation and self-mutilation. *The American Journal of Psychiatry, 159*, 672. doi:10.1176/appi.ajp.159.4.672

Shagle, S. C., & Barber, B. K. (1993). Effects of family, marital, and parent–child conflict on adolescent self-derogation and suicidal ideation. *Journal of Marriage and the Family, 55*, 964–974. doi:10.2307/352776

Shneidman, E. S. (1993). *Suicide as psychache: A clinical approach to self-destructive behavior*. Northvale, NJ: Aronson.

Skodol, A. E., Siever, L. J., Livesley, W. J., Gunderson, J. G., Pfohl, B., & Widiger, T. A. (2002). The Borderline Diagnosis II: Biology, genetics, and clinical course. *Biological Psychiatry, 51*, 951–963. doi:10.1016/S0006-3223(02)01325-2

Soloff, P. H., Lis, J. A., Kelly, T., Cornelius, J., & Ulrich, R. (1994). Risk factors for suicidal behavior in borderline personality disorder. *The American Journal of Psychiatry, 151*, 1316–1323.

Stone, M. H. (2000). Clinical guidelines for psychotherapy for patients with borderline personality disorder. *Psychiatric Clinics of North America, 23*, 193–210.

Swann, W. B., Hixon, J. G., Stein-Seroussi, A., & Gilbert, D. T. (1990). The fleeting gleam of praise: Cognitive processes underlying behavioral reactions to self-relevant feedback. *Journal of Personality and Social Psychology, 59*, 17–26. doi:10.1037/0022-3514.59.1.17

Tangney, J. P., & Dearing, R. L. (2002). *Shame and guilt*. New York, NY: Guilford Press.

Vinoda, K. S. (1966). Personality characteristics of attempted suicides. *The British Journal of Psychiatry, 112*, 1143–1150. doi:10.1192/bjp.112.492.1143

Weishaar, M. E., & Beck, A. T. (1992). Clinical and cognitive predictors of suicide. In R. W. Maris, A. L. Berman, J. T. Maltsberger, & R. I. Yufit (Eds.), *Assessment and prediction of suicide* (pp. 467–483). New York, NY: Guilford Press.

Welch, S. S., Linehan, M. M., Sylvers, P., Chittams, J., & Rizvi, S. L. (2008). Emotional responses to self-injury imagery among adults with borderline personality disorder. *Journal of Consulting and Clinical Psychology, 76*, 45–51. doi:10.1037/0022-006X.76.1.45

Zanarini, M. C., Frankenburg, F., Hennen, J., Reich, D. B., & Silk, K. (2005). Adult experiences of abuse reported by borderline patients and axis II comparison subjects after six years of prospective follow up. *Journal of Nervous and Mental Disease, 193*, 412–416. doi:10.1097/01.nmd.0000165295.65844.52

Zanarini, M. C., Frankenburg, F. R., Hennen, J., Reich, D. B., & Silk, K. R. (2006). Prediction of the 10-year course of borderline personality disorder. *American Journal of Psychiatry, 163*, 827–832. doi:10.1176/appi.ajp.163.5.827

Zanarini, M. C., Williams, A. A., Lewis, R. E., Reich, R. B., Vera, S. C., Marino, M. F., . . . Frankenburg, F. R. (1997). Reported pathological childhood experiences associated with the development of borderline personality disorder. *The American Journal of Psychiatry, 154*, 1101–1106.

Zimbardo, P., & Leippe, M. R. (1991). *The psychology of attitude change and social influence.* Boston, MA: McGraw-Hill.

11

POSTTRAUMATIC STRESS DISORDER AS A SHAME DISORDER

JUDITH LEWIS HERMAN

Posttraumatic stress disorder (PTSD) is classified as an anxiety disorder in the *Diagnostic and Statistical Manual of Mental Disorders* (American Psychiatric Association, 1994). This conceptualization has led to a fruitful line of investigation into the neurobiology of fear. Pathological derangements of the normal, innate fear signaling system have been demonstrated in PTSD (LeDoux, 2003; Perry, Southwick, Yehuda, & Giller, 1990), and effective treatments have been developed aimed at reducing pathological fear (Foa, Keane, & Friedman, 2000). Although this formulation seems accurate for single-impact traumas such as auto accidents, it is necessary but not sufficient to capture an essential characteristic of those traumas that are of human design, especially those that are repeated over a prolonged period of time. In these cases, in which a relationship of dominance and subordination is established, feelings of humiliation, degradation, and shame are central to the victim's experience. The resultant

This chapter is adapted from the John Bowlby Memorial Lecture delivered in London, England, in 2007, which was subsequently published in *Shattered States: Disorganized Attachment and Its Repair*, by J. Yellin and K. White (Eds.), 2011, London, England: Karnac. Copyright 2011 by the Bowlby Centre. All rights reserved. Adapted with permission.

posttraumatic condition can be conceptualized both as an anxiety disorder and a shame disorder.

At the Victims of Violence Program in the department of psychiatry at Cambridge Hospital, where I work, the majority of our patients report histories of abuse in childhood, and many report physical or sexual abuse by intimate partners in adult life as well. At the point of entry into treatment, the majority would easily fulfill diagnostic criteria for PTSD. On a commonly used measure, the Posttraumatic Diagnostic Scale (Foa, Cashman, Jaycox, & Perry, 1997), the mean PTSD score for patients entering treatment falls into the moderate to severe range. However, most of our patients do not cite their PTSD symptoms as their reason for seeking treatment. Rather, it is most commonly some breach in a relationship that acutely aggravates a profoundly damaged sense of self. In treatment, we find repeatedly that the core issue is shame.

This chapter briefly reviews the physiology, developmental origins, psychology, and social functions of shame and proposes that shame is intrinsic to the experiences of social subordination. With this understanding, one might expect to discover shame as a major issue among people who have been victims of interpersonal violence, and perhaps particularly among those with PTSD. The chapter then reviews some of the many ways that shame might be addressed in psychotherapy with trauma survivors. Case examples from the existing literature, from the practice of colleagues, and from my own treatment program are presented.

CHARACTERISTICS OF SHAME

Shame can be likened to fear in many respects. Like fear, it is a fast-track physiological response that in intense forms can overwhelm higher cortical functions. Like fear, it is also a social signal, with characteristic facial and postural signs that can be recognized across cultures (Darwin, 1872; Izard, 1971). The gaze aversion, bowed head, and hiding behaviors of shame are similar to appeasement displays of social animals (Keltner & Harker, 1998) and may serve a similar social function among human beings. From an evolutionary point of view, shame may serve an adaptive function as a primary mechanism for regulating the individual's relations both to primary attachment figures and to the social group (Gilbert & McGuire, 1998; Izard, 1977).

Like fear, shame is a biologically hardwired experience. Perhaps because we have not found a way to evoke shame in laboratory animals, however, understanding of the neurobiology of shame is rudimentary compared with the extensive literature on fear. Schore (2003) proposed that shame is mediated by the parasympathetic nervous system and serves as a sudden brake on excited arousal states. More than a century ago, Darwin (1872) described blushing as the most characteristic sign of shame and questioned "how it has arisen that the consciousness that others are attending to our personal appearance should have led to the capillaries, especially those of the face, instantly becoming filled with blood" (p. 327). This question remains unsolved. Leary, Britt, Cutlip, and Templeton (1992) noted that although some of the available evidence implicates the parasympathetic nervous system, "knowledge of the physiological basis of blushing is meager and clearly ripe for future research" (p. 449). In a meta-analysis of 208 laboratory studies, Dickerson and Kemeny (2004) demonstrated that socially embarrassing test conditions (e.g., public speaking) that might be expected to produce blushing also reliably produced elevated cortisol and adrenocorticotropic hormone—a stress response.

The subjective experience of shame is of an initial shock and flooding with painful emotion. Shame is a relatively wordless state, in which speech and thought are inhibited. It is also an acutely self-conscious state; the person feels small, ridiculous, and exposed. There is a wish to hide, characteristically expressed by covering the face with the hands. The person wishes to "sink through the floor" or "crawl in a hole and die." Shame is always implicitly a relational experience. According to Lewis (1987a), one of the early pioneers in the study of shame, shame is "one's own vicarious experience of the other's scorn . . . the self-in-the-eyes-of-the-other is the focus of awareness in shame" (p. 15). In addition, she observed, "the experience of shame often occurs in the form of imagery, of looking or being looked at. Shame may also be played out as an internal colloquy, in which the whole self is condemned by the 'other'" (pp. 18–19). Thus, shame represents a complex form of mental representation in which the person imagines the mind of another.

DEVELOPMENTAL ORIGINS OF SHAME

Developmentally, shame appears in the 2nd year of life. Erikson (1950) formulated the central conflict of this developmental stage as "autonomy vs. shame and doubt." Properly speaking, no toddler is autonomous; rather, one might formulate the toddler's developmental task as learning to regulate body, affect, desire, and will in attunement with others. Positive resolution of the conflicts of this stage of life creates the foundation for healthy pride and mutuality in relationships, including both self-respect and respect for others. Schore (2003) traced the origins of shame to the primary attachment relationship. Separations, which evoke fear and protest in normal toddlers, do not evoke shame; rather, shame can be seen in reunion interactions, when the toddler's excitement is met with indifference or disapproval. To a certain extent, such experiences are inevitable and normal, as no caregiver can be empathically attuned to her child at all times, and sometimes the caretaker must chastise the child. However, under normal circumstances, the child's shame reaction, like the appeasement displays of other primates, evokes a sympathetic response that in turn dispels the feeling of shame. The breach in attachment is thus repaired. Through repetition of this sequence, Schore postulated that the securely attached toddler learns the limits of the caregiver's tolerance and also learns to self-soothe and regulate shame states.

Although shame and guilt are often spoken of interchangeably, and although both can be considered social or moral emotions, the two states are quite distinct. Whereas shame is focused on the global self, guilt is focused on a specific action that the person has committed. Shame is an acutely self-conscious state in which the self is divided between imagining the contemptuous viewpoint of the other and feeling the impact of the other's scorn. By contrast, in guilt the self is unified; feelings of guilt or remorse seem to originate in the self. In shame, the self is passive; shame may be evoked by a sense of failure or disappointment or by being the object of ridicule, rejection, or rebuke. By contrast, in guilt the self is active; guilt is evoked by one's own transgressions. Shame is an acutely painful and disorganizing emotion; guilt may be experienced without intense affect. Shame engenders a desire to hide, escape, or lash out at the person in whose eyes one feels ashamed. By contrast, guilt engenders a desire to undo the offense, to make amends. Finally, shame is discharged in restored eye contact and shared, good-humored laughter, whereas guilt is discharged in an act of reparation (Lewis, 1987b).

SOCIAL FUNCTIONS OF SHAME

Originating in the primary attachment relationship, shame generalizes to become an emotion that serves to regulate peer relationships, social hierarchy, and all the basic forms of social life. Scheff and Retzinger (2000), building on the work of Goffman (1967), Lynd (1958), and Lewis (1971), described shame as the "master emotion of everyday life." In their conceptualization, shame is the "signal of trouble in a relationship." Shame, for example, serves to regulate social distance. People experience shame both if others are too distant, as in the extreme case of shunning or ostracism, and if others come too close, as in the extreme case in which personal boundaries are violated. Shame also mediates attunement to indices of social value or status. In its milder forms, shame is the result of social slights or ridicule. Mild experiences of shame are a part of ordinary social life. The everyday family of shame emotions includes self-consciousness, embarrassment, and feeling foolish or ridiculous. Through ordinary experiences of shame, individuals learn the boundaries of socially acceptable behavior.

In more extreme forms, shame is the reaction to being treated in a degrading manner. The extreme family of shame emotions includes humiliation and feelings of defilement, disgrace, or dishonor. In hierarchical societies, according to Miller (1997), disgust and contempt are "emotions of status demarcation" that consign to lower status those against whom they are directed. Relationships of dominance and subordination are inherently shaming. The social signals of subordinate status (bowed head and body, lowered eyes) are elaborated and ritualized expressions of the biological signals of shame. In slavery, the most extreme form of social subordination, the enslaved person exists in a permanently dishonored status that Patterson (1982) described as "social death."

Extreme social subordination is found in relationships of coercive control: in modern-day slavery, which takes the form of forced labor or prostitution (Bales, 2005); in political tyrannies; and in the private familial tyrannies of domestic violence and child abuse. Relationships of coercive control are established and perpetuated by an array of methods that are recognizable across cultures (Amnesty International, 1973). Among these methods, violence and threat of violence instill fear, whereas other commonly used methods, such as control of bodily functions, social isolation, and degradation, primarily evoke shame.

Extreme or catastrophic experiences of shame are a signal of profound relational disruptions or violations. When methods of coercive control are used within primary attachment relationships, as occurs in the case of child abuse, the developing child learns nothing of ordinary social shame. Rather, the child is overwhelmed with extreme shame states. Fonagy, Target, Gergely, Allen, and Bateman (2003) described the shame of the abused child as "an intense and destructive sense of self-disgust, verging on self-hatred." They explained that "the shame concerns being treated as a physical object in the very context where special personal recognition is expected" (p. 445).

N. Talbot (1996) elaborated on the reasons why shame is central for the sexually abused child. In the context of abuse, the child is rendered helpless, unable to control what is done to his or her body or how the body responds. The child is thereby deprived of normal experiences of pride and competence that come with basic bodily mastery. Moreover, the kind of empathic support that might mitigate shame is generally lacking in families in which abuse is occurring. The child "internalizes the message that she is not worthy of caring attention and that she is an object to be used" (p. 13).

Schore (2003) described catastrophic shame states as "self-disorganizing." Indeed, it is a characteristic of shame that it can feed upon itself. The shamed person feels ashamed of feeling ashamed, enraged and ashamed of being enraged. Lewis (1990) described these self-amplifying, disorganizing shame states as "feeling traps." She proposed that when shame states cannot be resolved, they are expressed as symptoms.

SHAME AS A PREDICTOR OF POSTTRAUMATIC SYMPTOMS

Although the literature on this subject is sparse, several recent studies have documented an association between shame and posttraumatic symptoms. Andrews, Brewin, Rose, and Kirk (2000) interviewed 157 victims of violent crime within 1 month of the incident and asked directly about shame experiences. Many victims felt shame in the immediate aftermath of the crime, but when they were interviewed again 6 months later, most reported that these feelings had diminished. A persistent feeling of shame was the only independent predictor of PTSD symptoms 6 months following the traumatic event. Similarly, in a longitudinal study of sexually abused youths, Feiring and Taska (2005) examined patterns of shame at the time of disclosure and 1 year and 6 years later. High shame was common in the immediate aftermath of disclosure, but for the majority, this had resolved by the 1-year follow-up. The minority (33%) of youths who reported high shame 1 year after disclosure were also likely to report persistent shame at the 6-year follow-up. Moreover, those who reported high shame at 1 and 6 years were also the most likely to report that they still had clinically significant levels of intrusive posttraumatic stress symptoms at the 6-year follow-up.

J. A. Talbot, Talbot, and Tu (2004) examined the relationship between shame proneness and dissociation in a sample of 99 hospitalized women with and without histories of childhood abuse. Shame proneness was measured with a modification of the Differential Emotions Scale (Izard, Libero, Putnam, & Haynes, 1993), using questions such as "In your daily life, how often do you feel embarrassed when anybody sees you make a mistake?" or "How often do you feel like people laugh at you?" Greater shame proneness was associated with higher levels of dissociation, especially among women who had experienced sexual trauma early in their development. Finally, Dutra, Callahan, Forman, Mendelsohn, and Herman (2008), in a study of 137 trauma survivors seeking outpatient treatment, measured self-reported shame schemas using a modified version of the Young Schema Questionnaire (Young & Brown, 1999). Shame schemas were measured by asking patients to rate statements such as "I'm unworthy of the love, attention and respect of others." Shame schemas were significantly correlated with measures of PTSD and dissociation. Furthermore, shame schemas were specifically correlated with self-reported suicidal risk variables, including recent suicide attempts, current suicidal ideation, and current suicidal plans. These data would support the inference that posttraumatic shame states can be life threatening.

ADDRESSING SHAME IN PSYCHOTHERAPY
WITH TRAUMA PATIENTS

Understanding that shame is a normal reaction to disrupted social bonds allows patients to emerge from the "feeling trap," in which they feel ashamed of being ashamed. According to Lewis (1981), addressing shame directly in the psychotherapy relationship facilitates therapeutic work by normalizing shame reactions and by giving patients a relational framework for understanding them. This is a task that challenges the tact and skill of even the most experienced therapist, however, because of the many disguised presentations of shame (Lewis, 1987a).

For patients suffering the sequelae of trauma, focusing on shame is particularly important because unacknowledged shame prevents any direct therapeutic approach to the trauma. As Kluft (2007) explained, "Since successful trauma treatment involves exposure to and mastery of what is upsetting . . . the operation of any shame script evades such material. . . . This freezes the patient in a posttraumatic or dissociative adaptation" (p. 375). In other words, as long as people are feeling ashamed about their traumatic experience, they cannot gain a sense of mastery over it.

The very fact of carrying a diagnosis of PTSD may evoke shame, as patients may view it as a sign of weakness and failure. The reticence of soldiers to seek mental health treatment for PTSD generally stems from the feelings of stigma and shame attached to the use of mental health services. In one large survey of members of the U.S. Army and the Marine Corps returning from combat operations in Iraq and Afghanistan ($N = 3,671$), feelings of shame and stigma were found to represent a major barrier to mental health care, particularly among those who appeared to be most in need of it. Statements such as "I would be seen as weak," "Members of my unit might have less confidence in me," or "My leaders would blame me for the problem" were endorsed by a majority of those respondents who met screening criteria for a mental disorder (Hoge et al., 2004).

Psychologist Jaine Darwin (personal communication, September 14, 2010) described the case of John, an infantryman who returned from a third deployment in Iraq suffering from flashbacks, nightmares, constant hypervigilance, and feelings of depersonalization. He was referred for mental health services after a medical hospitalization in which his psychiatric symptoms were observed during his medical care. He felt sheepish and embarrassed, variants of shame, because he could not "soldier through" these difficulties.

Psychologist Judith Himber (personal communication, March 13, 2008) emphasized the importance of psychoeducation regarding shame and the necessity to normalize the experience by explaining that everyone feels it: "It's so silent that just to name it is a piece of work." She found that even using the word *shame* is often too strong at first; synonyms with less extreme emotional resonance might include feeling *mortified, embarrassed,* or "lower than the lowest." Once shame becomes part of the conversation, the patient and therapist can become curious about it and can begin to explore the patient's personal shame experiences.

Numerous verbal, paralinguistic, and nonverbal cues should alert the therapist to shame states. The vocabulary of shame is extensive: words such as *ridiculous, foolish, silly, idiotic, stupid, dumb, humiliated, disrespected, helpless, weak, inept, dependent, small, inferior, unworthy, worthless, trivial, shy, vulnerable, uncomfortable,* or *embarrassed* may indicate feelings of shame. Paralinguistic cues include confusion of thought, hesitation, soft speech, mumbling, silences, stammering, long pauses, rapid speech, or tensely laughed words. Nonverbal cues include hiding behavior such as covering all or parts of the face, gaze aversion, eyes downcast or averted, hanging head, hunched shoulders, squirming, fidgeting, blushing, biting or licking the lips, biting the tongue, or false smiling (Retzinger, 1995).

Kluft (2007) reported a case of a patient with dissociative identity disorder; therapy was at an impasse because of a malignantly suicidal alter ego named "Asha." Curious inquiry about the meaning of this unusual name was met with the response, "My name is Asha, and I'm a medical student. That's all I have to say." The therapist deduced that "Asha-med" was the carrier of the patient's experiences of intense shame:

> I began to put her name and self-description together, and keeping in mind Poe's "hidden in plain sight" letter, and noting the shame signifier of the downward duck of her head, I said, "I guess I need to ask you . . . what are you Asha-med about?" (p. 378)

In this extreme case, the clue to the patient's disavowed shame experience was a verbal puzzle.

In another case contributed by Jaine Darwin (personal communication, September 14, 2010), a patient's vicarious posttraumatic symptoms resolved once shame issues were understood and directly addressed. Harriet was the wife of a wounded warrior who lost a leg in a Humvee explosion in Afghanistan. She spent months at his bedside as he convalesced, and she was regarded as the model of a loyal wife. When they returned home after his discharge from the hospital, however, she became panicky and showed symptoms of vicarious PTSD. Only with gentle urging was she able to admit to feeling repulsed by her husband's stump. She was filled with shame about these feelings, which had no place in her idealized image of a selfless caregiver.

Courtois (1988), in her description of therapeutic work with incest survivors, observed that shame may also be difficult to address directly because of the way it affects the transference. The patient may have difficulty trusting evidence of her therapist's positive regard because she expects the therapist to feel the same contempt for her that she has for herself. It may be necessary for the therapist to challenge this distorted perception gently but directly. A case example reported by Wagner, Rizvi, and Harned (2007) illustrates this point. The patient, Laura, an incest survivor, avoided sharing the most salient parts of her traumatic memories with her therapist because of her belief that the therapist would feel disgusted and repulsed. Because talking about the abuse was so difficult, the therapist suggested that she write about it and then read what she had written aloud in the session. Over time, Laura was able to read her account in a steady voice, "while occasionally making eye contact with the therapist . . . to reduce shame by gathering objective data that the therapist was not rejecting her" (p. 396). Though this case was conceptualized according to a behavioral model, the treatment required an emphasis on the therapist's empathic relational attunement and genuine expression of positive regard for the patient.

For survivors of childhood abuse, the patterns of relationship learned in early life may be reenacted in the therapy relationship. These transference reenactments may take the form of power struggles that carry the risk of humiliation and defeat, either for the patient or for the therapist. In this manner, one member of the dyad is cast in the role of the perpetrator, while the other becomes the victim or bystander. A frequent instance is the situation in which the patient is engaging in high-risk behavior and refuses to take self-protective action. In this case, the therapist is humiliated by being placed in the position of a helpless bystander. In the extreme case of the suicidal patient who refuses hospitalization, the patient is rendered helpless if the therapist hospitalizes her against her will; alternatively, the therapist is rendered helpless if he disregards evidence of high risk. Sharing the therapeutic dilemma with the patient brings the conflict into the room and allows the patient to own both sides of the conflict rather than projecting one side onto the therapist.

Shame also affects the countertransference; as Lewis (1987a) explained, shame is a contagious emotion, and the therapist may avoid addressing shame directly because of his or her own discomfort. A colleague, J (personal communication, March, 13, 2008), provided a case example of a countertransference shame reaction that became a fruitful source of therapeutic exploration once the therapist acknowledged her mistake without defensiveness. The patient was a female survivor of childhood abuse who came to treatment with a history of PTSD, major depression, and binge drinking. The patient was in both individual and couple therapy, with an understanding that confidential information could be shared freely between the two therapists. During one binge, the patient called J while drunk. In the next session, the patient asked J not to tell the couple therapist about the binge because she was so ashamed of it. In the moment, J agreed. Later, judging that this information was too important to withhold, she did inform the couple therapist, but uncharacteristically she did not tell the patient that she had done so. Thus, J, the therapist, mirrored her patient in attempting to harbor a secret.

As might be expected, the patient figured out what had happened and confronted her therapist. J's narrative continued:

> I said I was ashamed of having made a promise that I could not keep, sharing the information, and failing to notify the patient. I apologized and mused aloud, "I think I behaved this way because I don't know quite how to talk with you about your drinking. You feel so bad about it, and I don't want to make you feel worse." The patient *loved* this (seeing me admit I was in the wrong). We spent the rest of the hour talking about how to approach the problem. Lots more came out about shame, including early material from childhood which had never been revealed. When I acknowledged that I had made a mistake, felt ashamed, and tried to cover it up, I illustrated the things we do when we're ashamed. The patient really *got it.*

Cloitre, Cohen, and Koenen (2006), in their manual for treatment of survivors of childhood abuse, devoted a chapter to the creation of narratives of shame. They wrote,

> In the same way that narratives of fear must be titrated so that the client experiences mastery over fear rather than a reinstatement of it, so too narratives of shame should be titrated so that the client experiences dignity rather than humiliation in the telling. (p. 290)

These authors identified numerous reasons for telling about shameful events. They pointed out that shame perpetuates the bond with the perpetrator; as long as the patient guards her shameful secrets, she may feel that the perpetrator is the only person who knows her intimately. Disclosure in the context of a safe and securely established therapy relationship is a mastery experience that leads to greater self-knowledge, greater self-compassion, and reduced feelings of alienation.

Lewis (1987a) emphasized the importance of "good-humored laughter" in the discharge and resolution of the shame state. Laughing together *with* another person is a powerful antidote to the sense of acute shame and ostracism that one feels when one is the target of others' laughter. As Retzinger (1987) explained, shared laughter, when it is spontaneous and genuine, relieves shame and restores a sense of social connection:

> Shame is a major aspect of the human condition. It serves a fundamental purpose, enabling human beings to monitor their own behavior in relation to others. . . . When shame is too great, one feels alienated, disconnected from others, and alone in the world. Laughter serves to reconnect these severed ties, breaking the spiral of shame–

rage. . . . Without both shame and laughter, complex social life would be impossible. (p. 177)

Because of the power imbalance between patient and therapist, and because the patient exposes his or her most intimate thoughts and feelings without reciprocity, the individual therapy relationship is to some degree inherently shaming. For this reason, among others, group psychotherapy may be a particularly valuable treatment modality for traumatized people (Herman, 1992; Herman & Schatzow, 1984; Mendelsohn, Zachary, & Harney, 2007; N. L. Talbot et al., 1999; see also Chapter 5, this volume). The group members are peers who approach one another on a social plane of equality. Moreover, group members are in a position to give compassionate support as well as to receive it. Thus, they can feel themselves to be of value to the group and deserving of the support they receive.

Trauma-focused group treatment must be structured so that group members titrate their exposure and learn to stay present rather than dissociating, both while describing their own experiences and while listening to others. The resultant feeling of group acceptance and belonging is a powerful antidote to long-held feelings of shame and stigma (Herman & Schatzow, 1984). The case of Mary, from a trauma recovery group treatment guide (Mendelsohn et al., 2011), illustrates how the group leaders intervene to slow down the telling of the trauma story, how they invite the patient to reflect on the feelings evoked by her narrative, and, finally, how they guide the feedback process so that the patient can feel the compassion of the other group members.

During the introductory sessions of the group, Mary reported that she was consumed with feelings of shame and self-blame in response to flashback memories of childhood sexual abuse by her uncle. She stated that she knew intellectually that she was not responsible for the abuse but that she had difficulty believing that this was true at an affective level. She identified her goal for the group as transforming her feelings of shame and self-blame and indicated that she would know if she had made progress toward this goal if she was able to tell her story and experience some compassion for herself.

With a great deal of anticipatory anxiety, Mary used her time during this phase of the group to describe her memories of the abusive incidents. For the sake of Mary and the group, the coleaders initially intervened to slow down the pace of the telling, as Mary acknowledged a desire to "get it over and done with." As Mary told her story in a more emotionally connected way, it became apparent that much of her self-blame was rooted in statements made by the perpetrator during the abuse. She recalled him telling her that they were both "damned" and would go to hell for what they had done. During the feedback, group members commented on the powerful impact of such words in shaping Mary's self-blame and leading her to feel identified with the perpetrator, as though she were an equal participant in the abuse.

During her next turn to share, Mary took another risk and disclosed that one of the most shameful aspects of her experience was her memory of feeling sexually aroused during the abuse. A number of group members related to this disclosure. The group leaders also normalized this experience, pointing out that the fact that her body was responding did not make the experience any less abusive. Mary expressed great relief at receiving this feedback and not encountering the harsh judgment that she had anticipated. She referred to this moment several times, during subsequent sessions, as a turning point in her work toward being kinder to herself. At the conclusion of her group treatment, Mary's scores on measures of PTSD, dissociation, and depression had significantly decreased, and her scores on measures of self-esteem had significantly improved.

CONCLUSION

If the thesis of this chapter is correct, the role of shame in traumatic disorders should be a potentially fruitful area for further study. In particular, future research is needed to develop a fuller understanding of the neurophysiology of shame, to elucidate the role of shame in posttraumatic symptom formation, and, most important, to explore the potential therapeutic benefits of addressing shame directly in the treatment of trauma survivors. If, indeed, it is true that shame permeates every aspect of the treatment relationship, then it might be most fruitful to observe the skill and tact of master clinicians as they address the manifold presentations of shame and to learn from their wisdom and creativity as they and their patients work toward restored connection.

REFERENCES

American Psychiatric Association. (1994). *Diagnostic and statistical manual of mental disorders* (4th ed.). Washington, DC: Author.

Amnesty International. (1973). *Report on torture*. London, England: Duckworth.

Andrews, B., Brewin, C. R., Rose, S., & Kirk, M. (2000). Predicting PTSD symptoms in victims of violent crime: The role of shame, anger, and childhood abuse. *Journal of Abnormal Psychology, 109,* 69–73. doi:10.1037/0021-843X.109.1.69

Bales, K. (2005). *Understanding global slavery: A reader*. Berkeley, CA: University of California Press.

Cloitre, M., Cohen, L. R., & Koenen, K. C. (2006). *Treating survivors of childhood abuse: Psychotherapy for the interrupted life*. New York, NY: Guilford Press.

Courtois, C. A. (1988). *Healing the incest wound: Adult survivors in therapy*. New York, NY: Norton.

Darwin, C. (1872). *The expression of the emotions in man and animals*. London, England: John Murray. doi:10.1037/10001-000

Dickerson, S. S., & Kemeny, M. E. (2004). Acute stressors and cortisol responses: A theoretical integration and synthesis of laboratory research. *Psychological Bulletin, 130*, 355–391. doi:10.1037/0033-2909.130.3.355

Dutra, L., Callahan, K., Forman, E., Mendelsohn, M., & Herman, J. L. (2008). Core schemas and suicidality in a chronically traumatized population. *Journal of Nervous and Mental Disease, 196*, 71–74. doi:10.1097/NMD.0b013e318 15fa4c1

Erikson, E. H. (1950). *Childhood and society*. New York: Norton.

Feiring, C., & Taska, L. S. (2005). The persistence of shame following sexual abuse: A longitudinal look at risk and recovery. *Child Maltreatment, 10*, 337–349. doi: 10.1177/1077559505276686

Foa, E. B., Cashman, L., Jaycox, L., & Perry, K. J. (1997). The validation of a self-report measure of posttraumatic stress disorder: The Posttraumatic Diagnostic Scale. *Psychological Assessment, 9*, 445–451. doi:10.1037/1040-3590.9.4.445

Foa, E. B., Keane, T. M., & Friedman, M. J. (2000). *Effective treatments for PTSD*. New York, NY: Guilford Press.

Fonagy, P., Target, M., Gergely, G., Allen, J. G., & Bateman, A. W. (2003). The developmental roots of borderline personality disorder in early attachment relationships: A theory and some evidence. *Psychoanalytic Inquiry, 23*, 412–459. doi:10.1080/07351692309349042

Gilbert, P., & McGuire, M. T. (1998). Shame, status and social roles: Psychobiology and evolution. In P. Gilbert & B. Andrews (Eds.), *Shame: Interpersonal behavior, psychopathology and culture* (pp. 99–125). New York, NY: Oxford University Press.

Goffman, E. (1967). *Interaction ritual*. New York, NY: Anchor.

Herman, J. L. (1992). *Trauma and recovery*. New York, NY: Basic.

Herman, J. L., & Schatzow, E. (1984). Time limited group therapy for women with a history of incest. *International Journal of Group Psychotherapy, 34*, 605–616.

Hoge, C. W., Castro, C. A., Messer, S. C., McGurk, D., Cotting, D. I., & Koffman, R. L. (2004). Combat duty in Iraq and Afghanistan, mental health problems, and barriers to care. *New England Journal of Medicine, 351*, 13–22. doi:10.1056/NEJ Moa040603

Izard, C. E. (1971). *The face of emotion*. New York, NY: Appleton-Century-Crofts.

Izard, C. E. (1977). *Human emotions*. New York, NY: Plenum.

Izard, C. E., Libero, Z., Putnam, P., & Haynes, O. M. (1993). Stability of emotion experiences and their relations to traits of personality. *Journal of Personality and Social Psychology, 64*, 847–860. doi:10.1037/0022-3514.64.5.847

Keltner, D., & Harker, L. A. (1998). The forms and functions of the non-verbal signal of shame. In P. Gilbert & B. Andrews (Eds.), *Shame: Interpersonal behavior, psychopathology and culture* (pp. 75–98). New York, NY: Oxford University Press.

Kluft, R. P. (2007). Applications of innate affect theory to the understanding and treatment of dissociative identity disorder. In E. Vermetten, M. J. Dorahy, & D. Spiegel (Eds.), *Traumatic dissociation: Neurobiology and treatment* (pp. 363–384). Washington, DC: American Psychiatric Publishing.

Leary, M. R., Britt, T. W., Cutlip, W. D., & Templeton, J. L. (1992). Social blushing. *Psychological Bulletin, 112*, 446–460. doi:10.1037/0033-2909.112.3.446

LeDoux, J. (2003). *The synaptic self: How our brains become who we are.* New York, NY: Penguin.

Lewis, H. B. (1971). *Shame and guilt in neurosis.* New York, NY: International Universities Press.

Lewis, H. B. (1981). Shame and guilt in human nature. In S. Tuttman, C. Kaye, & M. Zimmerman (Eds.), *Object and self: A developmental approach* (pp. 235–265). New York, NY: International Universities Press.

Lewis, H. B. (1987a). Introduction: Shame, the "sleeper" in psychopathology. In H. B. Lewis (Ed.), *The role of shame in symptom formation* (pp. 1–28). Hillsdale, NJ: Erlbaum.

Lewis, H. B. (1987b). Shame and the narcissistic personality. In D. L. Nathanson (Ed.), *The many faces of shame* (pp. 93–132). New York, NY: Guilford Press.

Lewis, H. B. (1990). Shame, repression, field dependence, and psychopathology. In J. L. Singer (Ed.), *Repression and dissociation: Implications for personality theory, psychopathology and health* (pp. 233–257). Chicago, IL: University of Chicago Press.

Lynd, H. (1958). *On shame and the search for identity.* New York, NY: Harcourt.

Mendelsohn, M., Herman, J. L., Schatzow, E., Coco, M., Kallivayalil, D., & Levitan, J. (2011). *The trauma recovery group: A treatment guide.* New York, NY: Guilford Press.

Mendelsohn, M., Zachary, R. S., & Harney, P. A. (2007). Group therapy as an ecological bridge to new community for trauma survivors. *Journal of Aggression, Maltreatment & Trauma, 14*, 227–243. doi:10.1300/J146v14n01_12

Miller, W. (1997). *The anatomy of disgust.* Cambridge, MA: Harvard University Press.

Patterson, O. (1982). *Slavery and social death: A comparative study.* Cambridge, MA: Harvard University Press.

Perry, B. D., Southwick, S. W., Yehuda, R., & Giller, E. L. (1990). Adrenergic receptor regulation in post-traumatic stress disorder. In E. L. Giller (Ed.), *Advances in psychiatry: Biological assessment and treatment of post-traumatic stress disorder* (pp. 87–115). Washington, DC: American Psychiatric Press.

Retzinger, S. M. (1987). Resentment and laughter: Video studies of the shame–rage spiral. In H. B. Lewis (Ed.), *The role of shame in symptom formation* (pp. 151–181). Hillsdale, NJ: Erlbaum.

Retzinger, S. M. (1995). Identifying shame and anger in discourse. *American Behavioral Scientist, 38*, 1104–1113. doi:10.1177/0002764295038008006

Scheff, T. J., & Retzinger, S. M. (2000). Shame as the master emotion of everyday life. *Journal of Mundane Behavior, 1*, 303–324.

Schore, A. N. (2003). *Affect regulation and the repair of the self*. New York, NY: Norton.

Talbot, J. A., Talbot, N., & Tu, X. (2004). Shame-proneness as a diathesis for dissociation in women with histories of childhood sexual abuse. *Journal of Traumatic Stress, 17*, 445–448. doi:10.1023/B:JOTS.0000048959.29766.ae

Talbot, N. (1996). Women sexually abused as children: The centrality of shame issues and treatment implications. *Psychotherapy: Theory, Research, & Practice, 33*, 11–18. doi:10.1037/0033-3204.33.1.11

Talbot, N. L., Houghtalen, R. P., Duberstein, P. R., Cox, C., Giles, D. E., & Wynne, L. C. (1999). Effects of group treatment for women with a history of childhood sexual abuse. *Psychiatric Services, 50*, 686–692.

Wagner, A. W., Rizvi, S. L., & Harned, M. S. (2007). Applications of dialectical behavior therapy to the treatment of complex trauma-related problems: When one case formulation does not fit all. *Journal of Traumatic Stress, 20*, 391–400. doi:10.1002/jts.20268

Young, J. E., & Brown, G. (1999). *Young schema questionnaire: Short form*. New York, NY: Schema Therapy Institute.

12

BODY IMAGE AND EATING DISORDERS: A COMPELLING SOURCE OF SHAME FOR WOMEN

JENNIFER L. SANFTNER AND MARY TANTILLO

During my many years (especially in the early years) of the eating disorder, if you had asked me about shame, I would have looked blankly at you and not been able to answer. I would have shuddered at the question, looked away (or down at the floor), and not even have been able to make eye contact. The word (the feeling) was *that* intolerable. . . . I was truly operating from a deep place of "wrongness." Shame meant I was a bad person: "If you really know me and know how I am, you won't like me. " Shame fueled and, I believe, was one of the earliest negative feelings that started my illness. It was the gasoline constantly being poured over my eating disorder behaviors and beliefs. It was the lens I looked through and interpreted my world. This helped me hide and keep my eating disorder hidden. Shame totally validated my belief of being unacceptable. It became a vicious circle between the two: Shame was the feeling tied into painful experiences and memories, and the eating disorder was the vehicle that kept those numbed out, disconnected from my consciousness.

— Cindy Nappa Bitter, recovered eating-disordered person
(personal communication, 2008, printed with permission)

Eating disorders affect approximately 10 million women and 1 million men in the United States (National Eating Disorders Association [NEDA], n.d.). Lifetime prevalence estimates are 1.2% for anorexia nervosa (AN), 2.0% for bulimia nervosa (BN), and 2.7% for binge eating disorder (BED; Striegel-Moore & Bulik, 2007; Wade, Bergin, Tiggemann, Bulik, & Fairburn, 2006). It is estimated that when clinically significant partial syndromes are included, these figures double (Shisslak, Crago, & Estes, 1995). Thus, clinicians are likely to encounter these disorders in the course of their work.

Although rates of eating and body image disorders, such as muscle dysmorphia, are thought to be on the rise in men, women still constitute the vast majority of those with diagnosable eating disorders. In fact, gender is possibly the most influential of the sociocultural factors that affect eating disorders (Keel & Gravener, 2008). Examples of this can be found in the literature, as body image disturbances and poor self-esteem, both more common in girls than boys, have been identified as risk factors for the development of eating disorders (Elgin & Pritchard, 2006). Empirical studies reveal that gender moderates the link between body image disturbance and self-esteem—body dissatisfaction is significantly associated with self-esteem for women but not for men (Elgin & Pritchard, 2006). In addition, research has demonstrated a stronger association among women than among men between one's perception of how others evaluate one's body weight or shape and self-esteem (Davison & McCabe, 2006) and between satisfaction with specific body parts and self-esteem (Kashubeck-West, Mintz, & Weigold, 2005). Research has also shown that women are more likely than men to respond to body dissatisfaction with the use of weight loss strategies such as eating low calorie foods, eating according to special diets, and counting calories (Kashubeck-West et al., 2005). Although both women and men appear to be vulnerable to exposure to media messages concerning body image ideals, women's eating behavior has been seen to change in response to such images; women exposed to media images emphasizing a thin, idealized body shape ate less food than men in front of same-sex peers (Harrison, Taylor, & Marske, 2006). Thus, for women, low self-esteem and body dissatisfaction have been identified as factors in the etiology of eating disorders.

Shame, like low self-esteem and body dissatisfaction, involves negative evaluations of the self and is an integral part of the phenomenology of eating disorders. AN is characterized primarily by restriction of food intake, which results in abnormally low body weight, along with intense fear of gaining weight or becoming fat. Despite the more ego-syntonic nature of the symptoms associated with AN, there can be intense shame about one's size, because anorexic women never feel they are thin enough, as well as shame about the behaviors that characterize the disorder (e.g., the lengths one goes to in order to restrict food intake and the binging and purging that may be present). BN is characterized by episodes of binge eating accompanied by some form of compensatory behavior, such as self-induced vomiting, laxative abuse, or excessive exercise. Women with BN have intense negative feelings about their bodies that play prominently in their overall evaluation of themselves. There is shame inherent in this harsh self-scrutiny and painful negative body evaluation and shame about the out-of-control cycles of binge eating and compensation.

In addition to the diagnoses of AN and BN, approximately 30% to 60% of all eating disorder diagnoses fall into the category of eating disorder not otherwise specified (EDNOS; Andersen, Bowers, & Watson, 2001). Those with EDNOS experience clinically significant symptoms but not in a pattern or frequency that fits within the criteria for AN or BN. BED is also listed under the category of EDNOS and is characterized by binge eating without compensatory behaviors. BED is linked with obesity and is present in about 8% of obese individuals (Grillo, 2002). The tentative criteria for BED strongly suggest that shame, and perhaps guilt, are prominent factors in this disorder (e.g., "eating alone because of being embarrassed by how much one is eating" and "feeling disgusted with oneself, depressed, or very guilty after overeating"; American Psychiatric Association, 2000, p. 787). Feelings of shame among those diagnosed with BED and obesity are amplified as a result of the stigma associated with obesity in the dominant culture.

Because eating disorders occur predominantly in women, this chapter describes the numerous sources of shame that women with clinical and subclinical eating disorders experience. As the quotation that began this chapter illustrates, shame is often an important factor in the development and maintenance of eating disorders. Working with shame in the therapeutic relationship is key to helping women overcome these disorders. Relational-cultural theory (RCT; Miller & Stiver, 1997), a psychological theory initially based on the development of women, is described as a useful framework for understanding and working with women's shame in the therapeutic setting. This chapter also discusses the challenges related to dealing with shame in women with eating disorders; the therapist's possible feelings of shame, including those related to the therapist's own body image; and shame in the supervisory relationship.

THE ROLE OF SHAME IN BODY IMAGE

Shame has a long-standing place in the domain of women's feelings about their bodies. A core feature of shame, as defined by Lewis (1971), is the comparison of oneself against an internalized or imagined other. In our appearance-oriented and media-saturated culture, it is common for women to continually compare themselves against standards set by the culture. Given that these extreme standards for body image are increasingly underweight, artificial, and based on a narrow range of acceptable alternatives, they are unattainable for most women (Maine, 2000). Because many women feel that they are the object of scrutiny in a culture that values appearance over other characteristics (Silberstein, Striegel-Moore, & Rodin, 1987), and because most women come up short when making a comparison with an unrealistic ideal, shame is a common feeling that results from these comparisons (Markham, Thompson, & Bowling, 2005). In fact, in 1984, Rodin, Silberstein, and Striegel-Moore coined the term *normative discontent* to refer to American women's chronic dissatisfaction with their bodies and general appearance (p. 267). Believing that they have the wrong body or shape or are the wrong weight, women experience shame. In a culture that values a certain slender shape, women who are larger than the perceived ideal and/or who have larger hips, thighs, or stomachs; more flab or cellulite; or less muscle can be prone to self-consciousness and emotions such as shame. The teasing and social rejection that may accompany this sense of "wrongness" heighten feelings of shame.

To make matters worse, women also experience shame in response to failed attempts at dieting. They feel weak willed or unfeminine because of their seemingly insatiable appetites (Rodin et al., 1984). An implicit association is often made between femininity and being not hungry or having a mild appetite. This association stems from vestiges of a Victorian value system that equated appetite and eating in women with the unseemly qualities of sexuality and lack of self-restraint (Brumberg, 1989). For women, having an appetite continues to be considered vulgar, gluttonous, and ugly, even sexual (Brumberg, 1989), descriptors that may engender deep feelings of shame in the individual who perceives herself to be this way. Women may also experience shame about the very fact of having body consciousness (Silberstein et al., 1987). Modern women often believe that they should be above the obsession with weight and appearance, and admitting how this experience affects them can engender feelings of shame.

Central to women's feelings of shame about their natural body size and shape is the issue of obesity. Being obese has been a chronic source of self-loathing and shame for women, as described in seminal writings by Bruch (1973). The shame reported by obese girls and women in her practice left them feeling "ugly on the inside," with bodies that they perceived as "unpleasant, dirty, shameful, or disgusting" (Bruch, 1973, pp. 88, 100). The culturally based stigma of obesity (Puhl & Brownell, 2006; Puhl & Latner, 2007) has placed it squarely in the domain of psychological concerns, as obese women often feel intense shame about their bodies (Silberstein et al., 1987). Underlying this shame is the increased public scrutiny obesity has received in recent years. The health care industry's preoccupation with obesity fuels the media's obsession, which exacerbates obese women's sense of shame about their bodies, their appetites, and their weight. Added to this is the fear that nonobese women experience in association with gaining weight. With so much negative representation of obesity in the media, the fear of gaining weight and becoming obese is intensified for all women, and the stigma associated with being obese has been linked as a causal factor in the development of eating disorders (Puhl & Latner, 2007; Striegel-Moore & Bulik, 2007).

A sample news headline highlights this problem. In a story titled "Risk of Birth Defects is Linked to Obesity" (2003), the New York Times reported that obese women were reported to be more likely than nonobese women to have infants with birth defects, such as spina bifida and heart abnormalities. There was little mention in the story, however, of the correlational nature of the study or the resulting inconclusiveness with regard to whether body weight was the causal factor. Although those trained in research may assume that the causal factor will prove to be something other than weight per se, unfortunately the average woman is apt to take away from that news story the message that her children's problems are because of her weight, appetite, or inability to control her hunger. Thus, although obesity is a genuine health concern and a risk factor for a number of medical conditions for the individual herself, such media messages dealing with obesity are unduly alarming and may further intensify women's shame.

Researchers have begun to identify the pathways through which cultural standards set women up to experience shame related to their bodies. Objectification theory states that our culture views women's bodies as objects for criticizing, viewing, and obtaining sexual pleasure (Fredrickson & Roberts, 1997). Further, the theory suggests that women regularly have experiences that reduce them to their bodily parts or functions. These experiences make women feel devalued and lessen their ability to see themselves as whole persons. Growing up in a culture of objectification, particularly when there is little alternative information available from caregivers and important others, can lead a woman to internalize society's view of her. This process of self-objectification leads to a sense of vigilance, in which a woman is continuously scrutinizing herself for flaws and problem areas, and to the development of body shame, in which comparison against an ideal reveals her inadequacies and leaves her feeling that she is lacking (Moradi, Dirks, & Matteson, 2005). This model suggests that although we all may be exposed to a culture that objectifies women's bodies, it is the internalization of those messages and the resulting shame that lead some women to develop eating disorders.

For many women, the shame they experience in relation to their bodies becomes central to their psychological functioning, and this is particularly true if they develop eating disorders. Helping clients recognize and challenge the cultural messages with regard to the importance of appearance, particularly in terms of weight and body shape, can be useful in transforming shame about the body into a sense of acceptance and even pride. Group therapy may be helpful in getting women together to share experiences, thereby lessening shame. We say more about dealing with body shame in therapy later in the chapter.

THE ROLE OF SHAME IN EATING DISORDERS

Shame about the body is thought to be a critical factor in the development of eating disorders (e.g., Gilbert & Miles, 2002; Markham et al., 2005; Troop, Sotrilli, Serpell, & Treasure, 2006). For women with eating disorders, the sources of shame associated with body image are heightened.

This amplified sense of shame is related to their chronic experience of falling short in comparison to unrealistic internal and external ideals. For example, research findings have supported self-discrepancy theory, which posits that women with eating disorders tend to perceive a deficit in themselves that reflects a discrepancy between their perceived actual self-concept and a comparative ideal standard that they apply to themselves or believe others apply to them (Altabe & Thompson, 1996; Higgins, 1987; Strauman & Glenberg, 1994; Wonderlich, Mitchell, Peterson, & Crow, 2001). At the same time, women with eating disorders are bombarded with sociocultural messages and images that encourage them to internalize a thin ideal that the majority of women cannot achieve (Stice, 2001). Their attempts to meet this ideal fuel the illness and the associated shame of not being thin enough, as well as the shame associated with symptoms they experience in trying to attain the thin ideal. For example, for women who binge eat, shame is thought to fuel the drive to binge and to follow binge episodes. Although the act of purging may be an attempt to relieve the shame experienced by erasing the cause of the shame, it often leads to more shame, as does the bloating that accompanies frequent binge eating and purging. There is also shame about the behavior in general, and women with eating disorders go to great lengths to conceal their behaviors from others (Silberstein et al., 1987).

Although the eating disorders literature contains numerous references to both shame and guilt, empirical studies have been limited. Early researchers began to identify shame and guilt as emotions that women with eating disorders tend to experience both generally and surrounding episodes of binge eating and purging (e.g., Boskind-Lodahl & White, 1978; Cooper et al., 1988; Johnson, Stuckey, Lewis, & Schwartz, 1982; Larson & Johnson, 1985; Teusch, 1988). The first study to emphasize shame and guilt as central features of eating disorders was conducted by Frank (1991). This study found that women with eating disorders reported more shame and guilt than women with depression, who in turn reported more shame and guilt than women without a psychiatric disorder. This study used the Shame and Guilt Eating Scale (SGES), a four-item measure that asks how much shame and how much guilt respondents tend to feel about eating and overeating; items were combined into a composite shame/guilt score. Thus, initial research focused on identifying shame and guilt about eating or binging/purging without attempting to make a theoretical or empirical distinction between the two emotions. Measures were used that combined the constructs and/or simply asked participants how much shame and guilt they felt, a practice that does not reliably distinguish between shame and guilt (Tangney, 1990).

The first empirical attempt to examine shame and guilt as conceptually distinct constructs in relation to eating disorders was reported by Sanftner, Barlow, Marschall, and Tangney (1995). In this study of college students, proneness to shame and proneness to guilt were assessed using the Test of Self-Conscious Affect (TOSCA; Tangney, Wagner, & Gramzow, 1989), a scenario-based measure that assesses shame as an emotion involving a focus on the self ("I'm a bad person") and guilt as an emotion involving a focus on the action or behavior ("I did a bad thing"; Lewis, 1971). Proneness to shame was associated with a range of scales on the Eating Disorder Inventory 2 (EDI–2; Garner, 1991), whereas proneness to guilt was either negatively or negligibly associated with the EDI–2.

A subsequent study examined shame and guilt proneness, as measured by the TOSCA, in association with eating disorders in college students and women with BN (Hayaki, Friedman, & Brownell, 2002). These researchers found that shame proneness, but not guilt proneness, was significantly associated with more severe symptoms of bulimia in undergraduate women. When the community-based sample of women with BN was compared with women without an eating disorder, women with BN were found to have higher levels of shame proneness (Hayaki et al., 2002). However, this association was not independent of the shared relationship between shame proneness and the combined variable of depression and guilt proneness. Thus, whereas shame proneness has been shown to be clearly associated with eating disorder symptoms in college students and in women with BN, it is difficult to draw conclusions regarding the role of guilt proneness in eating disorder symptoms.

Burney and Irwin (2000) sought to investigate whether it is truly trait-based shame (i.e., shame proneness) and/or guilt that are associated with eating disorders, as opposed to the more domain-specific versions of shame and/or guilt that surround eating behavior. In a community-based sample of women, they compared the more broadly dispositional TOSCA with the domain-specific SGES scales, as used by Frank (1991), along with a measure of body-focused shame. They found that a generalized proneness to shame or guilt did not predict severity of eating disorder symptoms, whereas body shame, as well as shame and to a lesser extent guilt specifically associated with eating, did (Burney & Irwin, 2000). The authors concluded that it is not global proneness to shame that is associated with eating disorder behaviors, but shame and guilt about eating and shame about body size and shape.

Although this conclusion seems logical, closer inspection of the data suggests another explanation. The measure used in this study to assess domain-specific shame and guilt, the SGES, may not distinguish adequately between these constructs because, as noted earlier, it relies on participants' understanding the difference between shame ("I am a bad person because of what I ate") and guilt ("I did a bad thing by eating that"), which they may not be able to do. In fact, the questions are likely tapping into respondents' global sense of feeling bad about themselves surrounding their eating, which is consistent with shame and shame proneness. In contrast, the TOSCA measure presents respondents with phenomenological descriptions of shame and guilt experiences drawn from theory, clinical observations, and qualitative studies of these emotions. Respondents need not have a clear, a priori conception of the distinction between shame and guilt. Indeed, the correlations reported between TOSCA shame and SGES shame and guilt were high ($r > .3$) and significant, whereas correlations between TOSCA guilt and SGES shame and guilt were low ($r < .2$) and nonsignificant (Burney & Irwin, 2000). This suggests that both the shame and guilt scales of the SGES more directly assess shame than guilt regarding eating.

Another study (Sanftner & Crowther, 1998) sought to examine state-based shame and guilt by comparing women who binge with non-binge-eating women using the State Shame and Guilt Scale (SSGS; Marschall, Sanftner, & Tangney, 1994). The SSGS distinguishes between states of shame (e.g., "I want to sink into the floor and disappear") and guilt (e.g., "I feel remorse, regret"), although it does not specifically address eating behavior. Women who binge reported more daily fluctuations across a 7-day period in both state shame and state guilt compared with non-binge-eating women. In addition, higher levels of both state shame and state guilt were reported by women who binge before binge episodes compared with non-binge-eating women before eating episodes.

A few studies have focused on shame without attempting to measure guilt. For example, Swan and Andrews (2003) found that relative to non-clinical controls, women with eating disorders reported higher levels of several types of shame, including body shame, shame about one's character, shame about general behavior, and shame about eating behavior. Grabhorn, Stenner, Stangier, and Kaufhold (2006) found that women with eating disorders had higher general shame than women with anxiety or depressive disorders. Gee and Troop (2003) found that shame was related to eating disorder symptoms above and beyond depression in a sample of undergraduate women.

Taken together, the findings regarding proneness to shame and guilt across domains versus domain-specific shame and guilt are mixed. Generalized proneness to shame predicts severity of eating disorder symptoms in college women and women with BN. Shame specifically about eating behaviors also predicts eating disorder symptoms, as does body-oriented shame. Generalized proneness to guilt, on the other hand, does not reliably predict eating disorder symptoms or severity. However, when it comes to state shame and state guilt, both tend to fluctuate more for women with eating disorders, and these emotions appear to intensify prior to binge episodes. Thus, although evidence is clear that shame is a salient emotion for women with eating disorders, the extent to which guilt is relevant is less compelling. Given that previous research has found many aspects of disordered behavior (e.g., anxiety, depression, hostility, paranoia, somatization) to be associated with generalized shame proneness but not guilt proneness (Tangney, Wagner, & Gramzow, 1992), it is likely that if shame and guilt proneness were measured in a psychometrically distinct manner, shame proneness would continue to emerge as the main emotion relevant to women's struggles with food and eating. However, when looking at the cascade of changes in negative emotional states that immediately precede and follow episodes of binge eating and purging, both emotions might be important.

Although these findings offer hints of the nature of the role of shame and guilt in eating disorders, many questions remain for future research to address. For example, the causal nature of the link between shame and/or guilt and eating disorders is unknown. Are shame- and/or guilt-prone women more likely to develop eating disorders, or does having the disorder engender shame or guilt or both? Do women feel shame and/or guilt before a binge because they are about to binge, or do they binge because they feel shame and/or guilt? Do feelings of shame and/or guilt immediately follow binge episodes or both binge and nonbinge episodes of eating? Also unknown is the role shame and guilt play in various distinct manifestations of eating disorders. For example, what role does shame and/or guilt play in purging? Does shame and/or guilt inhibit women with AN from eating?

Several methodological limitations have made it difficult to study such intensely personal and painful feelings as shame and guilt surrounding the actual engagement in eating disorder behaviors. For example, women with eating disorders have great difficulty labeling emotion states (Cochrane, Brewerton, Wilson, & Hodges, 1993), particularly those that surround binge episodes or periods of restriction, and they are likely to experience shame frequently and in response to other negative emotions that they deem intolerable (Silberstein et al., 1987). Future researchers, however, may take advantage of advances in methodologies, such as ecological momentary assessment (e.g., Engel, Wonderlich, & Crosby, 2005), that make it possible to more reliably assess the subtle shifts and often rapidly changing emotional responses that are associated with eating disorder behaviors.

SHAME IN THERAPY WITH EATING DISORDERED WOMEN: AN RCT APPROACH

The role of shame in eating disorders can be understood in the context of relational-cultural theory (Miller & Stiver, 1997). According to RCT, healthy psychological development for women occurs through growth-fostering relationships (Jordan, 1991; Miller, 1986). Women who experience a pattern of numerous or severe disconnections in their formative relationships with important others (particularly, but not limited to, primary caregivers) are prone to a range of psychological disorders, including eating disorders (Surrey, 1991).

Disconnections occur when one's thoughts, feelings, needs, and/or behaviors are chronically ignored, invalidated, or denied by others (Miller, 1988). This may occur in a subtle manner (e.g., a caregiver changes the subject when the child expresses anger) or more obvious form (e.g., abuse, neglect). Either way, such disconnections are apt to result in the feeling that one's very self is not acceptable. Although times of disconnection are inevitable in any relationship, when these experiences are chronic and/or severe (and especially when they are not followed by relational repair), a psychological process unfolds in which a girl or woman begins to believe that her own feelings, needs, ideas, and so forth are not worthwhile or valued. Chronic disconnection results in what Miller (1988) called *condemned isolation*, the feeling that one is alone and that one is solely responsible for being alone: "It is because of who you are. And you feel helpless, powerless, unable to act to change the situation" (Miller, 1988, p. 7). Feelings of shame may result from this sense of condemned isolation, including the feeling that one is not worthy of being in connection with another person. There is a feeling of hopelessness that one will never receive empathic responses from others (Hartling, Rosen, Walker, & Jordan, 2000). Further, once a woman feels shame, her shame causes her to pull away from others, to disconnect not only from her own experiences but also from others around her who might be able to offer her a different experience (Hartling et al., 2000).

Once an individual develops a shame-prone style, the isolation is often further exacerbated by the feeling of blame the individual feels for situations in which shame occurs. According to Jordan (1989), there are several responses that are likely to occur in the context of a relational disconnection. One possibility is that the individual may become angry and defensively blame the other person. This response is characteristic of narcissistic defenses and is exemplified by Tangney, Wagner, Fletcher, and Gramzow's (1992) "shamed into anger" phenomenon, in which shame-prone individuals have been shown to be more prone to angry responses (e.g., "It's useless talking to him because he's a complete idiot!"). A second possible response, according to Jordan (1989), and the one most indicative of shame, is taking complete responsibility for the disconnection ("I'm so stupid for even asking him to understand— why do I always push him when I know he can't see it my way?"). A third, healthier option is when the individual engages in dialogue with the other that promotes a sense of mutuality and opens up the possibility of reconnection and relational movement toward understanding the processes that leave each individual feeling disconnected (Jordan, 1989). This is the kind of work that therapists can engage in with clients in order to help them transform the meanings they have constructed from their past experiences into newer, healthier meanings. An example of the third option is illustrated in the following vignette.

During the fifth session, the client stated that coming to therapy was probably a waste of the therapist's time because the client could not follow through on her homework. Even when she tried to do her journaling, she seemed to experience more binging and purging, not less. She wanted to terminate the therapy. The therapist first asked the client to examine the advantages of not doing her homework. The patient looked a bit surprised by this and stated there could be no possible advantage because she had wanted to get rid of her symptoms, and she was obviously sabotaging herself. However, in response, the therapist said that there were probably some very good reasons the client was not following through and that it was important for them to understand the pros of her not doing the homework. The client went on to address the possible pros for not doing homework, which included not having to sit with her feelings in the moment, not having to admit that she did not stick with her meal plan through the day, and not having to feel the embarrassment of discussing binge-purge episodes with the therapist.

The therapist also asked her to describe what feelings she was having as she stated these advantages of not doing her homework. This led the client to discuss how she felt ashamed and out of control. She also felt she was failing as a client because she could not consistently do her homework. The therapist did some quick education about how a behavior may initially tend to increase when one begins monitoring it. She told the client this had been the experience of other patients as well in an attempt to normalize the client's experience and decrease her shame. She then discussed how the client had listed many important advantages to avoiding her homework and that, in general, the homework challenged the existence of the eating disorder. The therapist explained how it may be scary and challenging for the client to give up her diagnosis when she is unsure of what the alternative is and how she can survive emotionally without the eating disorder. The therapist added that the client should not give up her symptoms until she first understands how they might help her. She stated that discussing the pros of not completing her homework helped them understand these things and would allow the client to explore other ways to meet her needs and manage her feelings.

The therapist also stated that she felt some sadness for the client as she spoke about the need to be a perfect client. She said the client was very hard on herself. It reminded the therapist of how the client spoke about being a disappointment to her mother and partner. She asked the client if she saw the parallel here and also stated that she did not want a perfect patient. She said that the desire to be perfect seemed to fuel the illness and that she really appreciated the patient taking the risk to return that day, to be imperfect and vulnerable, and to share her experience with the therapist. The client discussed how she had not thought of the parallel with her mother and partner until then, but that it made sense. She began to discuss what a painful week she had with both of them. She concluded that these interpersonal difficulties apparently also contributed to her not following her meal plan and not journaling.

According to an RCT model of development, proneness to shame develops because of the meaning one makes out of the sense of unavailability, unresponsiveness, criticism, inaccessibility, or invalidation perceived in primary relationships. The individual develops negative and/or distorted relational images and meanings (mental representations of one's relationships with others) in the face of repeated painful emotional experiences with others. These images (e.g., "What I say does not matter to my parents and is insignificant") and meanings (e.g., "This is because I am defective and unlovable") may produce a range of feelings, including shame, and may become the unconscious interpersonal blueprint for how the person interacts with others. This was evidenced in the above vignette; the patient wanted to quit therapy because she was not doing her homework. It is likely that she unconsciously was responding out of negative relational images and meanings associated with her relationships with her mother and her partner.

When clients present in therapy with feelings of shame, there is an opportunity to help them have a different relational experience, first with the therapist, and then with others in the client's life. This was what the therapist in the above scenario sought to do with the client. Clients who express feelings of shame are often experiencing the sense of condemned isolation discussed by Miller (1988). By being with them in the moment when they recall past or current shame experiences, a therapist has the opportunity to be present with and witness the client's painful feelings. As the therapist shows empathy and understanding in response to the client's deeply personal revelations, the client feels the therapist is with her in the moment, and this can help the client begin to have a different experience, one of "my feelings are justified, valid, even in this situation." Self-empathy grows in the context of mutual empathy and engagement that is encouraged by the therapist. More specifically, the client sees how she has moved the therapist with her feelings and thoughts, allowing her to realize that what she says or does is important and effectual. She reconnects with her own experience while experiencing a deepened relationship with the therapist, who also is changed in this interaction. This interactive effect was evidenced in the scenario above when the therapist disclosed that she felt some sadness in response to what the client experienced about not being a perfect patient. The client responded to this disclosure by revealing more about the pain that she experienced with her mother and her partner during the week and how this contributed to not being able to slow down, follow her meal plan, and do her journaling.

The experience of mutual empathy and empowerment (in which the patient and therapist are influenced by one another and grow in relationship to one another) transforms the client's isolated feeling of shame into one of "empathic respect," suggesting that she is not alone and that her genuine feelings, thoughts, and needs are acceptable given the context (Jordan, 1989). By having experiences with the therapist that bring an individual out of condemned isolation, a client has the opportunity to begin to transform feelings of shame into more affirming feelings about the self. As the spiral into shame lessens, other possible feelings may emerge in response to relational disconnections (e.g., justified anger, sadness, disappointment). By helping clients identify the sources of disconnection in their lives, the chronic patterns of disconnection that continually bring them into shame can be alleviated, and the path out of shame begins.

For shame-prone individuals, the therapeutic relationship provides an important arena for dealing with feelings of shame. As noted by Hartling et al. (2000), "If one cannot feel worthy of connection . . . within a therapeutic relationship, with whom can one feel worthy of connection?" (p. 4). Shame brings to therapy a sense of being fragile and helpless, which in the context of a culture that emphasizes always having the answer and being in control can be disorienting and frightening for even the most experienced therapists (Hartling et al., 2000). This experience can be amplified for individuals with eating disorders and for their therapists as issues of control and shame regarding not having control are key contributing factors in the development and maintenance of these disorders. Helping clients through the vulnerable state that shame evokes requires making an empathic connection that helps them feel that their fragility and helplessness are OK, that they can survive these feelings, and that they will not make the therapist turn away. Therapists are better able to respond in this way when they are comfortable with their own sources of shame and able to work through this feeling when it is elicited in the therapeutic encounter. When we show our empathy for clients and remain connected with them in their shame, clients can begin to develop more empathy for themselves and others (Hartling et al., 2000). As demonstrated in the vignette, the client felt less of a sense of isolation and shame about being ashamed and more of a sense of acceptance and connection with herself, specifically by having her shame acknowledged and named.

Identifying and working with client shame is particularly important when clients have eating disorders because there is so much shame surrounding the disorder and the accompanying behaviors (e.g., Serpell & Treasure, 2002). A client's willingness to accurately disclose details about the types of eating disorder behaviors she is engaging in, as well as the frequency and context of the behaviors, is crucial to effective therapy, much as accurate information about use of substances is central to effective substance abuse treatment. Shame about such behaviors can impede a client's willingness to share, particularly if he or she has had bad experiences with current or past therapists after revealing such information. Indeed, feelings of shame predict nondisclosure of eating-related details to therapists (Swan & Andrews, 2003). The therapist can help the client shed the overwhelming layers of shame that surround her sense of self in relationships with others by responding in ways that invite connection as the details of the disorder are revealed. An example of how to approach this is shown in the following vignette.

The client had not brought her self-monitoring log in two sessions ago, and she and the therapist had processed this to a certain extent. The client then missed the next session and showed up to the present session again without her self-monitoring log. The therapist reflected back on the missed appointment and validated that she had received the client's cancellation but also asked if anything had made it more difficult to attend last time. The client was initially quiet, and slowly a red flush climbed up her neck toward her face. The therapist asked what was going on, stating that it seemed the client was experiencing something difficult. The therapist said she was unsure if the client was feeling anxious or angry or something else. The client sighed and said she probably did not come because she did not want to discuss the fact that she had purged so much the last 2 weeks. She said she felt she had been doing so well and then she crashed. The therapist asked her to describe the thoughts and feelings she had about coming to the last appointment and how they were similar to or different from what she was experiencing now. The client went on to describe intense feelings of shame at having failed herself and the therapist. Eventually, she was able to tearfully describe how these feelings are similar to how she feels in relationships to others close to her. She said she was chronically worried about letting them down and not doing or being enough.

The therapist empathized with the client, stating she could understand why the client would feel this way based on her past assumptions about herself in relationships with others, but the therapist also pointed out how these negative and painful images of herself in relationships with others (relational images) and the meanings she ascribed to them (relational meanings) affected the client's relationship with the therapist. She asked the client if she wanted the therapist to share her thoughts and feelings in response to the missed appointment and the information that the client had just shared. The client nodded yes. The therapist shared how she had missed seeing the client and worried that she did not attend the session because of her anxiety about somehow not meeting expectations she thought the therapist had of her. She worried that the client was "doing the relationship for both of them"—using her own assumptions of what the therapist might feel and think versus letting the therapist share these herself. The client smiled and said she did tend to do this and that she was not always correct about what other people said they really felt and thought. She said it was hard for her to believe them, though, even when it was the complete opposite of what she expected, which was usually something negative.

The therapist asked the client how things would be different if they had not discussed all this. Would it have helped her feel more or less connected with herself? Would it have made her feel more or less connected with the therapist? She said, "less connected." Then the therapist asked whether the eating disorder got more intense when she was less or more connected with herself and others, and the client responded, "less." They discussed how important it was to stay connected at times when the client began to feel shame and was tempted to isolate and not discuss her symptoms, feelings, thoughts, and needs. The therapist asked about the frequency of the purging and did several behavioral chain analyses to help the client identify the triggers to her purging and the ways she could intervene more quickly in the chain of events as she had done in the past. She knew what to do, but she had been too emotionally dysregulated—shut down by her shame for not using various coping strategies—and so progressively isolated herself from others. As a consequence, she could not stop the purging. The therapist and client then talked about how the eating disorder had taken full advantage of how disconnected she felt and how it sought to keep her more disconnected from herself, the therapist, and others.

The therapist approach described above helped the client feel free and safe enough not only to disclose the specific behaviors she was engaging in (e.g., the frequency and nature of purge episodes) but also to begin to identify shame-related triggers to eating disorder behaviors. For example, negative thoughts like "I'm a bad person and I don't deserve to eat" could prompt women with AN to restrict food. Similarly, a negative thought like "I don't deserve nourishment" could prompt purging after a binge. In addition to these triggers, the aversive state of painful self-awareness that encompasses shame leads to the desire to temporarily escape, which can be achieved through the numbness of starvation or by binge eating and vomiting.

In addition to working with clients to identify negative and distorted cognitions and the associated emotional states that initiate eating disorder behaviors, it is essential to help them understand the relational disconnections that lead to shame. These disconnections may occur in the context of everyday life or, as frequently happens, because of the stress and tension experienced in relationships due to the eating disorder itself. As shown in the above vignette, the relational disconnections and, eventually, just the anticipation of them with the therapist or others lead to the use of eating disorder behaviors as a way to disconnect from the painful relational images, meanings, and feelings associated with these disconnections.

An additional source of stress for women with eating disorders is the perception many people have that those with eating disorders are simply not willing to eat or to exert enough control over their eating (Silberstein et al., 1987). This perception may come from comments made by family members and friends or from society in general and leaves women with eating disorders feeling that they are simply weak willed and that the disorders are self-inflicted. This sense of "I brought it on myself, and my inability to control it is evidence of my failing as a human being" creates shame, as they believe they are simply too inadequate to control themselves. As they attempt to change the eating disorder behaviors, an essential initial focus of therapy, clients are often left feeling, "Why can't I do this? Why do I keep binging, even though I want to stop?" As seen in the above vignette, a therapist can help by communicating to the client that he or she understands that the eating disorder is not in the client's control and assisting the client in identifying how the eating disorder helps and hurts her. Helping the client place the eating disorder behavior in the context of serving a valuable, even needed, function for the individual can help remove the blame she feels for her disorder and alleviate the shame that accompanies this feeling of self-blame. This was exemplified in the vignette described earlier.

An additional example is a client with AN who, when she eats a small meal, feels overwhelmed by fears of fatness and the shame of having fed her desire for food. By going to the gym immediately afterward, she can alleviate the intense shame and guilt. The relief provided by the exercise can be powerful and helps to maintain the behavior of exercise or any extreme method of attempting to counteract an eating episode. Or consider the woman with bulimia who binges after a fight with her husband. The act of binging helps her forget about her anger, thereby helping her to cope with the marital discord, perhaps by allowing her to symbolically swallow the anger that she is afraid to express. A third example may be seen with women who experience body shame with or without an eating disorder. A woman is given negative feedback about a project or task she completed at work and, without realizing it, begins to notice her stomach protruding from the lunch she ate. She begins ruminating about what or how much she ate and how her stomach looks in the clothes she is wearing. These thoughts distract her and to some extent keep her from experiencing painful emotions and thoughts associated with the work-related feedback. In all of these situations, the eating disorder behavior is, in a sense, helping the women cope with the situation at hand. By helping them to see how these behaviors serve needed functions, therapists can help women with eating disorders begin to let go of the feelings of shame and self-blame that they feel and explore other more healthy strategies for coping with the challenges of daily life. In addition, because the shame fuels the eating disorder behaviors, letting go of shame often leads to alleviation of the eating disorder symptoms.

THE CHALLENGE OF SHAME IN PARALLEL PROCESS: THERAPIST STANCE AND REFRAMING VULNERABILITY IN SUPERVISION AND THERAPEUTIC WORK

Clinical work is an extremely personal endeavor, and learning to be a clinician can elicit feelings of exposure, helplessness, and vulnerability. Even seasoned therapists may have difficulty sitting with a client through recollection of a painful shame experience (Jordan, 1989; Lewis, 1971). In American culture, feelings of helplessness and vulnerability are to be avoided, as a premium is placed on certainty and control in learning and in life. In many traditional training settings, this cultural value gets communicated through the unspoken idea that "therapist vulnerability is evidence of therapist ineptitude" (Walker, 2004, p. 12). These pressures can lead to an erroneous belief that the therapist–client relationship is built to fix the client and that the client is the sole source of vulnerability and shame. However, the learning of therapy and supervision depends on the presence of openness and flexibility, awareness of one's own patterns of disconnection from self and others, and a willingness to sit in uncertainty (Jordan, 2004). If a supervisor cannot do this with a supervisee, then the supervisee cannot do this with clients and cannot help them to be less fearful of experiencing these same things. Many beginning therapists feel extremely humbled by the work and are ashamed of their uncertainty, their lack of knowledge about clinical judgment and interventions, and their own human limitations.

Because the supervisee and client hold less power than the supervisor, they tend to bear the burden of vulnerability and shame in the clinical encounter. It is requisite that the supervisor reframe vulnerability to emphasize nonjudgmental awareness, curiosity, and self-empathy. These qualities allow the supervisor, trainee, and client (in parallel process) to view uncertainty and vulnerability as opportunities for growth in connections with others: "Making oneself vulnerable signals trust and respect, as does receiving and honoring the vulnerability of others" (Lawrence-Lightfoot, 2000, p. 93). This recognition allows the supervisor, trainee, and client to stop constructing and begin deconstructing the limited, perfectionistic, and unrealistic images of who they should be in relationships with others. This attitude is especially important in supervision of therapists working with eating-disordered patients who experience many constricted, unrealistic, and negative self-images. These self-images leave clients feeling they are never thin enough, smart enough, or good enough in relationships with others. Therapists need to help patients challenge these shame-based images and their associated negative meanings. Therapists can best do so in a supervisory relationship that allows them to acknowledge their own shame-related issues.

Because the work of therapy is so personal, and because for beginning therapists there is often a feeling of not knowing the trade secrets or the right thing to say, the therapist's experience of shame in supervision is important to address (Jordan, 1989). It is important for supervisors to be mindful of the feelings of shame beginning therapists often have regarding missed opportunities for exploration or important movement in therapy. The supervisor, by creating a sense of empathy and connection related to the missed opportunity or misstep, can help lessen the shame of the therapist and can serve as a model for the therapist in his or her clinical work.

The authors of this chapter were once supervisor (Mary Tantillo) and supervisee (Jennifer Sanftner) in an eating disorders rotation of the supervisee's clinical internship. Jennifer recalled one particular supervision session with Mary, in which they were reviewing a videotape of a group psychotherapy session. A group member was upset about a painful interaction with her father (a relational disconnection), when the group focus shifted to talking about feeling fat and how this made group members want to restrict eating, overexercise, vomit, and so forth. At that point, Mary had Jennifer stop the videotape so they could talk together about what had just happened in the group therapy session. Jennifer immediately began feeling shame prompted by unrealistic and negative thoughts like, "I should have seen that, I'm a terrible therapist, I should know this by now." Feeling that it would be wrong or inappropriate to share those thoughts and feelings further compounded the shame experience, causing Jennifer to be less focused on the videotape and group therapy session and what was happening in it, and more and more focused on what was happening in her own experience.

Sensing this, Mary quickly reframed the situation as one that beginning therapists commonly miss and something she missed when she was less experienced. She gave an example of this in her own training, as well as all the "shoulds" she felt in terms of her response to the group and her associated feelings of shame. This helped normalize the situation and allowed Jennifer to discuss similar thoughts and feelings with Mary. Mary also insisted on discussing what *could* have been done differently in the group therapy session, as opposed to what *should* have been done. By authentically self-disclosing, allowing herself to be vulnerable, and bringing herself into connection with Jennifer at a time when Jennifer was, without realizing it, disconnecting from Mary and moving into the condemned isolation experience of shame, Jennifer and Mary were able to diffuse Jennifer's shame together. This allowed them to return to a productive discussion of understanding the clients' interactions in the session. This supervisory model created a felt sense of empathic respect that grew from the supervisor's genuine self-disclosure in supervision. It was extremely helpful to Jennifer as she learned how to sit in vulnerability and uncertainty with patients, how to model a way for clients to be vulnerable and uncertain, and how to make decisions about when to use disclosure with patients.

CHALLENGES TO WORKING WITH SHAME IN THE TREATMENT OF WOMEN WITH EATING DISORDERS: THE THERAPIST'S OWN BODY IMAGE

An important additional challenge for trainees and seasoned therapists working with eating-disordered women, and women in general, is to become comfortable with their own weight and body image and to manage their own body shame (Silberstein et al., 1987). People who become therapists are not immune to the cultural pressures on women (and men) about their bodies or to experiencing the normative discontent about their bodies described by Rodin et al. (1984). Although both male and female therapists are affected by toxic sociocultural values, there are additional challenges associated with being a female therapist treating women with eating disorders. The combined effects of female socialization and sociocultural values in the dominant culture amplify the possibility of female therapists and clients experiencing shame, anxiety, or dissatisfaction or distortion in relation to their bodies. Because women are all called to come to terms with their feelings about their bodies as they change and develop over time, even women who develop a relatively healthy sense of body image early in life will have to struggle with how they see themselves as their bodies change over time and through developmental transitions in life (e.g., during adolescence, pregnancy, or through illness or aging). In addition, because weight is such a potent source of shame for women, it can be difficult for clients to discuss. Clients may expect the therapist to react to their concerns by brushing them off or causing them further shame, particularly if the therapist is female and particularly if other female role models have been shaming about body image.

Therapists who have considerable shame about their own bodies will feel uncomfortable in the face of client body shame and may offer subtle cues to clients about their discomfort in talking about it. Therapists whose bodies conform to social ideals may feel uncomfortable as well. Research shows that people tend to feel ambivalent about being the object of an upward comparison, in which someone is looking at you as being better than they are in some domain (Exline & Lobel, 1999). Therapists may feel the pressure of the comparison and experience distress, wishing to downplay the perceived difference in the service of preserving the relationship. In either case, clinicians working with women with eating disorders must always stand ready to discuss the meanings attached to the client's and therapist's body weight and shape. In some instances, therapist self-disclosure can be helpful to convey comfort with one's own weight and an openness to discussing this issue and how it is a metaphor for other aspects of the client experience. An example of such self-disclosure is as follows:

> In response to your question about my weight, I don't mind telling you the number, but I also want us to understand what prompted your question. A few minutes ago, you said you thought I was thin and about 100 pounds. Actually, I am 5 feet 5 inches and 131 pounds. Now, let's talk about what made you ask and what that might mean. We can figure out together if this question relates only to weight or to other things you may also be experiencing. Just before you asked me about my weight, you were talking about how badly you felt when comparing your body to another teacher at school. I am wondering if this might relate to your question to me as well.

If the therapist did not feel comfortable disclosing her exact weight, she could have said she does not generally share personal information, such as her weight, with clients, but she would need to state this in a way that leaves the client feeling that her question is a legitimate question (so she does not feel additional shame for asking) and reassured that the therapist is very interested in what it means for the client and for their relationship. In this scenario, it would be important for the therapist to explore how the client feels about the therapist not disclosing her weight.

This kind of therapist response can be used whenever a client raises a question and the therapist does not feel comfortable answering or somehow feels that a disclosure would not be in the client's best interest at the time. Alternatively, if the therapist is ambivalent or uncertain about a disclosure, she can share these feelings and say she wants more time to think about whether the disclosure is a good idea or not in terms of the client's present work. This response lets the client know that the therapist is being mindful of the client's question and its possible impact on the client, while at the same time allowing the client to know her question has moved the therapist. The response promotes mutuality because the therapist still shares her feelings about the request for disclosure (despite not sharing the requested personal information) and is modeling for the client how to sit with uncertainty and dialogue as one makes a decision about how to respond in relationships with others (Tantillo, 2004). Also in the case of male therapists treating women with eating disorders, they can disclose that they may not completely understand the client's experience, but they can convey an openness to learning and understanding it. This response models for the patient that the therapist has comfort in stating what he may not understand, an important strategy in life that helps lessen and/or avoid shame.

In other clinical situations, it may be wiser to have the client describe what she means first and decide on the basis of her feedback whether the therapist wants to self-disclose and how to frame the disclosure. One example of this is when a client asks the therapist if she ever felt fat. The therapist could say something like, "I'll tell you what. Let's you and I first discuss what made you ask me this and what it might mean. Then I can let you know my thoughts and feelings in answer to that question. It is a very good question." After hearing the patient's responses about how her feeling of fatness arose after she failed an entrance exam to college, the therapist might reply,

> Your answer helped me to understand where your question came from. Sounds like when you feel out of control or filled with intense feelings of shame or anxiety, your eating disorder tells you that you are fat, and you start focusing on your stomach and using more body talk to describe your experience. The eating disorder distracts you from how full you feel of your initial feelings and doesn't help you address them—just tempts you to solve how full you feel by restricting your food and numbing yourself. It works in the short run but does not help you in the long run. You still fill up again and then do not have a way to take care of what you are really full with. In answer to your question before about if I ever felt "fat," physically, I have felt bloated just before my period, and it feels uncomfortable, but I know it is temporary. And yes, I have felt full of feelings like anxiety or shame before in my life. I have had to find ways of constructively addressing these feelings so I could stop being so hard on myself and move on after mistakes or disappointments. It's not always easy to do this with or without an eating disorder. But the eating disorder will take full advantage of this opportunity and try to focus you on the fullness you start to feel in your belly when you actually feel very heavy or full in your heart.

Drawing women out about their body shame is important and will be potentially more healing therapeutically if therapists project a sense of comfort in their bodies regardless of their own weight. Seeking out their own support, whether through therapy, self-help, or informal peer support related to body image feelings, is important for therapists who work with women with eating disorders. Some excellent self-help sources are shown in Exhibit 12.1.

CONCLUSION

Eating disorders are a concern for many girls and women and for their families. It is likely that a therapist will encounter a woman struggling with an eating disorder at some point in his or her career. As can be seen in the quote

EXHIBIT 12.1
Self-Help Sources

Books

Cash, T. (1995). *What do you see when you look in the mirror?* New York, NY: Bantam Books.

Cash, T. (1997). *The body image workbook: An 8-step program for learning to like your looks.* Oakland, CA: New Harbinger.

Ensler, E. (2004). *The good body.* New York, NY: Villard.

Kano, S. (1989). *Making peace with food: Freeing yourself from the diet/weight obsession.* New York, NY: Harper & Row. (for children)

Kearney-Cooke, A. (2004). *Change your mind, change your body: Feeling good about your body and self after 40.* New York, NY: Atria Books.

Maine, M., & Kelly, J. (2005). *The body myth: Adult women and the pressure to be perfect.* New York, NY: Wiley.

Mills, A., & Osborn, B. (2003). *Shapesville.* Carlsbad, CA: Gurze Books. (for children)

Neumark-Sztainer, D. (2005). *I'm like, SO fat: Helping your teen make healthy choices about eating and exercise in a weight-obsessed world.* New York, NY: Guilford Press. (for adolescents)

Roth, G. (1998). *When you eat at the refrigerator, pull up a chair.* New York, NY: Hyperion.

Satter, E. (2005). *Your child's weight: Helping without harming.* Madison, WI: Kelcy Press. (for children)

Websites

National Eating Disorders Association (NEDA):
http://www.nationaleatingdisorders.org

Body Positive website: http://www.bodypositive.com

Website for eating disorders information: http://www.somethingfishy.org

Books and resources on eating disorders: http://www.gurze.com

Web site that challenges media images of all types: http://www.adbusters.org

that began this chapter, women with eating disorders suffer from extreme feelings of shame and isolation. Within the empirically based biopsychosocial etiological models of eating disorders, shame stands out as an important psychological component. Further, the RCT model of therapy provides an understanding of how relational disconnections cause a person to develop negative relational images and meanings that are infused with feelings of shame. Thus, eating disorder behaviors develop, in part, as a way of disconnecting from oneself in reaction to or as a way of coping with shame. In addition, the self-loathing and shame that result from eating disorder behaviors cause further disconnections from oneself and others. Addressing the disconnections from self and others, starting with the relationship with the therapist, is crucial to clinical work with women with eating disorders.

When working with women with eating disorders, clinicians need to be aware of several aspects of shame. It is important to work with clients in regard to past and present sources of shame that both fuel and result from the eating disorder, as well as the cultural shame related to the acceptability of women's bodies. A central part of this work for clinicians is developing and working toward a sense of comfort with and connection to their own bodies. Clinicians' experiences with supervisors are crucial to this process, as supervisors can model how to constructively identify sources of shame, process the associated relational images and meanings, and develop effective strategies for coping with these experiences. Because what happens in supervision and therapy is a parallel process, women with eating disorders benefit from the supervisor's and clinician's comfort with body image, uncertainty, and vulnerability—all potential sources of shame for women with eating disorders.

REFERENCES

Altabe, M., & Thompson, J. K. (1996). Body image: A cognitive self-schema construct? *Cognitive Therapy and Research, 20,* 171–193. doi:10.1007/BF02228033

American Psychiatric Association. (2000). *Diagnostic and statistical manual of mental disorders* (4th ed., text rev.). Washington, DC: Author.

Andersen, A. E., Bowers, W. A., & Watson, T. (2001). A slimming program for eating disorders not otherwise specified: Reconceptualizing a confusing, residual diagnostic category. *Psychiatric Clinics of North America, 24,* 271–280. doi:10.1016/S0193-953X(05)70223-9

Boskind-Lodahl, M., & White, W. C. (1978). The definition and treatment of bulimarexia in college women: A pilot study. *Journal of the American College Health Association, 27,* 84–86.

Bruch, H. (1973). *Eating disorders: Obesity, anorexia nervosa, and the person within.* New York, NY: Basic Books.

Brumberg, J. J. (1989). *Fasting girls: The history of anorexia nervosa.* New York, NY: Plume.

Burney, J., & Irwin, H. J. (2000). Shame and guilt in women with eating-disorder symptomatology. *Journal of Clinical Psychology, 56,* 51–61. doi:10.1002/(SICI)1097-4679(200001)56:1<51::AID-JCLP5>3.0.CO;2-W

Cochrane, C. E., Brewerton, T. D., Wilson, D. B., & Hodges, E. L. (1993). Alexithymia in the eating disorders. *International Journal of Eating Disorders, 14,* 219–222. doi:10.1002/1098-108X(199309)14:2<219::AID-EAT2260140212>3.0.CO;2-G

Cooper, J. L., Morrison, T. L., Bigman, O. L., Abramowitz, S. I., Levin, S., & Krener, P. (1988). Mood changes and affective disorder in the bulimic binge-purge cycle. *International Journal of Eating Disorders, 7,* 469–474. doi:10.1002/1098-108X(198807)7:4<469::AID-EAT2260070404>3.0.CO;2-O

Davison, T. E., & McCabe, M. P. (2006). Adolescent body image and psychosocial functioning. *Journal of Social Psychology, 146,* 15–30. doi:10.3200/SOCP.146.1.15-30

Elgin, J., & Pritchard, M. (2006). Gender differences in disordered eating and its correlates. *Eating and Weight Disorders, 11*, 96–101.

Engel, S. G., Wonderlich, S. A., & Crosby, R. D. (2005). Ecological momentary assessment. In J. E. Mitchell & C. B. Peterson (Eds.), *Assessment of eating disorders* (pp. 203–220). New York, NY: Guilford Press.

Exline, J. J., & Lobel, M. (1999). The perils of outperformance: Sensitivity about being the target of a threatening upward comparison. *Psychological Bulletin, 125*, 307–337. doi:10.1037/0033-2909.125.3.307

Frank, E. S. (1991). Shame and guilt in eating disorders. *American Journal of Orthopsychiatry, 61*, 303–306. doi:10.1037/h0079241

Fredrickson, B. L., & Roberts, T. (1997). Objectification theory: Toward understanding women's lived experiences and mental health risks. *Psychology of Women Quarterly, 21*, 173–206. doi:10.1111/j.1471-6402.1997.tb00108.x

Garner, D. M. (1991). *Eating Disorder Inventory 2 professional manual.* Odessa, FL: Psychological Assessment Resources.

Gee, A., & Troop, N. A. (2003). Shame, depressive symptoms and eating, weight and shape concerns in a non-clinical sample. *Eating and Weight Disorders, 8*, 72–75.

Gilbert, P., & Miles, J. (2002). *Body shame: Conceptualization, research, and treatment.* New York, NY: Brunner-Routledge.

Grabhorn, R., Stenner, H., Stangier, U., & Kaufhold, J. (2006). Social anxiety in anorexia and bulimia nervosa: The mediating role of shame. *Clinical Psychology & Psychotherapy, 13*, 12–19. doi:10.1002/cpp.463

Grillo, C. M. (2002). Binge eating disorder. In C. G. Fairburn & K. D. Brownell (Eds.), *Eating disorders and obesity* (2nd ed., pp. 178–182). New York: Guilford Press.

Harrison, K., Taylor, L. D., & Marske, A. (2006). Women's and men's eating behavior following exposure to ideal-body images and text. *Communication Research, 33*, 507–529. doi:10.1177/0093650206293247

Hartling, L. M., Rosen, W., Walker, M., & Jordan, J. V. (2000). *Shame and humiliation: From isolation to relational transformation* (Work in Progress No. 88). Wellesley, MA: Stone Center Working Paper Series.

Hayaki, J., Friedman, M. A., & Brownell, K. D. (2002). Shame and severity of bulimic symptoms. *Eating Behaviors, 3*, 73–83. doi:10.1016/S1471-0153(01)00046-0

Higgins, E. T. (1987). Self-discrepancy: A theory relating self and affect. *Psychological Review, 94*, 319–340. doi:10.1037/0033-295X.94.3.319

Johnson, C. L., Stuckey, M. K., Lewis, L. D., & Schwartz, D. M. (1982). Bulimia: A descriptive survey of 316 cases. *International Journal of Eating Disorders, 2*, 3–16. doi:10.1002/1098-108X(198223)2:1<3::AID-EAT2260020102>3.0.CO;2-K

Jordan, J. V. (1989). *Relational development: Therapeutic implications of empathy and shame* (Work in Progress No. 39). Wellesley, MA: Stone Center Working Paper Series.

Jordan, J. V. (1991). The meaning of mutuality. In J. V. Jordan, A. G. Kaplan, J. B. Miller, I. P. Stiver, & J. L. Surrey (Eds.), *Women's growth in connection: Writings from the Stone Center* (pp. 81–96). New York, NY: Guilford Press.

Jordan, J. V. (2004). Relational learning in psychotherapy consultation and supervision. In M. Walker & W. B. Rosen (Eds.), *How connections heal: Stories from relational-cultural therapy* (pp. 22–30). New York: Guilford Press.

Kashubeck-West, S., Mintz, L. B., & Weigold, I. (2005). Separating the effects of gender and weight-loss desire on body satisfaction and disordered eating behavior. *Sex Roles, 53,* 505–518. doi:10.1007/s11199-005-7138-4

Keel, P. K., & Gravener, J. A. (2008). Sociocultural influences on eating disorders. In S. Wonderlich, J. Mitchell, M. de Zwaan, & H. Steiger (Eds.), *Annual review of eating disorders (Part 2—2008)* (pp. 43–57). Oxford, England: Radcliffe Publishing.

Larson, R., & Johnson, C. (1985). Bulimia: Disturbed patterns of solitude. *Addictive Behaviors, 10,* 281–290. doi:10.1016/0306-4603(85)90009-7

Lawrence-Lightfoot, S. (2000). *Respect: An exploration.* New York, NY: Perseus.

Lewis, H. B. (1971). *Shame and guilt in neurosis.* New York, NY: International Universities Press, Inc.

Maine, M. (2000). *Body wars: Making peace with women's bodies.* Carlsbad, CA: Gurze Books.

Markham, A., Thompson, T., & Bowling, A. (2005). Determinants of body-image shame. *Personality and Individual Differences, 38,* 1529–1541. doi:10.1016/j.paid.2004.08.018

Marschall, D. E., Sanftner, J. L., & Tangney, J. P. (1994). *The State Shame and Guilt Scale.* Fairfax, VA: George Mason University.

Miller, J. B. (1986). *What do we mean by relationships?* (Work in Progress No. 22). Wellesley, MA: Stone Center Working Paper Series.

Miller, J. B. (1988). *Connections, disconnections, and violations* (Work in Progress No. 33). Wellesley, MA: Stone Center Working Paper Series.

Miller, J. B., & Stiver, I. P. (1997). *The healing connection: How women form relationships in therapy and in life.* Boston, MA: Beacon Press.

Moradi, B., Dirks, D., & Matteson, A. V. (2005). Roles of sexual objectification experiences and internalization of standards of beauty in eating disorder symptomatology: A test and extension of objectification theory. *Journal of Counseling Psychology, 52,* 420–428. doi:10.1037/0022-0167.52.3.420

National Eating Disorders Association. (n.d.). *Statistics: Eating disorders and their precursors.* Retrieved from http://www.nationaleatingdisorders.org/uploads/statistics_tmp.pdf

Puhl, R. M., & Brownell, K. D. (2006). Confronting and coping with weight stigma: An investigation of overweight and obese adults. *Obesity, 14,* 1802–1815. doi:10.1038/oby.2006.208

Puhl, R. M., & Latner, J. D. (2007). Stigma, obesity, and the health of the nations' children. *Psychological Bulletin, 133,* 557–580. doi:10.1037/0033-2909.133.4.557

Risk of birth defects is linked to obesity. (2003, May 5). *New York Times.* Retrieved from http://query.nytimes.com/gst/fullpage.html?res=9D03E6D8133CF936A35 756C0A9659C8B63

Rodin, J., Silberstein, L., & Striegel-Moore, R. (1984). Women and weight: A normative discontent. In T. B. Sonderegger (Ed.), *Nebraska Symposium on Motivation: Vol. 32. Psychology and gender* (pp. 267–307). Lincoln: University of Nebraska Press.

Sanftner, J. L., Barlow, D. H., Marschall, D. M., & Tangney, J. P. (1995). The relation of shame and guilt to eating disorder symptomatology. *Journal of Social and Clinical Psychology, 14,* 315–324.

Sanftner, J. L., & Crowther, J. H. (1998). Variability in self-esteem, moods, shame, and guilt in women who binge. *International Journal of Eating Disorders, 23,* 391–397. doi:10.1002/(SICI)1098-108X(199805)23:4<391::AID-EAT6>3.0.CO;2-D

Serpell, L., & Treasure, J. (2002). Bulimia nervosa: Friend or foe? The pros and cons of bulimia nervosa. *International Journal of Eating Disorders, 32,* 164–170. doi: 10.1002/eat.10076

Shisslak, C. M., Crago, M., & Estes, L. S. (1995). The spectrum of eating disturbances. *International Journal of Eating Disorders, 18,* 209–219. doi:10.1002/1098-108X(199511)18:3<209::AID-EAT2260180303>3.0.CO;2-E

Silberstein, L. R., Striegel-Moore, R. H., & Rodin, J. (1987). Feeling fat: A woman's shame. In G. B. Lewis (Ed.), *The role of shame in symptom formation* (pp. 89–108). Hillsdale, NJ: Erlbaum.

Stice, E. (2001). Risk factors for eating pathology: Recent advances and future directions. In R. H. Striegel-Moore & L. Smolak (Eds.), *Eating disorders: Innovative directions in research and practice* (pp. 51–73). Washington, DC: American Psychological Association. doi:10.1037/10403-003

Strauman, T. J., & Glenberg, A. M. (1994). Self-concept and body-image disturbance: Which self-beliefs predict body size overestimation? *Cognitive Therapy and Research, 18,* 105–125. doi:10.1007/BF02357219

Striegel-Moore, R. H., & Bulik, C. M. (2007). Risk factors for eating disorders. *American Psychologist, 62,* 181–198. doi:10.1037/0003-066X.62.3.181

Surrey, J. (1991). Eating patterns as a reflection of women's development. In J. V. Jordan, A. G. Kaplan, J. B. Miller, I. P. Stiver, & J. L. Surrey (Eds.), *Women's growth in connection: Writings from the Stone Center* (pp. 237–249). New York, NY: Guilford Press.

Swan, S., & Andrews, B. (2003). The relationship between shame, eating disorders and disclosure in treatment. *British Journal of Clinical Psychology, 42,* 367–378. doi:10.1348/014466503322528919

Tangney, J. P. (1990). Assessing individual differences in proneness to shame and guilt: Development of the Self-Conscious Affect and Attribution Inventory. *Journal of Personality and Social Psychology, 59,* 102–111. doi: 10.1037/0022-3514.59.1.102

Tangney, J. P., Wagner, P., Fletcher, C., & Gramzow, R. (1992). Shamed into anger? The relation of shame and guilt to anger and self-reported aggression. *Journal of Personality and Social Psychology, 62*, 669–675. doi:10.1037/0022-3514.62.4.669

Tangney, J. P., Wagner, P., & Gramzow, R. (1989). *The Test of Self-Conscious Affect (TOSCA).* Fairfax, VA: George Mason University.

Tangney, J. P., Wagner, P., & Gramzow, R. (1992). Proneness to shame, proneness to guilt, and psychopathology. *Journal of Abnormal Psychology, 101*, 469–478. doi: 10.1037/0021-843X.101.3.469

Tantillo, M. D. (2004). The therapist's use of self-disclosure in a relational therapy approach for eating disorders. *Eating Disorders: The Journal of Treatment & Prevention, 12*, 51–73. doi:10.1080/10640260490267760

Teusch, R. (1988). Level of ego development and bulimics' conceptualizations of their disorder. *International Journal of Eating Disorders, 7*, 607–615.

Troop, N. A., Sotrilli, S., Serpell, L., & Treasure, J. L. (2006). Establishing a useful distinction between current and anticipated bodily shame in eating disorders. *Eating and Weight Disorders, 11*, 83–90.

Wade, T. D., Bergin, J. L., Tiggemann, M., Bulik, C. M., & Fairburn, C. G. (2006). Prevalence and long-term course of lifetime eating disorders in an adult Australian twin cohort. *Australian and New Zealand Journal of Psychiatry, 40*, 121–128.

Walker, M. (2004). How relationships heal. In M. Walker & W. B. Rosen (Eds.), *How connections heal: Stories from relational-cultural therapy* (pp. 3–21). New York, NY: Guilford Press.

Wonderlich, S. A., Mitchell, J. E., Peterson, C. B., & Crow, S. (2001). Integrative cognitive therapy for bulimic behavior. In R. H. Striegel-Moore & L. Smolak (Eds.), *Eating disorders: Innovative directions in research and practice* (pp. 173–195). Washington, DC: American Psychological Association. doi:10.1037/10403-009

III

SHAME IN THE OTHER CHAIR

13

THERAPIST SHAME: IMPLICATIONS FOR THERAPY AND SUPERVISION

NICHOLAS LADANY, REBECCA KLINGER, AND LAUREN KULP

Much of this book has focused on shame experienced by the client. However, what happens when the therapist experiences shame? Many authors, including many who wrote for this volume, have noted that therapist shame can significantly influence the process and outcome of psychotherapy (Covert, Tangney, Maddux, & Heleno, 2003; Leith & Baumeister, 1998; Pope, Sonne, & Greene, 2006). For example, Pope et al. (2006) argued that embarrassing and shameful moments reveal unacknowledged, uncomfortable feelings of which the therapist is unaware that will likely have unknown effects on clients. Clearly, identifying therapist shame, and then working through the therapist's experience, can be critical given its potential influence on the therapist's ability to function effectively in clinical contexts. To that end, the purpose of this chapter is to define therapist shame, offer examples of types of therapist shame along with examples of therapist and client responses to therapist shame, and provide a case example of how therapist shame can be worked through in supervision. We propose the critical events model of supervision

---

The second and third authors contributed equally to this chapter, and their names are included alphabetically.

307

(CES) as a potential framework for working through therapist shame experiences within the context of supervision. Although this model was not developed specifically for addressing shame, it provides a useful context for identifying, addressing, and resolving shame that is experienced by therapists in the course of their clinical encounters.

DEFINING THERAPIST SHAME

Summarizing and expanding upon the literature (e.g., Gilbert, 1997; M. Lewis, 1993; Sorotzkin, 1985), we define *therapist shame* as an intense and enduring reaction to a threat to the therapist's sense of identity that consists of an exposure of the therapist's physical, emotional, or intellectual defects that occurs in the context of psychotherapy. For example, a therapist may experience shame if he or she fell asleep during a session. It would be particularly shameful if the therapist believed it reflected on his or her competence and if the emotional experience haunted him or her long past the time at which the event occurred.

It is important to distinguish between therapist shame and related, yet distinct, constructs of therapist embarrassment, humiliation, and guilt (Leith & Baumeister, 1998; H. Lewis, 1971; Tangney, Miller, Flicker, & Barlow, 1996; Tracy & Robins, 2004):

- Therapist embarrassment is most closely linked to shame and can be thought of as an experience on the other end of the shame-embarrassment continuum. Embarrassment, unlike shame, tends to be short lived and acute and is experienced mildly rather than intensely. In the previous example, rather than the therapist falling asleep, the therapist may have been distracted by something and recognized the distraction as an infrequent yet common and normal occurrence in therapy.
- Humiliation arises from the actions of others, and there is a minimal sense of disruption to identity. If, for example, a therapist trainee was distracted momentarily in a session, and later, in a classroom of peers, a supervisor angrily told the trainee that it was a stupid mistake, the therapist would likely feel humiliated but could attribute the experience to the supervisor's inappropriate behavior.
- Guilt results from a specific action that results in harm to others, in this instance specifically to the client (Leith & Baumeister, 1998; H. Lewis, 1971; Tangney et al., 1996; Tracy & Robins, 2004). In the running example, if the client abruptly terminated

shortly after the therapist fell asleep during session, the therapist may feel guilt for having fallen asleep.

In summary, shame distinguishes itself from other constructs in the following manner: It is more intense and extreme than embarrassment; it arises from the self more than from others as in humiliation; and the focus of attention pertains to the self, in contrast to guilt's focus on behavior.

EXAMPLES OF SHAMEFUL EVENTS AND THERAPIST AND CLIENT RESPONSES

Research on therapist shame appears to be almost nonexistent. Recently, Kulp, Klinger, and Ladany (2007) offered avenues for understanding therapist shame in the preliminary analyses of their studies on therapist and supervisor embarrassment and shame (more than 90 experienced therapists or supervisors in each sample). Although they combined embarrassment and shame events in their categorization (because they were deemed to be on a continuum and were difficult to distinguish in many ways, such as in cases of high-embarrassment or low-shame events), their results offer insight into the potential types of therapist shame events. The researchers examined shameful events identified by practicing therapists—specifically, the content of the event, the therapist's reactions to the event, and the client's reactions to the event.

Most notably, some of the more typical types of shameful events included the therapist falling asleep in session, chronic difficulties with time management, referring to a client by another client's name, forgetting significant client information such as a death in the family, bodily function difficulties, internal recognition that an intervention was failing miserably, and sexual behaviors by the client. In all of these instances, the therapists indicated that to various extents, the therapeutic relationship was affected, client outcomes may have been compromised, and their own self-efficacy was altered.

Therapist reactions to the shameful events included reactions at the moment of the event, such as changes in the therapist's body (e.g., tensing); reactions in the session subsequent to the event, such as apologizing to the client, using humor, processing the event with the client, or ignoring the event; and reactions that lingered past the event, such as persistent feelings of shame and recurring thoughts about the event. Therapists also identified client reactions to the events that included negative reactions (e.g., hostility, withdrawal, termination) and positive reactions (e.g., forgiveness, humor). As could be seen, at times the therapist shame event was used therapeutically and may actually have been beneficial to the therapeutic work, and at other times the event led to significant therapeutic problems.

WORKING THROUGH THERAPIST SHAME IN SUPERVISION

Experiencing shameful events is likely a normal therapy experience. As such, it seems important to consider what therapists should do once they've experienced a shameful event. In the case of embarrassing events and perhaps mildly shameful events, therapists may be able to put the event in context personally or share the event with a trusted colleague. However, psychotherapy trainees and master therapists alike would do well to work through moderately to significantly shameful events in supervision (Jennings & Skovholt, 1999). This section reviews a model of supervision suited for working through an event that caused a therapist shame—the critical events model of supervision (Ladany, Friedlander, & Nelson, 2005).

The CES was based on an extension of task analysis models developed to understand change in therapy (e.g., Greenberg, 1984, 1986; Safran, Crocker, McMain, & Murray, 1990) but expanded to recognize and integrate the unique differences and interpersonal dynamics that distinguish supervision from psychotherapy (e.g., evaluation, educational aspects). Moreover, five assumptions form the basis of the model. First, the CES was created to be pantheoretical such that it is applicable to multiple theoretical approaches to psychotherapy. Second, the model recognizes the interpersonal nature of supervision, thereby including the contributions of both the trainee and supervisor. Third, supervision is intended to facilitate supervisee growth as opposed to focusing on case management or being primarily administrative. Fourth, the process of supervision can be divided into a series of events, each having a beginning, middle, and end, and all of which can occur within a single session or across multiple supervisory sessions. Fifth, the events themselves are linked with specific supervision outcomes.

A number of common critical events have been identified and include remediating skill difficulties and deficits, heightening multicultural awareness, negotiating role conflicts, working through countertransference, managing sexual attraction, repairing gender-related misunderstandings, addressing problematic supervisee emotions and behaviors, facilitating supervisee insight, and facilitating a supervisee corrective relational experience. For the purposes of this chapter, we add an additional critical event: working through supervisee shame. According to Ladany et al. (2005), any event can be broken down into four components: (a) the supervisory working alliance, (b) the marker, (c) the task environment, and (d) the resolution.

Supervisory Working Alliance

The *supervisory working alliance* has been one of the most studied constructs of supervision, has been found to be related to a variety of supervision process and outcome variables, and has been considered to be the foundation on which effective supervision is based (Ladany & Inman, in press). The CES expands on Bordin's (1983) model of the supervisory working alliance and, like Bordin, deems the alliance to consist of three components: (a) mutual agreement between the supervisee and supervisor on the goals of supervision (e.g., increase therapy skills, enhance self-awareness), (b) mutual agreement between the supervisee and supervisor on the tasks of supervision (e.g., manner and type of feedback), and (c) an emotional bond between the supervisee and supervisor consisting of respect, caring, liking, and trusting. As a salient part of the CES model, the supervisory alliance acts as a figure-ground concept, whereby it rises to the figure early in the supervision relationship or following a rupture and recedes to the ground when adequate strength is reached.

The Marker

The *marker* occurs at the beginning of a critical event and signals that an event is about to take place. Markers are usually statements or a series of statements made by the supervisee asking for help. These statements may be simple, such as "I had this shameful experience with my client that I need to talk about." Alternatively, markers can take on a more subtle character, such as when a supervisee avoids talking about a particular client, forgets the client's name, or becomes uncharacteristically defensive when the supervisor brings up a client. At other times the supervisor, in the case of therapists in training, may observe the shameful event when watching a video recording of the therapy session. The marker, then, brings to the fore the next phase of the critical event, the task environment.

The Task Environment

The *task environment* is where much of the action takes place in a critical event. In the task environment, the supervisor engages in a series of interaction sequences, the 12 most common of which include (a) focusing on the supervisory working alliance (e.g., using empathy, reflections, and negotiations), (b) focusing on the therapeutic process (e.g., the interactions that transpired in therapy), (c) exploring supervisee feelings, (d) focusing on countertransference (e.g., biases that may be affecting the therapeutic work), (e) attending to parallel process (e.g., considering how therapy and supervision may be mimicking one another), (f) focusing on supervisee self-efficacy, (g) normalizing the experience, (h) focusing on therapy skills, (i) assessing knowledge (e.g., determining whether the event involved a skills or knowledge deficit), (j) focusing on multicultural awareness (e.g., gender, racial, sexual orientation identity), (k) focusing on evaluation, and (l) case review. The task environment typically consists of three to six interaction sequences of the 12 identified. For the purposes of demonstration, the interaction sequences are described in an order; however, the order, as well as the notion that the specific sequence occurs within a single session, is done for heuristic value.

In the context of working through a therapist shame event, we identified five likely interaction sequences that constitute the task environment: (a) focusing on the supervisory alliance, (b) exploring feelings, (c) focusing on countertransference, (d) focusing on self-efficacy, and (e) normalizing the experience (see Figure 13.1). Because feelings of shame are what characterize a shame event, it is critical that the supervisor empathize with the supervisee. Even with experienced clinicians in the role of supervisee, it is critical that an alliance is developed via empathy and understanding of the event and the supervisee's experience. The supervisor should also be collaborative in terms of negotiating the manner in which things will be discussed and the goal of these discussions. The effectiveness of the rest of the supervisory work is contingent upon the adequacy with which the alliance is strengthened.

For the shame experience to be fully understood, it is critical that the supervisor facilitate the exploration of the supervisee's feelings about the shame event. This exploration may involve deepening the supervisee's understanding of his or her reactions to the shame event by, for example, exploring possible links to previous shame events in the supervisee's life, as well as the similarities of the reaction to these previous experiences. Hence, exploration of feelings will likely lead to a focus on the countertransference or, simply put, the general internal struggles and biases that the therapist experiences in reaction to the client's presenting material. Next, because shame events, by definition, affect the therapist's sense of professional self, attention to the supervisee's self-efficacy is warranted, with perhaps statements that reinforce or rebuild the self-efficacy that was lost. Finally, the supervisor would do well to normalize the supervisee's experience. The recognition that therapists are human and that mistakes, even significant ones, are bound to happen can be quite validating to the supervisee and ultimately help him or her rebound effectively from the experience.

The Resolution

The end or outcome of a particular event is called the *resolution*. Resolution can occur in varying degrees (from totally unresolved to totally resolved) along four dimensions: self-awareness, knowledge, skills, and the supervisory working alliance. *Self-awareness*, the type most linked to a shame event, refers to changes in supervisees' understanding about how their feelings, beliefs, and behaviors are considered in the context of their psychotherapy work. So for a shame event, the therapist may have an enhanced understanding of how and

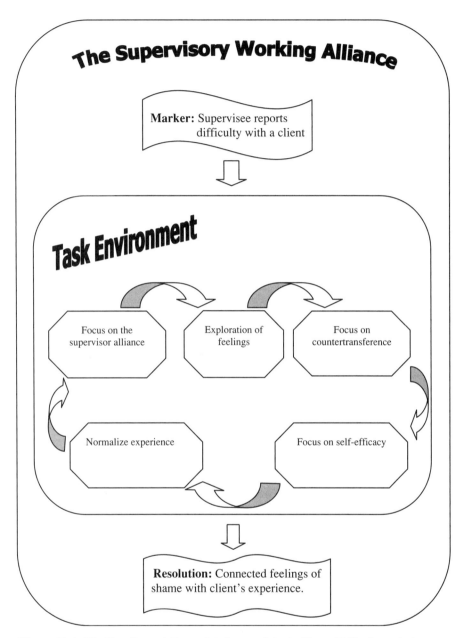

Figure 13.1. Working through therapist shame. Adapted from *Critical events in psychotherapy supervision: An interpersonal approach* (p. 12), by N. Ladany, M. L. Friedlander, and M. L. Nelson, 2005, Washington, DC: American Psychological Association. Copyright American Psychological Association.

why the shame event occurred and of the impact of the event on the client. Moreover, the therapist's self-efficacy may have been restored. All of these are positive resolutions. In the case of negative resolutions, the therapist may not have acknowledged feeling shamed by the experience and thus may not have gained in self-awareness. Knowledge about therapy would be increased if the supervisee gained an appreciation for how therapists can experience shame and learned ways to buffer himself or herself against the occurrence of such experiences in the future (i.e., change in approach or skills in relation to the therapeutic work). Finally, through all the work that is done during the event, the supervisory working alliance can become altered, preferably for the better, thereby serving as a foundation for future work. The following case example illustrates a process model for a successfully resolved supervisee/therapist shame event. Our example includes an intern in the role of the supervisee; however, we believe that similar processes would take place with more experienced psychotherapists.

CASE EXAMPLE

The supervisory dyad consisted of Nel, a 45-year-old supervisor who had 18 years of clinical experience and 10 years of supervisor experience, and Eva, a 31-year-old predoctoral intern. The setting was a university counseling center. Nel and Eva had met for seven supervisory sessions, and their alliance to date had been relatively strong. Eva had been open to discussing her personal issues and how they affected her work with clients. She was also aware of and insightful concerning her development as a psychotherapist.

The marker began when Eva reported being challenged by a new client, Silas, during their second session. Eva described to Nel how after engaging Silas in a breathing exercise to cope with his anxiety, Silas stated, "Well, that didn't work. Are you sure you know what you're doing?"

> *Eva:* I need to talk about something that happened with a new client I'm seeing.
>
> *Supervisor:* OK; tell me about it.
>
> *Eva:* Well, I got stuck when my client told me the intervention didn't work and challenged my ability.

At this point, the supervisor was unsure of what Eva needed and suggested they listen to the tape of the session.

> *Supervisor:* Wow, it sounds like he really challenged you there.
>
> *Eva:* Yes! I didn't know what to do! I felt so incompetent and embarrassed and . . .

> *Supervisor:* Sounds like it was difficult for you.
>
> *Eva:* Yeah, it really was. I guess I felt a lot of shame, like I failed.

The supervisor clearly saw the marker as Eva's reported feelings of shame due to a client challenge and recognized that the shameful feelings needed to be worked through. Because Eva's feelings had the potential to influence her therapeutic alliance with the client and the quality of treatment, the supervisor decided to address these feelings of shame. The supervisor recognized Eva's discomfort in disclosing her feelings of shame and therefore began the discussion with a focus on the supervisory alliance before moving into processing her feelings:

> *Supervisor:* I can imagine feeling that way, too.
>
> *Eva:* Yeah.
>
> *Supervisor:* This seems like a difficult topic for you. How does it feel telling me about this?
>
> *Eva:* Well, I feel comfortable talking to you about most topics, but I guess this is different because I feel like I failed and I want you to think I'm a good therapist.
>
> *Supervisor:* That makes sense. I appreciate you bringing this up, and I understand that you may question if I'm judging you.
>
> *Eva:* I don't know if I feel judged, but I know I don't want you to think negatively of me.
>
> *Supervisor:* That's understandable. I think the most important thing to remember is that we are working through these issues together, and I think we've done well with that so far.
>
> *Eva:* I do, too.
>
> *Supervisor:* What's most pressing for you to address with this client in relation to what happened?
>
> *Eva:* I think I would like to feel at ease with him and figure out what's preventing me from being able to work effectively with him.

Here the supervisor brought the focus back to Eva's work with the client. She also addressed the supervisory alliance by collaborating with Eva concerning the goals for the session. The supervisor was able to assess that the supervisory alliance has not been ruptured, as indicated by Eva's honest self-disclosure of her discomfort. By emphasizing the importance of the agreement of goals and Eva's contribution to the focus of the supervisory sessions, the supervisor strengthened the alliance.

Supervisor:	I know you haven't disclosed feeling this way with other clients. Beyond his statement, is there anything else about your interactions with him that contributed to your difficulties working with him?
Eva:	Well, there is something about him that makes me uncomfortable and reduces my confidence.
Supervisor:	Tell me more about what he does or says that creates this experience for you.
Eva:	I guess he pushes me for a solution, yet everything I offer him seems wrong. And this time, he really made a point of making me feel like an idiot!
Supervisor:	So it sounds like you feel pressured to give him an answer, but your efforts get rejected.
Eva:	Yeah, exactly. I feel rejected and so embarrassed.

The supervisor now had a better understanding of Eva's and her client's interactions. She recognized that the client's actions were triggering negative self-conscious emotions in Eva. Because Eva returned to her emotions by referencing feeling embarrassed, the supervisor further explored Eva's emotional experience to help her continue to process the event:

Supervisor:	What is that like for you—to feel embarrassed and rejected by this client?
Eva:	Horrible! I feel so small, like I don't know what I'm doing. I feel completely disempowered!
Supervisor:	That sounds overwhelming.
Eva:	Yeah, not only do I feel bad, but I started to second-guess my abilities as a therapist and feel worthless.

Here the supervisor noticed that Eva was doubting her abilities, which indicated she might be struggling with her self-efficacy. However, the supervisor decided to stay with Eva's emotions through a here-and-now focus and return to self-efficacy later:

Supervisor:	I notice you're looking down as you're describing this. What's going on for you right now?
Eva:	I'm just thinking about how he made me feel . . . it was like all my faults were exposed, and it was revealed that I'm not a very experienced therapist.
Supervisor:	That's a difficult place to be put as a young therapist. I can see it is still having a significant impact on you.

Eva: Yeah.

Supervisor: You mentioned before feeling a few different emotions, like embarrassment, rejection, and shame. I'm wondering if there is one emotion that stands out for you in your experiences with this client.

Because Eva disclosed feeling various emotions, the supervisor narrowed the focus of the emotions to gain clarity and work through the emotions to allow her to be more present with the client.

Eva: I hate to admit it, but I do feel a lot of shame with this client.

Supervisor: It seems like this is an emotion you move away from . . .

Eva: I guess you're right.

Supervisor: Let's just sit with this, then, for a moment to really take it in and stay with it.

Eva: OK.

Eva and her supervisor were silent for approximately 30 seconds to allow Eva to feel the emotion so she could begin to accept it. By having Eva sit with her feelings of shame, the supervisor was setting the stage to allow Eva to connect her experience with what the client was feeling. To deepen Eva's experience, the supervisor moved the discussion to an exploration of countertransference:

Supervisor: How was that moment of silence for you?

Eva: It was uncomfortable at first, but I think it helped me to understand how I am feeling and recognize the feeling as shame.

Supervisor: Now that you recognize this feeling, can you think back to when you have felt this way before?

Eva: Hmm. I remember feeling this way with my dad when I was younger.

Supervisor: Does anything specific come to mind?

Eva: Yes. I brought home a report card with two Bs and was expected to get all As. My dad was really angry and told me it wasn't good enough.

Supervisor: How did you feel when this happened?

Eva: I felt bad but didn't know what it was. Now I realize it was shame.

> *Supervisor:* It sounds like your father had high expectations of you, and you felt shame when you let him down, even though you were performing well.
>
> *Eva:* It's crazy how one person's opinion can shape the way I feel, even though I know inside I am doing OK.
>
> *Supervisor:* Similar to how one client can make you feel.
>
> *Eva:* Oh! You mean how Silas is making me feel.
>
> *Supervisor:* Exactly!

The supervisor highlighted the similarities between Eva's experience with her father and her interactions with her client.

> *Eva:* I never thought about it like that before, but it really does feel the same.
>
> *Supervisor:* Now that you recognize this, what can we do with it?
>
> *Eva:* I think being aware of it helps, but also I think I need to work through some personal issues with my dad.
>
> *Supervisor:* I think both of those are important. Now how can we bring it back to your work with Silas?
>
> *Eva:* I can be mindful of my feelings during the session to avoid them interfering with our work.
>
> *Supervisor:* OK, good. And how about Silas's feelings?
>
> *Eva:* Oh, I bet he could be feeling shame, too, about his anxiety and not being able to manage it.
>
> *Supervisor:* Right.
>
> *Eva:* Wow, I can't believe I missed that! I was so wrapped up in my own feelings.

Through exploring Eva's countertransference related to feelings of shame with her father, she was able to clarify her own emotional experience and that of her client. The supervisor recognized that this process was difficult for Eva, who was continuing to doubt her abilities as a counselor. Therefore, the supervisor transitioned the discussion to Eva's perception of herself as a competent therapist (i.e., self-efficacy):

> *Supervisor:* You mentioned before feeling incompetent working with this client, and I want to check in with you about that.
>
> *Eva:* Yeah. That is an issue, but I feel like this discussion has helped me to see more clearly what's going on with me and the client. I think I may be able to better relate to him now.

Supervisor:	I think you're right. How do you think you can better relate to him?
Eva:	Maybe by going back to exploring his feelings about his anxiety and not focusing so much on solving it.
Supervisor:	Like what we have been doing in here.
Eva:	Yeah, like that.
Supervisor:	How do you feel about this plan?
Eva:	I feel more prepared going into our next session, like I know what I am doing now.

To further attend to Eva's needs, the supervisor returned to her original concern of feeling incompetent. Through devising a plan for working with this client, Eva's confidence in her ability improved. At this point, the supervisor validated her concerns with this client and assured Eva that she was going through a normal developmental process (i.e., normalized the experience):

Supervisor:	Good. Supervision is often a difficult process, but it sounds like we both have done good work today and learned something new.
Eva:	Yeah, I knew I needed to discuss this today, but it is always hard to come in here when I feel like I haven't performed to the best of my ability.
Supervisor:	The way we improve our abilities so that we can perform our best is by being honest about our mistakes and working through our countertransference. And this is something that we all have to go through to become effective therapists.
Eva:	I know that's the case, but it is still comforting to hear it, especially after this session, because I never expected to feel so much shame with a client.
Supervisor:	It sounds like it was unexpected for you, and that's also something that is common for therapists to go through. We are often surprised when strong emotions come up for us in session. And the goal is to process these emotions so that we minimize the impact on the client.
Eva:	It's nice to hear that this is normal and all a part of my learning process.

The supervisor normalized Eva's struggle by validating her concerns and her feelings of shame. She also educated Eva about the process of becoming an effective therapist and emphasized the difficulty of this process. Moving into the resolution phase, the supervisor and Eva summarized their discussion by tying together Eva's insights about her feelings of shame and her process of working through it:

> Supervisor: Eva, we covered a lot of emotional material today, and I want to check in with you about how you are doing.
>
> Eva: It was hard to accept that my feelings of shame interfered with the session, but I learned a lot about what I should be aware of with my clients.
>
> Supervisor: All right; let's review what kinds of things you should be aware of.
>
> Eva: I should be aware of my feelings of shame and how they could be affecting my work with clients. If I recognize they are interfering, I need to check in with myself and work to resolve them. And then I could use my own experience to relate better to the client.
>
> Supervisor: It sounds like you did a lot of good work today and have a good handle on how to manage your feelings of shame with your clients. Maybe next week we can check in about your next session with Silas.
>
> Eva: Sounds good.

Eva was able to successfully work through her shame by exploring her interactions with her client and her own experiences with shame. Eva also made connections between her feelings of shame and her client's experience. The next step was for Eva to translate her work in supervision to her therapeutic work with her client.

CONCLUSION

The case example illustrates what can happen in relation to working through a therapist shame event. We recognize that the steps in real life may not be as orderly, sequential, and easily accomplished. However, we hope that the model offers therapists and supervisors a sense of what can occur when a therapist has experienced a shame event and perhaps provides avenues for discussion not considered previously. Clearly, more research on the model in relation to working through therapist shame events is needed to determine the utility of this approach. In addition, highlighting therapist shame experiences brings to the fore other issues in relation to shame, such as supervisee or supervisor shame that takes place in the context of supervision (Bernard & Goodyear, 2009; Kulp et al., 2007; Yourman, 2003). Therapist shame appears to be a prodigious and salient phenomenon that can have significant implications for therapy and supervision, and it therefore deserves continued recognition and study in the literature.

REFERENCES

Bernard, J. M., & Goodyear, R. K. (2009). *Fundamentals of clinical supervision* (4th ed.). Boston, MA: Allyn & Bacon.

Bordin, E. S. (1983). A working alliance based model of supervision. *Counseling Psychologist, 11*(1), 35–41.

Covert, M. V., Tangney, J. P., Maddux, J. E., & Heleno, N. M. (2003). Shame-proneness, guilt-proneness, and interpersonal problem solving: A social cognitive analysis. *Journal of Social and Clinical Psychology, 22,* 1–12. doi:10.1521/jscp.22.1.1.22765

Gilbert, P. (1997). The evolution of social attractiveness and its role in shame, humiliation, guilt, and therapy. *British Journal of Medical Psychology, 70,* 113–147.

Greenberg, L. S. (1984). Task analysis: The general approach. In L. N. Rice & L. S. Greenberg (Eds.), *Patterns of change: Intensive analysis of psychotherapy process* (pp. 124–148). New York, NY: Guilford Press.

Greenberg, L. S. (1986). Change process research. *Journal of Consulting and Clinical Psychology, 54,* 4–9.

Jennings, L., & Skovholt, T. M. (1999). The cognitive, emotional and relational characteristics of master therapists. *Journal of Counseling Psychology, 46,* 3–11. doi:10.1037/0022-0167.46.1.3

Kulp, L., Klinger, R., & Ladany, N. (2007, October). *Embarrassment, humiliation, and shame in therapy and supervision.* Poster presented at the meeting of the Mid Atlantic Society for Psychotherapy Research, New York, NY.

Ladany, N., Friedlander, M. L., & Nelson, M. L. (2005). *Critical events in psychotherapy supervision: An interpersonal approach.* Washington, DC: American Psychological Association. doi:10.1037/10958-000

Ladany, N., & Inman, A. G. (in press). Training and supervision. In E. M. Altmaier & J. C. Hansen (Eds.), *The Oxford handbook of counseling psychology.* New York, NY: Oxford University Press.

Leith, K. P., & Baumeister, R. F. (1998). Empathy, shame, guilt, and narratives of interpersonal conflicts: Guilt-prone people are better at perspective taking. *Journal of Personality and Social Psychology, 66,* 1–37.

Lewis, H. (1971). *Shame and guilt in neurosis.* New York, NY: International Universities Press.

Lewis, M. (1993). Self-conscious emotions: Embarrassment, pride, shame, and guilt. In M. Lewis & J. M. Haviland (Eds.), *Handbook of emotions* (pp. 563–573). New York, NY: Guilford Press.

Pope, K. S., Sonne, J. L., & Greene, B. (2006). *What therapists don't talk about and why: Understanding taboos that hurt us and our clients* (2nd ed.). Washington, DC: American Psychological Association. doi:10.1037/11413-000

Safran, J. D., Crocker, P., McMain, S., & Murray, P. (1990). Therapeutic alliance rupture as a therapy event for empirical investigation. *Psychotherapy: Theory, Research, Practice, Training, 27,* 154–165.

Sorotzkin, B. (1985). The quest for perfection: Avoiding guilt or avoiding shame? *Psychotherapy: Theory, Research, Practice, Training, 22,* 564–571. doi:10.1037/h0085541

Tangney, J. P., Miller, R. S., Flicker, L., & Barlow, D. H. (1996). Are shame, guilt, and embarrassment distinct emotions? *Journal of Personality and Social Psychology, 70,* 1256–1269. doi:10.1037/0022-3514.70.6.1256

Tracy, J. L., & Robins, R. W. (2004). Putting the self into self-conscious emotions: A theoretical model. *Psychological Inquiry, 15,* 103–125. doi:10.1207/s15327965pli1502_01

Yourman, D. B. (2003). Trainee disclosure in psychotherapy supervision: The impact of shame. *JCLP/In Session, 59,* 601–609.

IV

SHAME-FOCUSED
STRATEGIES

14

SHAME IN PSYCHOTHERAPY AND THE ROLE OF COMPASSION FOCUSED THERAPY

PAUL GILBERT

This chapter explores the nature of shame experiences and how they can interfere with the seeking of psychotherapy and the process of therapy. The latter half of the chapter outlines aspects of compassion focused therapy (CFT), which was specially developed for high shame problems.

THE NATURE OF SHAME

Shame is typically regarded as multifaceted, with feelings of anxiety, anger, disgust, and/or sadness and at times a "heart sink" feeling; a sense of self as inadequate, bad, or defective in some way; beliefs that other people look down on the self and hold us in a negative frame of mind; behavioral dispositions and urges to run away, freeze, hide, and avoid; and unpleasant physiological arousal. Shame differs from humiliation, which has its focus on the other as bad or harmful and feelings of anger and desire for revenge. It also differs from guilt, which is linked into caring-giving and harm avoidance mechanisms and is focused on sadness, sorrow, and remorse with a desire to repair any harm done (for reviews, see Gilbert, 1998, 2002).

Shame and that heart sink feeling that can come with anxiety and wanting to hide can affect any of us, especially when we have to open up to others and seek help. Indeed, when we consider what actually occurs in therapy, it is easy to see how shame can permeate so much of a process that involves revealing and discussing with a stranger intimate, painful, and difficult thoughts, feelings, fears, memories, and fantasies. People seeking therapy might discuss ways in which they feel they are not coping, such as losing control of their eating or drinking or their own emotions, feeling like a failure, being tormented by secret anxieties, making efforts to avoid things, or suppressing memories of past abuse. This degree of exposure of private experiences means that psychotherapy creates interactions that can be highly laden with shame (Gilbert, 2007c). However, shame in the therapy hour is not always focused on the client; therapists, too, can experience shame when clients criticize them or threaten litigation or suicide or because of their own fantasies and impulses (Pope, Sonne, & Greene, 2006). Indeed, avoiding the topic of shame can result in therapeutic ruptures and blocks (Gilbert, 2007b, 2007c; Retzinger, 1998; Safran & Muran, 2000).

Given that shame in psychotherapy is common and that healing of shame can be key to successful psychotherapy, it is important to outline the complexities of the shame experience because it can arise in different ways in different people. Here I explore the different elements of shame through the lens of client experiences and later those of therapist shame.

Shame is normally regarded as a secondary or self-conscious emotion, as contrasted with primary emotions (Tracy, Robins, & Tangney, 2007). Primary emotions are threat alerting and focused, such as anger, anxiety, and disgust. Shame belongs to a family of emotions that are linked to the very sense of oneself—the kind of person we feel we are (Gilbert, 1998; Kaufman, 1989; Tangney & Dearing, 2002; Tracy et al., 2007). However, the sense of self emerges from the confluence of two processes—how we believe we exist for others (e.g., as liked and valued or as disliked and devalued) and how we exist in our own minds (liking oneself or feeling oneself to be inadequate in some way). The two processes give rise to two forms of shame. The first is *external* shame, the shame that arises when we experience condemnation or disparagement in the mind of the other (or its anticipation—that "if they knew this about me, they would think badly of me"). The second is *internal* shame, which arises when we make negative judgments and have negative feelings about the self, such as being disappointed in oneself (Gilbert, 1998, 2002, 2007a; Whelton & Greenberg, 2005). Experiences of external and internal shame, in various combinations, can arise in both client and therapist and can script their interactions. Distinguishing external from internal shame in the therapist–client interaction can be helpful in recognizing the differences between each and contributing to their repair.

External Shame

A child excitedly puts on a new party dress, but her mother says, "Oh, that looks terrible on you"; a junior executive gives a presentation, but the director says he is disappointed in the quality; a client reveals that he has been drinking before therapy, and the therapist is angry and asks the client to leave; a client reveals that she suffered sexual abuse and that she did not resist it and thinks she sees a look of contempt on her therapist's face; a depressed person states that because of fatigue and anxiety he has avoided trying to get a new job and believes that the therapist sees him as lazy; a male client admits to beating his wife and "knows" the therapist will condemn him; a client listens to a cognitive therapist and believes that the therapist is basically saying, "You are simply thinking wrong" (i.e., "it is your fault you feel depressed because you can't think straight!"): External shame arises when we perceive our self as creating negative emotions (anger, disgust, contempt, ridicule) in the mind of the other. It arises when we experience others as looking down on us and deeming us unattractive, undesirable, incompetent, or inadequate in some way. This triggers a sense of threat because it brings up the possibility of rejection, marginalization, and even persecution, with a key fear that we will be cut off from sources of care and support (Gilbert, 2007c).

The reason we monitor so carefully how we exist for others and whether people like or dislike us, and the reason ruptures to potentially helpful relationships can be intensely threatening, can be understood against an evolutionary perspective (Barkow, 1989; Gilbert, 1989, 1998, 2007a; Hrdy, 2009). Throughout mammalian evolution, the abilities to elicit care (Bowlby, 1969; Mikulincer & Shaver, 2007), to be supported and accepted by others (Hrdy, 2009), to create and work with allies (Baumeister & Leary, 1995), and to navigate the challenges of the various competitions of life have played crucial roles in survival and reproduction (Gilbert, 1989, 2009a). There is now good evidence that the forms and quality of care in childhood affect brain development (Cozolino, 2007). In addition, throughout life, positive caring relationships have a significant impact on physiological systems, regulation of emotions, and sense of self (Cacioppo, Berston, Sheridan, & McClintock, 2000; Cozolino, 2007). We can see this in people's basic social motives and desires. For the most part, humans want to be seen as attractive social agents, loved and valued; they want to be chosen as (for example) a favored kin/family member, as a friend, a lover, and an employee (Barkow, 1989; Gilbert, 1998). Believing that we have created positive feelings and images about the self in the mind of the other gives rise to a sense of safeness within one's social network; we know that others will be positively disposed towards us, helpful and nonattacking. In contrast, being uninteresting or unattractive to others, such that one will not be chosen or valued, is threatening because one cannot count on others, and they may even become neglecting, rejecting, or hostile. Over millions of years, human survival has depended on gaining and maintaining good reputations among others and being able to count on others for sharing, support, and help (Barkow, 1989; Hrdy, 2009).

In addition to various motivational systems that orient us to seek out and develop sharing, supportive, and caring relationships, humans have a whole range of psychological abilities and mechanisms for working out and "guessing" what other people might be feeling and thinking about us. These have been labeled in various ways, such as perspective taking, mind-reading skills, mentalizing skills, and theory of mindskills (e.g., Allen & Fonagy, 2007; Hrdy, 2009; Malle & Hodges, 2005). These skills allow us to judge how we exist for others and thus the quality of our relationships with them. However, these competencies for mind reading are not always used appropriately or accurately (Nickerson, 1999). For example, people who feel badly about themselves (e.g., they are overweight) may assume others also will also judge them negatively. People may feel shamed in the eyes of others because they project (assume) negative emotions in the mind of others about the self, when others may actually have positive views (Hackmann, Surawy, & Clark, 1998). We can also read incorrect intentions in the minds of others. This can happen in therapy, too. For example, a therapist arrives late, and the client reads this as the therapist's disinterest in him or her before discovering that the therapist had been held up by a motorway crash. The client struggles to do a between-session piece of work and imagines that the therapist sees him or her as not trying or not up to it and, as a result, worries that the therapist will be critical or even want to end the therapy. Then there is the classic fear held by clients that the therapist will find out something about them that he or she doesn't like, and then the client will be stuck with a therapist who "does not really like me but has to pretend to like me." All these are examples of how people feel they exist in the minds of others. Clearly then, mind reading; how we think about the feelings, thoughts, motives, intentions, and mental states of others, especially what we think they think and feel about us; and how we experience ourselves in the minds of others all play a major role in the experience of external shame. It is the huge benefits that come from being seen as attractive and liked, in contrast to the major threat associated with being seen as unattractive or disliked, that may drive mentalizing abilities (Gilbert, 1998, 2002).

Internal Shame

Internal shame is related to internally focused attention (in contrast to externally focused attention, as in external shame) with negative feelings and judgments about ourselves— the dark mirror within. In internal shame, the feelings about oneself can vary from disappointment, frustration, and anger to disgust and contempt (Whelton & Greenberg, 2005). Accompanying negative feelings about oneself is *self-criticism*, the stream of negative thoughts, evaluations, and judgments about the self (Gilbert, Clarke, Hempel, Miles, & Irons, 2004). Internal shame can be focused on specific aspects of the self, such as body appearance or weight, or on more general abilities or inner experiences (e.g., feeling less intelligent than others, feeling out of control of one's emotions or moods, feeling damaged and flawed because of sexual abuse). People can also have a sense of shame about inner feelings or fantasies or images that "just pop into" one's mind (i.e., unwanted intrusions). Indeed, feeling there is something bad or shameful about oneself because of unpleasant, aggressive, sadistic, or sexual thoughts is the basis of some obsessional disorders, and deshaming people is an important therapeutic process (Baer, 2002).

Interactions Between Internal and External Shame: The Case of Tim

It is useful to tease out how memory of self and memory of others operate within the shame dynamic (Kaufman, 1989). For example, Tim had an aggressive, overly critical father. He had various experiences of being labeled stupid and lazy. Processing such a memory in detail can illuminate how such shame is manifested. Tim remembered a time when he brought his school report home and it wasn't very good. His father became extremely aggressive. Tim could remember his father turning red in the face and directing anger and contempt toward him. So Tim had a powerful experience (memory) of having stimulated rage in the mind of the other and of that rage being directed at him. There was also the fear that his father would lash out and hurt or harm him. In regard to his own emotions in that moment, he remembers feeling very vulnerable and small and trying to curl up to avoid being hit. He recalled his heart racing, with intense fear flushing through his body. Co-occurring with this high level of threat arousal, he was being verbally labeled as lazy and stupid (his father used more colorful language).

In addition to these traditionally understood aspects of a shame experience are others of importance. First, there was a feeling of being trapped. Tim felt he could not get away; there was nowhere he could run to hide from potential attack and what was happening to him. Indeed, the experience of being unable to get away yet wanting to run is common in shame, and these feelings can reemerge during a triggering of a shame memory in therapy or in the interaction (as a transference). Second, his mother was frightened of her husband, and so in that moment Tim felt totally alone—there was no rescue, no one to protect him. It is no surprise, then, that shame experiences often involve an intense sense of personal isolation, in part because in the original shame experience the person really was alone; there really was no rescue. For people whose shame is linked to school bullying, they, too, often have the same experience because the bully has frightened others so much that no one will come to rescue the victim.

So we can see that Tim's shame memory had different components relating to (a) his impression of what he stimulated in the mind of others, (b) feelings of being trapped but also stimulated defenses (e.g., fear and wanting to run or hide), (c) the self-defining labels that are being wired in in this high arousal state (e.g., "stupid"), and (d) what he can expect from others (e.g., absence and no rescue; being alone with the threat). For Tim, these emotional memories were fused together and could operate through fast processing roots and be (re)activated in a context of criticism. It is by carefully unpacking the emotions related to such memories and clarifying his experience of the other and of himself that Tim could begin to see the power of such experiences. A fifth element can be the postshame adaptation process in which Tim might apologize and try harder, avoid or stay quiet to avoid his father's anger, engage in dissociative defenses, or slip into a depression. It is always useful to explore the postshame safety strategies (e.g., things people do to try to avoid shame in the future; Gilbert, 2010).

If we look closely, we can also see that Tim's self-criticism was linked to fear. He noted that if he made mistakes, there was a kind of panic in him and an aggressive inner voice saying, "Oh, now look what you've done." He felt angry with himself for letting himself down and making himself vulnerable. Self-criticism also arose from internalizing a parental definition of self. Sachs-Ericsson, Verona, Joiner, and Preacher (2006) found that children who are shamed by their parents (they used the term *verbally abused*) by being called "stupid" or "bad" may be especially vulnerable to self-criticism by internalizing these labels. They found that self-criticism fully mediated the relationship between parental shaming (verbal abuse) and depression and anxiety, a finding replicated by Irons, Gilbert, Baldwin, Baccus, and Palmer (2006).

Self-criticism is a key mediator between traumatic or potentially shaming external events and psychopathology. Feiring, Taska, and Lewis (2002) found that in both children and adolescents, the ability to cope and come to terms with sexual abuse was significantly related to attributional style (self vs. other blame), with self-blaming and experience of shame (feeling bad and/or damaged) associated with vulnerability to psychopathology. Irons et al. (2006) found that self-criticism (and an inability to be self-reassuring) mediates the relationship between recall of overprotective and rejecting parenting and depression. Such data suggest that it is the way in which difficult, stressful, and traumatic experiences influence self-to-self relating that is key to vulnerability to psychopathology.

Dunkley, Zuroff, and Blankstein (2003) suggested that self-critical perfectionists experience chronic dysphoria "because they experience minor hassles in catastrophic terms and perceive others as condemning, unwilling or unavailable to help them in times of stress" (p. 235). Thus, the experience of being alone, beyond rescue, with no one to help is central to the shame experience.

RECOGNIZING SHAME IN THE THERAPEUTIC CONTEXT

So shame arises when the self experiences being devalued, marginalized, criticized, rejected, threatened, or harmed. Because psychotherapy focuses on negative feelings, worries, anxieties, and depression, which are often textured by a sense of inadequacy, and difficult, painful memories that may be textured by abuse and being intensely shamed, psychotherapy is an inherently shame managing process (Gilbert, 2002, 2007a, 2007b). So as people begin to engage with shame memories and themes, it is possible they will (a) feel increasing concerns about what the therapist is feeling about them; (b) become defensive; and (c) have unpleasant feelings within the self in that moment of being bad or inadequate, with a sense of being trapped, isolated, and alone. These experiences can flash though people like conditioned, body-based, emotional memories.

Client Shame

During conversations with clients, there are subtle indicators that we are touching on shame areas. Clients may go blank, show submissive crouched body postures, avoid topics (e.g., talk around topics but not clarify them), become anxious or angry, or point-blank refuse to reveal. Sometimes these clues are not obvious, except that the client is not improving. For example, a depressed man talked about problems at work and in his marriage, all of which seemed linked to his depression. It was some months before he told me that he was having a homosexual affair that was causing him considerable confusion and dilemmas. As a religious man, he thought he would go to hell. It was this that appeared to be at the root of his depression. He said he was ashamed to tell me and fearful of what I would think. This problem, in revealing the realities of his life, was clearly an inhibitor of our work together.

Not only can clients be ashamed to tell their therapist about life events or current behavior (e.g., abusing drugs or alcohol), they will rarely reveal behaviors that they know the therapist may disapprove of, such as being aggressive to their children or spouse. A client may present as depressed, but when the family is consulted, family members may complain of the client's irritability, anger, and unpleasantness at home. So shame can hinder accurate clinical formulation because clients are inclined to narrate their stories to minimize shame.

Clients can also be ashamed of their inner emotional and fantasy lives (Baer, 2002). Leahy (2002, 2005) pointed out that people can experience feelings and fantasies as major threats to self-integrity. These threats are linked to beliefs that certain emotions, desires, or fantasies are in some sense forbidden or a mark of sin or something bad about oneself. These unwanted emotions, desires, or fantasies might become overwhelming or confusing, or they may evoke shaming from others. Such urges may also be experienced as either of two types of "thought-action fusion." One type is focused on morality and a sense of shame and guilt: "If I think it, feel it, or imagine it, it's as bad as doing it." These intrusions are taken to imply something bad (shameful) about oneself as a person. The other type of thought-action fusion relates to thoughts producing events. For example, a client may believe that if he or she thinks of horrible events, such as a friend's car accident, then it could happen. The latter is more fear based, whereas the former is more shame based (Rachman & Safran, 1999).

The problem, of course, is that our minds can be susceptible to generating all kinds of strange and bizarre intrusive ideas, images, and fantasies that can be quite shocking to us (Baer, 2002). Some people are able to write them down and make a lot of money creating horror movies or books, but obsessional clients can become deeply ashamed and fearful of their fantasies (due to thought-action fusion). One of my first obsessional clients, who was in her 60s, had an intrusive image and thought of committing an illegal sexual act. This was so against her beliefs and religious values that she became severely depressed. The more she tried not to think about it, the more intrusive it became. She had suffered many years of depression and was very frightened, with deep shame. She was unable to talk to anybody, even her husband, about the things that went through her mind. Therapy progressed with discussion about the nature of intrusive fantasies, in general, and how we can become obsessively worried about them. She thought her troubling intrusive images had possibly been triggered by something she'd read in a newspaper.

When clients are frightened and deeply ashamed about their internal feelings, conflicts, or fantasies, the therapist can attempt to deshame such inner experiences so that they can be explored openly. The therapist can show nonjudgmental and caring curiosity to gather more information about the thoughts and other internal experiences that clients might feel ashamed of while conveying understanding that the human mind can easily create strange, unwanted, frightening, or unpleasant images, feelings, and ideas. This allows engagement with clients at a metacognitive level, such as addressing the meaning and interpretations given to intrusive feelings, thoughts, and images (Wells, 2000); developing a mindful stance toward them, and demonstrating acceptance or tolerance (Baer, 2002; Hayes, Strosahl, & Wilson, 2004).

Therapist Shame

A client tells his therapist that she is not as good as a prior therapist; a client tells her therapist that their work together is not helping and she is thinking of making a complaint; a client angrily accuses the therapist of "just sitting there, asking questions and not doing anything or giving anything back." A therapist recognizes that he or she has felt very affiliative or rescuing to a particular client and that he or she has actually been having sexual fantasies about the client. A therapist is overly critical to a client and then recognizes that the client reminds him of his own critical mother, whom he dislikes.

Therapists can be vulnerable to eruptions of shame over a whole range of issues, feelings, and difficulties (Pope et al., 2006). The way therapists recognize and cope with their own shame and fear of being shamed (e.g., with tolerance, mindfulness, or defensive acting out) can have a major impact on therapeutic outcomes (Safran & Muran, 2000). It is also extremely important in the supervisory relationship (see Chapter 13, this volume). Therapist shame episodes can arise from straightforward interactions in which clients imply that the therapy or therapist is inadequate, that the therapist is not helpful, or that the therapist is being unkind and doesn't understand the client. Therapists can react with mixtures of (a) external shame, worrying about what clients think about them, whether clients might spread negative information about them, and how that would affect their reputation with referring agents; (b) internal shame, reflecting on their own inadequacies and limitations; and (c) humiliation or feelings of anger at the client, with a desire to criticize him or her.

Early in my career, a client I had been working well with, a middle-aged woman who was improving, suddenly became acutely suicidal. My immediate anxiety was linked to anticipatory, external shame; I had visions of being taken to court for failing to stop her suicide, having all my case notes closely scrutinized, and being found deficient in some way. These thoughts flashed through my mind within seconds. These are not uncommon concerns; therapists are not immune from becoming frightened of external disapproval, criticism, and even prosecution. Ways of coping with external shame may involve trying to convince the client that one really is an adequate therapist or becoming more technique focused. If one is fearful of being scrutinized, criticized, disciplined, dismissed from service, or even prosecuted by external agents (e.g., because of a client's suicide), one might become highly defensive and seek hospital admission for the client even if this is not in the client's best interests. It is recognized that on psychiatric hospital wards, staff can become very defensive and unhelpful because they are working to avoid being externally shamed, criticized, or disciplined.

Another typical experience of therapist shame can occur when a client admits to falling in love with or having sexual fantasies about the therapist. While working in a day hospital some years ago, one of the female staff became very distressed when a male client admitted to falling in love with and fantasizing about her. This caused a serious rupture in the relationship, and she was unable to continue the therapy with the client. There are many reasons why therapists become disturbed by these transferences, but to avoid shaming the client it is possible simply to kindly and empathically reflect on "how painful it must be to fantasize and want things one can never have." The therapist can reflect that "perhaps these fantasies are only possible because you know the reality is not possible" (Gilbert, 2007c).

Therapists' internal shame reactions can involve confusion, anxiety, and difficulties responding to clients with confidence and clarity. The therapist may become very tentative and uncertain, and this can be picked up by the client. It is not just messages emanating from the client that can stimulate internal shame in the therapist. The therapist may have a number of unaddressed issues about his or her adequacy as a therapist. This is typically true for training and new therapists who worry whether they are doing things correctly, understanding the client sensitively, formulating accurately, and intervening appropriately. Shame may be a major reason that important material is not disclosed during supervision (Hahn, 2001; Yourman, 2003; Yourman & Farber, 1996; see also Chapter 13, this volume). Moreover, just as clients can feel ashamed of their emotions and fantasies, so can therapists. Areas of potential therapist shame have been explored in detail by Pope et al. (2006). Sexual, aggressive, or rejecting fantasies can be experienced as shaming by a therapist. Some therapists can feel self-conscious and ashamed if they are moved to tears with the client because they believe that they must always be in control and never show emotion.

It is possible, therefore, for different feelings, including anxiety, irritation, and even rage or sexual feelings, to be aroused in the therapist during the course of therapy. How the therapist is able to recognize, be mindful of, tolerate, and refrain from acting out these inner feelings can be key to the outcome. Recent research looking at the kinds of events that stimulate shame among therapists suggests that more attention needs to be given to training therapists to recognize and deal with their shame and shame reactions (Schroder, Gilbert, & McEwan, 2008).

The potential for shame, especially external shame, is clearly an issue in a group therapy context where one is "on display" to an audience and issues (for the therapist) of authority, safety, and control can be prominent. Shame and shaming can be one process by which hierarchies are established within group contexts (Gilbert & McGuire, 1998). So how the people in a group engage in such interactions, how the therapist works with them, and how he or she deals with personal attacks or time "hogging" can be important for creating a safe environment. A few writers have focused on clients' experiences of shame within therapy groups (Alonso & Rutan, 1988; Gans & Weber, 2000; Lear, 1990; Wyse, 1987; see also Chapter 5, this volume), and MacNab (1995) and Livingston (2006) provided experience-near personal accounts of their own shame experiences as group therapists.

DESHAMING

There are many ways in which therapists can engage in a process of deshaming. Providing psychoeducation, providing validation, reducing self-blame, distinguishing shame-based self-attacking from compassionate self-correction, distinguishing shame from guilt, and using the therapeutic relationship are a few of these ways.

Providing Psychoeducation

Psychoeducation on the complexities of our evolved and socially shaped minds can be an important early step in treatment. For example, the therapist can explain that our minds are the result of evolution, and as such they have different feelings, passions, desires, and fears, and sometimes these can be very intense. We did not design our brains; therefore, much of the potential for such feelings is part of that design, and it is not our fault that we have these potentials. Giving up self-blame and self-condemnation for our spontaneous feelings can open the door to becoming more mindful and compassionate with them and taking responsibility for actions (Gilbert, 2010).

Psychoeducation can also be important in helping people understand their own particular patterns of feelings associated with shame. For example, if a client presents a shame memory such as being bullied or criticized (as in the case of Tim), the therapist can help link feelings of shame, feelings of aloneness, and a sense of being trapped as understandable experiences flowing from a traumatic experience. So making sense of shame and depersonalizing can help some people.

Normalizing relates to psychoeducation and helps people understand that our minds can be full of conflicting and powerful feelings and emotions, simply because that's the way the brain functions (Baer, 2002). One can point to real-life events or novels and films as indicators of how many other humans can feel and think in these certain ways. Normalizing helps counteract shame that one's emotions are abnormal, are indicative of something wrong or flawed with the self, or cannot be revealed to others (Leahy, 2002). Normalizing can also help people recognize that we can fear being shamed by our emotions because our emotions can feel overwhelming or controlling and we could let something slip or act in shameful ways (e.g., become aggressive). These are represented in the popular media with films like *The Hulk* or classic literature such as *Dr. Jekyll and Mr. Hyde*, in which the character appears to be taken over by a potential within the self, which leads to subsequent shame. Similarly, we can be overwhelmed by anxiety or doubt and go along with others in a way that that we are then ashamed of, as did a recent client who had a one-night stand with a man at a party because she felt too submissive to resist and subsequently became ashamed of her feelings and actions.

Normalizing is also directed at helping clients recognize and cope with ambivalence, such as learning that we can have different and conflicting feelings for the same event. For example, having intense rage doesn't mean one is not a nice person, and having sexual feelings outside of marriage is not an indication of poor moral character. Leahy (2002) developed a useful measure for people to look at the degree to which they have shame-prone and simplistic views about emotions. He also suggested that people have these difficulties because of a lack of emotional coaching or not having had their feelings understood and validated by others as children.

Providing Validation

Validating clients' experiences and emotions and helping them make sense of these experiences and emotions are thus key to helping people reduce shame. The therapist can help the client make sense of and recognize the genuine basis of his or her feelings (e.g., "It is understandable that you feel threatened by this because . . . ," "It is understandable that you were enraged by this because . . . "). This is often in the face of the client's own invalidation when he or she experiences thoughts such as, "I should not feel like this; there is something wrong with me; I am bad or weak to feel like this. . . ." This does not mean that the therapist doesn't also try to help the client gain a different perspective on things, but if this is done too quickly, without validation, it's easy for shame-prone clients (in particular) to simply assume their feelings are wrong because they are "thinking wrong."

Reducing Self-Blame

Self-blaming and self-shaming occur for many reasons, some of which are defensive. For example, in the presence of powerful others, people who tend to be anxious and feel subordinate are more likely to self-blame than are people who are less anxious and more secure (Gilbert & Irons, 2005). Trower, Sherling, Beech, Horrop, and Gilbert (1998) asked socially anxious and non–

socially anxious students to engage in a conversation with a lecturer while being videotaped. The lecturer was part of the study and (unknown to the students) was instructed to break conversational rules, such as butting in and changing the subject. On viewing the videotape, socially anxious students blamed themselves for the problems in the conversation (e.g., they were being boring), whereas non–socially anxious students blamed the lecturer. Forrest and Hokanson (1975) found that depressed people were more self-punitive in a conflict situation than nondepressed people. The authors suggested that this self-blaming and submissive style was a learned coping response for dealing with conflicts.

Buchbinder and Eisikovits (2003) found that women often feel shame and self-blame in the presence of a powerful, hostile spouse and concluded that this is one reason women remain in violent and abusive relationships. Andrews and Brewin (1990) found that when women were in an abusive relationship, they tended to self-blame for the violence, but once they had escaped (and were safe), they blamed the abuser. Sharhabani-Arzy, Amir, and Swisa (2005) found that in the context of domestic violence, self-criticism (a form of internal shaming) significantly increased the risk of posttraumatic stress disorder. Hence, some elements of negative self-evaluations may be fueled by nonconscious submissive strategies to cope with hostile, rejecting others, which then become part of the sense of oneself (Gilbert & Irons, 2005; Gilbert & McGuire, 1998).

Therapists need to be aware of these tendencies for a number of reasons. First, self-blame can be a protective strategy, and therefore, trying to undermine it with only a cognitive focus might prove difficult (Gilbert, 2010). It is always useful to ask people what they would fear if they gave up their self-blaming and self-critical style. Second, if therapeutic ruptures are actually caused by the therapist, they may be attributed to the self by the client. The therapist's preparedness to acknowledge and accept responsibility for ruptures can be very important (Safran & Muran, 2000).

Distinguishing Shame-Based Self-Attacking From Compassionate Self-Correction

It is useful to help clients recognize that shame-based self-criticizing and attacking usually have emotions of anger, contempt, and disappointment as part of the emotional tone. Indeed, Whelton and Greenberg (2005) argued that the emotions of anger and contempt that accompany self-criticism and self-attacking are the main sources of feeling shame. The therapist can offer a compassionate, kind, and supportive model for dealing with setbacks and errors in nonshaming ways, helping people switch to "compassionate self-correction," with which one becomes motivated to recognize errors and to take responsibility to correct, grow, and improve (for further discussion, see Gilbert, 2009a, pp. 326–329).

Distinguishing Shame From Guilt

In some contexts, the therapist's role is not just to help clients lessen shame but also to help them face and take responsibility in contexts in which they may have acted harmfully. Here it helps if the therapist is clear on the distinction between shame and guilt.

First, guilt has a different focus from shame (Tangney & Dearing, 2002). In guilt, we usually focus on the harm or hurt we have caused other people by our actions. Shame is more about harm to oneself (being a bad person in some way or being seen as bad). Second, guilt tends to focus on specific events—"I feel guilty because I did this or failed to do that," whereas (again) shame is focused on feelings about the self, such as being inadequate, flawed, or unattractive. Third, whereas in shame we want to hide and cover up or be aggressive, in guilt we want to repair things and put things right. Fourth, guilt (often) arises when there are conflicts because what we want may adversely affect or harm others. For example, one may feel that a certain relationship is not working, that one doesn't love the person anymore and wants to leave, and at the same time one knows that breaking up would be very damaging to that person. These "guilt traps" can be a reason for people staying in relationships even when they are unsatisfactory and are causing low mood (Gilbert, 2007c). Guilt can also be associated with conflicts in which one person's gain is another person's loss (O'Connor, Berry, Weiss, & Gilbert, 2002).

The attention and ruminative focus in shame are on the self, with feelings of anxiety, anger, or depression. In contrast, when we have done something that has caused hurt or done harm, there can be feelings of sorrow linked to feelings of remorse and regret. It's these feelings that make us want to put things right. Guilt feelings require empathy and being able to imagine how we would feel in another person's situation. Mentalizing in shame is trying to work out what others think and feel about oneself, whereas mentalizing in guilt does not have this self-focused objective.

For example, a man accused of domestic violence might feel bad about himself, realizing that he lost control, and he might be worried about a conviction and what his wife now thinks of him. He may even want to make amends, but his focus is on the self, how bad he is and how others will blame him. If he is able to shift perspective from shame to guilt, he will begin to soften this shameful self-focus and self-attack and instead really try to work out how and why he acts violently toward his wife (e.g., perhaps he uses aggression to cope with feelings of vulnerability). He may then consider the harm he has done, become empathic to the distress he has caused, and become less self-focused.

Using the Therapeutic Relationship

The therapeutic relationship is one of the most important sources of deshaming because clients can experience themselves "in the mind of another" with acceptance and understanding. To feel understood and validated can be an important stepping-stone toward self-acceptance. The therapeutic relationship is, of course, a cocreation that emerges from the interaction between the client and the therapist (Gilbert & Leahy, 2007; Zuroff & Blatt, 2006). Nonetheless, the personal and trained skills of the therapist are key to the process and outcome, and therapist empathy and warmth are crucial in approaching and enabling shame material to be revealed and discussed. In addition, the therapist is sensitive to the possible internal shaming the client is engaging with and actively looks for these themes (e.g., "I am stupid to think like this"; "My therapist thinks I am immature with my emotions"; "These fantasies are perverted"). So to help clients overcome the difficulty of revealing potentially shaming material, the therapist needs to be to be empathically attuned with the client, with appropriate understanding of emotions and what the client fears. The therapist will cope more effectively with these client emotions if he or she is familiar with, and not shamed by, his or her own feelings. For example, if a therapist is fearful of his or her own sadistic fantasies, he or she may struggle to help clients compassionately understand and come to terms with sadistic fantasies of their own. Or if a therapist lacks confidence, he or she might struggle when clients are confrontational. In other words, as therapists, we need to feel safe enough with our own "shadow material" and competencies to invite exploration and tolerate being emotionally stirred up by clients.

The therapist helps the client (re)code his or her inner world as safe to the extent that although some memories, emotions, or fantasies are unpleasant or strange, they are normal to our humanity (Neff, 2003). These thoughts and emotions are manageable once we accept them and no longer fight to suppress or deny them or label ourselves negatively as a consequence of having them. This is a key component of a number of different schools of therapy, such as dialectical behavior therapy (Linehan, 1993) and acceptance and commitment therapy (Hayes et al., 2004), as well as being central to compassion-based approaches (Gilbert, 2000, 2010; Neff, 2003).

COMPASSION FOCUSED THERAPY

Compassion, with its focus on acceptance, understanding, and affiliation, can be a powerful antidote to the alienating experiences of shame (Gilbert, 2010). Indeed, compassion focused therapy was developed with and for people who have high levels of shame and self-criticism (Gilbert, 2000, 2007c, 2009a,

2010; Gilbert & Irons, 2005). These individuals often come from neglectful or abusive and harsh backgrounds. As a result, they often experience the external world and other people's minds as easily turning against them, becoming disapproving, critical, rejecting, or hostile. When setbacks occur, they experience their inner world and sense of self as also being harsh, empty, and critical. There is a kind of pincer movement of threat or attack from without and within. In essence, these individuals have few positive emotional memories to draw on and few skills to be self-reassuring, kind, and soothing.

Research on emotion regulation systems has suggested that there are two very different types of positive emotion system (Depue & Morrone-Strupinsky, 2005). One is a drive and activating system linked especially to dopamine. This system motivates us to achieve and gives us feelings of pleasure and excitement. For example, if a person wins the lottery and becomes a millionaire, he or she will likely become excited and restless and may find it difficult to sleep for a few days. In contrast, a very different type of positive emotion regulation system, linked to endorphin and oxytocin, gives rise to soothing and calming feelings. This system is linked to contentment and peaceful well-being (Carter, 1998).

Crucial to working with shame is the recognition that research has shown that the endorphin and oxytocin systems were central to the evolution of mammalian attachment systems (Bell, 2001; Lee, Macbeth, Pagani, & Young, 2009; Panksepp, 1998). Feelings of being cared for and caring about others stimulate this system and have soothing qualities, even in the face of threat (Carter, 1998). This means that kindness has innate qualities to soothe and down-regulate the sense of threat and to create feelings of closeness and connectedness (Heinrichs, Baumgartner, Kirschbaum, & Ehlert, 2003), whereas criticism and shame do the opposite (Dickerson & Kemeny, 2004). Indeed, there is good evidence that experiencing caring, kindness, and gentleness from others is a soothing and safe-creating experience that down-regulates the threat and stress system (Wang, 2005).

There is also evidence that being kind, reassuring, gentle, and supportive with ourselves (in contrast to being self-critical) is linked to low vulnerability to psychopathology (Neff, 2003; Neff & Vonk, 2009; Zuroff, Santor, & Mongrain, 2005). Gilbert et al. (2004) showed a negative relationship between depression and the ability to be self-reassuring when things go wrong. Gilbert, Baldwin, Irons, Baccus, and Palmer (2006) also showed that abilities to create compassionate images of oneself were negatively associated with depression. Furthermore, self-criticism was associated with difficulties in creating such images and was positively associated with difficulty in being self-reassuring. In a recent functional magnetic resonance imaging (fMRI) study, Longe and colleagues (2010) explored the neurophysiology of being self-reassuring in contrast to being self-critical regarding potential shame events (e.g., imagining getting a letter about a third job rejection). They found that efforts to be self-reassuring, in contrast to self-critical, activated different brain areas:

> Self-criticism was associated with activity in lateral prefrontal cortex regions and dorsal anterior cingulate, therefore linking self-critical thinking to error processing and resolution, and also behavioral inhibition. Self-reassurance was associated with left temporal pole and insula activation, suggesting that efforts to be self-reassuring engage similar regions to expressing compassion and empathy towards others. (p. 1849)

Self-critical people can struggle with cognitive interventions, commonly saying, "I understand the logic; it all makes sense, but I can't feel any different." CFT suggests that one reason for this is that the endorphin-oxytocin-linked soothing system that gives rise to feelings of reassurance and calm is not easily accessed by the client (Gilbert, 2010; Gilbert et al., 2006). The question is, Can we teach people how to practice and generate a particular type of self-to-self relationship that is based on self-compassion (Gilbert, 2009a; Neff, 2003) with the aim of stimulating the soothing system?

Compassionate Mind Training

In CFT, a compassion focus influences all aspects of the therapy, including the therapeutic relationship, assessment, and case formulation (Gilbert, 2007b, 2010). *Compassionate mind training* refers to the specific exercises and interventions that are compassion focused. Because high-shame and self-critical people may have had little experience of compassion from others and of being self-compassionate (Gilbert & Procter, 2006), we have to teach it.

The Dalai Lama (1995) defined *compassion* as a sensitivity to the suffering of self and others with a deep commitment to try to relieve it, thus underscoring sensitivity, awareness, and prosocial motivation as key components of compassion. CFT follows this approach but was also originally influenced by Fogel, Melson, and Mistry's (1986) model of nurturance and the neurophysiological model of affiliation as presented by Depue and Morrone-Strupinsky (2005). Following Fogel et al.'s (1986) outline, CFT distinguishes attributes and qualities of compassion from the skills of compassion (for details, see Gilbert, 2009a, 2010). While reading through these attributes, keep in mind that in a number of studies, Tangney and colleagues have shown that shame significantly interferes with key attributes of compassion and especially empathy (Tangney & Dearing, 2002).

Compassion Attributes

A crucial element of compassion is motivation to be caring, supportive, and helpful. So in therapy, compassion work involves working with the client's motivation to see compassion as desirable and to be motivated to become more (self-) compassionate. At this first point, there may be resistance in the form of client beliefs that self-compassion is a weakness or a self-indulgence or that the client doesn't deserve compassion. Because sensitivity and noting distress is important to compassion, we teach clients how to become more attentive to their feelings and needs—and to those of others. Indeed, during therapy, clients can become aware of feelings and issues they had not really been aware of before, and they sometimes describe these in shame terms, such as "opening a can of worms." This can be a difficult time with a risk of early termination if such insights are experienced as overwhelming or confusing or if the implications of working with these insights seem too much to cope with.

It is difficult to be compassionate if we are unmoved and unsympathetic to our (or others') pain, fear, or emotional distress. Sympathy is related to being emotionally moved by distress (Eisenberg, 2002). Clearly, to be unmoved by distress and/or to have no desire to do anything about it is not conducive to compassion.

A fourth quality and attribute is learning to face up to, tolerate, and accept painful feelings, memories, and fantasies, rather than becoming self-critical or avoidant (Hayes et al., 2004; Wilson, 2009). With some clients this can also mean learning to tolerate positive as well as negative emotions. Some clients are frightened of positive feelings, believing they will be punished for them (e.g., "If I am happy today, something is bound to go wrong tomorrow" or "I can't trust the loving feelings from others" or "I don't deserve to be happy or kind to myself"). For some clients, the experience of kindness and warmth activates the attachment system and its associated negative memories (Gilbert, 2009a, 2010). So it is important to learn to tolerate negative emotions (that might otherwise prompt avoidance), as well as to tolerate positive feelings. Guided exposure and practice are the major ways of doing this.

A fifth attribute of compassion is empathy, which concerns how we come to think about, reflect on, and understand our own and other people's feelings, thoughts, and behaviors. These abilities have been linked to those of mentalizing and theory of mind (e.g., Fonagy & Luyten, 2009). Self-empathy uses similar processes and curiosity about why we feel what we feel or why we think what we think. Psychodynamic therapists suggest this is easier said than done because some of our motives are unconscious, but it is the act of trying to understand how our minds work that is important. Therapists try to help clients develop empathic insight into their difficulties and to mentalize as therapy progresses. One way of doing this is to help clients recognize that some of their feelings and actions may be linked to basic safety strategies. For example, a child who was frightened of her parents and thus developed appeasing and submissive strategies to avoid harm from them may grow up to be submissive to authority figures in general. So seeing powerful others as threatening (rather than helpful) and controlling that threat through appeasement and behavioral inhibition can be seen as part of a safety strategy learned in childhood. In addition, she may also be self-critical and lack assertiveness skills as a result of never standing up for herself, may have a fear of not being loved, and may be frightened and ashamed of her anger at others. A strategy that served as a safety function in one context can become a source of pain and despair later in life.

A sixth attribute is linked to "becoming mindful without judgment" (Kabat-Zinn, 2005). CFT teaches people to become aware of thoughts and feelings from an observing point of view. We don't judge thoughts, nor do we try to suppress or push them out of our minds. Rather, we learn to notice but not act on our thoughts and feelings. This does not mean we do not have preferences—clearly, the Dalai Lama would prefer the world to be more compassionate. So *compassionate nonjudgment* refers to giving up condemning and learning emotional tolerance while still working toward our goals (Gilbert, 2009a).

Skills

The skills of compassion involve learning to direct our attention in compassionate and helpful ways. For example, in the context of a failure, one might become anxious, angry, and self-critical, whereas compassionate attention is focusing on the things that will be helpful in the context of a failure. This might involve bringing to mind past successes or remembering the helpfulness of others; much depends on what the person finds to be compassionate for himself or herself (Gilbert, 2009a, 2010).

Compassionate reasoning or thinking involves various cognitive skills for balanced, objective thinking but also focuses on the emotional tone of our thoughts. For example, noting that our thoughts can become a bit extreme and black and white and reminding ourselves to look at the evidence and take a different perspective can be done either in the spirit of kindness and support or in a more hostile tone of "pull yourself together and stop being so extreme." So the emotional tone of a client's thinking, not just the content, is important. To help generate compassionate thoughts to counter anxious or depressive ones, clients can be asked to take the perspective of a compassionate person or to think about how they would talk to somebody they really cared about who was in the same situation as they are—to ask themselves the question, "What is a helpful way for me to think about this problem, situation, or difficulty?" and to focus on a kind voice tone.

An additional skill centers on learning how to behave compassionately toward oneself (and others) in ways that will help clients with their difficulties and move them forward in their life's journey. Sometimes self-compassionate behavior can mean treating oneself kindly (e.g., recognizing that we need a holiday or that we need the support of others), but self-compassionate behavior also requires the courage to face painful feelings and memories in order to overcome them. So self-compassionate behavior can be acting against depression, anxiety, or shame—behaving, revealing, or talking about topics that have been avoided. For example, a person with agoraphobia behaves compassionately when he or she is kind and encouraging to himself or herself when initiating a program of going out. Courage is easier when the client develops a self-compassionate focus that helps mindfulness and counteracts fretting, anxious, overly critical thoughts and feelings.

Key to all of these interventions and practices is paying particular attention to the importance of generating feelings of warmth, kindness, and support. It's very important that clients learn to approach these trainings and procedures not by bullying or forcing themselves to get better, but in a kind, encouraging, and supportive way. Generating this kind of orientation in the skills training can be difficult with shame-prone clients, but it can also be the basis of successful therapy (Gilbert & Procter, 2006).

The Compassionate Self and Compassionate Other

Compassionate interventions are related to a range of therapeutic processes that include formulation, developing a compassionate orientation to one's difficulties, and understanding and engaging in different elements of compassionate attention, thinking, feeling, and behavior. As noted, therapists are confronted with a whole range of experiences, including past behaviors, desires, fantasies, emotions, conflicts, memories, and intrusions, that people can be ashamed of, frightened of, and alienated by. The therapist can help the client see that to better face and tolerate these issues, a compassionate stance needs to be developed. One type of exercise that we provide to begin this process is called *developing the compassionate self*.

Imagery

In compassion focused approaches, imagery is used to try to create particular feelings and states of mind to facilitate people's ability to engage with shame (Gilbert, 2009a, 2009b). For example, Sonia suffered from anxiety during the day while at home but was also rather ashamed of it because, in her words, "There is nothing for me to be anxious about. . . . I just don't seem able to cope. . . . I feel I am a rather weak sort of person." Imagery was used to address these concerns. First, she was invited to sit comfortably but upright in her chair and to engage in a breathing exercise called "soothing breathing rhythm" that involves breathing slightly deeper and slower than normal with a focus on how the breath can give a sense of slowing in the body. She was then asked to imagine being a compassionate person (like an actor might imagine being a particular character to get into role). She was asked to reflect on her voice tones and the way she thinks when she's in "compassionate self" mode. She was asked to create a compassionate expression on her face. In addition, we focused on imagining oneself to be wise, confident, and kind, while at the same time recognizing that we may not in reality feel like this, but like an actor getting into a role, we're imagining what it might feel like to have these qualities. (For more detailed instructions, see Gilbert, 2010.) Fredrickson, Cohn, Coffey, Pek, and Finkel (2008) showed that loving kindness meditations (compassion directed to self, then others, then strangers) increase positive emotions, mindfulness, feelings of purpose in life, and social support and decrease illness symptoms.

When people are able to begin to have pursuance of this aspect of the self, they can then use it to engage with other aspects of the self. So, for example, when Sonia began to feel a sense of her inner compassion, she was asked to imagine looking at herself as if watching a video, seeing herself getting up in the morning and walking about in the house, engaging in various activities, observing the expressions on her face, and having sensitivity to the feelings going on inside her. She was then asked to just feel compassion for whatever anxiety she experienced in herself as she watched the images of herself. If Sonia began to feel self-critical, she would be asked to let the image fade and go back to just focusing on becoming the compassionate self before reengaging in the imagery exercise.

The idea is to create experiences in which clients can engage with problematic aspects of themselves, but through the eyes of the compassionate self. So, for example, one could work up to a shame event and look at it through the eyes of the compassionate self. There is, in fact, a 1,000-year-old Buddhist practice that is very similar to this called *feeding your demons* (Allione, 2008). These types of exercises can be very useful in helping people to step back from aspects they feel ashamed of while at the same time creating a particular compassionate orientation that is designed to activate the soothing system. Indeed, throughout the therapy the main focus of the work is strengthening the sense of the compassionate self and helping people recognize that we all have a number of other possible selves (e.g., an angry self, anxious self, lonely self, happy self) and that the compassionate self can be strengthened and used through practice (Gilbert, 2009a, 2010). This compassionate self then becomes a center from which we can explore more difficult memories and feelings. Taking a compassionate self position is very helpful in counteracting the tendency to slip into an aggressive self-critical stance when working in these areas.

Compassionate Other

In many Buddhist practices, compassionate meditations focus on imagining the compassionate other (usually a Buddha figure called a *bodhisattva*). Bodhisattvas are of many kinds (Vessantara, 1993); the one seen as the bodhisattva of compassion is known as Avalokiteshvara, who has limitless compassion. Many spiritual traditions also involve praying to a deity who will then be helpful to the self. Newberg and Waldman (2007) used fMRI and found that even those who were atheist showed important neurophysiological changes when imagining a compassionate being having compassion for them (see the section "Evidence for the Value of Developing Compassion"). Compassion imagery can therefore involve helping people generate images of a compassionate other who is wise, strong, kind, and nonjudgmental and who is relating to them in various ways.

Fear of Compassion

Some people become very anxious about feelings of self-warmth because such feelings are alien to them, or feelings of self-warmth may activate enormous grief and recognition of feelings of isolation and aloneness. One patient acknowledged that she felt people had never been kind to her before, so focusing on feelings of kindness for the self in imagery felt sad, opening up yearning for connectedness feelings and resulting in overwhelming grief. There can be different fears associated with engaging in intense grief, one of which can be the fear of falling apart in front of the therapist. Another can be fear of overwhelming pain and loneliness and not being able to see a way out. Sometimes intense grief takes them back to a trauma memory. The therapeutic intervention is clarification with the client, creating a therapeutic process of engaging with the feared emotion in a step-by-step approach. In a way it follows a desensitization process that one would follow with other kinds of feared emotions.

There can also be various cognitive beliefs about compassion, that it's a weakness (going soft), that one is letting one's guard down, or that one does not deserve it. Not uncommonly, though, behind these metacognitive beliefs are deeper fears about being in touch with affiliative emotions and the implication of compassion for self-identity (Gilbert, 2010). Whatever the source of fear of compassion, there is increasing evidence that some individuals, especially self-critical people, respond to compassion and compassion imagery as if they are threats (Longe et al., 2010; Rockliff, Gilbert, McEwan, Lightman, & Glover, 2008).

Evidence for the Value of Developing Compassion

There is increasing evidence that focusing on compassion has a range of benefits for people's health and well-being. For example, practices of imagining compassion for others produce changes in the frontal cortex, the immune system, and physical and emotional well-being (Lutz, Brefczynski-Lewis,

Johnstone, & Davidson, 2008). Hutcherson, Seppala, and Gross (2008) found that a brief loving-kindness meditation increased feelings of social connectedness and affiliation toward strangers. Fredrickson et al. (2008) found that six 60-minute weekly group sessions with home practice based on a CD of loving-kindness meditations (compassion directed to self, then others, then strangers) increased positive emotions, mindfulness, feelings of purpose in life, and social support and decreased illness symptoms. Rockliff et al. (2008) found that compassionate imagery increased heart rate variability and reduced cortisol levels in low self-critics (but not in high self-critics). As noted above, Longe et al. (2010), using fMRI, also found differences in how self-critics respond to self-reassurance and compassion.

In a small, uncontrolled study of people with chronic mental health problems, compassion training significantly reduced shame, self-criticism, depression, and anxiety (Gilbert & Procter, 2006). Compassion training has also been found to be helpful for people who hear psychotic voices (Mayhew & Gilbert, 2008). In a study of group-based CFT for 19 clients in a high-security psychiatric setting, Laithwaite and colleagues (2009) found

> a large magnitude of change for levels of depression and self-esteem. . . . A moderate magnitude of change was found for the social comparison scale and general psychopathology, with a small magnitude of change for shame. . . . These changes were maintained at 6-week follow-up. (p. 521)

In the field of relationships and well-being, there is now good evidence that caring for others, showing appreciation and gratitude, and having empathic and mentalizing skills do much to build positive relationships, which significantly influences well-being as well as mental and physical health (Cacioppo et al., 2000; Cozolino, 2007). Evidence is increasing that the kind of self we try to become influences our well-being and social relationships and that compassionate rather than self-focused self-identities are associated with better outcomes (Crocker & Canevello, 2008). Taken together, there are good grounds for the further development of and research into CFT.

Neff (2003), a pioneer in studies of self-compassion, has shown that self-compassion can be distinguished from self-esteem and predicts some aspects of well-being better than self-esteem (Neff & Vonk, 2009). Self-compassion also aids in coping with academic failure (Neely, Schallert, Mohammed, Roberts, & Chen, 2009; Neff, Hsieh, & Dejitterat, 2005). Compassionate letter writing to oneself improves coping with life events and reduces depression (Leary, Tate, Adams, Allen, & Hancock, 2007). Taken together, these research results provide growing evidence for the value of developing compassion to enhance well-being, to improve social relationships, and as a focus for psychotherapy.

CONCLUSION

Humans have evolved to be highly regulated by their relationships. Caring, supportive, and protective relationships have major influences on physiological and psychological states. In contrast, critical, rejecting, and hostile relationships create stress and mental distress. In CFT, we suggest that the same is true of our internal relationships. If we have learned to be relatively self-accepting, kind, and self-soothing, this helps us deal with a range of difficulties that can arise in life. In contrast, if we are highly shame prone, have few memories of soothing, have many memories of shaming, and have a very critical self-evaluating relationship with ourselves, coping with life stresses becomes very tough. Developing compassion for ourselves and others is one way of healing shame.

REFERENCES

Allen, J. G., & Fonagy, P. (Eds.). (2007). *Handbook of mentalization-based treatment.* Chichester, England: Wiley.

Allione, T. (2008). *Feeding your demons.* New York, NY: Little, Brown.

Alonso, A., & Rutan, J. S. (1988). The experience of shame and the restoration of self-respect in group-therapy. *International Journal of Group Psychotherapy, 38*, 3–27.

Andrews, B., & Brewin, C. R. (1990). Attributions of blame for marital violence: A study of antecedents and consequences. *Journal of Family and Marriage, 52,* 757–767. doi:10.2307/352940

Baer, L. (2002). *The imp mind: Exploring the silent epidemic of obsessional bad thoughts.* New York, NY: Plume.

Barkow, J. H. (1989). *Darwin, sex, and status: Biological approaches to mind and culture.* Toronto, Ontario, Canada: University of Toronto Press.

Baumeister, R. F., & Leary, M. R. (1995). The need to belong: Desire for interpersonal attachments as a fundamental human motivation. *Psychological Bulletin, 117,* 497–529. doi:10.1037/0033-2909.117.3.497

Bell, D. C. (2001). Evolution of care giving. *Personality and Social Psychology Review, 5,* 216–229. doi:10.1207/S15327957PSPR0503_3

Bowlby, J. (1969). *Attachment: Attachment and loss* (Vol. 1). London, England: Hogarth Press.

Buchbinder, E., & Eisikovits, Z. (2003). Battered women's entrapment in shame: A phenomenological study. *American Journal of Orthopsychiatry, 73,* 355–366. doi:10.1037/0002-9432.73.4.355

Cacioppo, J. T., Berston, G. G., Sheridan, J. F., & McClintock, M. K. (2000). Multi-level integrative analysis of human behavior: Social neuroscience and the complementing nature of social and biological approaches. *Psychological Bulletin, 126,* 829–843. doi:10.1037/0033-2909.126.6.829

Carter, C. S. (1998). Neuroendocrine perspectives on social attachment and love. *Psychoneuroendocrinology, 23,* 779–818. doi:10.1016/S0306-4530(98)00055-9

Cozolino, L. (2007). *The neuroscience of human relationships: Attachment and the developing brain.* New York, NY: Norton.

Crocker, J., & Canevello, A. (2008). Creating and undermining social support in communal relationships: The role of compassionate and self-image goals. *Journal of Personality and Social Psychology, 95,* 555–575. doi:10.1037/0022-3514.95.3.555

Dalai Lama. (1995). *The power of compassion.* New Delhi, India: HarperCollins.

Depue, R. A., & Morrone-Strupinsky, J. V. (2005). A neurobehavioral model of affiliative bonding. *Behavioral and Brain Sciences, 28,* 313–350.

Dickerson, S. S., & Kemeny, M. E. (2004). Acute stressors and cortisol response: A theoretical integration and synthesis of laboratory research. *Psychological Bulletin, 130,* 355–391. doi:10.1037/0033-2909.130.3.355

Dunkley, D. M., Zuroff, D. C., & Blankstein, K. R. (2003). Self-critical perfectionism and daily affect: Dispositional and situational influences on stress and coping. *Journal of Personality and Social Psychology, 84,* 234–252. doi:10.1037/0022-3514.84.1.234

Eisenberg, N. (2002). Empathy-related emotional responses, altruism, and their socialization. In R. Davidson & A. Harrington (Eds.), *Visions of compassion: Western scientists and Tibetan Buddhists examine human nature* (pp. 131–164). New York, NY: Oxford University Press.

Feiring, C., Taska, L. S., & Lewis, M. (2002). Adjustment following sexual abuse discovery: The role of shame and attribution style. *Developmental Psychology, 38,* 79–92. doi:10.1037/0012-1649.38.1.79

Fogel, A., Melson, G. F., & Mistry, J. (1986). Conceptualising the determinants of nurturance: A reassessment of sex differences. In A. Fogel & G. F. Melson (Eds.), *Origins of nurturance: Developmental, biological and cultural perspectives on caregiving* (pp. 53–67). Hillsdale, NJ: Erlbaum.

Fonagy, P., & Luyten, P. (2009). A developmental, mentalization-based approach to the understanding and treatment of borderline personality disorder. *Development and Psychopathology, 21,* 1355–1381. doi:10.1017/S0954579409990198

Forrest, M. S., & Hokanson, J. E. (1975). Depression and autonomic arousal reduction accompanying self-punitive behavior. *Journal of Abnormal Psychology, 84,* 346–357. doi:10.1037/0021-843X.84.4.346

Fredrickson, B. L., Cohn, M. A., Coffey, K. A., Pek, J., & Finkel, S. A. (2008). Open hearts build lives: Positive emotions, induced through loving-kindness mediation, build consequential personal resources. *Journal of Personality and Social Psychology, 95,* 1045–1062. doi:10.1037/a0013262

Gans, J. S., & Weber, R. L. (2000). The detection of shame in group psychotherapy: Uncovering the hidden emotion. *International Journal of Group Psychotherapy*, *50*, 381–396.

Gilbert, P. (1989). *Human nature and suffering*. London, England: Erlbaum.

Gilbert, P. (1998). What is shame? Some core issues and controversies. In P. Gilbert & B. Andrews (Eds.), *Shame: Interpersonal behavior, psychopathology and culture* (pp. 3–38). New York, NY: Oxford University Press.

Gilbert, P. (2000). Social mentalities: Internal "social" conflicts and the role of inner warmth and compassion in cognitive therapy. In P. Gilbert & K. G. Bailey (Eds.), *Genes on the couch: Explorations in evolutionary psychotherapy* (pp. 118–150). Hove, England: Psychology Press.

Gilbert, P. (2002). Evolutionary approaches to psychopathology and cognitive therapy. *Cognitive Psychotherapy: An International Quarterly*, *16*, 263–294.

Gilbert, P. (2007a). The evolution of shame as a marker for relationship security. In J. L. Tracy, R. W. Robins, & J. P. Tangney (Eds.), *The self-conscious emotions: Theory and research* (pp. 283–309). New York, NY: Guilford Press.

Gilbert, P. (2007b). Evolved minds and compassion in the therapeutic relationship. In P. Gilbert & R. Leahy (Eds.), *The therapeutic relationship in the cognitive behavioural psychotherapies* (pp. 106–142). London, England: Routledge.

Gilbert, P. (2007c). *Psychotherapy and counselling for depression* (3rd ed.). London, England: Sage.

Gilbert, P. (2009a). *The compassionate mind*. London, England: Constable Robinson.

Gilbert, P. (2009b). Evolved minds and compassion focused imagery in depression. In L. Stropa (Ed.), *Imagery and the threatened self: Perspectives on mental imagery in cognitive therapy* (pp. 206–231). London, England: Routledge.

Gilbert, P. (2010). *Compassion focused therapy: The distinctive features*. London, England: Routledge.

Gilbert, P., Baldwin, M., Irons, C., Baccus, J., & Palmer, M. (2006). Self-criticism and self-warmth: An imagery study exploring their relation to depression. *Journal of Cognitive Psychotherapy: An International Quarterly*, *20*, 183–200. doi:10.1891/jcop.20.2.183

Gilbert, P., Clarke, M., Hempel, S., Miles, J. N. V., & Irons, C. (2004). Criticizing and reassuring oneself: An exploration of forms, style and reasons in female students. *British Journal of Clinical Psychology*, *43*, 31–50. doi:10.1348/014466504772812959

Gilbert, P., & Irons, C. (2005). Focused therapies and compassionate mind training for shame and self attacking. In P. Gilbert (Ed.), *Compassion: Conceptualisations, research and use in psychotherapy* (pp. 263–325). London, England: Routledge.

Gilbert, P., & Leahy, R. (Eds.). (2007). *The therapeutic relationship in the cognitive behavioural psychotherapies*. London, England: Routledge.

Gilbert, P., & McGuire, M. (1998). Shame, social roles and status: The psychobiological continuum from monkey to human. In P. Gilbert & B. Andrews

(Eds.), *Shame: Interpersonal behavior, psychopathology and culture* (pp. 99–125). New York, NY: Oxford University Press.

Gilbert, P., & Procter, S. (2006). Compassionate mind training for people with high shame and self-criticism: A pilot study of a group therapy approach. *Clinical Psychology & Psychotherapy, 13,* 353–379. doi:10.1002/cpp.507

Hackmann, A., Surawy, C., & Clark, D. M. (1998). Seeing yourself through others' eyes: A study of spontaneous occurring images in social phobia. *Behavioural and Cognitive Psychotherapy, 26,* 3–12. doi:10.1017/S1352465898000022

Hahn, W. K. (2001). The experience of shame in psychotherapy supervision. *Psychotherapy: Theory, Research, & Practice, 38,* 272–282. doi:10.1037/0033-3204.38.3.272

Hayes, S. C., Strosahl, K. D., & Wilson, K. G. (2004). *Acceptance and commitment therapy: An experiential approach to behavior change.* New York, NY: Guilford Press.

Heinrichs, M., Baumgartner, T., Kirschbaum, C., & Ehlert, U. (2003). Social support and oxytocin interact to suppress cortisol and subjective response to psychosocial stress. *Biological Psychiatry, 54,* 1389–1398. doi:10.1016/S0006-3223(03)00465-7

Hrdy, S. B. (2009). *Mothers and others: The evolutionary origins of mutual understanding.* Cambridge, MA: Harvard University Press.

Hutcherson, C. A., Seppala, E. M., & Gross, J. J. (2008). Loving-kindness meditation increases social connectedness. *Emotion, 8,* 720–724. doi:10.1037/a0013237

Irons, C., Gilbert, P., Baldwin, M. W., Baccus, J., & Palmer, M. (2006). Parental recall—Attachment relating and self attacking/self-reassurance: Their relationship with depression. *British Journal of Clinical Psychology, 45,* 297–308. doi:10.1348/014466505X68230

Kabat-Zinn, J. (2005). *Coming to our senses: Healing ourselves and the world through mindfulness.* New York, NY: Piakus.

Kaufman, G. (1989). *The psychology of shame.* New York, NY: Springer.

Laithwaite, H., Gumley, A., O'Hanlon, M., Collins, P., Doyle, P., Abraham, L., & Porter, S. (2009). Recovery after psychosis (RAP): A compassion focused programme for individuals residing in high security settings. *Behavioural and Cognitive Psychotherapy, 37,* 511–526. doi:10.1017/S1352465809990233

Leahy, R. L. (2002). A model of emotional schemas. *Cognitive and Behavioral Practice, 9,* 177–190. doi:10.1016/S1077-7229(02)80048-7

Leahy, R. L. (2005). A social-cognitive model of validation. In P. Gilbert (Ed.), *Compassion: Conceptualisations, research and use in psychotherapy* (pp. 195–217). London, England: Brunner-Routledge.

Lear, T. E. (1990). Shameful encounters, alienation, and healing restitution in the group. *Group Analysis, 23,* 155–161. doi:10.1177/0533316490232007

Leary, M. R., Tate, E. B., Adams, C. E., Allen, A. B., & Hancock, J. (2007). Self-compassion and reactions to unpleasant self-relevant events: The implications of treating oneself kindly. *Journal of Personality and Social Psychology, 92,* 887–904. doi:10.1037/0022-3514.92.5.887

Lee, H. J., Macbeth, A. H., Pagani, J. H., & Young, W. S., III. (2009). Oxytocin: The great facilitator of life. *Progress in Neurobiology, 88,* 127–151.

Linehan, M. (1993). *Cognitive behavioral treatment of borderline personality disorder.* New York, NY: Guilford Press.

Livingston, L. R. P. (2006). No place to hide: The group leader's moments of shame. *International Journal of Group Psychotherapy, 56,* 307–324. doi:10.1521/ijgp. 2006.56.3.307

Longe, O., Maratos, F. A., Gilbert, P., Evans, G., Volker, F., Rockliff, H., & Rippon, G. (2010). Having a word with yourself: Neural correlates of self-criticism and self-reassurance. *NeuroImage, 49,* 1849–1856. doi:10.1016/j.neuroimage.2009. 09.019

Lutz, A., Brefczynski-Lewis, J., Johnstone, T., & Davidson, R. J. (2008). Regulation of the neural circuitry of emotion by compassion meditation: Effects of the meditative expertise. *Public Library of Science, 3,* 1–5.

MacNab, R. T. (1995). Public exposure of shame in the group leader. In M. B. Sussman (Ed.), *A perilous calling: The hazards of psychotherapy practice* (pp. 115–126). New York, NY: Wiley.

Malle, B. F., & Hodges, S. D. (Eds.). (2005). *Other minds: How humans bridge the divide between self and others.* New York, NY: Guilford Press.

Mayhew, S. L., & Gilbert, P. (2008). Compassionate mind training with people who hear malevolent voices: A case series report. *Clinical Psychology & Psychotherapy, 15,* 113–138. doi:10.1002/cpp.566

Mikulincer, M., & Shaver, P. R. (2007). *Attachment in adulthood: Structure, dynamics, and change.* New York, NY: Guilford Press.

Neely, M. E., Schallert, D. L., Mohammed, S., Roberts, R. M., & Chen, Y. (2009). Self-kindness when facing stress: The role of self-compassion, goal regulation, and support in college students' well-being. *Motivation and Emotion, 33,* 88–97. doi:10.1007/s11031-008-9119-8

Neff, K. D. (2003). Self-compassion: An alternative conceptualization of a healthy attitude toward oneself. *Self and Identity, 2,* 85–101. doi:10.1080/152988603 09032

Neff, K. D., Hsieh, Y., & Dejitterat, K. (2005). Self-compassion, achievement goals and coping with academic failure. *Self and Identity, 4,* 263–287. doi:10.1080/1357 6500444000317

Neff, K. D., & Vonk, R. (2009). Self-compassion versus global self-esteem: Two different ways of relating to oneself. *Journal of Personality, 77,* 23–50. doi:10.1111/ j.1467-6494.2008.00537.x

Newberg, A., & Waldman, M. R. (2007). *Born to believe.* New York, NY: Free Press.

Nickerson, R. S. (1999). How we know—and sometimes misjudge—what others know: Inputing one's own knowledge to others. *Psychological Bulletin, 125,* 737–759. doi:10.1037/0033-2909.125.6.737

O'Connor, L. E., Berry, J. W., Weiss, J., & Gilbert, P. (2002). Guilt, fear, submission, and empathy in depression. *Journal of Affective Disorders, 71*, 19–27.

Panksepp, J. (1998). *Affective neuroscience*. New York, NY: Oxford University Press.

Pope, K. S., Sonne, J. L., & Greene, B. (2006). *What therapists don't talk about and why: Understanding taboos that hurt us and our clients* (2nd ed.). Washington, DC: American Psychological Association. doi:10.1037/11413-000

Rachman, S., & Safran, R. (1999). Cognitive distortions: Thought-action fusion. *Clinical Psychology & Psychotherapy, 6*, 80–85. doi:10.1002/(SICI)1099-0879(199905) 6:2<80::AID-CPP188>3.0.CO;2-C

Retzinger, S. M. (1998). Shame in the therapeutic relationship. In P. Gilbert & B. Andrews (Eds.), *Shame: Interpersonal behavior, psychopathology and culture* (pp. 206–222). New York, NY: Oxford University Press.

Rockliff, H., Gilbert, P., McEwan, K., Lightman, S., & Glover, D. (2008). A pilot exploration of heart rate variability and salivary cortisol responses to compassion-focused imagery. *Journal of Clinical Neuropsychiatry, 5*, 132–139.

Sachs-Ericsson, N., Verona, E., Joiner, T., & Preacher, J. K. (2006). Parental verbal abuse and the mediating role of self-criticism in adult internalizing disorders. *Journal of Affective Disorders, 93*, 71–78. doi:10.1016/j.jad.2006.02.014

Safran, J. D., & Muran, J. C. (2000). *Negotiating the therapeutic alliance: A relational treatment guide*. New York, NY: Guilford Press.

Schroder, T., Gilbert, P. & McEwan, K. (2008). *Shame, humiliation and guilt in psychotherapy: The therapist's tale*. Manuscript submitted for publication.

Sharhabani-Arzy, R., Amir, M., & Swisa, A. (2005). Self-criticism, dependency and posttraumatic stress disorder among a female group of help seeking victims of domestic violence. *Personality and Individual Differences, 38*, 1231–1240. doi:10.1016/j.paid.2004.08.006

Tangney, J. P., & Dearing, R. L. (2002). *Shame and guilt*. New York, NY: Guilford Press.

Tracy, J. L., Robins, R. W., & Tangney, J. P. (Eds.). (2007). *The self-conscious emotions: Theory and research*. New York, NY: Guilford Press.

Trower, P., Sherling, G., Beech, J., Horrop, C., & Gilbert, P. (1998). The socially anxious perspective in face to face interaction: An experimental comparison. *Clinical Psychology and Psychotherapy: An International Journal of Theory and Practice, 5*, 155–166.

Vessantara. (1993). *Meeting the Buddhas: A guide to Buddhas, bodhisattvas and tantric deities*. New York, NY: Windhorse Publications.

Wang, S. (2005). A conceptual framework for integrating research related to the physiology of compassion and the wisdom of Buddhist teachings. In P. Gilbert (Ed.), *Compassion: Conceptualisations, research and use in psychotherapy* (pp. 75–120). London, England: Brunner-Routledge.

Wells, A. (2000). *Emotional disorders and metacognition: Innovative cognitive therapy*. Chichester, England: Wiley.

Whelton, W. J., & Greenberg, L. S. (2005). Emotion in self-criticism. *Personality and Individual Differences, 38,* 1583–1595. doi:10.1016/j.paid.2004.09.024

Wilson, K. G. (2009). *Mindfulness for two: An acceptance and commitment therapy approach to mindfulness and psychotherapy.* Oakland, CA: New Harbinger.

Wyse, H. (1987). Towards a theology of shame in group analysis. *Group Analysis, 20,* 127–135. doi:10.1177/0533316487202004

Yourman, D. B. (2003). Trainee disclosure in psychotherapy supervision: The impact of shame. *Journal of Clinical Psychology, 59,* 601–609. doi:10.1002/jclp.10162

Yourman, D. B., & Farber, B. A. (1996). Nondisclosure and distortion in psychotherapy supervision. *Psychotherapy: Theory, Research, & Practice, 33,* 567–575. doi:10.1037/0033-3204.33.4.567

Zuroff, D. C., & Blatt, S. J. (2006). The therapeutic relationship in the brief treatment of depression: Contributions to clinical improvement and enhanced capacities. *Journal of Consulting and Clinical Psychology, 74,* 130–140. doi:10.1037/0022-006X.74.1.130

Zuroff, D. C., Santor, D., & Mongrain, M. (2005). Dependency, self-criticism, and maladjustment. In J. S. Auerbach, K. N. Levy, & C. E. Schaffer (Eds.), *Relatedness, self-definition and mental representation: Essays in honour of Sidney J* (pp. 75–90). London, England, and New York, NY: Routledge.

15

CONNECTIONS: A 12-SESSION PSYCHOEDUCATIONAL SHAME RESILIENCE CURRICULUM

BRENÉ BROWN, VIRGINIA RONDERO HERNANDEZ,
AND YOLANDA VILLARREAL

In early 2004, when shame resilience theory first emerged from a grounded theory study on women and shame (Brown, 2005), Brené Brown began teaching continuing education courses on shame resilience and giving public lectures. Surprisingly, although numerous mental health and addiction professionals expressed apprehension and concern about addressing the topic of shame with their clients, lay audiences appeared much more comfortable with the topic and often expressed relief after learning more about shame and shame resilience. In fact, whereas one of the most common questions from professionals was, "Do I have to use the word *shame* with clients?" one of the most common comments from lay audiences was, "I've been in therapy for years! Why hasn't anyone named this for me before? Why am I just now hearing about this? I thought it was just me." Brown heard "I thought it was just me" so often that it became the title of her book on shame resilience (Brown, 2007).

From interviews with more than 100 mental health and addictions professionals about this disconnect, three primary issues emerged:

1. The vast majority of clinicians have not studied shame. Brown is in the process of doing a content analysis of major texts used

by mental health professionals, and out of the 75 analyzed thus far, only one text includes information on shame.

2. Shame is a silent epidemic. It's universal, yet very few people are willing or able to discuss it. We need to develop the language to talk about shame before we can process our experiences in a meaningful way. This is why understanding shame and developing shame resilience require a learning component as much as an emotional process component. We believe that it's easier to teach someone about shame and shame resilience than it is to weave it into ongoing clinical work. For example, teaching shame resilience to 1,500 people in an auditorium is easier than breaking from the therapeutic process for didactic work or trying to weave educational content into that process. This is why psychoeducational group work is an invaluable tool in the shame resilience process.

3. Clinicians must do their own shame resilience work before they can ethically and effectively do shame work with clients. If shame comes up in the room, it will consume the clinician as quickly as possible. The only thing shame has to do to bring down the therapeutic process is trigger the clinician. Furthermore, most clinicians struggle to find a safe and effective place to do their own shame resilience work. The mandate that "we need to do the work before we do the work," combined with very few opportunities to do so, may explain why this critically important topic is often neglected in our work.

The Connections curriculum was developed in 2006 as a way to address both the needs of the clinical community and the needs of the lay community (Brown, 2009). The curriculum was originally piloted at the Menninger Clinic in Houston (2006–2007) and the Houston Area Women's Center (2006–2007). It has since been facilitated in a variety of settings across the United States and used with various populations, including residential psychiatric patients, residential substance abuse clients, high school students, women and men in state prisons, and nonresidential substance use groups of men and women. Although qualitative data have been collected over the past 2 years, the first formal evaluation of the curriculum was just completed by Virginia Rondero Hernandez, who field-tested Connections with women in three residential substance abuse treatment programs in central California. The sample included women from predominantly Latino backgrounds who were actively involved with child welfare or state correctional systems. Statistically significant differences were detected between pre- and posttest measures for general health, depression, internalized shame, and self-conscious affect. Statistically significant differences were also detected for each of the elements of shame resilience, indicating that the women involved in this research experienced gains in recognizing and understanding shame; identifying the individual, familial, and societal expectations that fuel shame; understanding the importance of reaching out for social support; and speaking out about shameful feelings and what they needed to reach treatment goals and sustain recovery (Rondero Hernandez, 2010).

The goal of this chapter is to briefly explain the research foundation of Connections, then to walk readers through the curriculum so that they may better understand how we introduce and explain shame and how resilience is taught and modeled through the psychoeducational process.

RESEARCH FOUNDATION OF
THE CONNECTIONS CURRICULUM

Using grounded theory methodology as developed by Glaser and Strauss (1967) and refined by Glaser (1978, 1992, 1998, 2001), Brown interviewed 215 women to understand how they experienced shame; how shame affected the way they live, love, parent, work, and develop relationships; and how they resolved their feelings and experiences of shame (for a full explanation of the research methodology, see Brown, 2005). Brown found that the research participants' main concerns related to shame were feelings of fear, blame, disconnection, and unworthiness. The following are representative responses from the female participants:

- "Shame is being rejected."
- "When you can't do it all and people know you're failing."
- "You work hard to show the world what it wants to see. Shame happens when your mask is pulled off and the unlikable parts of you are seen. It feels unbearable to be seen."
- "Shame is feeling like an outsider—not belonging."
- "Shame is being exposed—the flawed parts of yourself that you want to hide from everyone are revealed. You want to hide or die."

Over the subsequent 3 years, Brown continued to interview women and expanded her study to include men. After conducting more than 700 interviews with men and women, including more than 100 mental health professionals, she found that the main concerns of men were the same as those of women: Shame created pervasive feelings of fear, blame, disconnection, and unworthiness. The following are several of the responses from male participants:

- "Shame is failure. At work. On the football field. In your marriage. In bed. With money. With your children. It doesn't matter—shame is failure."
- "Shame is being wrong. Not doing it wrong, but being wrong."
- "Shame is a sense of being defective."
- "Shame happens when people think you're soft. It's degrading and shaming to be seen as anything but tough."
- "Showing fear is shameful. You can't show fear. You can't be afraid. No matter what."
- "Shame is being seen as 'the guy you can shove up against the lockers.'"
- "Our worst fear is being criticized or ridiculed—either one of these is extremely shaming."

On the basis of these interviews, Brown developed the following definition of *shame:* "the intensely painful feeling or experience of believing we are flawed and therefore unworthy of love and belonging" (Brown, 2007, p. 5). Additionally, shame, as described by the participants in Brown's research, emerged from the data as a psycho-social-cultural construct, not an experience or emotion that could be considered exclusively psychological, social, or cultural. The psychological component relates to the participant's emphasis on the emotions, thoughts, and behaviors of self. The social component relates to the way participants experience shame in an interpersonal context that is inextricably tied to relationships and connection. The cultural component points to the very prevalent role of cultural expectations and the shame or fear of shame related to not meeting or subscribing to those prescribed expectations.

Although the definition and conceptualization of shame emerged as the same for women and men, the data clearly demonstrated that the social-community messages and expectations that fuel shame are organized by gender. In other words, *how* we experience shame might be the same for men and women, but *why* we experience shame can be very different because the expectations and messages are driven by feminine and masculine norms.

Women reported experiencing shame as a web of layered, competing, and conflicting expectations that insist that they do it all, do it perfectly, and take care of everyone around them while they're doing it. For men, the expectations and messages center on masculinity and what it means to "be a man." Men did not talk about conflicting and competing expectations. They reported feeling trapped and confined by a single, suffocating message: Do not be weak. In her work, Brown (2007) used the metaphor of a web to describe shame for women and the metaphor of a small box to describe the stifling effect that shame has on men.

To live beyond the confines of shaming social-community expectations and to minimize feelings of fear, blame, disconnection, and unworthiness, men and women appear to have developed varying levels of shame resilience. After examining the interview data, Brown (2007) defined *shame resilience* as a person's ability to recognize and understand shame, move through it constructively while maintaining a basic level of authenticity, and increase his or her level of courage, compassion, and connection as a result of experiencing shame.

Brown (2007) found that men and women with high levels of shame resilience share four common characteristics that help them navigate shame and cultivate courage, compassion, and connection in their relationships with self and others: (a) understanding shame and recognizing triggers, (b) practicing critical awareness, (c) reaching out and sharing story, and (d) speaking shame. The four elements of shame resilience became the basis of the Connections curriculum and are explicated throughout the chapter as the sessions are explained (Brown, 2009).

THE CONNECTIONS CURRICULUM

The Connections curriculum consists of 12 sessions (Brown, 2009). Each session includes a didactic component that is available on a DVD or taught by the facilitator, an experiential exercise, and a process component that suggests ways the facilitator can engage participants to think more critically about the session topic. Facilitators are given specific objectives to achieve in each session. All of the session objectives relate to the propositions of shame resilience theory and provide consistency to the facilitators who use the Connections curriculum.

The following is an overview of the curriculum, including a summary of the session objectives, an explanation of how the work fits into the broader context of shame resilience, and some of the more universal challenges experienced by facilitators and participants who are immersed in this process. We provide the overview on a session-by-session basis to demonstrate how learning about and processing shame needs to be a gradual, active process in order to foster the development of effective shame resilience skills.

Session 1: Introduction

Vulnerability and establishing trust are necessary when discussing shame; therefore, the goals of the first session are for participants to recognize that shame is a universal, primitive emotion that we all experience and to understand how shame relates to the concepts of courage, compassion, and connection. Courage, compassion, and connection emerged from the data as the essential tools that women and men use to develop shame resilience.

The most significant barrier to this work is the individual's fear of shame. Participants often express significant relief when they hear what Brown (2007) referred to as the "quick three things about shame": (a) we all have shame, (b) we're all afraid to talk about it, and (c) the less we talk about it, the more we have it.

A large portion of early work in the curriculum is educational. Participants often are unaware that "this terrible feeling" has a name and that it's a universal struggle. Process, creativity, and homework exercises encourage participants to develop their own language and definitions of shame.

In addition to the focus on normalizing the experience of shame, two standardized measures—the Test of Self-Conscious Affect, Short Version 3 (TOSCA–3S; Tangney & Dearing, 2002; Tangney, Dearing, Wagner, & Gramzow, 2000) and the Self-Compassion Scale (Neff, 2003)—and a self-evaluation measure are administered to participants to give them an opportunity to evaluate their progression and gains related to the curriculum. The TOSCA–3S measures the amount of shame, guilt, and blame self-talk participants engage in. The Self-Compassion Scale (administered during Session 4) measures the three components of self-compassion: self-kindness, common humanity, and mindfulness. The curriculum also contains a shame resilience model handout (introduced in Session 2) that allows participants to track their progression along the four elements of the shame resilience model. Although the assessment instruments included in the curriculum are intended to be used as clinical assessment tools, they can be used to generate evidence of the curriculum's effectiveness.

To enhance clients' receptivity to the curriculum, it is important to develop a context for discussing shame and its implications for self, others, and society at large. Negotiation of group rules, emphasis on confidentiality (e.g., "what's said in group stays in group"), review of the curriculum's coping agreement, and emphasis on self-care principles during the first session contribute to the regulation of participants' behaviors and group interactions. A coping agreement is especially important because it conveys respect for an individual's tolerance and capacity to work on shame (e.g., not pushing oneself to share uncomfortable emotions, taking a break, stopping to think about the work group members are doing, reaching out for support). The coping agreement also helps to establish trust that the facilitator will refer the participant to a therapist or counselor if indicated. The agreement acknowledges that many clients participate in group work in addition to working with an individual therapist.

Session 2: Overview of the Curriculum and Defining Shame

The educational component of the curriculum begins with Session 2. Here participants expand their understanding of shame, learn to differentiate shame and guilt, and gain a better understanding of empathy. Exercises for this session ask participants to draw shame, assign colors to it, and think about what shame looks like, tastes like, and feels like. Once clients are able to assign the word *shame* to their experiences and feelings, facilitators begin talking about the differences between shame and guilt. Along with many other affect researchers, Brown (2007) defined the differences between shame and guilt as the differences between "I am bad" and "I did something bad."

Throughout this session, participants are asked to complete exercises designed to tap into thoughts, beliefs, values, feelings, sensations, and emotions associated with shame. They then share their responses to these exercises with the group. Identifying and discriminating between shame and guilt is the first step in the process of intrapersonal change. Doing so also sets the stage for a sequence or process that prompts group cohesion and generates a "constructive loop of trust, subsequent self-disclosure, feedback, and interpersonal learning" (Yalom & Leszcz, 2005, p. 375).

Comparing and contrasting shame and guilt allows participants to understand that they are not the only ones beset by shame experiences. This realization of shared experience further forges a common bond and provides a group vocabulary and definition of shame that facilitate transformative change at the individual and group levels. Because sharing stories of shame can prompt sadness, anger, and a sense of injustice, it is important that the facilitator be able to recognize signs of distress that may require clinical follow-up.

On reviewing the curriculum feedback forms and interviews with facilitators, we learned that after completing the Connections curriculum, clients consistently rated "having a definition for shame" and "knowing the difference between shame and guilt" as the two most valuable learning pieces. Additionally, many clinicians have identified developing a vocabulary and definition for shame as one of the most transformative components of this curriculum. Beginning to identify feelings of shame and understanding the differences between shame and guilt give participants knowledge as well as a sense of hopefulness. The idea that we can be "good people" and still make "bad choices" appears to immediately open up the idea that our worthiness doesn't always have to be tied to what we've done or failed to do.

Session 3: Big Webs and Small Boxes

Because shame is highly individualized, there are no universal shame triggers; however, Brown's (2007) research interviews allowed for classification of shame experiences into 12 primary categories: appearance and body image, money and work, motherhood or fatherhood, family, parenting, mental and physical health (including addiction), sex, aging, religion, speaking out, surviving trauma, and being stereotyped and labeled. Participant objectives for Session 3 include understanding the individualized nature of shame experiences, identifying the 12 shame categories that emerged from Brown's research, and understanding how gender-based messages and expectations fuel shame.

The curriculum's conceptual frameworks for shame (e.g., shame web for women and shame box for men) encourage participants to reframe their thinking about shame. They learn that sociocultural expectations and the shame related to not meeting those expectations are often imposed, enforced, or expressed by self, family and peer networks, and groups (e.g., educational systems, faith communities, neighborhoods, medical providers). These expectations are reinforced by larger influences (e.g., media culture of music, advertising, and film; Brown, 2007). Group facilitators have reported that participants easily relate to the sensation of feeling "trapped" in a web or box of societal expectations that define who the participant is supposed to be.

Participants also readily identify with the 12 categories of common shame triggers. Relating to the metaphor of the shame web or shame box exposes the faulty logic that one's self is the sole source of shame. According to Toseland and Rivas (2009), awareness of factors that shape and maintain belief systems, and how they might be modified, initiates and facilitates the process of cognitive restructuring and empowers a person with the choice to think differently about shame experiences. Shifting one's way of thinking about shame loosens the grip of shame-provoking experiences (e.g., victimization, transgressions, humiliation).

Session 4: Defining Resilience—Practicing Empathy

In Session 4, participants begin to define resilience and explore the critical role that empathy plays in shame resilience. The term *resilience* is often a new concept for clients, but as facilitators explain what resilience looks like and feels like, most quickly recognize it in their own behavior or in the behaviors of others. They mention famous figures and personal acquaintances who have "overcome the odds" of a divorce, bankruptcy, an addiction, and so forth. The process of identifying examples of resilient behaviors supports the development of *empathetic capacity*, a concept that, according to Yalom and Leszcz (2005), generalizes learning from what is gained in the group to a participant's everyday life.

A review of Wiseman's (1996) four attributes of empathy (seeing things from others' perspectives, withholding judgment, recognizing emotions, and communicating our understanding of emotions) sets the groundwork for operationalizing this concept. Practicing active empathy is a new behavior for many participants. They quickly realize that it is much easier to judge than to be empathic, and they often express worry about saying the wrong thing. An exercise in this session involves participants writing down what it means to feel understood and to understand others. Participants are asked to write down and discuss the experience of sharing something personal and vulnerable and the types of responses they would consider helpful and not helpful (Brown, 2007). This process lends insight into participants' personal strengths and their progression in cognitive restructuring of the shame experience.

Session 5: Practicing Empathy

In her research, Brown (2007) found that empathy is one of the strongest antidotes to shame. She wrote,

> It's not just about having our needs for empathy met; shame resilience requires us to be able to respond empathically to others. . . . If you put shame in a petri dish and cover it with judgment, silence and secrecy, it grows out of control. . . . On the other hand, if you put shame in a petri dish and douse it with empathy, shame loses power and starts to fade. Empathy creates a hostile environment for shame—it can't survive. (p. 32)

The goals for Session 5 are very specific to the practice of empathy. For example, participants learn to recognize the differences between sympathy and empathy, to understand how empathy requires us to connect to an emotion rather than an experience, and to understand how and why our beliefs about shame affect our ability to practice empathy (Brown, 2007).

This session also focuses on identifying barriers to empathy. Participants are invited to connect with the emotions expressed during others' shame stories. Although specific examples and experiences may be unique, being able to connect empathically with the emotions expressed by others further lends itself to fostering connection networks that help move people from shame to empathy. For instance, although all participants may not identify with the experience of being a victim of sexual assault, they have undoubtedly all experienced feelings of being labeled, misunderstood, and reduced.

Being able to practice empathy is predicated on a person's ability to relate to the shame experiences of another. This can be difficult because shame can cause physical and emotional discomfort for the listener. Even if the person is successful in withholding judgment and recognizing the emotion at hand, he or she may be swept up in the "sleeper" effect shame can have as he or she recalls personal shameful experiences (Lewis, 1987). To conceal the emotion that is elicited when listening to another's experience of shame, the listener may resort to sympathetic ("poor thing" or "it can't be that bad") versus empathetic responses.

Responding with concern often forces a person to dig deep into his or her own experiences to envision how another person may feel. Such responses can convey expressions of genuine concern even if the listener has not had the exact same experience (Brown, 2007). *Digging deep* is putting one foot in the world of the speaker and another in the world of the listener to bridge understanding and communication in spite of not having the exact same experience. Practicing empathy helps to move participants from the shame (e.g., fear, blame, disconnection) across the continuum to shame resilience. This session and the previous session promote participant self-efficacy in learning newly acquired behaviors and allow the facilitator "to adopt a position that maximizes members' sense of control and expertise" (Toseland & Rivas, 2009, p. 273).

Session 6: Recognizing Shame

The goal for Session 6 is for participants to be able to identify their own physical shame symptoms or sensations. To carry out this objective, participants are asked to identify a shaming moment that has occurred to them as well as the physical symptoms or sensations that accompanied this experience. This process allows participants to recognize the physical symptoms in the future, identify that they are feeling shame, and practice the resiliency techniques that they have learned to extract themselves from the experience quickly.

Participants are introduced to a simple explanation of how the brain responds to shame. They are reminded that the limbic system effectively "hijacks" rational thinking processes when the person is shamed, sometimes resulting in shame responses that can be hurtful to oneself and/or others. Feeling shame prompts inward hostility or anger at oneself, which can convert into outward forms of hostility and blame (Lewis, 1987; Tangney & Dearing, 2002). To support participants in making the shift from feeling shame to doing something productive about it, they are asked to complete worksheets that ask them to associate shame with emotional and physical states. Their responses are often graphic and even crude. However, asking participants to report where they "feel" shame in their body helps them learn that bodily reactions to shameful events are "cues" they can use to practice controlling their reactions to shame.

Participants also complete open-ended sentences that associate shame with feelings, tastes, smells, and touch. This cognitive-kinesthetic exercise reinforces the notion that shame is a "total body experience" (Brown, 2007) and that recognition of the core emotions shame provokes requires practice and self-reflection. Participants learn that recognizing shame and shame cues can be used to reduce or avert overwhelming shame experiences. Learning to recognize shame also promotes mindfulness, a practice that involves specific and purposeful attention on a subject (e.g., shame) while withholding judgment of self and others (Epel, Daubenmier, Moskowitz, Folkman, & Blackburn, 2009).

Session 7: Exploring Triggers and Vulnerabilities

The first half of the Connections curriculum sets the stage for advanced discussions about shame and movement toward critical awareness of shame (Brown, 2009). This session marks a vital stage in the development of shame resilience. In this session, participants are encouraged to (a) identify shame triggers related to two of the shame categories (unwanted and ideal identities), (b) increase their understanding of the origins of their triggers, and (c) identify their personal strengths related to two of the shame categories.

What makes us vulnerable to shame are the "unwanted identities" associated with each of the shame categories. For example, many women used adjectives like *loudmouth* and *pushy* to describe unwanted identities associated with speaking out. When discussing the category of fatherhood, men talked about *deadbeat* and *detached* as being hurtful unwanted identities. Ferguson, Eyre, and Ashbaker (2000) argued that "unwanted identity" is the quintessential elicitor of shame. They explained that unwanted identities are characteristics that undermine our vision of our ideal selves. Sometimes we perceive others as assigning these unwanted identities to us, and other times we pin them on ourselves.

In order to recognize their unwanted identities, participants are asked to list labels and words based on two-sentence stem exercises: "It is very important to me that I am perceived as _____." and "I do *not* want to be perceived as _____." They are asked to analyze the unwanted identities, to evaluate their meanings, and to determine why they are so unwanted and what messages fuel them. The intent of the exercise is to isolate, as best one can, the origin of the unwanted identity and to analyze, question, and challenge the messages and the beliefs attached to them. This process teases out cognitive distortions, challenges internal dialogues and negative self-talk, and supports the reframing of one's self-concept (Toseland & Rivas, 2009).

The work in this session challenges participants to identify and embrace their vulnerabilities. Participants who recognize their unwanted identities reduce the importance of these shame triggers, effectively helping them move from disconnection to connection or from shame to shame resiliency.

Session 8: Understanding Our Shame Screens

Once clients begin to recognize identities and messages that fuel their shaming experiences, we move to understanding how and why we protect ourselves from shame. The objectives for this session are to identify the basic shame screens participants use and understand why and when we use specific shame screens.

A *shame screen* is similar to a smoke screen: It is a reaction that individuals believe they can use to hide their shame. During this session we rely on the work of Linda Hartling, relational–cultural theorist at the Stone Center in Wellesley, Massachusetts (e.g., Hartling, Rosen, Walker, & Jordan, 2000). Hartling used Karen Horney's (1945) work on moving toward, moving against, and moving away to outline the strategies of disconnection we use to deal with shame. According to Hartling, to deal with shame, some of us move away by withdrawing, hiding, silencing ourselves, and keeping secrets. Some of us move toward by seeking to appease and please. And some of us move against by trying to gain power over others, being aggressive, and using shame to fight shame.

The activities and exercises during this session help participants identify which of these psychosocial processes (i.e., shame screens) they use when they are in a shaming experience. Learning about shame screens prompts introspection about how one disconnects from the world in the face of shame. Participants are quick to identify the strategy they use most and the situations in which they use a particular strategy. Moving away typically includes isolating and hiding out in one's own life. Moving toward prompts people-pleasing behaviors and seeking out of approval, primarily with people who are perceived to have more power. Moving against is often using shame to fight shame. Participants often tell stories of anger, violence, revenge, rage, and even harm against others. These self-disclosures test the adaptive functions of the group. In some groups, the opportunity to disclose shame responses prompts acceptance by others and redefines the responses as defense mechanisms against shame.

This session unmasks the typical ways participants defend themselves against shame. An astute facilitator must be able to differentiate between a healthy discharge of emotion and thought from one that requires further assessment for potential harm to self or others. The curriculum supports work and dialogues that help to advance participants through the curriculum, gaining deeper levels of understanding about shame and its personal implications for one's self. Over time, the group becomes a forum for interpersonal learning, offers corrective emotional experience, and functions as a social microcosm in which shame and the psychological threat it poses can be discussed and explored (Yalom & Leszcz, 2005).

Being aware of these shame screens, including what they look and feel like, helps participants identify when they are experiencing shame and engaging in shame screening instead of reaching out for empathy and connection with others. Facilitators report that simply describing these responses to shame helps participants practice mindfulness, which eventually leads them to identify effective coping strategies.

Session 9: Practicing Critical Awareness

In Session 9, we move from the first element of shame resilience—understanding shame and recognizing triggers—to the second element of shame resilience—practicing critical awareness. The goals for this session include demonstrating the skills related to "seeing the big picture" and "reality checking," understanding how and why social-community expectations fuel shame, and subjecting ideal and unwanted identities to a reality check.

This session challenges participants to begin the work of applying the concepts and strategies they have learned to circumstances outside the group. Doing so requires critical awareness about one's shame issues and increasing personal power and shame resilience by "understanding the link between our personal experiences and larger social systems" (Brown, 2007, p. 93). Specifically, participants are asked to select one of the shame categories and to construct a "big picture" of the expectations involved. They are asked several questions designed to help them analyze the nature, messages, and effects of expectations for a specific shame category. Joint examination of expectations around addiction, for instance, often prompts an effective brainstorming process characterized by the generation of ideas and encourages participants to participate fully (Toseland & Rivas, 2009).

This process helps participants to assess the realities of expectations placed on any given shame category and to evaluate who sets the expectations to begin with, how they are conveyed to the person and society, how all parties are affected, and who benefits from these expectations (Brown, 2007). Specifically, critical awareness skills allow clients to move away from reinforcing (I should feel shame), individualizing (I am the only one), and pathologizing (I'm not normal; something is wrong with me) shame to contextualizing (I see the big picture), normalizing (I'm not the only one), and demystifying (I'll learn more about this and share what I know with others) shame.

Discussions typically have a synergistic tone as participants take turns analyzing the effects of social-community expectations and critiquing how expectations converge or diverge from ideal and unwanted identities. For example, when working with a group of mothers struggling with postpartum depression (PPD), the facilitator asked, "What are the stereotypes about mothers struggling with PPD?" The group members came up with a list that included *unfit, unloving, crazy,* and *dangerous.* There was immediate relief among the group members when they realized that they were not the only ones facing these hurtful stereotypes. The remainder of the session was spent using facts about PPD to debunk the myths and strategizing about how the clients could talk to family and friends about their struggle.

Sessions 10 and 11: Reaching Out and Speaking Shame

Shame resilience requires us to practice all four of the shame resilience elements together. Sessions 10 and 11 work together as a unit to provide participants with the opportunity to begin to integrate the various pieces of the head (i.e., cognition) and heart (i.e., emotion) work they've done in group. These two sessions also begin to prepare participants to look outside of the group for the support necessary to continue this work by practicing how to share their feelings and ask for what they need. In this session, facilitators focus on the importance of recognizing and developing safe, mutually empathic relationships and the reasons why reaching out and sharing experiences and feelings in the context of those relationships is a critical element of shame resilience. Additionally, clients are encouraged to explore the barriers to reaching out— specifically, concepts relating to self-protecting and blaming.

The core tool used in Sessions 10 and 11 is a letter written by Jody Earle (n.d.), an infertility expert, during her 11-year struggle with infertility. In the letter, which was addressed to Earle's family and friends, she used very clear and explicit language to communicate her fears and feelings. She followed this by explicating exactly what she needed in the way of support and empathy (the focus of Session 11). The letter can be used as a guide or resource as the clients begin to compose their own letters. Facilitators have the option of giving clients a letter that is drafted with sentence stems based on Earle's letter. Examples of these sentences are as follows:

- I want to share my feelings about _____ with you, because I want you to understand my struggle. I know that understanding _____ is difficult; there are times when it seems even I don't understand.
- You may describe me this way: _____.
- My _____ makes me feel _____.

Every facilitator we've interviewed or spoken with about Connections has told us that the process of having clients read Jody Earle's piece and then write about their own feelings and needs has been the most emotional and healing aspect of this work. This process is where the elements of shame resilience come together. Shame is all about fear, blame, disconnection, and feelings of unworthiness. This exercise is all about courage, compassion, connection, and being worthy of love and belonging. Facilitators report the need to validate how scary it is to be emotionally honest and to ask for what we need, and they note that the healing comes from writing the letter, not receiving a response. This session also reinforces a message that is central to shame resilience work: The opposite of strength is not vulnerability; *vulnerability is strength*.

Session 12: Authenticity and Shame Resilience

The primary goals of the final session are to help clients develop a deeper understanding of the importance of practicing authenticity and to acknowledge and honor each member's personal growth in the shame resilience process. Shame is corrosive to our authenticity—it moves us away from believing that who we are is enough and that we are worthy of love and belonging. In her new research on wholeheartedness, Brown (2010) used grounded theory data to develop the following definition of *authenticity* (p. 50): "the daily practice of letting go of who we think we're supposed to be and embracing who we are." Choosing authenticity means the following:

- cultivating the courage to be imperfect, to set boundaries, and to allow ourselves to be vulnerable;
- exercising the compassion that comes from knowing that we are all made of strength and struggle and are connected to each other through a loving and resilient human spirit; and
- nurturing the connection and sense of belonging that can happen only when we believe that we are enough.

Authenticity demands wholehearted living and loving—even when it's hard, even when we're wrestling with the shame and fear of not being good enough, and especially when the joy is so intense that we're afraid to let ourselves feel it. Mindfully practicing authenticity during our most soul-searching struggles is how we invite grace, joy, and, gratitude into our lives. Facilitators use this definition of authenticity to help clients deconstruct the components of authenticity and recognize the relationship between shame resilience and feelings of worthiness. Many facilitators also report using a printed version of the definition as part of a closing ceremony or ritual (artful, printable versions are available to Connections facilitators).

CONCLUSION: MAKING THE CURRICULUM YOUR OWN

These sessions describe the fundamental and essential components of the curriculum; however, we advocate for facilitators to personalize their curriculum based on the needs of the group. Many clinicians have done this by combining elements of the curriculum with other therapy models such as cognitive behavioral therapy or by incorporating additional creative and artistic exercises. Creativity helps members disconnect from an overidentification with the cognitive aspects of shame and shame resilience and instead to tap into the emotional and spiritual elements of conducting this work. Others have personalized the curriculum by incorporating questions that help participants to share their shaming stories. This sharing allows individuals to practice sharing vulnerability, empathic listening, and compassion.

Shame is a universal, intensely painful feeling of unworthiness. However, beginning to have a discussion about shaming experiences, developing a vocabulary and definition around topics of shame, and ultimately building shame resilience can have profound effects on the lives of men and women. Many participants have expressed that their experiences within a shame resilience group have added to their relationships, reinforced healthy choices, given them insight to connect with others, and opened their awareness of authentic living. As one facilitator stated, "This work has the ability to change the lives of everyone it reaches" (C. Graves, personal communication, October 22, 2009).

REFERENCES

Brown, B. (2005). Shame resilience theory: A grounded theory study on women and shame. *Families in Society: The Journal of Contemporary Social Services, 87,* 43–52.

Brown, B. (2007). *I thought it was just me: Women reclaiming power and courage in a culture of shame.* New York, NY: Penguin Group.

Brown, B. (2009). *Connections: A 12-session psychoeducational shame resilience curriculum* (2nd ed.). Minneapolis, MN: Hazelden.

Brown, B. (2010). *The gifts of imperfection: Let go of who you think you're supposed to be and embrace who you are.* Minneapolis, MN: Hazelden.

Earle, J. (n.d.). *Infertility: A guide for family and friends* [Brochure]. Binghamton, NY: Educational Materials Advisory Committee of the Ferre Institute.

Epel, E., Daubenmier, J., Moskowitz, J. T., Folkman, S., & Blackburn, E. (2009). Can meditation slow rate of cellular aging? Cognitive stress, mindfulness, and telomeres. *Annals of the New York Academy of Sciences, 1172* (Longevity, Regeneration, and Optimal Health Integrating Eastern and Western Perspectives), 34–53.

Ferguson, T. J., Eyre, H. L., & Ashbaker, M. (2000). Unwanted identities: A key variable in shame-anger links and gender differences in shame. *Sex Roles, 42,* 133–157. doi:10.1023/A:1007061505251

Glaser, B. G. (1978). *Theoretical sensitivity.* Mill Valley, CA: Sociology Press.

Glaser, B. G. (1992). *Basics of grounded theory.* Mill Valley, CA: Sociology Press.

Glaser, B. (1998). *Doing grounded theory: Issues and discussions.* Mill Valley, CA: Sociological Press.

Glaser, B. (2001). *The grounded theory perspective: Conceptualization contrasted with description.* Mill Valley, CA: Sociological Press.

Glaser, B., & Strauss, A. (1967). *The discovery of grounded theory.* Chicago, IL: Aldine.

Hartling, L., Rosen, W., Walker, M., & Jordan, J. (2000). *Shame and humiliation: From isolation to relational transformation* (Work in Progress No. 88). Wellesley, MA: Stone Center, Wellesley College.

Horney, K. (1945). *Our inner conflicts.* New York, NY: Norton.

Lewis, H. B. (Ed.). (1987). *The role of shame in symptom formation.* Hillsdale, NJ: Erlbaum.

Neff, K. D. (2003). Development and validation of a scale to measure self-compassion. *Self and Identity, 2,* 223–250. doi:10.1080/15298860309027

Rondero Hernandez, V. (2010). *Shame resilience: A strategy for empowering women in treatment for substance abuse.* Manuscript submitted for publication.

Scheff, T. J. (1988). Shame and conformity: The deference-emotion system. *American Sociological Review, 53,* 395–406. doi:10.2307/2095647

Tangney, J. P., & Dearing, R. L. (2002). *Shame and guilt.* New York, NY: Guilford Press.

Tangney, J. P., Dearing, R., Wagner, P. E., & Gramzow, R. (2000). *The Test of Self-Conscious Affect—3* (TOSCA–3). Fairfax, VA: George Mason University.

Toseland, R. W., & Rivas, R. F. (2009). *An introduction to group work practice.* Boston, MA: Pearson Education.

Wiseman, T. (1996). A concept analysis of empathy. *Journal of Advanced Nursing, 23,* 1162–1167. doi:10.1046/j.1365-2648.1996.12213.x

Yalom, I., & Leszcz, M. (2005). *The theory and practice of group therapy* (5th ed.). New York, NY: Basic Books.

V

SHAME: FUTURE DIRECTIONS

16

WORKING WITH SHAME IN THE THERAPY HOUR: SUMMARY AND INTEGRATION

JUNE PRICE TANGNEY AND RONDA L. DEARING

It's ironic that it took 40 years from the publication of Helen Block Lewis's (1971) *Shame and Guilt in Neurosis,* in which Lewis laid out the self versus behavior distinction (as described in this volume's Introduction), for a clinicians' "handbook on shame" such as the present one to appear. Lewis was the quintessential scientist–practitioner—a collaborator on Witkin's classic research on field independence/dependence and a psychoanalytically trained clinician (Witkin et al., 1954; Witkin, Lewis, & Weil, 1968). *Shame and Guilt in Neurosis* was at heart a clinically oriented book, examining in detail the dynamics of shame and guilt in a series of clinical case studies. Yet it is in the domain of empirical research that Lewis's book has thus far had its greatest impact. The past 20 years have seen a virtual explosion of empirical research on shame and guilt, the majority of which has been directly or indirectly inspired by Lewis's groundbreaking differentiation between these often confused emotions. Two decades of research by social, personality, and developmental psychologists have confirmed Lewis's basic distinction between shame and guilt and her clinically informed speculations about the dynamics—both intrapersonal and interpersonal—of these distinct emotions. But surprisingly, comparatively little has been written to guide the clinician on how best to recognize, manage, treat, or capitalize on shame in the therapy hour. In this sense, this edited volume brings Lewis's influence full circle back to the therapy room.

What can master clinicians tell us about the effective management and treatment of shame? As it turns out, plenty. In developing this volume, we purposely sampled a broad range of clinicians in terms of theoretical orientation and clinical population of interest. What strikes us most are the many similarities among the suggested approaches for managing shame in the therapeutic context. In this final chapter, we summarize common themes that emerged across chapters, highlight intriguing and unique insights and treatment suggestions, and outline what we see as important future directions for clinically relevant treatment research.

COMMON THEMES AND INTRIGUING INSIGHTS

The following paragraphs describe themes and insights that appear across the chapters in this volume.

Shame Is Ubiquitous in the Clinical Context

One common theme emanating from the chapters is that although it is rarely mentioned in standard clinical training texts and articles, shame is ubiquitous in clinical settings. Shame may arise from at least three sources: the client, the therapeutic interaction, and the therapist himself or herself.

First, there is the shame that clients bring into the therapy room, shame born of experiencing psychological and behavioral problems—or symptoms of mental illness—that are a source of stigma and shame born of unsuccessful attempts (often over a period of years) to resolve such problems. Given the vast empirical research linking shame proneness to a range of psychological problems (Harder & Lewis, 1987; Tangney, Wagner, & Gramzow, 1992), it stands to reason that clients entering therapy are likely to be prone to shame from the start.

Second, the therapeutic process is, by its very nature, shame inducing. Clients who have unsuccessfully attempted to resolve problems or symptoms are expected to lay bare their failures and shortcomings before a therapist who is often imagined to be a paragon of psychological health. Greenberg and Iwakabe (Chapter 3) wrote:

> Shame operates everywhere in therapy because clients are constantly concerned about what part of their inner experience can be revealed safely and what part must be kept hidden. Clients' struggles with shame may start even before the therapy begins. . . . Seeking help from professionals about personal matters thus can evoke a sense of humiliation.

Herman (Chapter 11), too, observed the following: "Because of the power imbalance between patient and therapist, and because the patient exposes his or her most intimate thoughts and feelings without reciprocity, the individual therapy relationship is to some degree inherently shaming." Moreover, the process of psychotherapy, especially insight-oriented therapy, encourages an acute focus on self—especially the feared, problematic aspects of self. Not only is the reality of the therapeutic context likely to induce feelings of shame, but clients' experiences in therapy are often complicated by the process of transference, which elicits feelings typically associated with painful relationships from their past. In their quest for help, clients are apt to import more shame into this already shame-laden situation, and some of this shame may arise from envying the positive qualities (e.g., perceived emotional stability) of the therapist.

Third, as Ladany, Klinger, and Kulp (Chapter 13) and many others noted, the challenge of providing therapy, with all its uncertainty, can engender shame in a therapist who, rather than being a paragon of psychological health, brings to the therapeutic encounter very human limitations and vulnerabilities. In short, shame is apt to be found in all corners of the therapy room.

Shame Is Nonetheless Easily Overlooked (or Actively Avoided!)

Clients rarely spontaneously announce that they are feeling (or have felt) shame. In Western cultures, especially, shame is an emotion rarely discussed outside of academic circles and a few shame-focused methods for treating addiction (e.g., Bradshaw, 1988). Many authors in this volume noted how easily shame is overlooked by both clients and therapists in the therapeutic encounter. Greenberg and Iwakabe cautioned in Chapter 3 that "therapists need to be attuned and responsive to nonverbal as well as verbal indicators of shame-related experience in the session." To make matters even more complicated, as discussed by Teyber, McClure, and Weathers (Chapter 6), clinically relevant shame is easily disregarded because it is often actively avoided by the client, the therapist, or both. Thus, several master clinicians emphasize that it is important, from the outset, for therapists to be vigilant and probe for client shame. It is incumbent on therapists to be alert for nonverbal or therapy process-type cues of shame lurking beneath the various veneers that clients may present. (The trick, of course, is to probe carefully without inadvertently provoking additional feelings of shame.)

How to Recognize Client Shame

Our master clinicians were remarkably consistent in describing a common set of verbal, nonverbal, and paralinguistic cues that may signal underlying experiences of shame, including physical or emotional withdrawal (mentioned by Morrison, Chapter 1, among many other authors in this volume), decreased eye contact, slumped or rigid posture (Rizvi et al., Chapter 10), avoidance of "here-and-now" material (Shapiro & Powers, Chapter 5), freezing, stammering, tightened voice, self-deprecating comments that expand into hilarious monologues, and an "infinitesimal flash of irritation" before apology for a missing or incomplete homework assignment (Koerner, Tsai, & Simpson, Chapter 4). Similarly, Greenberg and Iwakabe (Chapter 3) cite downcast eyes, squirming or writhing in the seat, laughter or shrugging off that covers embarrassment, and indications that it is somehow degrading to be in therapy. In addition, as Gilbert (Chapter 14) described, shamed clients "may go blank, show submissive crouched body postures, avoid topics (e.g., talk around topics but not clarify them), become anxious or angry, or point-blank refuse to reveal" relevant clinical material.

Herman (Chapter 11) noted that client shame is frequently disguised by other emotions—most notably anger and rage, but also envy, contempt, and expressions of grandiosity. Such emotions are often prompted by initial feelings of shame, emerging as defensive reactions that serve to cover over the pain of shame. Herman also noted that "the vocabulary of shame is extensive." Code words for shame include "*ridiculous, foolish, silly, idiotic, stupid, dumb, humiliated, disrespected, helpless, weak, inept, dependent, small, inferior, unworthy, worthless, trivial, shy, vulnerable, uncomfortable,* or *embarrassed. . . .*" Recalling Helen Block Lewis's clinical observations, Herman further identified paralinguistic cues of underlying shame, including "confusion of thought, hesitation, soft speech, mumbling, silences, stammering, long pauses, rapid speech, or tensely laughed words." Yet in spite of such varied hints, many instances of client shame are overlooked or ignored by therapists not trained to recognize the many hidden faces of shame.

Common Causes of Shame

Client experiences of shame can arise from events both inside and outside the therapy session. Regarding shame arising from causes and events outside the therapy room, chapters by Rizvi et al. (Chapter 10); by Epstein and Falconier (Chapter 7); and by Brown, Hernandez, and Villarreal (Chapter 15) each advocated that, early in treatment, therapists routinely take a survey of the topics and situations that cause the client shame in the course of day-to-day life (i.e., domain-specific assessment, as discussed in Introduction and later in this section). Clinicians may also find it beneficial to assess clients' overall tendencies toward shame proneness and guilt proneness (i.e., dispositional shame and guilt), especially because of the differing and often clinically relevant outcomes associated with dispositional shame and guilt. Reviews of instruments for the assessment of dispositional shame and guilt can be found in Tangney and Dearing (2002) and Robins, Noftle, and Tracy (2007). For clinicians who are interested in dispositional assessment, we recommend use of the Test of Self-Conscious Affect, Version 3 (TOSCA–3; Tangney, Dearing, Wagner, & Gramzow, 2000), as suggested by Brown and coauthors (Chapter 15) and by Epstein and Falconier (Chapter 7).

Methods for domain-specific assessment are discussed in several of the chapters in this volume. For example, Rizvi and coauthors (Chapter 10) assessed clients' profiles of "shame triggers" using their Shame Inventory, composed of 98 situations or characteristics that might cause people to feel shame, to get an idiographic sense of client's personal areas of shame vulnerability. Brown et al. (Chapter 15) similarly assessed clients' idiographic shame triggers using 12 categories of potentially shame-inducing domains: appearance and body image, money and work, motherhood or fatherhood, family, parenting, mental and physical health (including addiction), sex, aging, religion, speaking out, surviving trauma, and being stereotyped and labeled.

Potter-Efron, in Chapter 9, suggested five sentences that convey different ways in which shame may be experienced: "I am not good," "I am not good enough," "I do not belong," "I am unlovable," and "I should not be." Clients may resonate with one or more of these if the therapist presents them as possible underlying themes (and then connects them with shame). Similarly, Gilbert (Chapter 14) emphasized as central to the shame experience feelings of being alone, disconnected from others, and in need of rescue but with no one there to help.

In addition, Shapiro and Powers (Chapter 5) and Sanftner and Tantillo (Chapter 12) expanded on the idea of the body as a potent source of shame. Shapiro and Powers noted,

> Whether it is sexual arousal, flatulence, or the loss of hearing, there is something deeply personal about bodily functions. A primitive vulnerability is awakened by these situations, and a profound threat to one's sense of bodily integrity and personal cohesion can be experienced.

Episodes of body-related shame often lead to a desire to hide or avoid on the part of both clients and therapists. Because avoidance is apt to lead to even greater shame, it is important for therapists to make use of encounters that focus attention to the body—the therapist's or a client's. Shapiro and Powers also point out that client efforts to (apparently shamelessly) reveal or put on display shame-provoking aspects of the body can be seen as a defensive maneuver to disguise more profound and troubling aspects of the self.

Regarding shame arising from the context of treatment itself, Koerner and coauthors (Chapter 4) identified four common classes of shame-inducing clinical material that may help the therapist anticipate when problematic shame responses are apt to occur in therapy: shame related to purpose (e.g., feeling ashamed of desires, dreams, fantasies, or sense of purpose), shame related to affect (e.g., regarding specific emotions such as anger or pride or regarding intense emotional experience), shame related to sexual drives and hunger drives, and shame related to interpersonal needs.

As described by Sanftner and Tantillo (Chapter 12) in their discussion of the treatment of eating disorders, some clients secretly wish to be "the perfect patient," which sets the stage for inevitable failure and attendant shame experiences. In such cases, it may be helpful for the therapist to reassure the client directly that he or she does not want a "perfect client."

We were surprised to find that only two chapters mentioned money and billing issues as a potential source of shame between clients and therapists (Koerner et al., Chapter 4; and Shapiro & Powers, Chapter 5). Enforcing fee policies (e.g., dealing with cancellations and missed sessions) and addressing late payments can be shame inducing for both client and therapist, whether in the context of individual therapy or (especially) in the context of group therapy. For the therapist, enforcing fee policies—explicitly asking for money—may seem incongruous with the role of therapist as other-oriented, empathic helper; the notion of not only expecting but also requiring money in exchange for caring and concern may be shame inducing. More generally, both therapist and client may share a widespread societal discomfort with owing or being owed money.

Shame's Insidious Impact on the Therapeutic Process

Many chapters echoed Helen Block Lewis's observation that shame can wreak havoc on the therapeutic process. Most obviously, to the extent that clients are inclined to hide shameful thoughts, emotions, and behaviors, important material is missing and the therapeutic process is adversely affected (see, e.g., Sanftner & Tantillo, Chapter 12). As Gilbert (Chapter 14) observed, shame can "hinder accurate formulation because clients are inclined to narrate their stories to minimize shame." Even worse is the shame-based anger and rage that can be directed toward the therapy work and/or the therapist. This dynamic is eloquently demonstrated in a clinical vignette in which a client storms out of an appointment because his therapist arrives for the session a few minutes late (Morrison, Chapter 1). Morrison explained that the incident of the therapist arriving late confirmed the client's feelings of being small and insignificant. Not only does client shame pose a challenge to the therapy work—so, too, does therapist shame. As Ladany et al. (Chapter 13) noted, "identifying therapist shame, and then working through the therapist's experience, can be critical given its potential influence on the therapist's ability to function effectively in clinical contexts."

Other Hidden Dangers: The Link Between Shame and Suicide

A major danger of shame-related depression is suicide. In fact, the link between shame and suicide is mentioned specifically in seven chapters—by Potter-Efron (Chapter 9); Rizvi et al. (Chapter 10); Herman (Chapter 11); Gilbert (Chapter 14); Morrison (Chapter 1); Teyber et al. (Chapter 6); and Epstein and Falconier (Chapter 7). As Morrison (Chapter 1) noted, "the relationship of shame to suicide has been grossly underestimated in psychodynamic assessment. . . . " Morrison observed that shame-induced suicide is especially likely when clients feel exposed to public observation and condemnation (e.g., a government official about to be exposed for a scandal) or when clients feel deep despair for their failure to live up to life aspirations and ideals. Under such circumstances, careful assessment of suicide risk is warranted, and efforts to take appropriate action to ensure client safety may be necessary.

Suicidal clients can also elicit shame in the therapist. For example, Gilbert (Chapter 14) described how therapists may experience anticipatory shame when faced with a suicidal client, envisioning the shame of failing as a therapist should the client actually commit suicide and the shame and humiliation of being taken to court for failing to prevent the suicide. He noted that therapists' anticipation of shame can cloud their professional judgment when dealing with suicidal clients—for example, therapists may take unnecessarily conservative measures, seeking hospital admission even if this is not in the best interest of the client with the aim of avoiding even the remote possibility of being shamed or criticized.

Herman (Chapter 11) described the bidirectional dynamic of shame that can arise between suicidal clients and their therapists when transference reenactments of early childhood experiences take the form of power struggles in which both the patient and the therapist are at risk of humiliation and defeat:

> In the extreme case of the suicidal patient who refuses hospitalization, the patient is rendered helpless [i.e., humiliated and shamed] if the therapist hospitalizes her against her will; alternatively, the therapist is helpless [i.e., humiliated and shamed] if he disregards evidence of high risk." Herman recommends that, in such instances, clinicians explicitly describe the therapeutic dilemma, thus allowing the client to recognize and own both sides of the conflict rather than projecting one side (the role of victim or perpetrator) onto the therapist.

What to Do: Managing and Treating Client Shame

The master clinicians who contributed to this volume offer a wealth of insights and innovative techniques for managing and treating client shame.

Their ideas are apt to be useful for both beginning and seasoned clinicians. Trained in two quite different clinical programs, on opposite coasts, at different points in time, neither of us (Tangney or Dearing) recalls client shame being a focus of our clinical training (other than questions initiated by Dearing during supervision and coursework as a result of working in the Tangney's shame-focused research lab). We suspect the same is true of many clinicians trained in between us, temporally and geographically. As noted by Brown and coauthors (Chapter 15), few texts on psychotherapy training even mention client shame. Explicit attention to client shame in clinical supervision is equally rare in our experience and that of our colleagues. Yet the foregoing 15 chapters written by experienced, practicing clinicians show remarkable depth and continuity in how they address and transform maladaptive shame.

In an effort to integrate and summarize the authors' many rich observations and suggestions, we found the four domains identified by Greenberg's emotion-focused therapy framework to be a useful organizational scheme. Common themes are described in sections defined by Greenberg's four domains—relational validation, accessing and acknowledging shame, shame regulation, and transformation of shame—followed by a section describing more specific approaches and techniques that we hope will serve as the beginnings of a toolbox for clinicians as they encounter client shame daily.

Relational Validation

The authors were unanimous in emphasizing the importance of developing a supportive, validating, empathic, and affectively attuned relationship. As a sense of safety is established, clients can allow themselves to acknowledge and experience painful feelings of shame. To this end, therapists may find it helpful to state at the outset of treatment that a key goal is to create a safe, collaborative atmosphere in therapy.

Although not explicitly mentioned by our authors, we think the "MI spirit" of motivational interviewing/motivational enhancement therapy (MI/MET) is essentially a shame-reducing approach by virtue of relational validation. In MI/MET, therapists validate and empower clients by working from the client's values (rather than therapist-imposed values, which implicitly suggests there is something wrong with the client's own values and goals). MI/MET therapists also validate (and thereby "de-shame") clients by emphasizing equality in the relationship (e.g., asking permission to give advice), by eschewing the role of expert, and by providing frequent affirmations.

Helping Clients to Access and Acknowledge Shame

Our clinician–authors were also unanimous in emphasizing the importance of helping clients to recognize and identify shame as a first step in helping clients manage and ultimately resolve or positively transform painful feelings of shame. As both Morrison (Chapter 1) and Greenberg and Iwakabe (Chapter 3) noted, a key to successful treatment is bringing client shame out of hiding and concealment (its natural state). Shapiro and Powers (Chapter 5) further stated,

> So, as with any avoidance, that which is most feared most needs to be faced. The most natural response to the experience of shame (i.e., to hide) is the most toxic, whereas the least automatic or natural (i.e., to expose the source of the shame) is the most healing. As the old adage goes, one needs to "let the air get at it." It is only when shame reaches the light of day that the healing process can begin.

Simply verbalizing shame-inducing events and associated experiences can help reduce the pain of shame. As clients translate into words their preverbal, global shame reaction, they bring to bear a more logical, differentiated thought process that may prompt them to spontaneously reevaluate the global negative self-attributions associated with the experience. In fact, therapists can help clients come to realize that most flaws, setbacks, and transgressions really don't warrant global feelings of worthlessness or shame.

Efforts to help clients access and acknowledge their underlying feelings of shame can be a tricky business. Greenberg and Iwakabe (Chapter 3) observed that "drawing attention to the shameful experience often only intensifies the impulse to retreat and close down emotionally." Herman (Chapter 11) underscored the importance of "titrating" shame so that the client will not become overwhelmed, but instead "experiences dignity in the telling"— a process reminiscent of graded exposure. In this regard, it is helpful to reflect and empathize with the client's discomfort and to normalize the desire to hide. More generally, therapists can help embolden their clients to access and acknowledge painful hidden feelings by normalizing the experience of negative emotions such as shame, guilt, sadness, and anger. Here, too, psychoeducation may be useful in the form of a brief discussion of the functionalist perspective on emotions in lay terms. From this perspective, all emotions evolved for good reason—they are (or were) useful in some contexts but not in others (e.g., Izard, 1977). Shame, in particular, was likely adaptive in more primitive, preverbal, hierarchical societies but is less adaptive than behavior-focused guilt in most modern contexts (Tangney & Salovey, 2010). In the case of shame, normal does not necessarily equate with adaptive.

Therapists need to monitor their own natural tendency to collude with clients in avoiding or prematurely trying to eradicate client shame (Teyber et al., Chapter 6). Potter-Efron (Chapter 9) cautioned that therapists must "accept the client's shame rather than try to argue it away." In our rush to "help," therapists are understandably drawn to try to wipe away clients' shame—to make them feel better in the moment. (We guess this may be especially true for new therapists in training.) But such well-intentioned efforts are apt to be experienced on some level as invalidating. Therapists need to tolerate, accept, and "hold" clients' shame in order to provide them with an opportunity to constructively manage and resolve this most unpleasant emotion.

Sometimes clients express anger that serves as a cover for shame. Greenberg and Iwakabe (Chapter 3) suggested that in such instances clients be encouraged to express their reactive anger at being shamed, but interventions should acknowledge such anger as a secondary reaction—a face-saving, coping response—while at the same time highlighting the underlying core experience of shame. For those who are defended by grandiosity and sense of unique specialness (in essence, a reaction formation), Morrison (Chapter 1) suggested that therapists look for cracks in the clients' defenses to elicit and discuss feelings of underlying shame.

Although painful and fraught with potential pitfalls, the process of helping clients access and acknowledge feelings of shame can be healing in and of itself. Identifying shame in the moment can lead to "an 'aha!' experience of recognition and relief that these long-held self-loathing feelings are, perhaps, tolerable and acceptable" (Morrison, Chapter 1). At the same time, it is important to not to encourage clients to unduly perseverate on shame. Too much shame is a problem. As Epstein and Falconier (Chapter 7) noted, the goal is not to express shame and perseverate but to express shame and resolve it.

Is it necessary to identify shame as such? This is a question we frequently encounter from students and colleagues: Is it necessary to use the term *shame* in session to label such feelings? Our clinician experts' views on this matter varied widely. Epstein and Falconier (Chapter 7) stated unambiguously that no, it's not necessary for client or therapist to label shame as *shame*. They can use other, more descriptive terms (e.g., negative self-evaluation and feelings of worthlessness associated with violation of personal standards). In contrast, Rizvi et al. (Chapter 10) suggested that therapy benefits from "direct attention to the shame when it arises, by labeling it as shame and discussing it openly as an obstacle to successful problem-solving efforts." Brown and coauthors (Chapter 15) were even more adamant that labeling shame as such is essential, stating, "We need to develop the language to talk about shame before we can process our experiences in a meaningful way." In fact, a substantial portion of the early work in their treatment program is "educational." They reported that "many clinicians have identified that developing a vocabulary and definition for shame is one of the most transformative components of [the shame resilience] curriculum."

From our perspective, the use of the term *shame* is a matter of choice depending in part on the needs of a given client and in part on the orientation of the therapist. Some clients may spontaneously offer their own idiosyncratic descriptions of the shame phenomenon (e.g., "that dark, awful, sinking feeling"). In such cases, Tangney has found it effective to adopt the clients' personal terminology, with shame work proceeding effectively. Other clients may bristle at the mention of shame, especially shame-prone clients early in treatment. They may benefit initially from alternative, less threatening terms, such as *embarrassment*. We agree, however, that psychoeducation in the emotional realm can be extremely helpful. Expanding clients' shame-relevant "emotion knowledge" (Denham, 1998) can be a powerful intervention in and of itself, enhancing their ability to reexamine and better regulate the pain of shame. In particular, as discussed below, simply educating clients about the distinction between shame and guilt can result in dramatic positive change.

Shame Regulation

The next task for clients, upon recognizing and acknowledging shame, is learning skills to regulate this often pernicious affective experience. Our authors had many thoughts on how to help clients develop such skills. Some approaches (e.g., Greenberg & Iwakabe, Chapter 3) focused directly on self-soothing or distraction techniques, such as taking a bath or engaging in pleasurable exercise. A number of authors have emphasized meditative practice and self-acceptance, such as that those espoused by acceptance and commitment therapy (Hayes, Strosahl, & Wilson, 1999) and dialectical behavior therapy (DBT; Linehan, 1993). More specifically, both Greenberg and Iwakabe (Chapter 3) and Rizvi and coauthors (Chapter 10) encouraged clients to practice mindful non-judgment. In stepping back and simply observing their thoughts and feelings, clients learn to describe internal and external experiences, "sticking to the facts" rather than engaging in shame-inducing processes of evaluation and judgment. Another key component of acceptance and commitment therapy and DBT, developing tolerance for negative affect, is also advocated (see also Koerner et al., Chapter 4).

We were struck by how many authors identified the development of self-compassion as an especially effective method for regulating shame. Gilbert (Chapter 14), for example, believes that compassion—for the self and for others—is an especially potent antidote for shame. As Gilbert noted, however, because shame-prone (i.e., self-critical) people have had little experience with compassion (from others or toward the self), it is incumbent upon therapists to teach it. A key aim of Gilbert's compassion focused therapy is to teach clients to become more attentive to and accepting of their feelings and needs. One method for enhancing self-compassion, suggested by Furukawa and Hunt (Chapter 8), is to ask the client to imagine giving advice or comfort to a real or imaginary friend who has a similar shame-inducing problem. Furukawa and Hunt described the advantages of "taking the self" out of the equation, noting that people are usually much better able to forgive and comfort others than the self.

Transformation of Shame

From Greenberg and Iwakabe's perspective (Chapter 3), the ultimate goal of emotion-focused therapy is to transform problematic emotional experiences into more adaptive, empowering, and meaningful emotions that can then serve as a source of strength, as an internal resource. Our clinician–authors had much to say about ways in which shame can be meaningfully transformed in affective, cognitive, and behavioral terms.

Cognitive-Affective Transformations. In our view, the transformation of shame into guilt is one of the most common and effective means of resolving problematic shame, resulting in an enhanced capacity for adaptive moral motivation and behavior. Sometimes all that's needed is to educate clients about the difference between shame and guilt. We have been surprised to find in our clinical work that many clients have not considered the difference between condemning a behavior versus condemning the self. They had not considered the possibility that there might be "good ways" and "bad ways" to feel bad in response to failures and transgressions. People seem to readily understand that it is better to teach a child that he or she did a bad thing than to point a finger and say, "You are a bad kid." Shame-prone people have a harder time recognizing that during shame experiences, they are essentially pointing the finger at themselves and saying, "You are a bad person." When this is pointed out and they are given an explicit choice, many spontaneously shift to more adaptive (and less aversive) behavior-focused feelings of guilt.

Some forms of treatment implicitly support the transformation of self-focused shame into behavior-focused guilt. For example, Potter-Efron (Chapter 9) observed that participation in Alcoholics Anonymous can promote such a transformation as members are "encouraged to separate their character flaws from their core selves (Step 4) and to make amends for what they have done wrong during their addictions (Steps 8 and 9)," thus moving from a shame to guilt focus.

From a social cognitive perspective (Maddux & Tangney, 2010), therapists can support the transformation of shame into guilt by encouraging clients to make cognitive reevaluations using key cognitive–behavioral techniques described by, for example, Beck (1983) and Ellis (1962) to challenge internal, stable, and global attributions (i.e., irrational beliefs) that are associated with shame (Tracy & Robins, 2006).

More generally, therapists may find it useful to help clients reexamine cognitions about the nature and degree of self-punishment necessary for violating personal standards by reexamining and modifying perfectionistic standards (How flexible are they? What are the advantages and disadvantages of living according to such high standards?), by challenging excessive concerns about others' evaluations of the self, and by examining clients' early family experiences concerning shame and expectations.

Potter-Efron (Chapter 9), too, emphasized cognitive–behavioral techniques such as "exploring the exceptions," (e.g., in response to "I'm a failure" or "I'm not good enough," acknowledging "Well, I did win an athletic scholarship to the university"). In response to "I'm not good enough," therapists can ask, "As compared with whom? Some idealized self? An idealized parent, peer, or recovering addict? An idealized version of the self conjured up by a parent or significant other?" We believe it is often extraordinarily useful to guide clients in a reexamination of the advantages and disadvantages of seeking to become a "perfect person." In addition to underscoring the impossibility of achieving such a goal, it is helpful to appeal to the client's rationality and good sense, discussing the fact that there's a point of seriously diminishing returns: The effort required to go from an A to an A+—or from a really, really good person to a perfect person—is enormous (and, quite probably, impossible). One could better use that time and energy to earn three other As—to become really, really good along three other valued dimensions as a person. Not infrequently, clients idealize the therapist himself or herself. Thus, it can be therapeutic for clinicians to allow clients to see therapists as real human beings who have their own frailties and shortcomings. (See the section later in this chapter on the value of therapists acknowledging their own shame.) For some people, addressing spirituality and self-forgiveness (e.g., using symbolic rituals as discussed by Furukawa and Hunt, Chapter 8) in therapy can be a useful tool for moving in a positive direction of personal growth.

When working with clients, Rizvi et al. (Chapter 10) find it useful to explicitly distinguish between justified versus unjustified shame. Rizvi et al. defined *justified shame* as a reaction to behavior that would lead to rejection from important others. Also relevant, we believe, are the answers to questions such as Did you really do it? Did you mean to do it? Is it contrary to your own personal values and code of ethics? Rizvi et al. described strategies for addressing justified shame, including apologizing and repairing the damage, committing to and implementing an effective plan to solve the problem (e.g., anger management therapy), and accepting consequences. Each of these strategies for justified shame involves an emphasis on a shift toward guilt rather than shame-related responses.

In what scenarios is it inappropriate to frame the therapeutic goal as one of shifting from shame to guilt? As emphasized by Rivzi et al., it is important to determine if there's a rational basis for shame or guilt—that is, to collaboratively determine whether the client actually *is* responsible for the shame-eliciting (or guilt-eliciting) event(s). If so, many of the suggestions provided by our authors on cognitively restructuring shame into guilt would be relevant. In cases of justified guilt, the focus can be on reparation (e.g., apology, resolution to do things differently in the future). But in other cases, clients experience shame owing to misplaced responsibility—for example, when someone feels shame for being a victim of physical or sexual abuse or simply for not living up to a significant other's expectations that are at odds with one's own values. What is the therapeutic goal when shame or guilt is an inappropriate response? In our view, when clients feel shame irrationally for some outcome over which they had no responsibility, it is useful to encourage clients to reassess attributions of culpability. Cognitive–behavioral techniques informed by concepts from attribution theory can help guide such interventions. Further guidance is offered within several of the foregoing chapters (e.g., Rivzi et al., Chapter 10; Greenberg & Iwakabe, Chapter 3).

Greenberg and Iwakabe (Chapter 3), for example, noted that survivors of maltreatment and abuse are especially apt to become shame prone, often feeling somehow responsible for the abuse. In such cases, it may be especially healing to help survivors appropriately externalize the blame back onto the abuser—"putting the blame where it belongs," to coin Greenberg and Iwakabe's (Chapter 3) phrase. With this deserved shift in blame often come empowered anger and pride as the client constructs new meaning for long-standing wounds. As Greenberg and Iwakabe observed,

> Sadness or anger can be fundamentally growth producing in that they point to adaptive actions appropriate to the situation. For example, sadness can lead to reaching out to connect to others, or anger can lead to asserting one's right to live one's own life without shame.

Here, too, it is important to distinguish adaptive, empowering anger from maladaptive rage born of narcissistic slights and reactions to humiliation. "Maladaptive rage is overly intense, chronic, destructive, and/or inappropriate and is often in reaction to minor insults or failure experiences. . . . The focus of such work is on asserting the self rather than destroying the other" (Greenberg & Iwakabe, Chapter 3).

Modifying Behavior to Transform Shame. A unique approach to treating shame endorsed by Rizvi et al. (Chapter 10) centers on the concept of "opposite action," a technique derived from DBT (Linehan, 1993). The notion is to encourage actions that are incompatible with urges that arise from the client's unwanted emotion. In the case of shame, therapists may encourage clients to behave "as if" they are not ashamed, to approach rather than hide, to hold one's head high rather than shrink, to proclaim one's worth rather than communicating shame. The effectiveness of opposite action derives from cognitive dissonance. As Rizvi et al. noted, countless cognitive dissonance studies have shown that "getting people to act contrary to their attitudes (when they believe they have freely chosen to do so) is a powerful way to change beliefs and attitudes, including low self-esteem."

Koerner et al. (Chapter 4), too, advocated an action-oriented approach to the treatment of shame. Functional analytic therapists endeavor to create conditions that help clients learn to respond with skill and flexibility to situations that evoke problematic shame—even while feeling intense shame. To this end, therapy often focuses on practical skills (e.g., organization, public speaking) to help clients remedy skills deficits and/or develop new skills and abilities.

More Approaches and Techniques: Expanding the Clinician's Shame-Focused Toolbox

Our master clinicians offered a number of approaches and techniques that may expand the toolbox of clinicians working with clients who are troubled by maladaptive shame. Among these approaches and techniques are recording of sessions, two-chair dialogue, interpersonal coping, group therapy, and therapists acknowledging their own shame.

Recording Sessions

One of the most intriguing approaches, suggested independently in two chapters, is the notion of audio- or videotaping sessions so that both client and therapist are able to catch "lightning fast" shame episodes and subject them to more careful scrutiny and analysis (Koerner et al., Chapter 4; Teyber et al., Chapter 6). Episodes of shame are apt to erupt unbidden and unexpectedly. The intricate dynamics of shame intertwined with anger, deflection, and defense can play out within seconds, unnoticed and unprocessed by both clients and therapists in the moment. To make matters worse, while in the midst of a shame experience, clients are apt to be temporarily cognitively impaired— overwhelmed and absent a cool head—and unable to coolly process the emotionally laden and complex shame-provoked processes occurring at both the intrapersonal and interpersonal levels (Lewis, 1971). As Stadter (Chapter 2) noted, when clients are in the midst of a shame experience, "they may be too disrupted to be able to process it." With the benefit of time to recover and some emotional distance, clients and therapists may be better placed to objectively observe and explore shame-induced behaviors and shame-inducing interactions. Stadter suggested that it may be necessary to revisit such interactions in a subsequent session. Audio- or videotaped records of these subtle but powerful shame triggers and their ensuing effects can be an invaluable tool in this regard. Recordings offer clients (and therapists) a second chance to observe and process such events from a more objective perspective at a time when they are more cognitively able.

Two-Chair Dialogue

Greenberg and Iwakabe (Chapter 3) identified two-chair dialogue as the intervention of choice for clients mired in self-criticism. By encouraging clients to take on the dual roles of condemner and condemned, therapists can help them in capturing

> the expressive quality of contempt, specifying the shame-producing cognitions, heightening awareness of agency in the shame-producing process, and countering shame by supporting the emergence of the healthy part of self with feelings of pride. An example of the contempt expressed from the Critic's chair (i.e., the self's critical voice) might be "You're pathetic," and this will evoke shame expressed from the other aspect of self: "I feel so worthless, like curling up into a ball and hiding." In this dialogue people come to see that by denigrating themselves, they are agents in the production of their experience of shame and that they can change how they relate to themselves. People resolve this split as more adaptive feelings such as anger and sadness and later more self-assertion such as "Leave me alone; stop attacking me like that" evolve to counteract the shame. Resolution of the split is seen when the Critic softens into compassion, saying, "I don't want to make you suffer; I do care about you." An integration of the two aspects can then occur, resulting in self-acceptance and a stronger sense of self.

A key insight gained from such two-chair dialogues is that current shame-producing messages are internally generated by the client and therefore amenable to change.

Interpersonal Coping

Although this was implicit in many chapters, Epstein and Falconier (Chapter 7) focused most explicitly on the process of recovering from an experience of shame in-the-moment. Like others, Epstein and Falconier emphasized the importance of sufficient self-awareness so clients can identify their own shame experience. Once recognized, clients have open two major pathways toward managing and resolving the pain of shame: (a) individual coping (e.g., cognitive restructuring or reframing, self-soothing) and (b) reassuring interactions with a partner (or significant other). The latter interpersonal pathway is not much discussed in other chapters, but we imagine it is a strategy that is more common than recognized in well-functioning individuals. Fighting the natural urge to hide, resilient people may be especially adept at seeking out social support from safe others—a supportive spouse, a close friend, a trusted colleague. Epstein and Falconier emphasized that to effectively use the social support pathway, the shamed individual must be aware of the shame experience and willing to share that information "clearly and constructively" with the significant other. One of the key elements of Brown's shame resilience curriculum (Brown, 2009; Brown et al., Chapter 15) is teaching clients to "speak shame." Specifically, within the context of the therapy group, clients are taught to become more comfortable sharing their shame experiences. Eventually, group participants are encouraged to identify others outside of the group with whom it is safe to talk about occurrences of shame.

For less resilient individuals, the very act of seeking professional help and of struggling to explore shame is a hopeful and important first step toward developing effective interpersonal methods of coping with and alleviating shame. Daring to share one's shame and experiencing its transformation into something more useful in a reassuring therapeutic relationship can then serve as a template from which to generalize. Therapists can explicitly encourage clients to reach out for interpersonal support when experiencing shame in the course of daily life; such behaviors can be reinforced by shame-alleviating client–therapist encounters.

In the context of couples or family therapy, therapist and client can explicitly recruit a partner or other family member more directly to serve as an ally in helping correct unrealistic standards and other shame-inducing cognitions in the course of real life, outside of session. In cases in which partners or family members tend to be less constructive and more inclined to induce client shame, therapists can directly coach such significant others to reexamine beliefs about the advantages of punitiveness. Do people who behave badly deserve to be reminded of it? Do they deserve to be made to feel awful, to be severely punished? Such shame-inducing significant others can be directly coached to express concerns and dissatisfaction in a more constructive way (e.g., requesting a positive change in behavior rather than denigrating the client as a person). In coaching partners or other family members, Potter-Efron's (Chapter 9) Five As of positive interactions may be especially useful:

- Attention: I have time for you.
- Approval: I like what you do.
- Acceptance: It's OK for you to be you.
- Admiration: I can learn from you.
- Affirmation: I celebrate your existence.

In fact, these Five As can be used more generally to coach families, couples, parents, teachers, and even beginning therapists in concrete ways to affirm, not shame, individuals.

Group Therapy

Group treatment is rife with additional sources of shame beyond the many operating in the context of individual therapy. But when facilitated by a clinician who is sensitive to shame issues, group therapy can be a powerful context for resolving shame-based concerns. In fact, the authors of four chapters (Brown et al., Chapter 15; Herman, Chapter 11; Furukawa & Hunt, Chapter 8; and Shapiro & Powers, Chapter 5) independently suggested that if it is well managed, group therapy can be the optimal environment for treating shame.

First, group therapy can be helpful in normalizing shame experiences by showing that others are facing similar issues (Furukawa & Hunt, Chapter 8). As Shapiro and Powers (Chapter 5) noted, "Universality . . . can mitigate the feeling of aloneness and individual corruptness that often accompanies shame." Second, even when a group member may not yet be ready to face his or her own feelings of shame directly, the experience of seeing another, less defended member process his or her own shame can help desensitize the reluctant client and provide an indirect learning experience. Third, because of the shame-inducing power imbalance inherent between client and therapist, Herman (Chapter 11) suggested that group psychotherapy may be especially useful for traumatized (and other shame-prone) clients. In group therapy, many clinical interventions come from directly from peers.

Therapists Acknowledging Their Own Shame

A number of chapters explicitly discussed the power of therapists acknowledging their own shame experiences (e.g., Herman, Chapter 11; Morrison, Chapter 1; Koerner et al., Chapter 4; Potter-Efron, Chapter 9; see also Sanftner and Tantillo's discussion in Chapter 12 of the utility of supervisors sharing their own shame experiences). As Potter-Efron (Chapter 9) noted, "Clients need to see that their counselors are human." The notion that it is normal and potentially useful for therapists to experience shame is apt to be reassuring to beginning therapists who fear not being adequate enough. But this raises the sticky issue of how much personal material to reveal and how to do so while still maintaining appropriate boundaries. On this point, Koerner et al. (Chapter 4) offered the following:

> There are times when disclosing to clients one's own thoughts, reactions, and personal experiences regarding shame is helpful to the therapeutic process. A major factor to take into account in making a decision to disclose is whether such disclosure will facilitate clients having greater contact with their shame issues or whether it will take them away from their own focus. . . . Disclosures should be titrated to what the client can handle and should almost always include a discussion of how the client is reacting to the disclosure and why the disclosure was offered.

Supervision can be invaluable for helping to determine when and how much to self-disclose without weakening appropriate client–therapist boundaries.

Ways Therapists Inadvertently Shame Clients
(and What to Do About It)

Despite their very best intentions, therapists can inadvertently induce feelings of shame in the very clients they seek to help. Stadter (Chapter 2) discussed several ways in which clients may feel "objectified," and thus shamed, by well-meaning therapists. Therapists can unintentionally shame clients by focusing on or reifying a psychiatric diagnosis. Clients may end up feeling that the therapist sees them not as a person but "objectified" as a diagnostic category. Clients are also apt to feel neglected and "not really seen" when therapists use a one-size-fits-all "cookbook" approach to treatment. Or they may feel objectified "as merely the therapist's 3 p.m. Monday appointment." (Morrison, in Chapter 1, provided a moving case example of the shame that can arise from such a perception.) To avoid the shame of objectification, Stadter recommended that diagnoses, interventions, and even scheduling of appointments should be done "in a manner that promotes collaboration rather than a situation" totally driven by the "expert therapist."

In addition, Stadter (Chapter 2) cautioned that clients are apt to feel neglected, "not really seen," and thus shamed when interpretations are delivered with certainty and are off the mark. Even well-conceived interpretations can be experienced as shaming. Clients may experience the process of interpretation as intrusive, omniscient, and uncovering and as an attack on one's intrapsychic privacy. Moreover, a therapist's interpretation may be seen as implying inadequacy and a lack of insight on the part of the client. Stadter recommended that interpretations be

> presented in a style conveying lack of certainty but also an invitation to explore . . . (e.g., "I'm not sure of this, but I had a sense that your daughter's comment hurt you more than you might have thought. Is there anything to that impression of mine?").

When therapists shame clients, it's not simply an error; it's a golden opportunity to process and resolve shame. As Greenberg and Iwakabe (Chapter 3) pointed out, healing such shame-induced ruptures in the client–therapist relationship can be highly therapeutic. A therapist's unwitting error presents an opportunity for a valuable corrective experience, one that may be generalized to similar shame-inducing misunderstandings outside of the therapy room.

Sensitivity to Cultural Factors

Furukawa and Hunt (Chapter 8) advised that when working with clients from different cultures, backgrounds, or ethnicities, therapists engage in "an ongoing questioning of our assumptions about other cultures and our own reactions to them. It requires therapists to be humble." Perhaps more than any other emotion, culture colors how, when, and why shame is experienced and expressed, thus further complicating an already complicated picture.

As noted by Greenberg and Iwakabe (Chapter 3), in collectivist cultures that emphasize group harmony, social hierarchy, and interdependence, expressions of shame or embarrassment may be used for instrumental purposes—to convey submission or to smooth over social interactions in order to maintain group harmony and to preserve culturally defined hierarchical roles: "Being humble and acting with reserve are considered virtuous and respectful." Furukawa and Hunt (Chapter 8) suggested being sensitive to such practices by looking to the client for cues regarding direct eye contact, direct questioning, handshakes, and power relations within families.

One implication of such instrumental uses of shame is that Western therapists should guard against overinterpreting initial expressions of shame and embarrassment as necessarily maladaptive or problematic. Alternatively, although some shame may be normative, this is not to suggest that clients from collectivistic cultures are immune to problems with shame (or that their experiences of shame are necessarily adaptive). In fact, Greenberg and Iwakabe (Chapter 3) pointed out that shame plays a prominent role in a variety of mental health problems among individuals from Asian collectivist cultures. They cited, as an example, a class of phobic disorders associated with fear of being publicly shamed. No one, it seems, is immune to maladaptive shame!

Greenberg and Iwakabe (Chapter 3) encouraged therapists working with clients from collectivist cultures to make sure clients understand the rationale for accessing, tolerating, expressing, and understanding shame and other related emotions in therapy: "In particular, they need to know that expression of negative emotions in front of the therapist is not only allowed but also is essential to therapeutic work." Culturally prescribed "display rules" may dictate that negative emotions such as anger and sadness (and the positive emotion of pride) be inhibited. Clients from such backgrounds may benefit from special permission or invitation to experience and express emotions in the context of therapy (and perhaps in their everyday life).

Furukawa and Hunt (Chapter 8) identified numerous sources of shame that may be overlooked by therapists working with immigrant and refugee clients from culturally diverse backgrounds. Although stigma associated with mental illness persists in the United States, such stigma is more pronounced in many other cultures. Clients from such cultures may feel deeply shamed simply for seeking help for mental health issues. Furukawa and Hunt recommended that, early in treatment, it may be helpful to emphasize how common and acceptable it is in the United States to seek help from psychologists and other mental health professionals.

Clients' shame may be further compounded by difficulty speaking English and by language barriers more generally. Furukawa and Hunt recommended that in such instances, the therapist reassure clients that English is difficult to learn and acknowledge the therapist's own shortcoming in not knowing clients' native language. To further reduce feelings of incompetence and shame, Furukawa and Hunt suggested that therapists request forgiveness when asking clients to repeat themselves and show a willingness to work hard together toward effective communication.

It is useful to bear in mind that when immigrants and refugees seek professional help, the presenting problem is often a more immediate survival issue (e.g., financial problems, children's school-related issues, need for shelter) than a psychological concern:

> Practical survival problems may be associated with feelings of incompetence, worthlessness, and shame and cannot be ignored. The challenge for the therapist is to deal with these external but serious case management problems that clients face while being aware of and addressing underlying psychological issues. (Furukawa & Hunt, Chapter 8)

An intriguing approach suggested by Furukawa and Hunt to ease the burden of shame is the use of culturally relevant rituals. They cited, as an example, sweeping rituals common in many cultures of Central and South America that can be drawn upon to help clients resolve shame related to past traumatic events. Alternatively, intense shame and guilt associated with deceased loved ones can be alleviated through traditional mourning rituals, as described by Furukawa and Hunt. With an open mind and a sincere effort to understand the nuances of the client's cultural background, therapists can creatively adapt treatment strategies to help clients regulate and transform difficult experiences of shame.

Therapists Experience Shame, Too

Shame is not solely the domain of clients. Therapists experience shame, too. As both Morrison (Chapter 1) and Herman (Chapter 11) independently observed, shame is contagious—therapists can catch it from their clients. Herman emphasized the bidirectional dynamic of shame in the therapeutic relationship. Shame-prone clients are apt to inadvertently shame therapists (projecting their own shame onto the therapist), and (as noted earlier) therapists can inadvertently shame clients. Stadter (Chapter 2), too, observed that therapists are vulnerable to shaming and being shamed by clients. The former is especially problematic in that it is so inconsistent with the ideal therapist role of empathic, caring helper.

In fact, as discussed by Sanftner and Tantillo (Chapter 12) and by Ladany and coauthors (Chapter 13), therapists often struggle with fears about adequacy and competence. This may be especially the case for therapists in training, who are apt to "worry whether they are doing things correctly, understanding the client sensitively, formulating accurately, and intervening appropriately. Shame may be a major reason that important material is not disclosed during supervision" (Gilbert, Chapter 14). But even seasoned therapists are not immune. Chapters by Morrison (Chapter 1) and by Koerner et al. (Chapter 4) identified numerous sources of therapist shame, including identification with a client whose shame issues are similar to those of the therapist, mistakes made in session, unsuccessful treatment outcomes, and unfavorable comparisons with colleagues, to name a few. Moreover, because shame is incongruous with the role of therapist, we think that mental health workers may be further vulnerable to the double whammy of "metashame"—feeling ashamed of being ashamed!

Group therapists may be especially vulnerable to being shamed in the therapy hour because group members may be emboldened by numbers. Shapiro and Powers (Chapter 5) observed that group therapy members not infrequently disparage and devalue the group leader. Disparagement of the leader may represent an effort to distract the group from more difficult material, or it may arise from projections of unacceptable parts of the self. Regardless, such encounters should be anticipated, and group leaders need to have a pretty hardy level of professional esteem to weather the shame that these attacks are apt to induce.

Shapiro and Powers also remarked that therapists are at times devalued (shamed) by other professionals. They noted that in the "pecking order" of the mental health professions, group therapy has been perceived for many years as occupying a lower position despite empirical evidence supporting the efficacy of group therapy. Morrison (Chapter 1), too, referred to one-upmanship in the institutional hierarchy as a source of therapist shame.

The impact of therapist shame on the therapy process can be dramatic. Koerner et al. (Chapter 4) cited shame as the potential culprit when therapists avoid dealing with problematic client behaviors (e.g., chronic lateness, not paying therapy bills) and when they do not observe limits and boundaries (e.g., answering client phone calls late at night). Koerner et al. advocated supervision in such instances, asserting that "seeking consultation from a trusted colleague when one's own shame issues interfere with treatment is both courageous and ethical."

Numerous authors in this volume stressed the importance of therapists being aware of areas of vulnerability, recognizing (and managing) shame quickly when it arises in session, and dealing with shame issues and shame vulnerability in the therapists' own personal therapy. Similarly, Brown et al.

(Chapter 15) advocated that therapists "do their own shame resilience work before they can ethically and effectively do shame work with clients . . . 'we need to do the work before we do the work. . . .'"

Importance of Supervision

In addition to personal therapy, supervision is an ideal setting in which to "do the work." Our guess, however, is that most supervision, as currently practiced, does not address shame—either on the part of clients or on the part of supervised therapists. Tangney, for example, has had some outstanding supervisors over the years, yet she cannot recall a single instance in which client shame or her own shame was broached in supervision. (In retrospect, she certainly can recall multiple instances of shame—both client and therapist shame—in the therapy room!)

Because shame can be profoundly unsettling and, at the same time, hidden or disguised, Shapiro and Powers (Chapter 5) strongly advised professional or peer supervision when shame issues arise. They noted that supervision is invaluable not just in instances of already perceived shame experiences but also when therapists find themselves feeling confused, stymied, or ineffective: "It is useful to suspect shame as the culprit and valuable to allow another set of eyes to ferret out the potential manifestations of shame and the defenses aroused in response to its presence" (Shapiro & Powers, Chapter 5).

Ladany et al. (Chapter 13) advocated that supervisors adopt a collaborative approach from the outset, negotiating the goals of supervision and the manner in which things will be discussed. For supervisee shame experiences to be fully understood, the supervisor must facilitate exploration, deepening the supervisee's understanding of his or her reactions and exploring possible links to previous shame events in the supervisee's life (i.e., countertransference). Because shame events are apt to affect the therapist's sense of professional self, efforts are needed to reinforce or rebuild the supervisee's self-efficacy. It is also helpful to normalize the supervisee's experience, underscoring that therapists are human and that mistakes, even significant ones, are bound to happen.

Sanftner and Tantillo (Chapter 12) observed that because supervisees have less power in the supervisory relationship (and less experience), they are especially vulnerable to shame. Supervisors can enhance effectiveness by "[reframing] vulnerability to emphasize nonjudgmental awareness, curiosity, and self-empathy" and by presenting "uncertainty and vulnerability as opportunities for growth." There is also use in reexamining perfectionistic and unrealistic images of what a therapist should be. By encouraging novice therapists to abandon perfectionistic standards and by helping them develop self-compassion, episodes of shame can be viewed as a unique opportunity for nonjudgmental inquiry and professional growth.

Finally, we think it is useful to consider clinicians' irritation with clients (or subtle denigration when talking about clients during supervision) as a possible sign of therapist shame. Research consistently shows a link between shame and hostility or anger (for reviews, see Tangney & Dearing, 2002; Tangney, Stuewig, & Mashek, 2007). On occasion, therapists find themselves irritated or annoyed with clients—an inevitable, if occasional, human response to the difficult work of helping others who do not always respond immediately to treatment efforts. When a therapist finds himself or herself feeling uncharacteristically aggravated, exasperated, or even scornful toward a difficult client, the possibility of unrecognized shame should be considered, and peer or professional supervision can be invaluable.

Is Shame Ever Adaptive?

In line with empirical research (for reviews, see Tangney & Dearing, 2002; Tangney et al., 2007), clinicians' sense of the psychological and social implications of shame is grim. Shame is uniformly portrayed in the chapters in this volume as the root of multiple forms of psychopathology and as the source of disruptions to the psychotherapeutic process. The question arises: Is shame ever adaptive? Why in the world do humans have the culturally universal capacity to experience this painful, often devastating emotion?

Contributing clinician–authors were mixed in this regard. Epstein and Falconier (Chapter 7) believed that mild to moderate (but not intense) shame can motivate people to make positive changes. The theory underlying emotion-focused therapy (Greenberg & Iwakabe, Chapter 3) explicitly acknowledges an adaptive form of shame. *Primary adaptive shame* is conceptualized as a direct, initial, rapid reaction to a situation. Similar to the functions of self-esteem in Leary's (2005) sociometer theory, shame can serve as a source of adaptive information, informing us that we are too exposed and that other people will not support our actions. From an emotion-focused therapy perspective, shame can inform us that we have violated important standards or values. Moreover, displays of shame can function to reduce the likelihood of others' retaliatory aggression, evoking instead affiliative responses, such as sympathy and forgiveness from others (Greenberg & Iwakabe, Chapter 3; Gilbert, Chapter 14).

More broadly, Koerner et al. (Chapter 4) posited that access to vital resources depends on membership in groups and on one's rank within the group. Feelings of shame aid us by alerting us when our behavior is apt to result in a demotion in status or exclusion from the group. It prompts us (sharply) to inhibit offending behaviors and to strive to correct them. Shame signals us to shift behavior in order to reduce the threat of rejection.

In contrast, Morrison's (Chapter 1) answer to the question "In what ways can shame be adaptive?" is unambiguous: None. Morrison wrote, "I find it difficult to find any redeeming qualities in shame per se, in contrast with the clear benefits of self-awareness. Rather, I believe that what can be useful about shame lies only in its resolution."

From our perspective, shame is a relatively primitive emotion that served adaptive "appeasement" functions in the distant past among ancestors whose cognitive processes were less sophisticated and in the context of much simpler societies. This sociobiological approach taken by Gilbert (1997) and others (de Waal, 1996; Fessler, 2007; Keltner, 1995; Leary, Britt, Cutlip, & Templeton, 1992; Leary, Landel & Patton, 1996) emphasizes the appeasement functions of shame that reaffirm the relative rank in a dominance hierarchy and minimize harmful intragroup aggression. In short, shame evolved as an important damage limitation strategy in contexts in which the likelihood of aggression was high and the consequences often life threatening.

Humankind, however, has evolved not only in terms of physical characteristics but also in terms of emotional, cognitive, and social complexity. With increasingly complex perspective-taking and attributional abilities, modern human beings have the capacity to distinguish between self and behavior, to take another person's perspective, and to empathize with others' distress. Whereas early moral goals centered on reducing potentially lethal aggression, clarifying social rank, and enhancing conformity to social norms, modern morality centers on the ability to acknowledge one's wrongdoing, accept responsibility, and take reparative action (Tangney & Salovey, 2010). In this sense, guilt is today the moral emotion of choice.

EMPIRICALLY SUPPORTED TREATMENTS TARGETING SHAME: STATE OF THE FIELD AND FUTURE DIRECTIONS

No doubt about it: Shame is ubiquitous in the therapy room. Clients frequently present with shame-related issues. The process of therapy often provokes experiences of shame. And therapists are by no means immune to the dark pain of shame.

This volume represents a first compendium of master clinicians' approaches and techniques for addressing shame in the context of mental health treatment. The vast majority of contributors work from theoretical perspectives that do not explicitly consider shame as a focus of treatment. Yet whether cognitive–behavioral, psychodynamic, or humanistic in orientation, these clinicians had much to say about managing and treating shame in the therapy hour.

At present, there exist only a few explicitly shame-focused therapies: Gilbert's compassion focused therapy (Chapter 14), Rizvi et al.'s shame-enhanced DBT for the treatment of borderline personality disorder

(Chapter 10), and Brown's Connections curriculum for shame resilience (Chapter 15). In addition, Greenberg and colleagues' emotion-focused therapy addresses shame as one of several emotions of particular clinical relevance (Chapter 3).

The field is in its infancy in terms of empirical validation of shame-focused therapies. In a pilot study of five women with BPD, Rizvi and Linehan (2005) evaluated an 8- to 10-week manualized shame-enhanced DBT, a cognitive–behavioral intervention based on an expansion of the DBT principle of opposite action (Linehan, 1993) for shame. Results indicated that the intervention reduced shame about a specific event for some of the clients. An unanticipated but clinically significant finding was the high level of client motivation, as indicated by the absence of treatment dropouts and unplanned missed sessions and by the high compliance with homework assignments—both unusual in the treatment of individuals with BPD. As noted by Rizvi et al. (Chapter 10), the sample size was small; future research is needed on a larger scale to replicate the promising findings.

Several nonexperimental evaluations have been conducted on Gilbert's (2010) compassion focused therapy with promising results. In a small study of people with chronic mental health problems, compassion training was associated with reduced shame, self-criticism, depression, and anxiety (Gilbert & Procter, 2006). Compassion training appears helpful for people who hear psychotic voices (Mayhew & Gilbert, 2008). And group-based CFT with 19 clients in a high-security psychiatric setting was associated with decreases in shame, depression, and general psychopathology and increases in self-esteem (Laithwaite et al., 2009).

Brown's (2009) Connections, a psychoeducational shame resilience curriculum, has yet to be empirically evaluated, but it is manualized and ready for empirical study.

Together, these shame-focused therapies break important new ground. We hope that in the coming years, the many rich ideas presented in this volume will provide the basis for additional treatment development in this important but long-neglected area. What's needed next is much more scientifically informed outcome research using randomized experimental designs to clearly document treatment the efficacy and effectiveness of shame-focused interventions. Once efficacy has been demonstrated, efforts to "decompose" treatments to identify their most "active ingredients" will further our understanding of optimal strategies for managing and treating maladaptive shame.

Research indicates that the propensity to experience shame is associated with a broad range of psychological disorders (for reviews, see Tangney & Dearing, 2002; Tangney et al., 2007). It may be necessary to develop shame-focused interventions tailored to the specific needs of particular disorders and/or populations. Rizvi and Linehan's (2005) shame-enhanced DBT for the treatment of borderline personality disorder may serve as a model for other disorder-specific treatment approaches. We can imagine the utility of shame-focused treatment for individuals suffering from eating disorders, from depression, from post-traumatic stress disorder, from social anxiety, from sexual dysfunction, and from substance use disorders, to name but a few. As Rizvi et al. (Chapter 10) observed, "The treatment of maladaptive shame has been largely overlooked in treatment models and manuals across all disorders."

Classes of clients not addressed in this volume include those who present with conduct disorder, antisocial personality disorder, and psychopathy. Virtually no research has been conducted on shame among children with conduct disorder to guide clinicians who work with such difficult clients, and systematic research on the dynamics of shame in adult antisocial personality is in its infancy. In our own research with adult felony offenders (Tangney, Mashek, & Stuewig, 2007), we have begun to explore the moral affective characteristics associated with antisocial personality and its more serious variant, psychopathy. In a study of 550 jail inmates (Tangney, Stuewig, Mashek, & Hastings, 2010), we found that antisocial personality disorder, as assessed by the Personality Assessment Inventory (Morey, 1991), was negatively correlated with guilt proneness but positively correlated with shame proneness. Psychopathy, as assessed by the Psychopathy Checklist: Screening Version (Hart, Cox, & Hare, 1995), was negatively correlated with guilt proneness but unrelated to shame proneness. These findings suggest that although some psychopathic individuals may be truly absent the capacity for both "moral emotions," some psychopaths (and many individuals with antisocial personality) are vulnerable to shame. Our guess is that such individuals do not necessarily experience shame for their crimes against society, but instead may be vulnerable to shame in connection with personal failures and shortcomings, with substance abuse (a prevalent comorbid condition), and with other stigmatizing personal characteristics. Much research remains to be done to help guide clinicians and others committed to the rehabilitation of individuals with antisocial spectrum disorders.

Finally, an exciting avenue for future clinically relevant research concerns the role of shame (in both client and therapist) in shaping the therapeutic process, including its impact on the therapeutic alliance. Helen Block Lewis (1971) identified this as an area ripe for empirical study nearly 40 years ago, and it remains so today. We hope the current volume will also stimulate clinically relevant research on effective strategies for addressing shame in the context of clinical training and supervision.

In editing this volume, we have been struck by how much we can learn from each other about optimal clinical intervention once the veil of silence is lifted from shame. We are forever indebted to Helen Block Lewis for paving the way.

REFERENCES

Beck, A. T. (1983). Cognitive therapy of depression: New perspectives. In P. Clayton & J. Barrett (Eds.), *Treatment of depression: Old controversies and new approaches* (pp. 265–290). New York, NY: Raven Press.

Bradshaw, J. (1988). *Healing the shame that binds you.* Deerfield Beach, FL: Health Communications.

Brown, B. (2009). *Connections: A 12-session psychoeducational shame resilience curriculum* (2nd ed.). Minneapolis, MN: Hazelden.

Denham, S. A. (1998). *Emotional development in young children.* New York, NY: Guilford Press.

de Waal, F. B. M. (1996). *Good natured: The origins of right and wrong in humans and other animals.* Cambridge, MA: Harvard University Press.

Ellis, A. (1962). *Reason and emotion in psychotherapy.* New York, NY: Lyle Stuart.

Fessler, D. M. T. (2007). From appeasement to conformity: Evolutionary and cultural perspectives on shame, competition, and cooperation. In J. L. Tracy, R. W. Robins, & J. P. Tangney (Eds.), *The self-conscious emotions: Theory and research* (pp. 174–193). New York, NY: Guilford Press.

Gilbert, P. (1997). The evolution of social attractivenenss and its role in shame, humiliation, guilt, and therapy. *British Journal of Medical Psychology, 70,* 113–147.

Gilbert, P. (2010). *Compassion focused therapy: The distinctive features.* London, England: Routledge.

Gilbert, P., & Procter, S. (2006). Compassionate mind training for people with high shame and self-criticism: A pilot study of a group therapy approach. *Clinical Psychology & Psychotherapy, 13,* 353–379. doi:10.1002/cpp.507

Harder, D. W., & Lewis, S. J. (1987). The assessment of shame and guilt. In J. N. Butcher & C. D. Spielberger (Eds.), *Advances in personality assessment* (Vol. 6, pp. 89–114). Hillsdale, NJ: Erlbaum.

Hart, S. D., Cox, D. N., & Hare, R. D. (1995). *The Hare Psychopathy Checklist: Screening version.* Toronto, Ontario, Canada: Multi-Health Systems.

Hayes, S. C., Strosahl, K., & Wilson, K. G. (1999). *Acceptance and commitment therapy: An experiential approach to behavior change.* New York, NY: Guilford Press.

Izard, C. E. (1977). *Human emotions.* New York, NY: Plenum Press.

Keltner, D. (1995). Signs of appeasement: Evidence for the distinct displays of embarrassment, amusement, and shame. *Journal of Personality and Social Psychology, 68,* 441–454. doi:10.1037/0022-3514.68.3.441

Laithwaite, H., Gumley, A., O'Hanlon, M., Collins, P., Doyle, P., Abraham, L., & Porter, S. (2009). Recovery after Psychosis (RAP): A compassion focused programme for individuals residing in high security settings. *Behavioural and Cognitive Psychotherapy, 37,* 511–526. doi:10.1017/S1352465809990233

Leary, M. R. (2005). Sociometer theory and the pursuit of relational value: Getting to the root of self-esteem. *European Review of Social Psychology, 16*, 75–111. doi:10.1080/10463280540000007

Leary, M. R., Britt, T. W., Cutlip, W. D., II, & Templeton, J. L. (1992). Social blushing. *Psychological Bulletin, 112*, 446–460. doi:10.1037/0033-2909.112.3.446

Leary, M. R., Landel, J. L., & Patton, K. M. (1996). The motivated expression of embarrassment following a self-presentational predicament. *Journal of Personality, 64*, 619–636. doi:10.1111/j.1467-6494.1996.tb00524.x

Lewis, H. B. (1971). *Shame and guilt in neurosis.* New York, NY: International Universities Press.

Linehan, M. M. (1993). *Skills training manual for treating borderline personality disorder.* New York, NY: Guilford Press.

Maddux, J. E., & Tangney, J. P. (Eds.). (2010). *Social psychological foundations of clinical psychology.* New York, NY: Guilford Press.

Mayhew, S. L., & Gilbert, P. (2008). Compassionate mind training with people who hear malevolent voices: A case series report. *Clinical Psychology & Psychotherapy, 15*, 113–138. doi:10.1002/cpp.566

Morey, L. C. (1991). *Personality Assessment Inventory: Professional manual.* Odessa, FL: Psychological Assessment Resources.

Rizvi, S. L., & Linehan, M. M. (2005). The treatment of maladaptive shame in borderline personality disorder: A pilot study of "opposite action." *Cognitive and Behavioral Practice, 12*, 437–447. doi:10.1016/S1077-7229(05)80071-9

Robins, R. W., Noftle, E. E., & Tracy, J. L. (2007). Assessing self-conscious emotions: A review of self-report and nonverbal measures. In J. L. Tracy, R. W. Robins, & J. P. Tangney (Eds.), *Self-conscious emotions: Theory and research* (pp. 443–467). New York, NY: Guilford Press.

Tangney, J. P., & Dearing, R. L. (2002). *Shame and guilt.* New York, NY: Guilford Press.

Tangney, J. P., Dearing, R., Wagner, P. E., & Gramzow, R. (2000). *The Test of Self-Conscious Affect—3 (TOSCA–3).* Fairfax, VA: George Mason University.

Tangney, J. P., Mashek, D., & Stuewig, J. (2007). Working at the social-clinical-community-criminology interface: The George Mason University Inmate Study. *Journal of Social and Clinical Psychology, 26*, 1–21. doi:10.1521/jscp.2007.26.1.1

Tangney, J. P., & Salovey, P. (2010). Emotions of the imperiled ego: Shame, guilt, jealousy, and envy. In J. E. Maddux & J. P. Tangney (Eds.), *Social psychological foundations of clinical psychology* (pp. 245–271). New York, NY: Guilford Press.

Tangney, J. P., Stuewig, J., & Mashek, D. J. (2007). Moral emotions and moral behavior. *Annual Review of Psychology, 58*, 345–372. doi:10.1146/annurev.psych.56.091103.070145

Tangney, J. P., Stuewig, J., Mashek, D., & Hastings, M. (2010). Feeling bad about the behavior or the self? Assessing jail inmates' proneness to shame and guilt:

Reliability, validity, and relation to key criminal justice constructs. Manuscript submitted for review.

Tangney, J. P., Wagner, P. E., & Gramzow, R. (1992). Proneness to shame, proneness to guilt, and psychopathology. *Journal of Abnormal Psychology, 101*, 469–478. doi:10.1037/0021-843X.101.3.469

Tracy, J. L., & Robins, R. W. (2006). Appraisal antecedents of shame and guilt: Support for a theoretical model. *Personality and Social Psychology Bulletin, 32*, 1339–1351. doi:10.1177/0146167206290212

Witkin, H. A., Lewis, H. B., Hertzman, M., Machover, K., Meissner, P. B., & Wapner, S. (1954). *Personality through perception: An experimental and clinical study*. New York, NY: Harper.

Witkin, H. A., Lewis, H. B., & Weil, E. (1968). Affective reactions and patient-therapist interactions among more differentiated and less differentiated patients early in therapy. *Journal of Nervous and Mental Disease, 146*, 193–208.

INDEX

characteristic of shame, 5, 25, 32, 83,
175–176, 186–189, 247,
262–263
couple therapy guidelines for, 177
guilt focused on, 7–11, 19, 25, 26,
47, 52, 54, 71, 127, 168–169,
181, 182, 184, 185, 187, 196,
197, 203, 209, 219–220, 225,
230, 264, 279, 282–285, 292,
308–309, 338, 383, 386–388
impulsive, 237, 238
influence of, on partner, 174–175
maintenance of problematic,
103–106
modification of, 388–389
moral, 8
offending, 93–94, 398
the self vs., 8, 9, 51, 83, 186, 197,
225, 283, 309, 375, 386, 399
of therapist, 33, 63, 76, 82, 96,
106–109, 128, 131, 132, 160,
161, 207, 230, 249, 269, 309,
327, 328, 337, 339, 379, 380,
393, 395
Behavioral activation activities,
103–104
Behavioral analysis, 246. See also
Functional analytic approach
Behavioral inhibitions, 342–343
Behavioral interventions, 170, 185,
188–190, 244, 245, 400
Behavior analytic approach, 100
Belief systems
in addiction treatment, 226
as coping/healing mechanism,
206–211, 395
in immigrant communities, 200–201
Westernized, 207
Belonging, sense of, 76, 80, 86, 121,
201, 220, 223, 225, 271, 357,
358, 368, 369
Bibring, E., 30
Billing issues, 129–130, 380
Binge eating disorder (BED), 277, 279
Biosocial theory, 239–241
Bitter, Cindy Nappa, 277
Blame. See also Self-blame
in couple therapy, 172–173
externalization of, 6, 82, 184, 388
Blankstein, K. R., 330–331

Blushing, 262–263
BN. See Bulimia nervosa
Bodhisattva, 345–346
Bodily functions, 131, 379
Body image
and eating disorders, 279–281
and gender, 277–278
of therapist, 295–297
Borderline personality disorder (BPD),
237–255
biosocial theory of, 239–241
clinical example, 251–254
opposite action in, 244–251
overview, 237–239
research on shame and, 241–244
and shame-focused therapy, 399, 400
Bordin, E. S., 311
Borrowed shame, 232
Boundaries, 55, 122, 125, 199, 229–230,
264, 392, 396
BPD. See Borderline personality disorder
Brain development, 157
Brain function, 335, 340–341
Brain responses, 364
Brandchaft, B., 144, 160
Brewin, C. R., 266, 337
Bridging questions, 108
Britt, T. W., 263
Bromberg, P., 154, 161
Broucek, F., 26
Brown, B., 355, 357–359, 361, 363, 369,
378, 379, 382, 384, 391, 396, 400
Bruch, H., 280
Buchbinder, E., 337
Buddhist practices, 345–346
Bulimia nervosa (BN), 277, 278, 283, 292
Burney, J., 283

Callahan, K., 266
CBCT. See Cognitive–behavioral
couple therapy
Center for Multicultural Human
Services, 196
Central American cultures, 207, 395
CFT. See Compassion focused therapy
Child abuse and maltreatment
and abusive shaming other, 51–52
and attachment, 141–143
and borderline personality disorder,
239–240

Dalai Lama, 341, 343
Darwin, C., 262–263
Darwin, Jaine, 267, 268
DBT. *See* Dialectical behavior therapy
Dearing, R. L., 3–10, 12, 14–18, 46, 52,
    55, 61, 71, 167, 168, 184, 196,
    198, 219, 234, 242, 243, 326,
    338, 360, 364, 370, 379, 382,
    398, 400
Death, of loved one, 208
Defectiveness, 221–223
Defective shamed self, 53, 60
Defense mechanism(s)
    anger as, 28–29, 176
    contempt as, 29–30
    and defensive sphere of self, 227
    and disconnection, 286
    in group therapy, 118–124
    from a psychodynamic perspective,
        28–33
    with shame, 23
Defensive grandiosity, 31
Defensive sphere of self, 227
Deficiency statements, 224–226, 379
Depression, 6, 9
    and childhood experiences, 37
    cultural factors in, 204
    dysphoria, 330–331
    and eating disorders, 282–284
    in identification of shame, 30–31
    in immigrant/refugee clients, 204, 207
    postpartum, 367
    and self-criticism, 338, 340, 347
    and shame, 81, 83, 96, 172, 179
    and suicide, 242, 381
    treatment recommendations for,
        245, 400–401
Depue, R. A., 341
Deshaming, 335–339
Devaluation, 120, 130, 396
Developmental factors, 5, 157, 263–264
*Diagnostic and Statistical Manual of
    Disorders*, 24, 238, 261
Dialectical behavior therapy (DBT)
    for borderline personality disorder,
        244–251
    opposite action in, 388
    as shame-focused therapy, 399, 400
    shame regulation methods in, 385
Dieting, 280

Differential Emotions Scale, 266
Direct shaming other, 49
Disconnection, 285–286, 289, 291,
    357–358, 366
Disgust, 265
Disparagement, 396
Dispositional tendencies to shame,
    10–11, 378–379
Dissociation, 54–55, 266
    of rage, 143
    of shamed self, 54–55, 60
Domestic violence, 337, 338
Dopamine system, 340
Drug dependency. *See* Addiction
Dubus, A., 199
Dunkley, D. M., 330–331
Dutra, L., 266
Dyadic factors, 40, 93, 170–171,
    178–182
Dysfunctional behaviors, 73, 83, 170,
    238, 239
Dysfunctional beliefs, 78, 86, 208–209,
    247, 249
Dysregulation, 106, 237, 239

Earle, J., 368
Early experiences
    of abusive treatment, 157
    in family system, 118
    and intergenerational shame, 154
    of interpersonal relationship pat-
        terns, 269
    and maladaptive core shame, 81
    of trauma, 142–143
Eating Disorder Inventory 2 (EDI–2), 283
Eating disorders, 28–29, 33, 277–299
    and body image, 279–281
    and guilt, 282–285
    not otherwise specified, 278–279
    overview of, 277–279
    in parallel process of therapy,
        293–295
    perfectionism in, 380
    relational-cultural theory approach
        to, 285–293
    self-help sources for, 297, 298
    and therapist body image, 295–297
Ecological momentary assessment, 285
Ego
    antilibidinal, 57

Enuresis, 140–141
Envy, 30
Epstein, N. B., 170, 183, 189, 378, 379, 384, 390, 398
Erikson, E. H., 142, 263
Escape conditioning, 95–96
Evaluations
    comparative, 117, 118, 225
    negative, 185, 199
    self-, 11, 85, 128, 133, 173, 178–179, 182, 183, 185, 337, 384
Evans, S., 228
Evidence-based treatment, 245
Evocative imagery, 76
Evolutionary perspective, 92–94, 327–328, 335, 399
Exhibitionism, 227
Existential awareness, 226
Expansive pole (of self), 25
Expectations
    in couple relationships, 167
    as cultural factors, 197–198, 358
    of family members in home country, 200–201
    gendered, 358
    of immigrant parents, 201, 210
    with shame categories, 367
    sociocultural, 295, 362
Exposure
    in group therapy, 116, 129, 133
    and opposite action, 245
    repeated, 125
    as treatment for shame, 102–103, 125, 129–130, 245, 248, 267, 271, 342
Externalization, 6, 82
External shame
    and compassion, 327–328
    in group therapy, 334–335
    and internalized shame, 72–73
    in therapeutic relationship, 326

Fairbairn, W. R. D., 56, 57
Falconier, M. K., 378, 379, 384, 390, 398
Family systems
    with addiction, 230–234
    avoidance in, 231–232
    expectations in, 200–201
    and group therapy, 118
    of immigrants/refugees, 200–201

isolation from, 232–233
    loyalty and honor in, 231–232
    nonshaming communication in, 233–234
    patterns in, 159–161
    roles in, 233
    transferred shame in, 232
    unrealistic standards in, 185–186
Family therapy, 137–164
    and development of shame, 141–143
    establishing new family patterns in, 159–161
    exploring origins of shame in, 150–154
    helping client feel understood in, 148–150
    initial family interview, 138–141
    not ignoring shame in, 154–156
    process of, 161–163
    psychoeducation and feedback in, 156–158
    safe environment and connection in, 143–147
    the self in, 158–159
    therapist ally in, 391
    therapist shame in, 147–148
Fantasies, 332, 334
Fear, 357–358
    cues related to, 249
    in group therapy, 119
    pathological, 261–262
    and self-criticism, 330
    of shame, 346, 360
    in therapist, 396
Fear disorders, 245
"Feeling traps," 266
Fee policies, 380
Feiring, C., 266, 330
Felony offenders, 401
Finances, 129–130, 380
Finkel, S. A., 345
Flawed self, 227–228
Fletcher, C., 286
Fogel, A., 341
Fonagy, P., 143–144, 265
Forgiveness, 187–188, 207
Forman, E., 266
Formation phase, 120–121
Forrest, M. S., 337
Frank, E. S., 282, 283

Kaufman, G., 99
Kilborne, B., 42
Kinzie, J. D., 204
Kirk, M., 266
Kleinian perspective, 30
Klinger, R., 309, 377
Kluft, R. P., 267, 268
Koenen, K. C., 270
Koerner, K., 379, 389, 392, 396, 398
Kohut, H., 24–26, 29, 30, 37, 40, 150
Kulp, L., 309, 377
Kurdish culture, 203–204

Ladany, N., 309, 310, 377, 380, 396, 397
Laithwaite, H., 347
Language barriers, 199, 203, 205, 395
Laughter, 270–271
Leahy, R. L., 332, 336
Lear, T. E., 126
Learning histories, 93–97
Leary, M. R., 263, 398
Leszcz, M., 362
Lewis, H. B., 7–9, 25, 27, 29, 40, 46,
    115, 182, 196, 263–265, 267,
    269, 270, 279, 375, 378, 380, 401
Lewis, M., 330
Limbic system, 364
Linehan, M. M., 98, 239–241, 244–246,
    249, 400
Livingston, L. R., 129, 133–134, 335
Longe, O., 340–341, 347
Loss, 84, 117–118
Loyalty, 231
Lynd, H., 264

MacNab, R. T., 129, 335
Maladaptive anger/rage, 82–83, 388
Maladaptive emotions, 72
Maladaptive shame, 78, 94, 97, 394
Maltreatment survivors, 82
Markers, 311, 313
Marlatt, G. A., 249
Marschall, D. M., 282–283
Masterson, J. F., 150
McClure, F. H., 377
Medication, 38, 205
Meditation, 77
Meers, D., 24
Melson, G. F., 341
Memories, 73, 118, 329–330

Mendelsohn, M., 266
Menninger Clinic, 356
Mentalization, 144, 338, 342
Middle Eastern cultures, 207
Miller, J. B., 286, 288
Miller, W., 265
MI/MET (motivational
    interviewing/motivational
    enhancement therapy), 382
Mindfulness, 162, 226, 249, 342–343,
    385
"Mind in mind," 143–144
Mind reading, 328
Mirroring self-object, 25, 26
Mirroring self-object, failure of, 26
Mishima, Y., 31
Misplaced responsibility, 388
Mistry, J., 341
Money, 129–130, 380
Moral behavior, 8
Moral emotions, 5, 195, 264
Morrison, A. P., 116–117, 120, 126,
    381, 383, 395, 396, 398–399
Morrone-Strupinsky, J. V., 341
Motivational interviewing/motivational
    enhancement therapy
    (MI/MET), 382
Mourning rituals, 395
Multicultural perspective, 195–211
    belief systems in, 206–211
    intergenerational issues in, 201–203
    past experiences in, 196–198
    and receiving professional help,
        204–206
    resettlement in, 198–201
    therapeutic engagement in, 203–204
Multigenerational transmission, 147, 154
Mutuality, 296

Nakken, C., 222
Narcissism
    and anger, 29
    dialectic of, 24–25
    and ego ideal, 27–28, 46–47
    and self, 41
Narcissistic defenses, 286
Narcissistic rage, 29
Narcissistic vulnerability, 38
Narratives, 79–80, 270
Neff, K. D., 347

Negative attributions, 186–187
Negative emotions
   in couple therapy, 167
   cultural factors in, 85–86, 394
   function of, 71
   tolerance of, 342
Negative self-evaluations, 185
Neglectful shaming other, 50, 62
Neuropsychoanalytic theory, 47
Newberg, A., 346
Noftle, E. E., 379
Nonjudgment, 343, 385
Nonshaming family patterns, 233–234
Nonverbal cues
   with addictive disorder clients, 230
   with borderline personality disorder
      clients, 243–244
   in compassion focused therapy, 331
   in emotion-focused therapy, 74–75,
      84
   in functional analytic approach,
      97–98
   with posttraumatic stress disorder
      clients, 268
   in recognizing client shame,
      377–378
Normalization, 177, 335–336, 383, 392
Normative discontent, 279–280
Norms, 117–118, 125, 358

Obesity, 33, 280–281
Objectification, 281, 393
Objective self-awareness, 26
Object relations perspective, 45–66
   clinical example, 58–61
   conceptualization of shame in, 46–47
   on group therapy, 119
   overview, 47–49
   regressed libidinal ego in, 56–58
   shamed selves in, 52–56
   shaming internal others in, 49–52
   therapy setting for, 61–66
Obsessional clients, 332
Oedipal guilt, 53–54
Offending behaviors, 398
On Narcissism (S. Freud), 27
Opposite action, 244–251, 388–389, 400
The other, 49–52, 116–117
Overinterpretation, 394
Oxytocin system, 340

Pakistani culture, 202
Palmer, M., 330, 340
Paralinguistic cues, 84, 268, 377–378
Parents
   contempt from, 137
   cultural variations in, 182
   elderly, 202–203
   immigrant, 201
   rejection by, 225–226
Passivity, 24
Past experiences
   of early family system, 118
   of immigrant/refugee clients,
      196–198, 209
   unconscious patterns from, 48
Pathological fear, 261–262
Patterson, O., 265
Pavio, S. C., 243
Pek, J., 345
Perception, selective, 174
Perfectionism, 128, 287, 330–331, 387
Personal Feelings Questionnaire
   (PFQ2), 184
Personality Assessment Inventory, 401
Personality change, 58
Personality theory, 56
Personal meaning, 71
Personal standards, 80–81, 185–188
PFQ2 (Personal Feelings
   Questionnaire), 184
Phobic disorders, 86
Physical abuse
   and abusive shaming other, 51–52
   and borderline personality disorder,
      239–240
   and primary maladaptive core
      shame, 81–82
   and shame in abuser, 181
Physical states, 46, 54–56, 364
Piers, G., 27, 29
Pines, M., 46
Pope, K. S., 307
Positive communication skills, 189–190
Positive consequences, 180–181
Positive emotions, 79, 340, 342
Positive psychology, 226
Postpartum depression (PPD), 367
Posttraumatic Diagnostic Scale, 262
Posttraumatic stress disorder (PTSD),
   33, 261–272

Self-objects, 26, 116–117
Self-organization, 150–151
Self–other pairings, 57
Self-punishment, 241, 386–387
Self-regulation, 53, 143
Self-report questionnaires, 184
Self-reproach, 119
Self-shame, 222–223
Self-shaming other, 52
Self-soothing, 77–78, 102, 340, 385
Self-verification theory, 241
Self-warmth, 346
Self-worth, 71–72, 198–199
Sense of belonging, 223, 225, 233
Sense of purpose, 99
Sensitivity, 76, 109, 393–395
Seppala, E. M., 347
Sexual abuse
    and abusive shaming other, 51–52
    and attributional style, 330
    and borderline personality disorder,
        239–240
    and dissociated shamed self, 54–55
    and primary maladaptive core
        shame, 81–82
    as relationship of coercive control,
        265
    and shame proneness, 266
    trauma-focused group treatment for,
        271–272
Sexual fantasies, 334
Sexual identity, 210–211
Sexuality, 99–100, 127, 131, 332, 379
Shame, 378–379. *See also* Therapist
        shame
    and addiction, 219–222
    affect regulation for, 77–78
    with antisocial personality
        disorder, 401
    with borderline personality
        disorder, 239
    borrowed, 232
    common themes of, 375–381
    conceptualization of, 10, 46–47,
        241–242, 358, 361–362
    core, 81–83, 182–183, 222–223
    in couple therapy, 181–182,
        184–190
    covert, 171
    defined, 4–5, 8, 358

and depression, 9, 30–31, 36, 37, 42,
    81, 83, 86, 96, 120, 175–176,
    179, 183, 195, 204, 282–285,
    344, 347, 388, 400
development of, 26–27, 141–143,
    150–154, 288
and dissociation, 266
domain-specific assessment of,
    283–284
and eating disorders, 283–285
as emotion, 3, 23, 31, 39, 41, 42,
    45, 51, 76, 79, 82, 87, 88,
    102, 115, 133, 167, 196,
    224, 232, 246, 264, 269,
    283–285, 326, 377, 384,
    388, 394, 398, 399
fear of, 346, 360
guilt vs., 7–11, 25–26, 168–169, 264,
    325, 338, 361
instrumental, 73
instruments for assessment of, 184
in-the-moment, 5, 11, 390–391
justified, 247–249, 387
metashame, 396
negative attributions with, 186–187
outcomes of, 8–9
and parental rejection, 225–226
from past experiences, 196–198, 209
and primary caregiver, 142
as problematic, 5–7, 99–100, 109,
    211, 379, 386, 389
problems linked with, 6
in psychological interventions, 6–7,
    62, 63, 72–76, 84, 103, 117,
    126, 138, 159, 169, 170,
    174–177, 184–185, 188–190,
    224–230, 244–250, 341–344
of receiving professional help,
    204–206
recognition of, 32, 76, 331–335,
    364–365, 384
regulation, 385–386
secondary, 34, 73, 83–85
and self-esteem, 241–242
and self-organization, 150–151
situational, 169
situational shame vs., 169
social functions of, 5, 80–81,
    180–181, 211, 264–266,
    398–399

Traumatic events, *continued*
    in posttraumatic stress disorder, 267
    and primary maladaptive shame,
        72–73
Traumatization, interpersonal, 46, 59
Treatment recommendations, 381–401
    for adaptive shame, 398–399
    for addiction, 224–230
    with borderline personality
        disorder, 238
    for client acknowledgment of shame,
        382–385
    cultural factors, 393–395
    and empirically supported treatment,
        399–401
    interpersonal coping, 390–392
    narratives of shame, 270
    recording of sessions, 158, 389
    relational validation, 382
    shame regulation, 385–386
    for supervision, 397–398
    for therapist shame, 392, 395–397
    for therapist shaming of client, 393
    and transformation, 386–389
    two-chair dialogue, 390
    for unbearable shame, 33
Triggers
    in Connections curriculum,
        361–362, 365
    in couple relationships, 181–182
    domain-specific assessment of, 379
    in dyadic interactions, 183–184
    in eating disorders, 291
Troop, N. A., 284
Trower, P., 336
Trumbull, D., 46
Trust, 208, 359–360
Tu, X., 266
Two-chair dialogue, 76–77, 83–85,
    390

Unbearable shame, 32–33
Unique specialness, 31–32, 384
Universality, 125, 392
Unjustified emotions, 246–248
Unjustified shame, 248, 387
Unrealistic standards, 185–188, 282
Unwanted identities, 170, 365
Unworthiness, 357–358
"Urge surfing," 249

Validation, 154–155, 336, 382
Values in Action–Inventory of
    Strengths, 226
Verbal abuse, 330
Verbal cues
    with addictive disorder clients, 230
    in compassion focused therapy, 331
    in couple therapy, 179
    in emotion-focused therapy,
        74–75, 84
    in functional analytic approach,
        97–98
    with posttraumatic stress disorder
        clients, 268
    in recognizing client shame,
        377–378
Verbalization, 383
Verona, E., 330
Vicarious experience, 124–125, 392
Victims of Violence, 262
Victorian value system, 280
Videotaping, 158, 389
Vietnamese culture, 199, 200, 204, 206,
    210–211
Villareal, Y., 378
Vulnerability
    areas of, 10
    in Connections curriculum,
        359–360, 365, 368
    empathic affirmation of, 82
    narcissistic, 38
    reframing of, 293–295
    related to bodily functions, 131
    in supervisor/supervisee relationship,
        293–295
    of therapist, 397
    therapist awareness of, 396–397
    in Western cultures, 293

Wagner, A. W., 269
Wagner, P., 286
Waldman, M. R., 346
War situations, 196–197
Weakness, 162, 292, 342
Weathers, R., 377
Weber, R., 115, 116, 118, 128, 129,
    131, 132
Weight gain, 280
Well-being, 346–347
Western cultures, 85, 293
Westernized beliefs, 207

Whelton, W. J., 337
When–then sequences, 158
Whole self, 23
Wiseman, T., 362
Withdrawal
    in couple therapy, 189
    as defense mechanism, 32
    and group therapy, 118
    and primary maladaptive shame,
        72–73
    from the self, 56–58

Women
    and body image, 279–281
    and eating disorders, 277–278,
        295
    experience of shame in, 357–358
    shame resilience in, 359

Yalom, L., 124, 133, 362

Zaslav, M. R., 64
Zuroff, D. C., 330–331

ABOUT THE EDITORS

Ronda L. Dearing received her PhD in clinical psychology from George Mason University, followed by a postdoctoral fellowship specializing in alcohol research at the Research Institute on Addictions (RIA) of the University at Buffalo and funded by the National Institute on Alcohol Abuse and Alcoholism (NIAAA). Upon completion of her fellowship appointment, she continued at RIA, where she currently works as a research scientist. Dr. Dearing is coauthor of *Shame and Guilt* (2002, with June Tangney) and *Alcohol Use Disorders* (2007, with Stephen Maisto and Gerard Connors). Her scientific publications have appeared in a number of professional journals, and her research has been recognized by awards from the Research Society on Alcoholism. She has received research funding from NIAAA for her work as principal investigator of a Mentored Research Scientist Development Award to study help-seeking behaviors among at-risk drinkers and as a co-investigator on a grant to study impulsivity as a mechanism of change during treatment for alcohol dependence. Dr. Dearing's research interests include help-seeking for alcohol problems, treatment engagement and outcome, and issues related to shame and guilt.

June Price Tangney received her PhD in clinical psychology from the University of California, Los Angeles (UCLA). After teaching for 2 years at Bryn

Mawr College, she joined the Psychology Department at George Mason University (GMU) in 1988, where she is currently professor of psychology. In 2007, she was honored to become University Professor at GMU. A Fellow of the American Psychological Association's Division of Personality and Social Psychology and the American Psychological Society, Dr. Tangney is coauthor (2002, with Ronda Dearing) of *Shame and Guilt*, coeditor (2007, with Jess Tracy and Richard Robins) of *The Self-Conscious Emotions: Theory and Research*, and coeditor (2003, with Mark Leary) of the *Handbook of Self and Identity*. She has served as associate editor for *Self and Identity* and consulting editor for the *Journal of Personality and Social Psychology*, *Personality and Social Psychology Bulletin*, *Psychological Assessment*, the *Journal of Social and Clinical Psychology*, and the *Journal of Personality* and is currently associate editor of *American Psychologist*. Her research on the development and implications of moral emotions has been funded by the National Institute on Drug Abuse, the Eunice Kennedy Shriver National Institute of Child Health and Human Development, the National Science Foundation, and the John Templeton Foundation. Currently, her work focuses on moral emotions among incarcerated offenders. A recipient of GMU's Teaching Excellence Award, Dr. Tangney strives to integrate service, teaching, and clinically relevant research in both the classroom and the lab.